ab. . . . . . . Spell out abbreviation (M7b)

adv. . . . . . . Use adverb form (U2c)

agr. . . . . . . Make verb agree with subject
(or pronoun with antecedent) (U3a, U3b)

ap. . . . . . . Use apostrophe (M2b)

cap. . . . . . . Capitalize (M2a)

coll. . . . . . . Use less colloquial word (U2a)

CS . . . . . Revise comma splice (M4a)

d. . . . . . Improve diction (W4)

dev. . . . . . Develop your point (C2a)

div. . . . . . . Revise word division (M7a)

DM . . . . . . Revise dangling modifier (U3c)

frag. . . . . . . Revise sentence fragment (M3a)

FP . . . . . . Revise faulty parallelism (U3f)

gr. . . . . . . Revise grammatical form or construction (U3d)

awk. . . . . . Rewrite awkward sentence (U4)

lc. . . . . . . Use lower case (M2a)

MM . . . . . . Shift misplaced modifier (U3c)

p. . . . . . . Improve punctuation (M3, M4, M5)

¶. . . . . . . New paragraph (C1)

no ¶. . . . . . . Take out paragraph break (M7a)

ref. . . . . . . Improve pronoun reference (U3b)

rep. . . . . . . Avoid repetition (U4)

shift . . . . . . Avoid shift in perspective (U3e)

sl. . . . . . . Use less slangy word (U2a)

sp. . . . . . . Revise misspelled word (M1)

st. . . . . . . Improve sentence structure (U3)

t. . . . . . . Change tense of verb (U1a)

trans . . . . . . Provide better transition (C2d)

w. . . . . . . Reduce wordiness (U4)

American English Today

American English Today

General Editor and Senior Author: **Hans P. Guth**

Third Edition

WEBSTER DIVISION/McGRAW-HILL BOOK COMPANY
New York   St. Louis   San Francisco   Dallas   Atlanta

Editorial Development: *John A. Rothermich*

Managing Editor: *Hester Eggert Weeden*

Design: *Bennie Arrington*

Production: *Judith Tisdale*

Acknowledgments—see page 470

Library of Congress Cataloging in Publication Data

Guth, Hans Paul, date
    The uses of language.

    (His American English today, [5])
    Includes index.
    SUMMARY: An 11th grade text offering instruction in composition, word
            study, grammar, usage, mechanics, and speech.
1. English language—Grammar—1950–
2. English language—Composition and exercises.
[1. English language—Composition and exercises.
 2. English language—Grammar]   I. Title.
PE1408.G933   1980 vol. 5   [PE1112]   428'.2   79-13730
ISBN 0-07-025021-9

THE AUTHOR

HANS P. GUTH

General Editor and Senior Author

Dr. Guth is a widely published teacher-scholar who writes about effective communication with the authority that comes from successful practice. He is widely known for his work in workshops and in-service meetings for teachers of language and composition. His first book on the teaching of English, *English Today and Tomorrow,* was widely praised and hailed as a "milestone" and as a book "with no equal in its field." His recent book for teachers, *English for a New Generation,* has been called "a book that every teacher of the language arts should read." Through his college textbooks—especially the widely used rhetoric handbook, *Words and Ideas* (Wadsworth)— Dr. Guth has become known as a leading authority on teaching composition to today's students. He has spoken at numerous regional and national conferences and in institutes sponsored by Stanford University, University of Illinois, and University of Hawaii.

Consultants and Contributors

Student Writing **Gabriele Rico,**
San Jose State University

Cultural Minorities **Carol Kizine,**
Kansas City Public Schools

Linguistics **Edgar H. Schuster,**
Allentown (Pa.) Public Schools

Teaching Suggestions **Barbara Johnston,**
San Jose, California

Testing and Measurement **William Kline,**
California Test Bureau

Graphics **Herbert Zettl,**
San Francisco State University

The Authors and the Publishers also thank the following teachers who evaluated manuscript, provided hundreds of examples of student writing, and tried out *American English Today* in their classrooms:

Marge Archer, Lawrenceville, New Jersey
James Conway, St. Louis, Missouri
Jeanne Irwin, Los Angeles, California
Cherry Mallory, Kansas City, Missouri
Donald Mayfield, San Diego, California
Virginia McCormick, Allentown, Pennsylvania
Jane McGill, Chula Vista, California
Janet Minesinger, Columbia, Maryland
Nancy Mitchell, Lakewood, California
Richard E. Roberts, Clinton Corners, New York
Margaret Timm, Bay City, Michigan
Marilyn Walker, Salem, Oregon

To the Teacher

American English Today, Third Edition, offers solid productive work in the basic areas of language and composition. Its aim is to provide materials that are intelligible, workable, and motivating for today's students. The following are key features of the new Third Edition:

1. More varied, effective, and interesting exercises than any competing series.

2. A functional, plain-English approach designed to help students defeated by awkward, elaborate terminology or theory.

3. Streamlined, compact presentation for efficient study and reference.

4. A positive, constructive teaching program systematically developing the students' skills and proficiencies.

5. Frequent provision for measurement of student achievement, with new unit review exercises, diagnostic tests, and achievement tests. A new section on how to take tests, complete with sample tests, appears in the resource chapter of each volume.

6. High-interest materials designed to help teachers overcome students' resistance to English as a subject.

7. Effective use of charts and other visuals designed to help students take things in at a glance.

8. A positive, habit-building program for teaching standard English.

9. Proven step-by-step instruction in the process of composition.

10. Special attention to familiar trouble spots and problem areas for students.

Chapter Table of Contents

TABLE OF CONTENTS

Chapter 1

WORDS   Building Your Vocabulary

Chapter 2

SENTENCES Writing Better Sentences 53

Chapter 3

COMPOSITION   Writing for a Purpose   135

Chapter 4

USAGE   Using Standard English

Chapter 5

MECHANICS   Words on a Page

Chapter 6

ORAL LANGUAGE You and the Audience 411

Chapter 7

RESOURCES   Special Helps for Writers   429

PROSE MODELS

To the Student

What does it take for you to use language well? As you watch effective speakers or writers in action, ask yourself what their attitude is toward language. You will discover the following:

(1) *Good speakers and writers have learned how to learn.* Over the years, they build up the vocabulary that enables them to choose the right word, with just the right shade of meaning. Over the years, they learn how to pack a sentence with information. As the result of trial and error, they know how their audience will react to different ways of saying things.

(2) *Good speakers and writers know the power of language.* Success on the job depends on how well people use words. How well people do depends on how they talk during a job interview; what they say to a dissatisfied customer; how well they understand what they are told to do. Words arouse people to action. Look at words and phrases like "corruption," "censorship," "law and order," "crime in the streets." Such words have the power to change our thinking, and to change the society in which we live.

(3) *Good speakers and writers enjoy using language.* A rousing talk or a good magazine article never makes us feel: "The author did this only because he or she *had* to." Instead, we feel: "This speaker enjoyed giving a talk as much as the audience enjoyed listening to it." Or we feel: "The author got as much out of writing this as I got out of reading it."

Chapter 1

Words
Building Your Vocabulary

Chapter
Preview 1

IN THIS CHAPTER:

- How to keep up with new words that reflect our changing world.

- How to know words better by studying their different meanings.

- How to recognize the contributions of other languages to our vocabulary.

- How to keep language fresh, vivid, and direct.

- How to avoid prejudiced language, exaggeration, and jargon.

Keep improving your knowledge of words.

If we want to use language well, the most basic requirement is that we have a good knowledge of words. To use the right word, we have to be able to choose. We have to know different words that might fit the situation. We have to choose the one that is just right. Tests that predict how well someone will do in school or on a job often measure above all that person's knowledge of words. How well we do in our private lives and in public often depends on whether we know the right words and use them at the right time.

As you study how words work, and how you can make them work for you, remember: When words are not related to experience, they remain just words. When you learn new words, be sure to ask: "What does this word stand for in my own experience? What things, feelings, events does it describe? When people hear this word, what picture does it bring to their minds?"

PREVIEW EXERCISE

To make better and fuller use of language, you have to become interested in words as words. How many of the following questions can you answer? Pool the information you can give with the information provided by your classmates.

1. A conductor on a train helps people get to where they are going. What does a "conductive" substance do? What do we mean when we say a substance is "nonconductive"?
2. The "rear guard" brings up the rear. What does the "vanguard" do?
3. What common meaning connects the "extra" of a newspaper and an "extra" on a movie set? What does the word *extraordinary* mean? What does *extraterrestrial* mean?

4. What does the *inter-* mean in *international, interstate,* and *intercontinental?* What does the word *interval* mean?

5. What common meaning connects words like *transportation, transit, transatlantic,* and *transmission?*

6. What does *martial* mean in "martial law" and "court-martial"?

7. A "seismograph" registers—or "writes down"—earthquakes. What other words that you know contain the root *graph* and have something to do with writing?

8. How is a "supreme court" different from ordinary courts? When people are "supreme" in a society, we say that they have "supremacy." What does the word mean?

9. Animals are living things. An "animated" conversation is lively, full of life. What kinds of things do we call "*in*animate"?

10. When we "revoke" an order, we "call it back" and thus cancel it. People sometimes announce an "irrevocable" decision. What do they mean by *irrevocable?*

Keep adding new words to your vocabulary.

As long as we continue to grow and learn, our language grows along with us. It helps us label and understand the things we see in the society around us. It helps us identify and take in things that are new and strange. Look at three kinds of words to study and make your own.

Make the right word stand for the right thing.

People with adequate vocabularies do not have to say that they saw "a funny little animal." They call it a chipmunk, or a squirrel, or a raccoon. They do not have to say that someone "walked in a funny way." They use a word like *stride, stalk,* or *prance* instead. Avoid the word that gives only a blurry, general notion. Learn the word that clearly pins down something specific. Use the word that points accurately to what you have in mind:

(1) Use the word that points accurately to one of several kinds. Our language is rich in resources. We can often choose from a whole range of words the one that comes closest to what we mean. Look at the way the following sets of words enable us to choose the one that is just right:

PLACE TO LIVE: house, duplex, tenement, cottage, mansion, cabin, hut, trailer, high-rise

KIND OF BREAD: wheat, rye, pumpernickel, bagel, pretzel, scone, muffin, corn pone

Words

KIND OF SNOW: sleet, slush, powder, hail

HORSES: bay, roan, mustang, bronco, mare, foal, pinto, pony, steed, mount

CARS: sedan, wagon, van, limousine, convertible, jeep

(2) Use words that call to mind specific shapes, sounds, textures, colors, motions. Such words help us imagine that we see and hear what is being described. Language that appeals to our senses is called **concrete** language. Many of the concrete words in the following passages help us *see* what is going on:

> He and Tennie's Jim held the passive and still trembling bitch while Sam *daubed* her *tattered* ear and *raked* shoulder with turpentine and axle grease. . . . The dogs were there first, ten of them *huddled* back under the kitchen, himself and Sam *squatting* to peer back into the obscurity where they *crouched.* . . . (William Faulkner)

(3) Use words that accurately label specific parts and functions. The following passage is from a humorous article on what it used to be like to drive a Model T. Note how specifically it describes the operation of starting the car:

> The trick was to leave the *ignition switch* off, proceed to the animal's head, pull the *choke* (which was a little wire *protruding* through the *radiator*), and give the *crank* two or three *upward lifts.* Then, whistling as though thinking about something else, you would saunter back to the driver's cabin, turn the ignition on, return to the crank, and this time, catching it on the *down stroke,* give it a *quick spin* with plenty of That. If this procedure was followed, the engine almost always responded—first with a few scattered explosions, then with a tumultuous gunfire, which you checked by racing around to the driver's seat, and retarding *the throttle.* (Lee Strout White)

In many of the practical dealings of every day, the person who knows the right word or the accurate word has the advantage. The right word helps us explain what we need and what we want. Precise language helps us understand the needs and purposes of other people.

EXERCISE 1

Test your knowledge of accurate words. Number your paper from 1 to 10. In each group of three, match the right definition with the right word.

EXAMPLE: **A. hop**   a. leap into the air
             B. skip   b. move by repeated short leaps
             C. jump   c. bounce along with light, springy motions

(Answer)   *Ab, Bc, Ca*

1. A. lope   a. skip quickly along the surface
   B. trot   b. run with a long, easy stride
   C. skitter   c. run moderately fast with short, regular steps

2. A. winch   a. hoisting tackle with ropes running over wheels
   B. pulley   b. beam or tower with hoisting tackle
   C. derrick   c. hoisting tackle with drum for coiling rope

3. A. chisel   a. trace with acid in metal
   B. carve   b. cut in wood, as with a knife
   C. etch   c. cut in stone by pounding sharp metal tool

4. A. ditch   a. narrow slit dug for protection or access
   B. trench   b. body of water surrounding town or castle
   C. moat   c. narrow channel for carrying water

5. A. prance   a. move in a playful, skipping manner
   B. frisk   b. move along ploddingly
   C. trudge   c. move in lively, proud manner

6. A. muzzle   a. a faucet
   B. nozzle   b. open end of a weapon
   C. spigot   c. spout at the end of hose or pipe

7. A. soar   a. fly very high, without effort
   B. hover   b. stay over the same place in the air
   C. glide   c. move along smoothly, without effort

8. A. roam   a. move freely over a large territory
   B. prowl   b. move aimlessly, without clear direction
   C. ramble   c. move about in search of prey

9. A. furrow   a. a smooth, regular track
   B. groove   b. track cut in the ground by wheels
   C. rut   c. a long, narrow, somewhat irregular track

10. A. march   a. walk leisurely, for pleasure
    B. stroll   b. walk firmly, with a definite goal
    C. straggle   c. walk in a tired or disorganized manner

EXERCISE 2

How much of the *language of business* should every consumer and employee know? Do you know all of the words italicized in the following sentences? After the number of the sentence, write the letter for the explanation that best sums up the meaning of the italicized word.

1. We thank you for your payment and remind you that the next *installment* is due October 15.
2. We urge you to take advantage of this offer, which will *expire* in March.
3. The company will *repossess* the car unless you keep up the payments.

4. The *warranty* covered all original parts for three years.
5. We took the set back to the store and asked for a *refund*.
6. After studying the ads, the judge accused the company of *misrepresentation*.
7. The gas company credited the *rebate* to our current gas bill.
8. The owners complained they could not afford to pay the new *minimum wage*.
9. When her workload was stepped up, she complained to her *supervisor*.
10. When he looked at his first paycheck, he was discouraged by the many *deductions*.
11. When I wanted to buy four more glasses to complete the set, I found that the style had been *discontinued*.
12. We discovered we could not make the candles ourselves and sell them at a *competitive* price.
13. I was asked if I would be willing to *relocate* if the plant moved to another state.
14. When he was fired, he sued the company and was *reinstated*.
15. As a messenger, I had to be familiar with the *layout* of the plant.
16. Many car buyers are surprised by the price of the various *options*.
17. If you buy your car in another town, *maintenance* can be a problem.
18. We received two copies of the *invoice* with the books we ordered.
19. People mailing things to you need to be informed of any change of *residence*.
20. My friends bought all their furniture *on credit*.

MEANINGS:

   a. force customer to give back merchandise
   b. promise to make good any defects
   c. extras a customer may choose
   d. floor plan and general arrangement
   e. rehired
   f. a partial payment
   g. run out
   h. statement asking for payment due
   i. money taken out for taxes, dues, and the like
   j. return of money paid
   k. reduction in price
   l. misleading claims about a product
   m. with payment later at an agreed time and rate
   n. place where someone lives
   o. service to keep something in good condition
   p. the least wage that it is legal to pay
   q. no longer manufactured
   r. in the same range as that of other competing sellers
   s. move
   t. someone directing the work of others

How many specific words do you know in each of the following general categories? Without consulting a reference book, write down *as many words as you can think of* under each heading. Which of your lists is the longest? which the shortest? Compare your lists with those of your classmates. What accounts for the differences?

EXERCISE 3

1. kinds of birds
2. kinds of ships
3. kinds of dogs
4. parts of a bicycle
5. kinds of tools

Keep up with the language of specialized areas that are of concern to you.

W1b

Technical Terms

Each trade or profession has its own vocabulary. No trade can get along without shoptalk. No industry or science can operate without exact **technical terms.** Railroad supervisors cannot always say, "the little car that rides at the end of a freight train." They need a word like *caboose.* Mechanics cannot always say, "the gadget that allows one of the rear wheels to turn faster than the other." They need the word *differential.*

Technical terms easily confuse the outsider. Follow these rules of thumb when you encounter technical terms:

(1) Try to get the exact technical meaning of a term. In your own words, what does each of the following dictionary entries tell the reader? What questions would you like to ask the dictionary makers who wrote the following entries? What help could you provide on the basis of your own reading and experience?

> **mo·gul** \'mōgəl\ *n* -s [prob. of Scand origin; akin to Norw dial. *muge* heap, pile, fr. ON *mūgi* — more at MOW] : a bump in a ski run
> —*Webster's Third New International Dictionary*

> **diesel engine,** an internal-combustion engine that burns oil with heat caused by the compression of air. [named after R. *Diesel,* 1858–1913, its inventor]
> —*Webster's New Students Dictionary*

> **mod·ule** \'mäj-ül\ *n* [**L** *modulus,* dim. of *modus* measure] **1 :** a standard or unit of measurement **2 :** a usu. packaged functional subassembly of parts (as for an electronic device)
> —*Webster's New Students Dictionary*

(2) Learn about technical terms from how and where they are used. Look for the explanations and details an effective speaker or writer uses with key terms. Sum up in your own words what each of the following passages tells you about the word printed in bold letters:

The river's earliest commerce was *in great barges* —**keelboats, broadhorns.** They *floated and sailed from the upper rivers to New Orleans,* changed cargoes there, and *were tediously warped and poled back by hand.* (Mark Twain)

By a **faction,** I understand *a number of citizens,* whether amounting to a majority or minority of the whole, who are *united and actuated by some common impulse of passion, or of interest, adverse to the rights of other citizens.* . . . A **pure democracy,** by which I mean a *society consisting of a small number of citizens, who assemble and administer the government in person.* . . . (James Madison)

(3) Pay attention to words used to distinguish two closely related terms from one another. In the following passage, two shipwrecked sailors discuss a distinction of vital importance to them:

The cook and the correspondent argued as to the difference between a *life-saving station* and a *house of refuge.* The cook had said: "There's a house of refuge just north of the Mosquito Inlet Light, and as soon as they see us, they'll come off in their boat and pick us up."

"As soon as who sees us?" said the correspondent.

"The crew," said the cook.

"Houses of refuge don't have crews," said the correspondent. "As I understand them, they are only places where clothes and grub are stored for the benefit of shipwrecked people. They don't carry crews." (Stephen Crane)

EXERCISE 1

In which of the following six areas are you most interested? Choose *one* area. Write a one-sentence explanation for each of the ten terms listed. (Share your information with your classmates.)

A. THE MECHANIC'S LANGUAGE—Write one sentence about each of the following terms used by people who work on cars:

1. **ignition**	6. **differential**
2. **carburetor**	7. **radiator**
3. **cylinder**	8. **gasket**
4. **piston**	9. **thermostat**
5. **accelerator**	10. **camshaft**

B. THE LANGUAGE OF SCIENCE—Pretend you have been appointed science teacher for a day. Study the following terms. Explain each briefly and accurately in one sentence:

1. **nucleus**	6. **formula**
2. **vacuum**	7. **prism**
3. **generator**	8. **monitor**
4. **oscillation**	9. **molecule**
5. **equilibrium**	10. **prototype**

C. THE LANGUAGE OF LAW—Suppose you have a friend who is soon going to spend a day in court. Brief your friend on the following lawyers' terms:

1. petition
2. larceny
3. infringement
4. compensation
5. indigent
6. counsel
7. due process
8. defendant
9. appeal
10. felony

D. THE LANGUAGE OF POLITICS—Suppose you have a friend who is soon going to vote for the first time. Brief your friend on the following terms that have played a role in American politics:

1. emancipation
2. anarchist
3. reconstruction
4. monopoly
5. suffrage
6. incumbent
7. vigilante
8. isolationist
9. amendment
10. prohibition

E. THE LANGUAGE OF SURVIVAL—Suppose you and your friend are going to be student representatives at a conference studying ways to protect the environment. Brief your friend on the following terms:

1. contamination
2. derivatives
3. fossil fuel
4. conservation
5. erosion
6. food cycle
7. sediment
8. synthetics
9. additives
10. reforestation

F. THE LANGUAGE OF COOKING—Suppose you and your friend are in charge of the annual class dinner. Define the following culinary terms:

1. baste
2. wok
3. mince
4. double boiler
5. mayonnaise
6. sauté
7. whisk
8. tablespoon
9. soufflé
10. batter

Test your knowledge of *sailing terms* that the reader is likely to encounter in the sea stories of nineteenth-century American writers. Match the right word with the right explanation, such as *9d* or *5t*.

EXERCISE 2

1. bowsprit
2. quarterdeck
3. packet
4. sloop

a. sailors' quarters forward of the foremast
b. away from the wind
c. heavy spar projecting ahead of ship
d. shallows

Words

5. forecastle   e. the rear area of a ship's upper deck
6. shoal   f. broken fibers of flax or hemp
7. lee   g. boat carrying mail and people on regular schedule
8. galley   h. crane used to lower lifeboats
9. gunwale   i. sailboat having one mast
10. tow   j. ship's kitchen
11. davit   k. sailing vessel with two masts
12. mole   l. top of a ship's mast
13. starboard   m. lookout's platform
14. brig   n. left side
15. larboard   o. upper edge of a boat's side
16. masthead   p. breakwater
17. crow's nest   q. tackle for working masts, yards, and sails
18. wake   r. handle used to turn the rudder
19. tiller   s. track left by a moving ship
20. rigging   t. right side

EXERCISE 3

Prepare a report in which you *explain half a dozen technical terms* of a profession, trade, hobby, or craft. Choose one of the areas listed below. (Your teacher will tell you whether to prepare notes for oral presentation or a *written report* to be read in class or handed in.)

1. Working for the Railroad
2. Dressmakers' Language
3. CB Talk
4. Talking to Counselors (Bankers) (Police Officers)
5. Pilots' Talk
6. The Language of French (Mexican) (Italian) (Jewish) (Southern) Cooking
7. Logging Camp Talk
8. Hobby Talk: Painting (Ceramics) (Folk Dancing)
9. Musicians' Talk
10. How Carpenters (Nurses) (Plumbers) (Electricians) Talk

W1c

New Words

Keep up with new words that mirror the changes in our society.

Changing institutions, new discoveries, and passing fashions create a need for new labels. What would a modern Rip Van Winkle, just back from half a century in the hills, need to know to understand the following passages?

After three days in the *space capsule,* the *astronauts debriefed* aboard a navy *carrier.*

Huddled over their *hi-fi sets,* thousands listen to the balance of *stereo* sound flowing from their twin batteries of *tweeters* and *woofers.*

NEW WORDS IN OUR DICTIONARIES

Why were these words added recently to the words listed in dictionaries? For each of these words, provide a brief definition that would help explain the word to the ordinary person.

1. **abort** *n :* the premature termination of an action, procedure, or mission relating to a rocket or spacecraft < a launch ~ >

2. **doggie-bag** *n* [²*doggy* + *bag;* fr. the original assumption that such leftovers were destined for the diner's dog]: a bag used for carrying home leftover food and esp. meat from a meal eaten at a restaurant

3. **granny glasses** *n pl :* spectacles with usu. small oval, round, or square lenses and metal frames

4. **hot line** *n :* direct telephone line in constant readiness to operate so as to facilitate immediate communication (as between heads of two governments)

5. **life-support system** *n :* a system that provides all or some of the items (as oxygen, food, water, control of temperature and pressure, disposition of carbon dioxide and body wastes) necessary for maintaining (as in a spacecraft or on the surface of the moon) the life and health of a person

6. **mafia** *n, often cap :* a group of people of similar interests or backgrounds prominent in a particular field or enterprise: CLIQUE

7. **macrobiotic** *adj :* of, relating to, or being an extremely restricted diet (as one containing chiefly whole grains) that is held to promote health and well-being even though deficient in essential nutrients

8. **su·per·son·ic** 1 : having a frequency above the human ear's audibility limit of about 20,000 cycles per second—used of waves and vibrations; compare SONIC 2 : utilizing, produced by, or relating to supersonic waves or vibrations 3 : of, being, or relating to speeds from one to five times the speed of sound in air—compare SONIC 4 : moving, capable of moving, or utilizing air currents moving at supersonic speed 5 : relating to supersonic airplanes or missiles < the ~ age >

9. **third world** *n, often cap T&W* 1 : a group of nations esp. in Africa and Asia that are not aligned with either the Communist or the non-Communist blocs 2 : an aggregate of minority groups within a larger predominant culture

10. **wipeout** *n -s* [fr. the phrase *wipe out*] : a fall from a surfboard caused usu. by losing control, colliding with another surfer, or being knocked off by a wave
    —*Webster's Third New International Dictionary* and *New Collegiate*
    Copyright © 1966, 1971 by G. & C. Merriam Co.

Words

Do the following to keep up with our changing language:

(1) Study the way dictionaries deal with new words and meanings. Study the following dictionary entry. What was the original meaning of the word? What are several modern uses of the word that had to be added to this entry in recent years? Explain each of these modern uses briefly in your own words:

> **car·tridge** (kär′trij) *n.* **1.** cylindrical case, as of metal or paper, usually containing a percussion cap, a propelling charge of gunpowder, and a bullet. **2.** roll of camera film enclosed in a protective case which fits into a camera as a unit. **3.** device that holds a phonograph needle and transforms its vibrations into an electric current as the needle follows the groove of a record. **4.** small container, designed for easy replacement as a unit, as in a pen or tube. **5.** case designed to hold magnetic tape for easy insertion into a tape player.
> —*The Macmillan Dictionary*

(2) Look for new words in areas of our lives where there is rapid change. Why do you think each of the following words became part of our language? (Where did some of these words come from?)

MODERN LIVING: freeway, litterbug, smog, stereo, low-calorie, disposable, laundromat

TECHNOLOGY: jet, transistor, computer, teleprompter, microwave, printout, satellite, videotape

MEDICINE: tranquilizer, antibiotic, transplant, transfusion

POLITICS: integration, redevelopment, ethnic, mobility, sun belt

ARTS AND FASHIONS: Levis, disco, collage, mobile

EXERCISE 1

Assume that you are in charge of new words for the next edition of a dictionary. Write a one-sentence definition for each word below:

1. customized
2. eye bank
3. zoom lens
4. collage
5. teleplay
6. one-upmanship
7. lift-off
8. skycap
9. nose cone
10. cassette

EXERCISE 2

Changes in language often come about by contact with *a different culture*. The following is a list of words that have become familiar to English-speaking people as a result of British and, later, American influence in India and Pakistan. How many of these do you know? Match the right explanation with the right word, such as *2d* or *3o*.

1. **yoga**
2. **guru**

a. ultimate peace and happiness
b. "Sir" or "Master"

3. nirvana	c. spiritual teacher and guide
4. bazaar	d. unit of currency
5. Brahmin	e. seasonal wind
6. caste	f. hereditary social class
7. Koran	g. Moslem scriptures
8. monsoon	h. passageway lined with shops
9. pundit	i. voluntary cremation of a widow
10. purdah	j. Hindu system of meditation and exercise
11. rupee	k. expert
12. sahib	l. veil for women kept in seclusion
13. sari	m. priest or teacher of top caste
14. suttee	n. Hindu scriptures and poetry
15. Vedas	o. women's dress

Look at the three possible meanings for each numbered word. Put the letter for the right meaning after the number of the word.

1. disposable	a. can be bent	b. can be dumped	c. now due
2. rebate	a. money back	b. long talk	c. hookup
3. invoice	a. whispering	b. sound track	c. bill
4. repossess	a. give back	b. remodel	c. take back
5. felony	a. accident	b. companionship	c. serious crime
6. supersonic	a. noiseless	b. beyond sound	c. four-speed
7. moat	a. sweet bread	b. water trench	c. long delay
8. equilibrium	a. balance	b. electric bolt	c. horse show
9. pundit	a. outcast	b. prizefighter	c. expert
10. ethnic	a. of a minority	b. very moral	c. illegal
11. trudge	a. skip ahead	b. plod along	c. walk swiftly
12. installment	a. investigation	b. credit rating	c. part payment
13. reforest	a. replant trees	b. live in woods	c. retrain
14. etch	a. erase	b. enamel	c. trace by acid
15. options	a. obstacles	b. choices	c. copies
16. expire	a. start up	b. do again	c. run out
17. soar	a. fly high	b. flap clumsily	c. swerve
18. prototype	a. large print	b. first model	c. imitation
19. reinstate	a. rehire	b. hook up	c. disconnect
20. suffrage	a. right to vote	b. much pain	c. tolerance

Study the meanings and exact shades of meaning of words.

W2

WORDS AND MEANINGS

Most of our words do not have one simple meaning and one clearly limited use. Most words have several related meanings. We have to watch them in action to see how they are being used. Often, we have a choice between two words that are very similar in meaning but are not exactly the same.

W2a
Words in Context

Use context as a guide to meaning.

To know a word, we have to see how it works *with other words* — in a sentence or in a paragraph. We have to see the word in **context.** This is how dictionary makers pinpoint the meaning of a word in the first place. They collect and study citations showing its typical uses:

These men of the back country seemed born actors; they had a sense of display, the theatrical temperament. They could instantly eradicate expression from their faces; the blank countenance, the poker face, the *dead pan* were already American accomplishments. . . . (Constance Rourke)

A grimly serious person, Richard wears a *dead pan* on and off the ice.

When we study these passages, we gather that *dead pan* must mean something like "grimly serious in appearance," "keeping the face deliberately without expression." This is the conclusion we find recorded in the dictionary:

dead·pan *n* **1** : a completely expressionless immobile face < wears a *dead pan* on and off the ice —*Newsweek* > **2** : a deadpan manner of behavior or of presentation (as of comedy) < a master of *dead pan* > —*Webster's Third New International Dictionary*

Learn to study context as a clue to meaning. Look for and try to remember sentences that help fix the meaning of a word in your mind. Here are some familiar context clues:

(1) PARAPHRASE—A writer will often give the meaning of a word in *slightly different words* in the same sentence or passage:

jeopardize   Never eager to *take serious risks,* Vera did not want to jeopardize her grade average by taking a difficult new course.

(2) EXAMPLE—A speaker or writer will often describe an incident that shows the *word in action:*

ingenious   When the top of a truck was stuck under the arch of an overpass, the ingenious driver *let just enough air out of the tires to lower the truck to the point where it could pass.*

(3) COMPARISON—We can often tell what a word stands for if we are told *what it is like:*

authoritarian   My aunt was still her old authoritarian self, ordering her family around *like an old-fashioned schoolmaster.*

(4) CONTRAST—We can often tell what a word stands for if we see something that is *its opposite:*

deadpan   The two girls handed us the packages, the one *grinning broadly,* the other deadpan.

SORRY—WRONG WORD

How much context contributes to meaning is well illustrated by **malapropisms.** When people use the wrong word by mistake, we can often tell *what word they meant to use.* For each malapropism, write the word that should have taken its place. Write on a separate sheet of paper.

1. (Voter to senator) "What a wonderful speech! It was absolutely *superfluous!*"
2. The first-aid course offered instruction in mouth-to-mouth *recreation.*
3. By the time the fire department arrived, the burning house was totally *diminished.*
4. Timothy and Edgar had long been *insufferable* friends.
5. The heroes of Alger's novels were *ragged* individualists.
6. Shakespeare wrote his plays in *dynamic* pentameter.
7. She had traveled in France and the *contagious* smaller countries.
8. Librarians should see to it that *immortal* books are removed from the libraries.
9. Like other famous musicians, Mozart had been a child *protégé.*

EXERCISE 1

Look at the three possible meanings listed for each italicized word. Choose the meaning that *fits the context.* Put the letter for the right meaning after the number of the sentence.

EXAMPLE: 7. The unwelcome visitor apologized for the *intrusion.*
    a. unwanted company b. noise c. high price
(Answer) *7a*

1. The people were supposed to be *gregarious,* but they slammed doors in my face.
 a. seriously ill   b. crowd-loving   c. awake
2. He had been getting better, but during the night his condition *deteriorated.*
 a. got worse   b. improved   c. was recorded
3. The investigators *scrutinized* all our records carefully.
 a. threw out   b. rejected   c. studied closely
4. Ticks and other *parasites* were living off the huge animals.
 a. exploiting others b. scars   c. layers
5. Fog can *impair* a driver's vision even more than a heavy rain.
 a. sharpen   b. question   c. make worse
6. He always wanted to be *inconspicuous,* like an ordinary shopper in a department store.
 a. unusual   b. unnoticed   c. incompetent

7. The company paid the workers *incapacitated* in the accident.
   a. disabled   b. responsible   c. fired
8. To the visitors from an advanced civilization, the houses might have seemed like *primitive* huts.
   a. cozy   b. backward   c. well-insulated
9. Visitors to the castle were amazed at the contrast between the modern conveniences and the *anachronistic* surroundings.
   a. ahead of their time   b. wrong for the time   c. well-run
10. The wary officials *disclaimed* all responsibility.
    a. took over   b. shared   c. refused
11. There was strong applause for several speakers, but only *perfunctory* applause for our candidate.
    a. energetic   b. shouted   c. lukewarm
12. Though the gorilla is often shown as a *ferocious* animal, it is in fact a gentle creature.
    a. easily taught   b. savage   c. thoughtful
13. The African nations were asked to set aside land for game *preserves*.
    a. protected areas   b. factories   c. training grounds
14. The passenger pigeon, once numbering in many millions, is now *extinct*.
    a. numerous   b. very tasty   c. died out
15. She answered our questions with an impressive *array* of facts.
    a. spotty sampling   b. ordered collection   c. wild search
16. The invaders melted down many of the priceless golden *artifacts*.
    a. inscriptions   b. temples   c. art objects
17. The United Nations planned a *global* offensive against hunger.
    a. worldwide   b. unnecessary   c. humorous
18. After the war, the tank factories were *converted* to other uses.
    a. expanded   b. adapted   c. closed down
19. We watched a *sentimental* story about an abandoned baby.
    a. sugary   b. adventure   c. newspaper
20. They worked with tireless *perseverance,* like beavers building a dam.
    a. taking things easy   b. aimlessness   c. keeping at it

---

EXERCISE 2

In the following sentences, *context* helps show the meaning of the italicized words. Match each word with the right meaning from the list given on page 18, for instance *4c* or *5f*.

1. **cadge**   It is generally considered low and shameful to *cadge* a consultation from a doctor or a lawyer.

2. **incentive**   The promise of a two-weeks' vacation was an added *incentive* for the people working on the project.

3. **resilience**   My aunt, who used to be a bundle of energy, has lost some of her old *resilience* and resourcefulness.

4. tawdry   The souvenir shop offered nothing but *tawdry* scarves and gadgets.

5. provincial   Nothing can broaden a *provincial* outlook faster than life in a foreign country.

6. consensus   The President had hoped for a broad *consensus* rather than for support by a slim partisan majority.

7. corrupt   His originally noble motives were *corrupted* by constant pressure from dishonest associates.

8. scruple   Her ruthless partners were impatient with the *scruples* that kept her from taking advantage of the customers.

9. encroachment   The mayor objected to the *encroachments* of the city council on his authority.

10. avid   Burning with ambition, Sue became an *avid* reader of the paper's business pages.

11. conspicuous   Jerry had selected an eye-catching red convertible, but his fiancée made him choose something less *conspicuous*.

12. decorous   The dances at the club had always been highly *decorous*, with everyone well behaved and politely bored.

13. untenable   As more and more staff members denied him their support, the official's position became *untenable*, and he resigned.

14. compulsory   When voluntary enlistments fell off, military service had to be made *compulsory*.

15. exempt   The speaker protested against the kind of favoritism that makes us *exempt* nonprofit institutions from taxes.

16. inert   For once a political issue had stirred up the usually *inert* masses of voters.

17. expedient   Since the governor's views on the new tax were not shared by the majority, she found it *expedient* not to mention them in public.

18. relentless   Candidates used to a leisurely style of campaigning found to their sorrow that Hogan was a *relentless* competitor.

19. logistics   Hampered by lack of shipping, the movement of new divisions and supplies to the islands proved an almost insoluble problem in *logistics*.

20. frenzy   Their efforts threatened by the steadily rising water, the volunteers engaged in a *frenzy* of activity.

MEANINGS:

a. narrow-minded	k. military deployment and supply
b. encouragement	l. free from a requirement
c. very eager	m. very noticeable
d. sponge	n. gradual taking over
e. cheap, shoddy	o. turn evil
f. bouncy energy	p. mad rush
g. meeting of minds	q. without letup
h. qualm of conscience	r. without movement
i. impossible to hold on to	s. enforced as a requirement
j. wise for practical purposes	t. very dignified and proper

W2b
Word Meanings

Study the full range of uses for words with many different meanings.

Few of our words have one simple and limited meaning. Most of our words have several meanings and several major uses, depending on the context.

Remember:

(1) Two or three words of different origin and meaning may have come to look and sound alike. We call such words **homonyms.** A dictionary will usually have separate numbered entries for such words:

bat[1]   wooden stick or club
bat[2]   a mouselike mammal with wings

bay[1]   arm of a sea or lake
bay[2]   deep, long drawn-out barking of a dog
bay[3]   small, ornamental tree
bay[4]   reddish-brown color

(2) Many words have several different meanings that have branched out from a common core. A dictionary usually gives several numbered meanings for each entry. Here are some of the meanings a dictionary would list for the word *beam:*

> **beam** 1. a heavy piece of timber used as a support. 2. a large piece of steel or other material used in construction. 3. a ray or shaft, like of light. 4. a steady radio signal sent in one direction to guide pilots.

Typically, a dictionary will list several *major* uses of a word. It may subdivide some of them further. Are all of the meanings listed for the following word familiar to you? How closely related are the various meanings?

¹dis·charge \dis-'chärj, 'dis-,\ *vb* **1 a :** to relieve of a charge, load, or burden **:** UNLOAD **b :** to throw off or deliver a charge **2 :** SHOOT ⟨*discharge* a gun⟩ **3 :** to set free ⟨*discharge* a prisoner⟩ **4 :** to dismiss from service or employment ⟨*discharge* a soldier⟩ **5 :** to let go or let off ⟨*discharge* passengers⟩ **6 :** to give forth fluid or other contents ⟨this river *discharges* into the ocean⟩ **7 :** to get rid of by paying or doing ⟨*discharge* a debt⟩ ⟨*discharge* a function⟩ **syn** see FREE — **dis·charg·er** *n*

—*Webster's New Students Dictionary*

(3) Be prepared to find a word used with a limited or technical meaning in a special setting. Dictionaries often use **subject labels,** like *Naut.* for "nautical"—navy talk, or sailors' talk. The italicized words in the following sentence would have special meanings in a description of farming country:

> We found the town a thriving place, with rich *country* behind it, an *elevator* in front of it, and in the center a fine *mill* for the manufacture of cottonseed oil.

What kind of *elevator* is meant? How does the use of the word *country* here differ from its most common use? Have you encountered the word *mill* the way it is used here?

(4) Look out for earlier meanings that have gone out of use. Dictionaries use the label **archaic** for very old-fashioned words, like the biblical *thou* and *thee*. They use the label **obsolete** for words that have gone out of use altogether. Here are some examples of earlier meanings:

nice	8. *Archaic.* particular, fussy.
impress	2. *Archaic.* to force into military service, especially in the navy.
cunning	3. *Archaic.* skillful, expert.
curious	3. *Archaic.* taking great care, careful.

In each of the following, the same word is used with two different meanings. For each use, write down a word or phrase that means roughly the same. Write your answers on a separate sheet of paper.

EXERCISE 1

1. cut	(a) *cut* bread	(b) *cut* an acquaintance
2. odd	(a) *odd* number	(b) *odd* appearance
3. stand	(a) *stand* in line	(b) unable to *stand* it
4. mind	(a) *mind* the store	(b) if you don't *mind*
5. right	(a) turn *right*	(b) do it *right*
6. bank	(a) *bank* on a raise	(b) *bank* a fire
7. living	(a) make a *living*	(b) *living* quarters
8. overlook	(a) *overlook* a mistake	(b) hills *overlook* the city
9. shop	(a) machine *shop*	(b) dress *shop*
10. game	(a) play a *game*	(b) *game* preserve

Words

EXERCISE 2

Each of the following sets shows the same word used with three different meanings. Match the number of the sample sentence with the letter for the right meaning, such as *2b* or *3a*.

(A)   1. All our *records* were lost in the fire.
      2. We should study the candidate's *record*.
      3. Attendance broke all *records*.
         a. past performance   b. document   c. best performance

(B)   4. My grandmother tired of the visitors' *attentions*.
      5. The study of plants requires careful *attention*.
      6. The soldiers came to *attention*.
         a. rigid posture   b. courtesy   c. observation

(C)   7. Angela was reading a book of ancient *legends*.
      8. The *legend* identified the coin as late Roman.
      9. The *legend* was so unclear that the map was useless.
         a. inscription   b. story   c. key

(D) 10. Everyone praised her sunny *disposition*.
    11. Her *disposition* of the property pleased nobody.
    12. People are showing a *disposition* to invest more freely.
       a. settlement   b. temper   c. inclination

(E) 13. My English teachers have always had high *standards*.
    14. The emperor's *standard* was planted in front of the tent.
    15. Her achievement will serve as a *standard* of excellence.
       a. model   b. banner   c. yardstick

(F) 16. The legislature amended the state *constitution*.
    17. Her grandmother was a person of strong *constitution*.
    18. The president did not like the *constitution* of the committee.
       a. physical state   b. basic laws   c. makeup

(G) 19. Theory is useless without *practice*.
    20. *Practice* makes perfect.
    21. It had been his *practice* to interview the candidates.
       a. regular training   b. application   c. custom

(H) 22. The Red Cross organized *relief* for the flood victims.
    23. The guard posted at the gate was waiting for *relief*.
    24. Local homeowners were hoping for tax *relief*.
       a. lessening   b. aid   c. release

(I) 25. The prisoners were treated according to the Geneva *Convention*.
    26. *Convention* required men to open doors for women.
    27. The state *convention* will be held in July.
       a. meeting   b. agreement   c. custom

(J) 28. A gray *substance* had formed at the bottom of the jar.
    29. The article gave the *substance* of the governor's speech.
    30. His cousin was a person of *substance* in the community.
       a. importance   b. main content   c. matter

Some common words like *body* or *head* have dozens of meanings and uses. Suppose one of your friends is an exchange student bewildered by the English language. Help him or her tell apart the words in each of the following sets. Explain each phrase in a few words of your own.

EXERCISE 3

(A)   1. body English
     2. body language
     3. bodyguard
     4. body stocking
     5. body snatcher
     6. busybody
     7. homebody
     8. body building
     9. body surfing
   10. body shop

(B) 11. headcount
   12. head office
   13. figurehead
   14. make headway
   15. a head of steam
   16. a head for figures
   17. head off
   18. thunderhead
   19. headlight
   20. headline

Learn about words by studying synonyms and antonyms.

W2c
Synonyms and Antonyms

When we study a word, we often ask: What are possible **synonyms**—words that mean roughly the same? Synonyms of *vow* are *pledge* and *promise*. A vow is a very solemn kind of promise. Often we learn by looking not only at synonyms but also at **antonyms**—words with roughly the *opposite* meaning. *Latent* means something like "dormant"—the opposite of *active*. A "latent" talent is a potential talent not yet in action.

Remember:

(1) We usually have a choice of several words that mean roughly but not quite the same thing. We call such words **synonyms.** Dictionaries often use synonyms to explain the meaning of a word:

bau·ble	a showy *trinket*, a *trifle*
in·hib·it	*hold back, check, restrain*
junk	*rubbish, trash*

A good dictionary offers frequent "synonymies" comparing and contrasting a term with other related words.

> **syn** DISCUSS, ARGUE, DEBATE mean to talk about in order to reach conclusions or to convince others. DISCUSS implies a presentation of considerations pro and con and suggests an interchange of opinion for the sake of clarifying issues; ARGUE implies the marshaling of evidence and reasons to support a proposition or proposal; DEBATE stresses formal or public argument between opposing parties
>
> —*Webster's New Students Dictionary*

(2) Articulate people usually have a whole range of related words at their disposal. First-rate speakers or writers do not seem to be groping for a word. They have a plentiful supply of words ready to do their bidding. For each major idea, they have a whole arsenal of terms and expressions:

"give up"	abandon, surrender, resign, yield
"reject"	renounce, repudiate, disclaim
"pay"	reward, compensate, remunerate
"get back"	regain, recover, retrieve, recoup, recuperate
"do offhand"	improvise, extemporize, ad-lib
"lengthen"	stretch, extend, prolong, elongate

(3) The right synonym has just the right shade of meaning. Often the meanings of two words merely overlap, with important differences. Possible synonyms of *pretext* are *alibi* and *excuse*. But a "pretext" is usually an excuse we offer *before* we do something. An "alibi" is an excuse we offer *after:*

She went back on the *pretext* of looking for her tennis racquet.
Illness was his *alibi* for not returning the book on time.

Study the shades of meaning that set apart synonyms like those in the following pairs:

evident—apparent	Something that is evident is more *certain* than something that is apparent, since appearances may deceive.
request—demand	A demand is a *strong* request, asking for something *due.*
modest—diffident	A diffident person is so *extremely* modest that he or she lacks self-confidence.
agree—concur	We concur when we do not just agree generally but *specifically,* on definite points.
discover—invent	We discover something that was there for us to find all the time. We invent something by putting things together in a *new* combination.
conceit—disdain	Conceit is a proud person's too high opinion of *herself* or *himself.* His or her disdain shows a too low opinion of *others.*
glib—pat	A ready answer sounds glib when it was made up too *quickly,* without thinking. It sounds pat when it was made up *ahead of time* and perhaps used before.

mutual—reciprocal	"Mutual" refers to things shared in a general way. "Reciprocal" refers to *specific* obligations or transactions that work both ways.
statute—ordinance	A statute is a law passed by a legislature. An ordinance is passed by a more *limited* local authority and often in a less elaborate way.
aloof—shy	An aloof person may stay away from people because he or she feels *superior*. A shy person stays alone because he or she feels *inferior*.

A. Of the three words that follow each listed word, two mean roughly the same as the original word. Find the word that is *not* a synonym. Put its number after the letter of the original word.

EXERCISE 1

EXAMPLE: 7. *fictitious* a. invented b. serious c. imaginary   *opposite*
(Answer) *7b*

1. **exaggerated**   a. overdone   b. extravagant   c. watertight
2. **disclose**   a. expose   b. tighten   c. reveal
3. **prevent**   a. circle   b. obstruct   c. hinder
4. **lenient**   a. irritable   b. mild   c. forgiving
5. **retaliation**   a. retribution   b. repetition   c. revenge
6. **flaw**   a. defect   b. blemish   c. reward
7. **discourage**   a. deter   b. dishearten   c. accuse
8. **courage**   a. stubbornness   b. fortitude   c. bravery
9. **polite**   a. courteous   b. sly   c. mannerly
10. **obey**   a. comply   b. submit   c. question

B. Of the three words that follow each listed word, two mean roughly the opposite as the original word. Find the word that is *not* an antonym. Put its number after the letter of the original word.

EXAMPLE: 13. *fictitious* a. real b. existing c. awkward
(Answer) *13c*   *same*

11. **shy**   a. aggressive   b. pleasant   c. assertive
12. **simple**   a. profitable   b. complicated   c. elaborate
13. **hesitant**   a. eager   b. questioning   c. ready
14. **permanent**   a. temporary   b. provisional   c. well-built
15. **rigid**   a. flexible   b. slanted   c. elastic
16. **interest**   a. promise   b. indifference   c. apathy
17. **weaken**   a. fortify   b. strengthen   c. explore
18. **slavery**   a. freedom   b. possession   c. liberty
19. **hypocritical**   a. delayed   b. sincere   c. candid
20. **biased**   a. impartial   b. fair   c. alien

Words

EXERCISE 2

A. How many rough synonyms do you know for each of the following? (Write on a separate sheet.)

1. lengthen _____
2. beat _____
3. throw out _____
4. get _____
5. move forward _____

B. How many rough antonyms do you know for each of the following? (Write them on a separate sheet.)

6. awkward _____
7. happy _____
8. freedom _____
9. informal _____
10. construct _____

EXERCISE 3

For each sample sentence, write down the *synonym that fits best.* Write on a separate sheet of paper.

1. **conceit — disdain**
None of us had attended college, and he looked at us with _____ .

2. **retrieve — recoup**
For years my uncle had waited for a chance to _____ his losses.

3. **evident — apparent**
The inspector admitted he was skeptical of the _____ suicide.

4. **elongate — prolong**
The emcee did her best to _____ the agony of the contestants.

5. **aloof — shy**
Tim secretly admired Herbert but was too _____ to try to make friends with him.

6. **glib — pat**
Afraid to discuss the subject freely, the governor always gave the same _____ answer to questions about the scandal.

7. **pretext — alibi**
No one was allowed into the building on any _____ whatever.

8. **mutual — reciprocal**
The details for the exchange were worked out on a strictly _____ basis.

9. **repudiate — disclaim**
The accused writer continued to _____ authorship of the anonymous pamphlet.

10. **compensate — reward**
The government refused to _____ him for his losses.

How good are you at explaining the *shades* of meaning that set apart similar words? Explain each of the following distinctions in a few words of your own.

EXERCISE 4

1. What's the difference between a *riot* and a *panic?*
2. What makes a *hoax* different from a *swindle* and a *dodge?*
3. What's the difference between a *vision* and a *sight?*
4. Would you rather seem *suave, nonchalant,* or *blasé?*
5. What is worse: *apathy* or *indifference?*
6. Is being *insolent* exactly the same as being *arrogant?*
7. What's the difference between *competition* and *rivalry?*
8. Do you do the same thing when you *mimic* and when you *impersonate* someone?
9. Is there any difference between being *passionate* and being *emotional?*
10. What's the difference between something that is *mechanized* and something that's *automated?*

Look at the word in parentheses that follows each sentence. Does it give the right meaning of the italicized word? Does it give the opposite meaning? Does it give a meaning different from the one that fits in this sentence? After the number of the sentence put the right abbreviation:

UNIT REVIEW EXERCISE

> *S*—synonym of the italicized word the way it is used in this sentence;
>
> *A*—antonym of the italicized word the way it is used in this sentence;
>
> *D*—a meaning of the italicized word that is different from the meaning used in the sample sentence.

EXAMPLE: The owner *discharged* the clerk that had made the mistake. (dismissed)

(Answer) *S*

1. By drinking the polluted water, the villagers *jeopardized* their health. (endangered)
2. The pickpocket tried to be *inconspicuous* in the crowd. (noticeable)
3. Her friends attended a *convention* of government workers. (custom)
4. The family of the accused was thankful for the *lenient* sentence. (mild)
5. All their expressions of support for us had been *hypocritical.* (sincere)
6. A pioneer needed an iron *constitution* in order to survive in the wilderness. (basic laws)
7. All *records* of their business were lost in the fire. (documents)
8. The comedian *improvised* many of his most successful lines. (ad-libbed)
9. The tribe went to war in *retaliation* for the attack. (retribution)
10. The investigators handed in a clearly *biased* report. (impartial)

11. The radio *beam* helps pilots find the airport at night. (wooden shaft)
12. Grain was stored in big *elevators* close to the highway. (transportation between floors)
13. The Olympic Games have always had high *standards.* (yardsticks)
14. Her great-grandfather had been *impressed* into the royal navy. (made to admire)
15. Nothing of any *substance* happened at the meeting. (importance)
16. My grandparents' *disposition* had been affected by years of poverty. (settlement)
17. My brother and I were too *diffident* to ask for directions. (confident)
18. It was *evident* that the cabin had not been used for years. (obvious)
19. All arrangements between the two companies were strictly *reciprocal.* (one-sided)
20. The arrangements for custody of the children were only *provisional.* (permanent)

W3
WORDS AND THEIR SOURCES

Study the sources from which our language draws its rich variety.

The basic stock of our language comes to us from the language of Germanic seafarers and farmers who lived in Denmark and Northern Germany two thousand years ago. These "Anglo-Saxons" came over to England between 450 and 600 A.D. As they took over the country, their language —**Old English**—came to be spoken in most of the British Isles. Old English was close to the dialects from which modern German, Dutch, and Danish have developed. After centuries of change, it still provides the basic framework for our language. Many of our most common words go back to it:

- house, hand, foot, finger, bone, book;
- eat, drink, see, hear, have, find, answer;
- good, evil, young, old, strong.

But since the days when the Germanic tribes first brought English to England in their dragon ships, our language has traveled far and changed a great deal. It has taken over thousands of words from other languages. These words came into our language whenever and wherever our ancestors came in contact with other peoples.

W3a
Latin and Greek Roots

Expand your knowledge of Latin and Greek roots.

Thousands of words came into English from Latin and Greek. For centuries, educated people learned Latin as a second language, and sometimes Greek as a third. Throughout the Middle Ages, most education was in the hands of the Roman Catholic Church, with Latin as its official language. Later, Latin and Greek were widely studied as interest revived in the literature of ancient Rome and Greece. Latin was the international language of early modern science —physics and mathematics.

We constantly encounter words that English has borrowed from Latin and Greek. Here are some examples of words from Latin:

> education, progress, state, pure, certificate
> permanent, construct, permit, transportation

Here are some examples of important words from Greek:

> cycle, hygiene, anatomy, democracy, cosmic

Latin and Greek **roots** appear as parts of English words. *Autobiography,* for instance, includes three familiar roots: *auto* (self), *bio* (life), and *graph* (write). When a famous tennis star writes her autobiography, it is the story of her life, written by herself.

These Latin and Greek roots help you build your vocabulary.

LATIN ROOTS

ROOT	MEANING	EXAMPLES
ann-, -enn	year	*annual* yearly *perennial* through the years
audi-	hear	*auditorium* place to listen *audible* can be heard
cent-	hundred	*century* hundred years
cred-	believe	*incredible* unbelievable *credibility* believability
culp-	guilt	*culprit* guilty party
dec-	ten	*decimal* tenth part
doc-	teach	*docile* easily taught *indoctrination* forced teaching
gress-	march	*progress* marching forward
laps-	fall	*relapse* fall or slide back *collapse* fall in a heap
loqu-, loc-	talk	*eloquent* talking well *colloquial* chatty
magn-	great	*magnify* make larger *magnitude* size

Words

	ROOT	MEANING	EXAMPLES
LATIN ROOTS	meter-	measure	*chronometer* measures time *barometer* measures pressure
	mill-	thousand	*millimeter* one thousandth of a meter
	pos-	put	*compose* put together *impose* put upon
	scrib-, script-	write	*describe* write about something *manuscript* "written by hand"

	ROOT	MEANING	EXAMPLES
GREEK ROOTS	auto-	self	*automatic* works by itself *automobile* moves by itself
	bibl-	book	*bibliography* list of books *bible* "sacred books"
	bio-	life	*biography* life story *biology* life science
	chron-	time	*chronological* in time order *anachronistic* out of its time
	geo-	earth	*geography* charting the earth *geology* soil study
	graph-	writing	*autograph* writing one's name
	hydr-	water	*hydrant* water hookup *hydraulic* through water pressure
	path-	feel, suffer	*sympathy* feeling for or with *pathology* study of diseases
	phil-	friend	*philosopher* friend of wisdom *philanthropist* friend of humanity
	phys-	body	*physically* bodily *physiology* study of the body
	psych-	mind	*psychology* study of the mind
	pyr-	fire	*pyre* pile for burning the dead *pyrotechnics* fireworks
	thermo-	heat	*thermometer* measures heat

A. Often, Latin and Greek words provide us with a "second language" for everyday things and ideas. Match the number of each of the following words with the letter for the right meaning.

1. edible	a.	on foot
2. manually	b.	of stars
3. pedestrian	c.	for eating
4. dormant	d.	by hand
5. hibernation	e.	of God, like God
6. aquarium	f.	from the sun
7. solar	g.	of the moon
8. lunar	h.	sleeping
9. stellar	i.	winter rest
10. divine	j.	water tank

B. Often, the original meaning of a Latin or Greek word gives us something to visualize and remember. Match the number of each of the following words with the letter for the right meaning.

11. dependent	k.	"puts something over"
12. impostor	l.	"being carried away"
13. possess	m.	"speaks first"
14. rapture	n.	"a branching out"
15. unanimous	o.	"going way out"
16. lucrative	p.	"brings in money"
17. recalcitrant	q.	"kicks back" (like a mule)
18. prologue	r.	"of one mind"
19. extravagant	s.	"sit on something"
20. ramification	t.	"a hanger-on"

After the number of each sentence, write the missing word. Write on a separate sheet.

1. A *physician* heals the _____ .
2. A *bibliography* lists _____ and articles.
3. A *centimeter* is one _100_ of a meter.
4. A *ventriloquist* _____ from the stomach.
5. A *psychopath* is sick in the _____ .
6. A *thermostat* regulates _____ .
7. A *magnificent* athlete does _____ things.
8. Most of the world's great religions have *scriptures* that put their beliefs in _____ .
9. A *pyromaniac* likes to start _____ .
10. A *doctrine* is something that is _____ .
11. A *decade* is a period of _____ years.
12. When a reply is *inaudible,* it cannot be _____ .

13. When food is *dehydrated,* the _____ is taken out of it.
14. A *centennial* comes every hundred _____ .
15. When we *synchronize* two things, we make them show the same _____ .
16. *Geothermal* heat is heat from inside the _____ .
17. A *deposition* is something that has been _____ down for the record.
18. When our course of action has been exactly *prescribed,* it is as if it were _____ down for us to follow.
19. *Credulous* people _____ everything very easily.
20. A *stenographer* learns a very speedy way of _____ .

EXERCISE 3

Each of the following sets of words uses an *additional* famil-iar root word. Put the letter for the meaning of the root word after the number of the set. (Be prepared to discuss in class how the common root helps explain the meaning of each word listed.)

1. foliage, defoliate
2. associate, social, society
3. capital, per capita
4. videotape, evident, providence
5. science, scientific, omniscient
6. voluntary, involuntary, benevolent
7. capture, captive, captivity
8. vital, vitality, revitalize
9. temporary, contemporary
10. sanctuary, sanctity

MEANINGS: a. see   f. life
           b. head   g. catch
           c. companion   h. will
           d. holy   i. leaf
           e. time   j. know

W3b

Prefixes and Suffixes

Expand your knowledge of common prefixes and suffixes.

In learning new words, draw on your knowledge of the inter-changeable parts that often come before or after the main part of a word. A **prefix** like *re–,* meaning both "back" and "again," appears in front of many different roots:

> *repel* (push back), *reject* (throw back), *retrench* (cut back), *recur* (come again), *resume* (take up again), *renovate* (make new again)

A **suffix** like *–cide,* meaning "kill," appears after many words:

> *suicide* (killing oneself), *fratricide* (killing a brother), *regicide* (killing a king)

Here is an overview of important prefixes and suffixes:

PREFIX	MEANING	EXAMPLES
ab–	away	*abduct* carry away, kidnap
ad–	to, toward	*adhere* stick to something
anti–	against	*antidote* remedy against poison
con–, co–	together	*conspire* plot together
contra–	against	*contradict* say something against
de–	down	*depressed* in a very downcast mood
dis–	apart, opposite	*disperse* spread far apart, scatter *disloyal* opposite of loyal
ex–, e–	out of	*extract* pull out
inter–	between	*interval* space between two events
mon–	one	*monarch* one ruler, king
post–	after	*postpone* leave till after
pre–	before	*predict* tell beforehand
pro–	forward	*provident* planning ahead
re–	back	*rejuvenate* take back to youth
sub–	under	*submerge* put under water
super–, supra–	above	*supernatural* above and beyond the natural
trans–	beyond	*transition* going beyond one stage to another

COMMON PREFIXES

SUFFIX	MEANING	EXAMPLES
–cide	kill	*pesticide* pest killer
–cracy	rule	*democracy* rule by the people
–esce	grow	*coalesce* grow together
–fy	make	*glorify* make seem glorious
–lateral	sided	*unilateral* one-sided
–logy	study	*meteorology* study of the weather
–meter	measure	*altimeter* device to measure altitude

COMMON SUFFIXES

Words

NOTE: The common prefix *in–* has two very different meanings:

in, into :   *inter* (put in the ground), *inflammable* (easily bursts into flames)

not :   *inedible* (cannot be eaten), *incoherent* (not hanging together)

Prefixes like *in–* and *ad–* often blend with the word that follows:

in- :   *illegible, irresponsible*
ad- :   *attach, ascend*

EXERCISE 1

After the number of each sentence, write the missing word. Write a word that best translates the prefix or suffix used. (Write on a separate sheet.)

EXAMPLE: By *extending* our vacation, we tried to stretch _____ our stay.
(Answer) *out*

1. A *postscript* is written _____ the rest of the letter.
2. The person who *dissented* had the _____ opinion.
3. A *monotonous* conversation often deals with _____ topic.
4. There was a long *intermission* _____ the two parts of the play.
5. *Mineralogy* is the _____ of minerals.
6. An *exclusive* group keeps many people _____ .
7. An airplane that *emerges* from clouds comes _____ .
8. When family life is *disrupted*, the people may be torn _____ .
9. When we *rescind* an order, we take it _____ .
10. *Subsidizing* something is putting financial support _____ it.
11. *Progressive* people want to move _____ .
12. A *bilateral* agreement is agreed to by two _____ .
13. When legislators *ratify* a treaty, they _____ it official.
14. *Antipathy* is a strong feeling we have _____ somebody.
15. Goods in *transit* will go on _____ their present location.
16. *Contraband* is merchandise taken across a border _____ the law.
17. A *premeditated* crime was planned _____ the event.
18. People who are *demoted* are moved _____ in rank.
19. People who *cooperate* work _____ .
20. When we *advance*, we move _____ a goal.

EXERCISE 2

In each of the following pairs, the same root word is used with two different prefixes. Explain briefly the difference between the two words in each pair. Try to show how the prefix makes the difference.

1. prediction, contradiction
2. concord, discord
3. rejected, dejected
4. export, import
5. submerge, emerge
6. extinguish, distinguish

7. prescription, postscript   14. supersonic, subsonic
8. prelude, interlude   15. interrupt, disrupt
9. admonition, premonition   16. inhale, exhale
10. international, supranational   17. dissolve, absolve
11. promotion, demotion   18. ascend, descend
12. reclaim, disclaim   19. convert, subvert
13. convention, prevention   20. superhuman, inhuman

Study the contributions other languages have made to our vocabulary.

W3c

Word History

English is basically a Germanic language. But it has a strong overlay of material directly from Latin, or from modern languages that have developed from Latin. The most important of these is French. In 1066, the French-speaking Normans conquered England. They made French the language of law, administration, and culture. The king and the nobles at his court spoke Norman French. During much of the **Middle English** period (roughly 1150 to 1500), English was a language spoken by peasants and servants rather than by their masters. By the fourteenth century, English had re-established itself as the language of political and cultural life. In the process, it took over thousands of words that the Norman knights had brought into the country:

- castle, chair, table, envy, praise;
- avoid, demand, desire, catch, quit, require;
- just, gentle, double, foreign, honest, safe.

After the Norman conquest, many French words replaced native words. Many other French words *joined* native words in pairs with similar or related meanings:

| **English:** | pigout | cow | "lambert" | calf | stool y |
| **French:** | porkout | beef | mutton up | veal | chair |

Remember:

(1) Many of the French words that the English took over dealt with war, government, and upper-class social life. How would you explain each of the following?

| besiege | garrison | homage | mansion |
| revenue | sovereign | warrant | noble |

(2) Many words have come into our language of law from French sources. What is the meaning of each of the following?

| arraign | bailiff | forfeit | indictment | inquest |
| plaintiff | trespass | jury | perjury | attorney |

(3) During the Age of Discovery, English took over many Spanish and Portuguese words. French is not the only modern language that has supplied English with a ready-made vocabulary for major new areas of experience. The Spanish and the Portuguese led the other European nations in the exploration and exploitation of overseas territories. They brought back with them words like the following:

adobe   alligator   banana   canoe   corral
maize   mosquito   hacienda   potato   tobacco

(4) Italy led Europe in architecture, music, and opera. Italian words like the following came into the English language. Do you know all of them?

aria   cupola   solo   sonata   crescendo
soprano   duet   trio   baritone   finale

During the last few centuries, as travel and trade have become worldwide, English has absorbed words from many other languages around the globe.

EXERCISE 1

What is the meaning of the italicized word in each of the following sentences? Select the right meaning from the three choices that follow each sentence. Write the letter for the right meaning after the number of the sentence.

1. Her people had once been a *sovereign* nation.
   a. foreign   b. independent   c. proud
2. Several of the relatives were present at the *inquest.*
   a. burial   b. formal hearing   c. award ceremony
3. Myrna almost *forfeited* her winnings.
   a. lost   b. doubled   c. split
4. The concert was planned as *homage* to the dead composer.
   a. replacement   b. insult   c. honoring
5. She looked forward to her first *solo* flight.
   a. accompanied   b. alone   c. blind
6. The children loved the *trio* of acrobats.
   a. crowd   b. group of five   c. group of three
7. The audience especially liked the *crescendo* at the end.
   a. low volume   b. high volume   c. growing volume
8. We all knew the performance would soon reach its grand *finale.*
   a. dead end   b. high point   c. spectacular ending
9. The news was about the *indictment* of several officials.
   a. formal accusation   b. firing   c. rehiring
10. The judges decided the case in favor of the *plaintiff.*
    a. person who sues   b. accused person   c. heir

11. The conquerors expected much *revenue* from their territories.
    a. trouble   b. income   c. glory
12. A large army *besieged* the city.
    a. kept attacking   b. relieved   c. conquered
13. Juan and his friends spent several days at the *hacienda*.
    a. folk festival   b. rural market   c. ranch
14. The scouts were warned about *trespassing*.
    a. unallowed entering b. falling behind c. taking shortcuts
15. Fred Astaire and Ginger Rogers were singing a *duet*.
    a. love song   b. song for two   c. Spanish song
16. The witness was accused of *perjury*.
    a. false swearing   b. being biased   c. failure to appear
17. They had searched the house without a *warrant*.
    a. owner's permission b. legal permission c. definite goal
18. The *bailiff* was talking to the witness.
    a. custodian   b. lawyer   c. court officer
19. The suspect wanted to talk to an *attorney*.
    a. reporter   b. lawyer   c. junior judge
20. The Spaniards had left a small *garrison* in the town.
    a. armed force   b. supply dump   c. fuel depot

What does your dictionary tell you about the origin of each of the following words? From what language did each of the following words come into *American English?* For each word, write down the earlier language. Can you see how or where or why some of these words were adopted? Write on a separate sheet of paper.

EXERCISE 2

1. accolade	11. haiku	21. piano
2. banjo	12. judo	22. pizza
3. bayou	13. kimono	23. polka
4. bazaar	14. kindergarten	24. premiere
5. café	15. kosher	25. rodeo
6. camouflage	16. liverwurst	26. sierra
7. coolie	17. luau	27. succotash
8. corridor	18. Mardi Gras	28. waltz
9. debut	19. menu	29. yacht
10. forte	20. patio	30. yam

Which of the three possible meanings is the right one for each listed word? Write the correct letter after the number of the word.

UNIT REVIEW EXERCISE

1. **conspire**   a. take away   b. plot together   c. meet
2. **ascend**   a. go up   b. revise   c. take out
3. **premeditated** a. unnatural   b. mixed unevenly   c. planned ahead

4. **decade**	a. accident	b. privilege	c. ten years
5. **distinguish**	a. put out	b. tell apart	c. tear down
6. **ratify**	a. check out	b. stretch out	c. make official
7. **eloquent**	a. talking well	b. chatty	c. long-lasting
8. **warrant**	a. discount	b. official order	c. space between
9. **credulous**	a. believing easily	b. unbelievable	c. creditable
10. **psychology**	a. bodily illness	b. mental illness	c. study of mind
11. **unanimous**	a. without name	b. unregistered	c. of one mind
12. **revenue**	a. remainder	b. income	c. rotation
13. **discord**	a. quarreling	b. exile	c. low cost
14. **provident**	a. planning ahead	b. hostile	c. lenient
15. **subsidize**	a. demolish	b. let drop	c. support
16. **disperse**	a. repeat often	b. scatter	c. different
17. **perjury**	a. false oath	b. prejudice	c. complaint
18. **plaintiff**	a. accuser	b. court officer	c. defendant
19. **unilateral**	a. agreed by all	b. one-track	c. one-sided
20. **rescind**	a. knit together	b. push forward	c. cancel

W4
EFFECTIVE WORDS

Know how to choose words that are fresh, lively, and direct.

Words can be confusing, awkward, and dull. They can also be clear, lively, and just right. Study some of the things that make the difference.

W4a
Figurative Language

Draw on the resources of figurative language.

When we reach the limits of our language, we extend it further *by comparison*. When we do not have a word for something, we ask: "What does it look like? What does it act like? What does it feel like?" A place where several roads meet to cause heavily congested traffic narrows things like the neck of a bottle. We call it a "bottleneck."

When we use the word *bottleneck* in reference to an actual bottle, we use it in its **literal** sense. When we use the word to help us picture something else, we use it in its **figurative** sense. We can usually tell from the context whether a word is used literally or figuratively:

LITERAL: The farmer *plowed* the field.
FIGURATIVE: The train *plowed* into the stalled truck.

LITERAL: The holdup occurred *at the crossroads*.
FIGURATIVE: Their friendship is *at the crossroads*.

LITERAL: The water in the pot is reaching *the boiling point*.
FIGURATIVE: My temper is reaching *the boiling point*.

Here are three major kinds of figurative language:

• A **simile** is a short comparison using words such as "as if" or "like":

Central heating plants under the long black street puff away through its many manholes *like geysers on the moon.* (Cyril Connolly)

• A **metaphor** is a shortened comparison that is *merely implied.* We understand it when we realize that the literal meaning of a statement does not fit:

The misted early mornings will be cold;
The little puddles will be *roofed* with glass.
                                 (Elinor Wylie)

(Puddles do not literally have roofs, but on a winter morning the thin new ice covers them *like* a roof.)

• **Personification** is a comparison that treats *things* as if they were capable of the actions and feelings *of people.* A traveler uses personifications when describing a wild mountain stream, swollen by melting snow, as "*brawling* continually in sight"; or describing the narrow mountain path as "*squirming* around corners."

Remember the following guidelines for using figurative language:

(1) Use figurative language that will effectively help others see and imagine what you have in mind. When someone speaks of "*cementing* the friendship" between two nations, we can visualize it being firmly locked into place. An argument described as "*flaring up again*" produces in us some of the startled sensation we feel when a smolder-fire leaps back into flame.

(2) Avoid figures of speech that have become trite. In routine conversation, we encounter many metaphors that have become mere fillers. We have heard them so often that they no longer make us pay attention. They have lost all power to call up a clear or striking image. We call such tired expressions **clichés.** Do without expressions like the following:

blind as a bat
sharp as a tack
hot as blazes
dull as dishwater
know her like a book, like the back of my hand
throw in the sponge
stick to your guns
been through the mill
when the chips are down

A SHORT HISTORY OF THE CLICHÉ

Many clichés, but not all, are trite figurative expressions. In the following article, a writer makes fun of many familiar phrases. How many of them do you recognize? Write down the ten clichés from this article that in your opinion are the most common or the most often heard.

The cliché is as American as apple pie. An integral part of our way of life, it has become an American institution. Passed from generation to generation by word of mouth, the cliché is among the treasures that make up our rich national heritage.

As every schoolchild knows, the cliché has a long and glorious history here in the land of the free. Clichés were here long before I was born and they'll be here long after I'm dead and buried. Clichés traveled from the Old World to the New to follow their manifest destiny. They crossed the Great Plains, forded the rushing rivers and traversed the burning sands of the steaming deserts of this teeming continent until they stretched from sea to shining sea. And each succeeding wave of immigrants assimilated into the melting pot by learning to mouth our clichés.

And these clichés did not crawl out of the woodwork. Many of our Founding Fathers added their 2 cents to the nation's great storehouse of clichés. Jefferson, Lincoln and Roosevelt created enough clichés to choke a horse, and Franklin coined more phrases than Carter has pills.

Since then, these immortal words of wisdom have become landmarks on the American scene.

Today, however, the cliché is under siege. In an age when traditional values are falling by the wayside like dominoes, nothing is sacred—not even clichés. . . .

But talk is cheap. It's easy to criticize but it's a whole different kettle of fish to propose a practical alternative. And these critics have been unable or unwilling to come up with a single concrete proposal.

Common sense dictates, therefore, that we hold our horses. If we get rid of the cliché before we find something to replace it with, we will be opening a Pandora's box. Charging into this like a bull in a china shop would be putting the cart before the horse and creating a dangerous precedent. The vast majority of average Americans of all races, creeds and colors will have to take the bull by the horns and unite in a rare outpouring of bipartisan support for the beleaguered cliché. Let's face facts: you can't change human nature.—Peter Carlson, "Food for Thought," *Newsweek,* May 29, 1978

NOTE: Tired expressions sometimes come back to life when some-one gives them a new twist. We take notice when one politician calls another "a sheep in sheep's clothing." We remember the Speaker of the House who said of the President, "He keeps his ear to the ground so close that he gets it full of grasshoppers much of the time."

(3) Avoid the kind of mixed figure that leaves the reader or listener entangled. When you shift too quickly from one picture to another, the result may be a blur. The following are examples of **mixed metaphor:**

MIXED: The industries of our great state help *forge* the *sinews* of freedom.
(Implements made of iron are *forged*. Sinews *grow*.)

MIXED: The poet seems to come out of a dream world to *step* into the *face* of reality.
(The poet might *step* into reality, or *face* it, but hardly step into its face.)

(4) Avoid figures of speech that bring in the wrong associations. What is wrong in the statement that "students should be well *soaked* in the values of serious literature"? "Soaking" leaves us soggy—rather than inspired.

In each of the following pairs, a *familiar word or expression* is used once in its more literal sense, once in a figurative sense. After the number of each pair, write the letter for the sentence with the *figurative* meaning, such as 7b or 9a.

1. (a) The *blackout* kept enemy planes from spotting the city's lights.
   (b) The army caused a *blackout* of news from the besieged city.

2. (a) *Railroading* a law through the legislature was their specialty.
   (b) *Railroading* had been my uncle's career and lifetime hobby.

3. (a) The Christmas decorations were *shelved* in the back room.
   (b) The proposal was *shelved* until the next meeting.

4. (a) My sister had been on *edge* all morning.
   (b) The knife had a razor-sharp *edge*.

5. (a) Her move *opened the door* to further negotiations.
   (b) Gerald *opened the door* for the guests.

6. (a) Their policy aimed at *driving a wedge* between the allies.
   (b) We split trees by *driving a wedge* into the wood.

7. (a) We preferred a car with *well-cushioned* seats.
   (b) Government spending *cushioned* the economy against depression.

8. (a) The candidate wanted to put a *ceiling* on government spending.
   (b) Rain coming through the *ceiling* had damaged the furniture.

9. (a) He decided to *swallow* the insult.
   (b) He found he could *swallow* only with difficulty.

10. (a) The runner had cleared the last *hurdle*.
    (b) The proposal had cleared the last *hurdle*.

EXERCISE 2

Which of the following uses of figurative language are effective? After the number of each sentence, write one of the following abbreviations:

E   for effective;
M   for mixed metaphor;
C   for cliché;
I   for inappropriate, bringing in wrong associations.

(Be prepared to defend your decisions in class discussion.)

1. Specialized study in voice or piano and participation in chorus or band make up a perfect diet for the future musician.
2. Character is a sturdy cloth woven of hundreds of threads, and every thread is important.
3. The main characters of the novel all had faults, but to unleash these faults into a tragic chain of events a sparkplug was needed.
4. Often a textbook has been quarried out of a larger treatment of the same subject.
5. To be effective in the world of advertising, a man has to be able to get down on his hands and knees and talk to the consumer.
6. The average young person becomes like a lamb in the jungle when leaving the snug harbor of school to step out into the employment arena.
7. Teenagers should not be placed in an aquarium tank for exhibition and analysis.
8. I tried to change his mind but felt as if I were hitting my head against a stone wall.
9. Rising to the bait of a reporter's needle, the candidate unleashed a bitter blast at her rival for the nomination.
10. When a few points on a test score make the difference between success and failure, a miss is as good as a mile.
11. A popular speaker must have a talent for wrapping the bitter facts of life in bandages of soft illusion.
12. We drove along streets so thick with traffic they were like sluggish rivers of gleaming painted steel.
13. Today's teenager has never been taught to put a shoulder to the wheel and strike the iron while it is hot.

14. Painting and sculpture are gymnastics of the eye.
15. The failure of the program proves again that you can lead a horse to water but you cannot make him drink.
16. His struggle was a long, hard climb up the ladder, interrupted by occasional bouts of depression.
17. Too many people try to get ahead by polishing the apple instead of using old-fashioned elbow grease.
18. To be successful, the members of a comedy team have to work together well, like two people riding a bicycle built for two.
19. The little child they had brought with them looked pretty as a picture.
20. The person who just wants to sit under a tree or pick flowers will always be the caboose on the train of life.

Select *three* of the following model sentences. Fill in each sentence frame with a figurative expression of your own. Use it to create a vivid image of something you have observed or felt.

EXERCISE 3

1. There are a thousand hacking at the branches of evil to one who is striking at the root. (Thoreau)
   FRAME: There are a thousand _____ to one who _____ .
   (Answer) There are a thousand waiting to pick the apples to one who helps with pruning the tree.

2. If a man does not keep pace with his companions, perhaps it is because he hears a different drummer. (Thoreau)
   FRAME: If a man (woman) does not _____ , perhaps it is because _____ .

3. What does education often do? It makes a straight-cut ditch of a free, meandering brook. (Thoreau)
   FRAME: What does education do? It _____ .

4. An abode without birds is like meat without seasoning. (Hariwansa)
   FRAME: A(n) _____ without _____ is like _____ .

5. The soul selects her own society,
   Then shuts the door. (Emily Dickinson)

   FRAME: The _____ , then _____ .

Take into account the connotations of words.

We seldom just give information without showing approval or disapproval. We do not always have to ask outright: "What do you think of manual labor?" We can tell that people look down on it if they call working with their hands "menial tasks." We can tell they think highly of manual labor if they call it "honorable toil."

W4b

Words and Connotations

The same word often carries two different kinds of meaning at the same time. The **denotation** of a word is the part of its meaning that carries neutral information. It is part of the meaning that signals to us: "Here it is. I am merely pointing it out." The **connotation** of a word is the part of its meaning that carries personal preference, approval or disapproval. The denotation of *cur* is simply: "This is a dog." The connotation is: "This is a dog. What a miserable creature!"

Remember the following guidelines:

(1) Distinguish neutral words from words with favorable or unfavorable connotations. Know which word is likely to be considered flattering, which insulting, and which is "straight talk," plain and simple.

NEUTRAL	FAVORABLE	UNFAVORABLE
thin	slender	skinny
group	circle	clique
project	enterprise	scheme
determined	resolute	stubborn
official	public servant	bureaucrat
careful	discreet	sneaky
reproach	admonish	nag

(2) Practice restraint in using words that express disgust or contempt. The damage done by **invective,** or name-calling, is not easily patched up. Be careful how you call someone an "opportunist" or a "snob." Call someone a "coward" or a "slob," and you may make a lifelong enemy. Such words are the true "fuse blowers" of argument and discussion. Among heated charges guaranteed to blow the fuse are:

- accusing a book of "poisoning the minds of children";
- calling a person of conservative views a "fascist";
- calling unwelcome new ideas "subversive";
- calling a lawyer a "shyster";
- calling a doctor a "quack."

(3) Resist being swayed by mere words. Remember to ask: "What's in a name?" A political candidate or an advertiser will naturally choose of two different names the one that suits his or her purpose best:

"patronage"	or	"spoils system"	"accusation"	or	"smear"
"negotiation"	or	"bickering"	"order"	or	"regimentation"
"investigation"	or	"witch-hunt"	"freedom"	or	"lawlessness"

The publishers of early American newspapers editorialized freely and used strong "loaded language" to express their views.

 BUCKSKIN BUGLE

☆ ☆ ☆ ☆ The Colorado Chieftain, Pueblo, 7/22/1869. ☆ ☆ ☆ ☆

Viewed With Alarm

A Mr. Vincent Colyer, who is in some way connected with the Indian commission, has been traveling in the Indian Territory and through New Mexico, attended by escorts of United States troops. This man has trumpeted himself through the newspapers in such a way as to show that he is ambitious of cheap notoriety. He has been furnishing to the public, observations he has made among the Indians of southern Kansas and in the Indian country generally. The red man and woman are the objects of his unqualified admiration. The Kansas Indians are superior to the white of that state.

The rascally whites are credited with all the blame for the unpleasant relations which exist between the races. With this sort of disgusting twaddle, Colyer regales the pseudo philanthropists of the East, and demonstrates that he is a cheap humbug and unmitigated liar.

> How many different words (and hints) in this excerpt are unflattering or downright insulting?

CHIEFS SEEK PEACE

A long conversation this morning with Major Wynkoop has considerably changed our opinion respecting the pending council — if one is to be held — with the Arapahoe and Cheyenne Indians. With a full statement of the facts, such as will be made in the council today, we believe it is the part of prudence to compromise with the tribes named upon the terms which they propose. They have unquestionably had great provocation for hostilities, and were not the first to violate friendly relations.

The Major is confident that the Chiefs now here can and will control all the warriors of their tribes and that a treaty with them will be faithfully and honorably kept on their part. The Rocky Mountain News, 8/24/1864.

> What feelings or emotions are associated with the following words?
> PRUDENCE • PROVOCATION
> VIOLATE
> FAITHFUL • HONORABLE

Words

EXERCISE 1   On a separate sheet of paper, write down the more *appealing* or more flattering term in each pair. (What does it add to the common meaning of the two words?)

1. house—home
2. kinfolk—relatives
3. youngster—child
4. farm—homestead
5. thrifty—stingy
6. foreign—imported
7. customer—client
8. train—drill
9. handcrafted—handmade
10. limited—exclusive

EXERCISE 2   On a separate sheet of paper, write down the more *unfavorable* word in each pair. (Be prepared to explain what the word adds to the common meaning of the two words.)

1. firm—ruthless
2. domineering—masterful
3. paint—daub
4. boast—brag
5. haggle—bargain
6. clever—tricky
7. error—blunder
8. amateur—dabbler
9. fanatic—dedicated
10. reckless—daring
11. shoddy—cheap
12. talk—chatter
13. panacea—remedy
14. friend—crony
15. gaudy—colorful
16. fashion—fad
17. withdraw—back out
18. handle—manipulate
19. indecisive—flexible
20. politician—public figure

EXERCISE 3   What differences in connotation are there among the synonyms in each group? What feelings, attitudes, or associations does each word bring to mind? Compare your reactions with those of your classmates. (Prepare notes for class discussion.)

1. dog:	mongrel, hound, mutt, pup, pooch
2. car:	auto, motor vehicle, jalopy, hot rod, crate
3. prisoner:	convict, felon, criminal, inmate, captive
4. work:	toil, labor, drudgery, exertion, task, chore
5. be idle:	relax, loaf, dawdle, loiter, rest
6. group:	gang, troop, crew, team, clique, horde, mob, clan
7. quarrel:	feud, spat, run-in, vendetta, argument, confrontation
8. investigate:	check, snoop, pry, spy, expose, sleuth
9. oppose:	resist, thwart, obstruct, sabotage
10. custom:	tradition, routine, ritual, rut

Know how to use English that is plain, simple, and direct.

Words that are too fancy or too roundabout interfere with communication. Look out for the following:

(1) **Superlatives**—*do not overuse.* Some people habitually use superlatives, words that express the strongest possible enthusiasm or praise. They may use these words to encourage or inspire us, or to impress us with an idea or product. When overused, superlatives sound gushy and insincere. Before you use one of the following words, ask yourself: "Can I really deliver on the promise this word implies?"

> great, exciting, wonderful, marvelous, lavish, tremendous, gorgeous superb, colossal, spectacular, lovely, magnificent, sublime

(2) **Euphemisms**—*do not use to deceive.* Euphemisms are soothing words for harsh facts. We use them to soften unpleasant realities, to spare a person's feelings. We call a child "handicapped" rather than "crippled." We say that someone "has been in trouble with the law" instead of calling the person an "ex-convict." At times, however, we *do* want to know the facts, unpleasant or not. Sometimes, euphemisms are merely ridiculous, as when an airline calls throw-up bags for airsick passengers "discomfort containers."

EUPHEMISTIC	BLUNT
affluent	rich
underprivileged	poor
speech defect	stammer
problem drinker	alcoholic
financial straits	bankruptcy
inexpensive	cheap

(3) **Jargon**—*do without.* People using jargon want us to feel for them the respect we feel for scientists and scholars. They therefore dress up simple ideas in fancy *scientific-sounding* words. They say "underprivileged preadolescent" instead of "poor child." Symptoms of jargon are the frequent use of:

- **"–ize" words** *verbalize* (put into words), *personalize* (give a personal touch), *finalize* (put into final shape)

- **"–ation" words** *implementation* (putting into effect), *stratification* (layers), *beautification* (making more beautiful)

- **"two-for-one"** *home environment* (home), *basic fundamentals* (fundamentals), *real-life situation* (real life), *observable phenomena* (facts)

Words

JARGON: Family-group maladjustments may manifest themselves in socially unacceptable behavior in the classroom.

PLAIN ENGLISH: A student in trouble at home may act up in class.

EXERCISE 1

Translate the following examples of jargon into plain English. Compare your versions with those of your classmates.

1. When asked whether the food met with their approval, a majority of the students replied in the affirmative.
2. Upon entering the residence, I perceived the presence of a faint odor.
3. In case of adverse weather conditions, the meeting will adjourn to the cafeteria.
4. My dexterity in manipulating mechanical contrivances is limited.
5. Skill in personal relations is a contributing factor in the success of candidates for student government.
6. Final evaluation of these theories must await their implementation in a real-life situation.
7. Adequate monetary funds are a must for anyone contemplating a trip abroad.
8. Employees who verbalized their grievances were threatened with termination of employment.
9. The student's scholastic experience should provide proper orientation to adult responsibilities in a democracy.
10. My parents consulted with the rest of the family concerning the acquisition of a new automobile.

EXERCISE 2

Look at the glamor words in the following list. What are the plain, ordinary words that they are meant to replace? Why did people make up the new word? What does it add that the other word lacks? Which word do you like better? Why do you prefer it? (Prepare some notes for class discussion.)

1. disposal company
2. custodian
3. sanitary engineer
4. educator
5. funeral director
6. flight attendant
7. sales representative
8. waste-material dealer
9. hair stylist
10. security officer

What other "glamor words" have you recently seen substituted for more ordinary names of jobs or occupations?

In each pair, find the sentence with the more effective choice of words. Choose the sentence in which the words are more lively, or fresher, or more appropriate, or more direct. Put the letter for the effective sentence after the number of the pair. Write on a separate sheet of paper.

1. (a) Like anyone else, teachers can lead a horse to the water but they can't make him drink.
   (b) Teachers can make students listen but they cannot force them to think.

2. (a) A clumsy person often has trouble trying to do anything right.
   (b) A person who is physically poorly coordinated often experiences difficulty with manipulative skills.

3. (a) Trying to build a dramatic arts program in this school is like pulling teeth.
   (b) Trying to build a dramatic arts program in this school is like trying to get to the top of the Empire State Building using the backstairs.

4. (a) Most Americans came out of the great melting pot with a tough backbone.
   (b) Having to mix with many different people helped make Americans tough and self-reliant.

5. (a) We should give our wholehearted support to the mayor's project—building a new freeway.
   (b) We should give our wholehearted support to the mayor's scheme—building a new freeway.

6. (a) We want to thank our great committee for the marvelous job they did on these gorgeous decorations.
   (b) We want to thank our committee for the imaginative job they did on these colorful decorations.

7. (a) A sufficient supply of provisions is an absolute requirement for those undertaking an excursion into the wilderness.
   (b) Hikers should be sure to carry enough food.

8. (a) The governor has forwarded your proposal to our committee of experts.
   (b) The governor has forwarded your proposal to our little clique of bureaucrats.

9. (a) We should hold our horses before we jump feet first into this half-baked enterprise.
   (b) We should think things over carefully before we rush into this poorly planned enterprise.

10. (a) Once a candidate picks up enough steam, everyone jumps on the bandwagon.
    (b) Once a candidate picks up enough steam, everyone wants to get aboard the train.

THE POWER OF WORDS

To use words well, we have to know more than their dictionary meanings. We have to know the associations they bring to mind. We have to know how they reveal the attitudes of the people who use them. We have to know what purposes a word can serve. The following activities will give you a chance to explore the way our thoughts and feelings are brought into play when we react to words.

ACTIVITY 1

Do you recognize the *figurative* element in each of the following expressions? What is its origin or original meaning? What picture does it bring to mind? Write one brief sentence of explanation for each of the italicized words in the following sentences.

1. Aunt Harriet's legacy was the kind of *windfall* he hoped for.
2. She did not want to run the *gauntlet* of hostile criticism.
3. Even when writing a postcard, he wants it to bear the *hallmark* of his personality.
4. Simply evicting these people goes against the *grain*.
5. The buyer wanted an *ironclad* guarantee of satisfactory performance.
6. In the poem, a grieving father gives free *rein* to his emotions.
7. Unable to face the *ordeal,* she stayed away from the courtroom.
8. Jim realized that his last desperate *gambit* had failed.
9. For many an athlete, the emotional *backlash* of failure is profound.
10. The constant struggle to stay ahead had been *sapping* her energies.

ACTIVITY 2

Words have the power to make us feel comfortable or uncomfortable, to make us feel happy or depressed. Look at the italicized words in the following passage. What or how would they normally make you feel? What or how do they make you feel in the context of this passage? (Do any of your classmates have reactions to these words that differ from your own?)

On seasonable Sunday afternoons the *burghers* of Cordelia Street usually sat out on their front "stoops," and talked to their *neighbors* on the next stoop, or called to those across the street in neighborly fashion. The men sat *placidly* on gay cushions upon the steps that led down to the sidewalk, while the women, in their Sunday "waists," sat in *rockers* on the cramped porches, pretending to be greatly at their ease. . . . The men on the steps—all in their *shirt sleeves,* their vests unbuttoned—sat with their legs well apart, their stomachs comfortably *protruding*, and talked of the prices of things, or told anecdotes of the *sagacity* of their various chiefs and *overlords*. They occasionally looked over the multitude of *squabbling* children, listened affectionately to their *high-pitched, nasal* voices, smiling to see their own proclivities reproduced in their *offspring*, and interspersed their *legends* of the iron kings with remarks about their sons' progress at school.—Willa Cather, "Paul's Case"

Do you ever find that the words you choose rub someone the wrong way? Here is what one reader said after she read an article about how children are taught. The article was entitled, "How Should We *Retool* Our Schools?" Can you explain in your own words what made this reader angry?

ACTIVITY 3

The Education Factory

A "tool" is an instrument of manual or mechanical operation, a machine for shaping metal, wood or other inanimate matter. One shapes, forms or finishes with a *tool*. It is used, relating to human affairs, in a highly derogatory sense, as of a person used to accomplish another's ends; a dupe; a tyrant's *tool*. Used as a verb, it means to equip a plant or industry (for volume production, for instance). "Retooling" a school might accurately mean equipping it with a cafeteria or a wood- or metal-working shop. But what are the "tools" with which one equips, shapes, forms or finishes a child, a youth, a human character, a human mind?

Words exercise a powerful influence upon the human mind and psyche and are essential to human communication. In that sense they are tools. But they are not analogous to a tool that works on matter. One does not speak of retooling a growing plant. One *nurtures* it, feeding it, pruning out dead wood, pulling up weeds that would choke it, giving it sun or shade according to its nature, in order that it should grow to fullest strength and beauty. One does not "process" a plant, nor does one assign it permanently to a place in the garden. One watches and aids its growth, always with a view to its essential nature. The same necessity for nurture, requiring loving care, holds for animals and humans. A kindergarten is a children's garden, not a factory. If children are "rubber-stamped," "pigeonholed," "channeled," or graded by mechanical or essentially mechanical tests, they wither. —Dorothy Thompson, from *Ladies' Home Journal*

1. Explain briefly each of the following: *inanimate, derogatory, dupe, psyche, analogous, nurture.*

2. Pretend you are Dorothy Thompson. How do you react to the following sentences?

   "People in the schools will have to learn how to step up efficiency, utilizing the plant better and turning out a better product."

   "Tests are being engineered that will enable teachers to channel students into the right grooves and train them to perform efficiently in a technological society."

3. Do you yourself have objections to the way people sometimes use words? How would you fill in the following statement?

   "I don't like it if people talk about _____ as if they were _____."

   Explain your objection.

ACTIVITY 4

Newswriting is not produced by a machine. Journalists and newspaper publishers are people—with preferences, feelings, and standards of their own. If you were to read the following passages in a newsmagazine, could you tell *how the writer felt* about the person described? What attitudes, favorable or unfavorable, does each passage suggest? Point out words likely to steer the reactions of the reader.

1. A slender man with jodhpured legs and a rosebud in his buttonhole scooted in and out of the diplomatic conference rooms with whispered propositions on his lips. The diplomat from India wanted to be helpful.
2. Into a large Detroit studio strides a trim, lean man with the suave good looks of an ambassador. His bright blue eyes sparkle like a newly polished car; his smile is as broad as a Cadillac grille. But under the hood there throbs a machine with the tireless power of one of his own 260-horsepower engines.
3. The senator returned to Washington after careening about his old stamping grounds. Scowling, puffy-eyed, he lumbered into the hearing room, elbowing his way through the crowd.
4. At the Versailles Peace Conference, the young revolutionary trotted up to President Wilson to badger him about the "liberation" of his country.
5. After nearly running down a photographer's assistant with the old taxicab he uses for buzzing around the island, the congressman brandished a shotgun and snarled, "I'll kill you if you set foot on my property."

ACTIVITY 5

The following *euphemisms* have been recommended to teachers for use in conferences with the parents of their students. For each pair, compare the two choices and discuss the pros and cons of each. If you were a teacher, counselor, friend, or parent of the student in question, which of the two would you *prefer* other people to use, and why?

1. lazy — can do more when he or she tries
2. troublemaker — disturbs class
3. cheats — depends on others to do his or her work
4. stupid — can do better work with help
5. steals — takes without permission
6. uninterested — not challenged
7. insolent — outspoken
8. sloppy — could do neater work
9. clumsy — not physically well coordinated
10. rude — inconsiderate of others

ACTIVITY 6

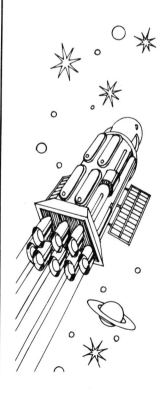

Words serve many purposes besides giving information.

- We use language to be polite:

Thank you for a wonderful time.
It is a real privilege to be with your group today.

- We use language to express attitudes or emotions:

Oh, it's *you* again.
Some people never learn!
He better not repeat that when I am around!

- We use language to impress:

My aunt has her own private plane.
My great-grandfather was the first settler in this county.

Assume that a strange craft has just arrived from the far reaches of outer space and that its passengers are about to debark. They have monitored our language on their long journey and are ready to communicate in English. Prepare a sentence (or a short paragraph) for each of the following purposes:

to make them welcome;
to impress them with Earth civilization;
to explain how we govern our society;
to discourage them from planning any permanent settlement;
to express your personal feelings about their arrival.

Chapter 2

Sentences
Writing Better Sentences

Chapter
Preview 2

Make full use of the resources of the English sentence.

The sentence is the basic resource of every speaker and writer. Studying it, and understanding it, helps us to use it better. When we study sentences, we look at the way they are put together. We look at what holds them together and enables them to do their work. Though each sentence is different, they all share basic common features. Some basic tools are used over and over again. Remember the three most basic tools we use in putting together an English sentence:

(1) To build an English sentence, we put words in the right order. The most basic tool we use in sentence building is word order. A dictionary lists separate words, in alphabetical order. To communicate, we have to arrange words so that they will make sense.

Here are some English sentences first without, and then *with,* the right word order:

RANDOM: Afar—hunter—moose—from—roar—the—of—heard— the—the

RIGHT ORDER: The hunter heard the roar of the moose from afar.

RANDOM: The—Mexico—uncle—from—my—officials—had—barred

RIGHT ORDER: The officials had barred my uncle from Mexico.

THE ENGLISH SENTENCE
A Bird's-Eye View

KINDS OF WORDS

Nouns	*The batter* hit *the ball*.
Pronouns	*She* knew *everything*.
Verbs	My friends *worked* on weekends.
Adjectives	We have *curious* neighbors.
Adverbs	She looked at us *curiously*.
Prepositions	We were driving *without* a map.
Connectives	They sang *and* danced around the fire.

SEVEN SENTENCE PATTERNS

S–V	Dogs bark.
S–V–O	The dog chased the cat.
S–LV–N	Sue was her cousin.
S–LV–Adj	Her eyes were brown.
S–V–IO–O	Father gave Jim a dime.
S–V–O–OC	Tom called Harry his friend.
S–V–O–Adj	The hecklers made the speaker angry.

ADAPTING THE SIMPLE SENTENCE

Questions	*Do* your parents *know?*
Requests	*Leave* the house!
The Passive	The cat *was chased* by the dog.

KINDS OF CLAUSES

Independent	He slipped, *but* the rope held.
Adverbial	Catch me *if* you can.
Relative	We asked people *who* knew.
Noun Clause	I know *that* you care.

SPECIAL SENTENCE RESOURCES

Appositive	Marie Curie, *a French scientist,* discovered radium.
Present Participle	*Buzzing* bees surrounded us.
Past Participle	We stared at the *broken* vase.
Verbal Noun	*Seeing* is *believing*.
Infinitive	*To err* is human.

Even minor changes in word order may produce major changes in meaning:

The dentist *had pulled* a tooth.
The dentist *had* a tooth *pulled*.

Everybody *had to tell* a story.
Everybody *had* a story *to tell*.

I know the man *that you met*.
I know *that you met* the man.

I *need* all the money I *get*.
I *get* all the money I *need*.

(2) We use the right **word forms** *to turn a group of words into an English sentence.* Most English words have more than one form: *dog* and *dogs, ask* and *asked, fast* and *faster, I* and *me.* Each form of a word gives us the same basic meaning with a slight difference added. The difference fits it for a different role in a sentence. We use different forms of the same word in the sentences in each of the following groups:

child	The _____ was acting strange.	(child)
	The _____ were acting strange.	(children)
	The _____ mother punished him.	(child's)

work	At present she _____ nights.	(works)
	She has always _____ hard.	(worked)
	She was _____ full time.	(working)

fast	Jim is a very _____ runner.	(fast)
	Henry is _____ than Jim.	(faster)
	June is the _____ of the three.	(fastest)

The most common way of changing the form of a word is to add one of the endings usually spelled *–s, –ed,* and *–ing: work, works, worked, working.* But another possible way is to make changes in the word itself: *sing, sang, sung; man, men.* Such changes are often irregular and unpredictable:

| go | *goes, went,* has *gone,* is *going* |
| be | *am, is, are, was, were,* will *be,* has *been* |

(3) We use **function words** *to help make separate words a part of a whole sentence.* Function words help the parts of a sentence go together. They do work, or serve a function, for the main parts of a sentence. For example, the most common function words are the **articles:** *the, a,* and *an.* See how these words can make the parts of a skeleton sentence work together in different ways:

STUDENT DEMANDS CHANGE
    (1) *A* student demands *a* change.
    (2) *The* student demands change.

CHICAGO OUTLAWS STRIKE
    (1) Chicago outlaws *a* strike.
    (2) *The* Chicago outlaws strike.

MAYOR SETS POOR EXAMPLE
    (1) *The* mayor sets *a* poor example.
    (2) *The* mayor sets *the* poor *an* example.

Other common function words are the **prepositions:** *at, of, with, to, about, until, during, from, without, into, under, among, for, between, by, in, through, before, after,* and many others. Many of them establish relationships in space and time or between cause and effect:

At noon, several *of* my relatives arrived *by* car.
During the break, we looked *for* seashells *on* the beach.
The trees *around* the house were damaged *by* the storm.

Function words make the parts of a sentence work together smoothly. They show us how these parts are related.

Arrange the words in each of the following groups to make a satisfactory sentence. Use *all* the words in the group.

PREVIEW EXERCISE 1

EXAMPLE: unreliable called her friend Mary
(Possible   *Mary called her friend unreliable.* or,
Answers)   *Her friend called Mary unreliable.* or,
           Mary called her unreliable friend.

1. his Harold parrot called Fred
2. only followed the boy the dog
3. carefree make cheerful people songs
4. Chicago from my sad received a letter friend
5. green with the man threatened the cane the boys
6. in the natives river ate huge the crocodiles
7. a stepped from the tiny green metallic space traveler capsule
8. the had found missionary friendly the villagers
9. the hit the man with stick the rock
10. driver confused the exhausted the noise
11. welcomed the beady scientists with the Martian tiny eyes
12. the the killed dragon knight ferocious
13. the Ellen made pizza happy
14. spoiled Paul him child a called
15. teacher student the disliked unfriendly the math

Sentences

PREVIEW EXERCISE 2

Change the form of the word in the left margin to make it fit into the blank space in the sentence that follows it. On a sheet of paper, write the changed form after the number of the sentence.

EXAMPLE: **good**   His grades are _____ than hers.
(Answer) *better*

1. **boy**   This _____ score was lower than usual.
2. **alarm**   Her report had _____ the villagers.
3. **break**   She gathered the pieces of the _____ vase.
4. **leave**   The sailors had already _____ the boats.
5. **be**   Your help _____ needed right now.
6. **go**   Yesterday everything _____ wrong.
7. **tooth**   Her _____ are in marvelous shape.
8. **swerve**   He jumped out of the path of the _____ car.
9. **quick**   Air mail is _____ than ordinary mail.
10. **enjoy**   Nowadays old age _____ little respect.
11. **sink**   The boat had _____ without a trace.
12. **teach**   The experience has _____ us a lesson.
13. **child**   The other _____ were waiting for him.
14. **smart**   She was the _____ of them all.
15. **be**   Until recently, his customers _____ always satisfied.
16. **drive**   He went to have his _____ license renewed.
17. **know**   Years ago, Margaret _____ everyone in town.
18. **man**   He kept telling me it was a _____ world.
19. **woman**   Several _____ had applied for the job.
20. **choose**   The gang had already _____ a new leader.

PREVIEW EXERCISE 3

Turn each of the following groups of words into an English sentence. Do not change the words or their order. Add only the connecting words needed to turn each group into a statement that makes sense. Use only articles and prepositions.

EXAMPLE: undertow—was—danger—swimmers
(Answer)   *The undertow was a danger to the swimmers.*

1. city—raised—pay—police captain
2. trees—courtyard—were—bloom
3. censors—rewrote—speech—general
4. visitor—raincoat—studied—inscription—stone
5. hecklers—audience—kept—candidate—finishing—speech
6. blanket—fog—hung—lake—mountains
7. representative—company—met—delegates—airport
8. friend—asked—information—contest
9. girls—met—cup—coffee—concert
10. Fred—talked—friends—intermission

Know the major building blocks that we use in English sentences.

We use a few kinds of words over and over when we put together English sentences. The five major kinds are nouns, pronouns, verbs, adjectives, and adverbs. In addition, we use two kinds of words to link other sentence parts: connectives and prepositions. These **word classes,** traditionally called the "parts of speech," are the building blocks that we use over and over again in putting together sentences.

Review the signals that help us recognize nouns.

Nouns are words like *bird, street, tree, dog, house, program, invitation, disturbance,* and *freedom.* They name things, people, places, animals, ideas. The name of any article you order from a catalogue is a noun. The name of any object you see in a department store is a noun.

Review the features that help us recognize nouns:

(1) Most nouns can show the change from one to several by a change in the word itself. The form we use for one of a kind is the **singular** form: *dog, house, program.* Most English nouns have a separate **plural** form to point to several of a kind. In most cases we form the plural by adding the ending spelled –s, or –es: dog*s* house*s*, program*s*, invitation*s*, disturbance*s*. Some unusual plurals:

SINGULAR:	child	mouse	leaf	tooth	foot
PLURAL:	children	mice	leaves	teeth	feet

Remember: Most English nouns have two different forms to show the difference in **number.**

(2) Nouns often come after noun markers. Noun markers give us the signal that a noun is about to follow. The following are three different kinds of noun markers. (They are often grouped together as "determiners.")

		NOUN MARKERS
articles	*the, a, an* the car, a tree, an error	
possessive pronouns	*my, your, his, her, its, our, their* my eyes, his sister, their idea, our car	

demonstrative
  (pointing)
  pronouns
	this, that, these, those
	this street, that question, these coins	

Other words may come between the noun marker and the noun:

The fast-talking *owner* talked to *the* reluctant *customer.*
His criminal *career* reached *its* inevitable *end.*
This timely *warning* should stop *these* dangerous *experiments.*

(3) Many nouns have typical noun endings. Often we can make a new noun by starting with some other word and adding a noun-making **suffix** like *–ation, –ness, –hood, –ance,* or *–ence.* All the following are typical English nouns: invit*ation,* organiz*ation;* kind*ness,* rough*ness,* clever*ness;* nation*hood,* mother*hood,* neigh-bor*hood;* disturb*ance;* prefer*ence,* confer*ence.*

NOTE: Common, or ordinary, nouns help us put labels on everything in the world around us. When a noun is the special name of one person or thing, we call it a **proper noun:**

COMMON NOUN: friend, tree, mountain, newspaper
PROPER NOUN: Ralph, the Rockies, *Herald Tribune*

Many nouns stand for ideas in our minds or for qualities that exist as part of something else. We cannot easily point to or touch what they stand for. We call the labels of such things "beyond our touch" **abstract nouns.**

ABSTRACT NOUN: friendship, height, idealism

See **M2a** for capital letters with proper nouns.

EXERCISE 1

For many English nouns, we produce a plural form by simply adding an *–s: car/cars; tree/trees; house/houses.* But some words do not follow this simple pattern. They illustrate ways of forming the plural forms that were at one time more common in our language. Or they brought a plural form with them when they were borrowed from a foreign language. Write down the plural form for each of the following. Write the form that you would use after "several" or "many."

1. arm	11. ox	21. professional
2. bicycle	12. loaf	22. analysis
3. louse	13. license	23. die (for gambling)
4. container	14. shelf	24. deer
5. goose	15. freshman	25. elevator
6. woman	16. thief	26. intersection
7. application	17. medium	27. sheep
8. crisis	18. wolf	28. blues
9. knife	19. building	29. emergency
10. penalty	20. series	30. exit

After the number of each sentence, write down every noun that (1) appears in a plural form, or (2) follows a noun marker (or both). Include the noun marker but omit any words that come between the noun marker and its noun.

1. Charlotte Brontë and Emily Brontë were sisters.
2. Their family lived in the English countryside.
3. They each wrote a novel that made its author famous.
4. Their stories were about strong-willed characters.
5. These people often live in a gloomy mansion.
6. They have strong feelings and deep loyalties.
7. The heroine of the book may reach her goal after many years.
8. *Jane Eyre* is the story of an orphan.
9. She comes to a mansion that seems haunted by ghosts.
10. Events happen which could cause nightmares.
11. Her marriage is stopped at the last minute.
12. The big house burns down in a spectacular fire.
13. The owner is crippled when the staircase collapses in the fire.
14. In the end, the two lovers are united.
15. In some ways, this story is similar to the book by the other sister.
16. In that book, the hero is also a homeless child.
17. A life full of disappointments makes him bitter.
18. He loses the dearest friend of his childhood.
19. He gets his revenge against those people who persecuted him.
20. These two books are still among our most widely read novels today.

Charlotte Bronte

Review the pronouns that can replace a noun.

Pronouns are words that can take the place of a noun. Where a noun gives us a full description, a pronoun can give us a quick, short pointer. Look at the pronouns used as noun substitutes in the following pairs:

NOUN: *The coach* inspired *our team.*
PRONOUN: *He* inspired *us.*

NOUN: *Her assistant* applied for *the job.*
PRONOUN: *She* applied for *it.*

Know how to recognize four major kinds of pronouns:

(1) The most common pronouns are the **personal pronouns.** They replace a noun already mentioned, or one understood as part of the situation: *I (me), you, he (him), she (her), it, we (us), they (them).*

FIRST MENTION: *The principal* asked *Gino* into the office.
SECOND MENTION: *She* asked *him* a question.

We choose *I* or *me, he* or *him*, or *she* or *her* depending on how the pronoun is used in the sentence. *Me* or *him* is the right form when we are talking about the target or object of an action: They questioned *me*. They arrested *him*.

See **U2b** for standard uses of pronoun forms.

(2) We use **possessive pronouns** *to show where or to whom something belongs.* We use the following forms to introduce a noun: *my, your, his, her, its, our, their.* These are the forms we use as noun markers. But we also have forms that can replace a noun: *mine, yours, his, hers, its, ours, theirs.*

NOUN MARKER: *Her check* has already arrived.
NOUN SUBSTITUTE: *Yours* will be sent with *mine*.

NOUN MARKER: *Our horses* were already tired.
NOUN SUBSTITUTE: *Theirs* were rested.

(3) We use the **demonstrative pronouns** *as "pointing pronouns."* The same forms can either introduce a noun or replace a noun: *this, these; that, those.*

NOUN MARKER: *That road* is shorter.
NOUN SUBSTITUTE: *That* is true.

NOUN MARKER: *These contestants* have been eliminated.
NOUN SUBSTITUTE: *Those* are still in the running.

(4) We use **indefinite pronouns** *when we are not pointing to any specific person or thing.* We call them indefinite because they are more open-ended than other pronouns: *somebody (someone), something; anybody (anyone), anything; everybody (everyone), everything; nobody (no one), nothing.* These words take the place of a more specific noun in the following examples:

Everybody had heard the news.
Anyone can come to the meeting.
Your threats frighten *nobody*.

EXERCISE 1

How many pronouns can you find in each of the following sentences? After the number of each sentence, write down all pronouns that were used in it.

EXAMPLE: We buy everything at this store.
(Answer)   *we, everything, this*

1. We had never seen this kind of plane.
2. Her Chinese parents taught their children by a strict method.
3. They were as proud of their victory as we had been of ours.

4. Somebody had changed everything in the room.
5. She remembered everything I had said to her.
6. Someone left these packages on our doorstep.
7. I helped with his homework, and he helped with mine.
8. For her, everything depended on this tryout.
9. Nobody seemed to remember him or his friends.
10. You will have to choose between these boots and those.
11. Harriet Tubman risked her life to help her people.
12. Everyone in the city had heard these rumors.
13. This parrot repeated everything its owner said.
14. Anyone could have opened this door and ransacked our office.
15. Everyone found it hard to believe this.
16. They had lost their shovel, so we let them use ours.
17. They had never done anything for me or my family.
18. Everyone in that part of the country knew this dialect.
19. Those letters are yours, and these are mine.
20. She told no one her secret.

Because pronouns can take the place of nouns, they provide us with a test for recognizing nouns in a sentence. If a word is used as a noun, *he (him), she (her), it,* or *they (them)* can take its place. Look at the italicized words in each of the following sentences. Which of them are nouns? After the number of the sentence, write the word or combination of words that could be replaced by one of the above pronouns. Write the pronoun that could replace it in parentheses after the noun. (NOTE: The pronoun takes the place of a noun and any noun marker that goes with it.)

EXERCISE 2

EXAMPLE: *The hikers* had *left* very *early.*
(Answer) *the hikers (they)*

1. *Busy* workers *were* unloading *crates.*
2. *Regulations* are not *always* easy to *follow.*
3. Her *good* advice *has kept* us out of *trouble.*
4. *Jefferson* helped *start* the *American* Revolution.
5. *Large* crowds *lined* the streets to see *the Queen.*
6. *Rita* always *organized* our *daring* expeditions.
7. *The whole* neighborhood *is angry* at *my brother.*
8. *Her fine* work *finally* earned *Linda* a promotion.
9. *The angry* voters sent *new* representatives to *Congress.*
10. *Ceres* was *the ancient* goddess *of* the harvest.
11. She wrote *the letter to* complain *angrily.*
12. *Lights lit* the *dingy* streets.
13. *Jim closed* the book *and left* the library.
14. *The scheme* proved *a huge* success.
15. *The* dock was *swarming* with *swimmers.*

S1c
Reviewing Verbs

Review the signals that help us recognize verbs.

Verbs are words like *see, know, work, ask, organize, investigate*. Verbs point to actions and events as they happen (or could happen) in time. Some verbs point to conditions as they exist in time.

The following features help us recognize verbs:

(1) A verb can signal a difference in time by a simple change in the form of the word itself. The technical term for the different kinds of time shown by verbs is **tense.** With most English verbs, we can add the ending spelled *–d* or *–ed* to add the idea of "past time." For instance, we attach *–ed* to the word *ask* to get *asked*. We call verbs that use the *–d* or *–ed* ending **regular** verbs. Contrast the present and past tenses in the following pairs:

PRESENT:	You ask.	I complain.	We try.	They work.
PAST:	You ask*ed*.	I complain*ed*.	We tri*ed*.	They work*ed*.

With some English verbs, we produce the past form by a change in the word itself. If we want to add the idea of past time to the word *break,* we change it to *broke*. We *sing* now, but we *sang* in the past. Planes *fly* today, but they *flew* yesterday. We call such verbs **irregular** verbs:

PRESENT:	I *see*.	We *know*.	They *dig*.	We *teach*.
PAST:	I *saw*.	We *knew*.	They *dug*.	We *taught*.

For standard forms of irregular English verbs, see **U1a.**

(2) Often the complete verb includes one or more **auxiliaries,** *or helping verbs.* The two most common auxiliaries are *be* (with its various different forms: *am, are, is, was, were*) and *have* (with its two other forms: *has* and *had*). Other important auxiliaries are *will (would), shall (should), can (could), may (might),* and *must:*

AUXILIARIES	BE	HAVE	CAN, MAY, WILL
	am waiting	have agreed	can happen
	is cooking	has left	could try
	are working	has objected	may proceed
	was asked		might fail
	were invited		will check
			would break
			should change
			must stop
			shall listen

Often two or three auxiliaries appear together. They are typically arranged in the following order:

(CAN, MAY)	HAVE	BE	MAIN VERB
may			*ask*
will		be	*asking*
	has	been	*asked*
might	have	been	*asked*
should	have		*asked*
could		be	*asked*
	had	been	*asking*
would	have	been	*asking*

(3) Verbs can show many differences in time and point of view. Together, the different forms and auxiliaries of the verb make it possible for us to express time distinctions, or **tenses,** as shown in the following table:

TENSES

PRESENT: (now or usually)	I *work* nights.
SIMPLE PAST: (in the past and done with)	Her grandmother *lived* in Oregon.
PERFECT: (completed recently)	We *have received* your invitation.
PAST PERFECT: (in the more distant past)	Germany *had invaded* the Soviet Union.
FUTURE: (still to come)	Our friends *will help* us.

Forms of *be* combine with forms like *talking* or *cooking* to make up the **progressive** forms of a verb. For each tense, these give us an *alternative* form. It shows that something is currently happening or "in progress":

PROGRESSIVE	
PRESENT:	We *are building* a new fence.
PAST:	She *was finishing* the job.
PERFECT:	The dog *has been barking* all night.
PAST PERFECT:	The campers *had been sleeping* outdoors.
FUTURE:	Tim *will be selling* tickets.

The place of an auxiliary is often taken by such familiar expressions as *ought to, used to, am going to,* or *am about to:*

He *will come* back.
He *is going to come* back.

The show *must go* on.
The show *ought to go* on.

(4) Often the plain form of a verb shows typical verb endings. We can often make up a new verb by starting with some other word and adding a verb-making **suffix** like *–ize, –en, –fy,* or *–ate:* organ*ize,* systemat*ize,* popular*ize;* deep*en,* black*en,* soft*en;* glori*fy,* beauti*fy;* alien*ate,* activ*ate.*

(5) Many English verbs are two-word combinations. These are used as a single unit of meaning: *get up, get by; give in, give up; come in.* Notice how these combinations take the place of a single word:

ONE WORD:	He *rose.*	We *manage.*	They *yielded.*
TWO WORDS:	He *got up.*	We *get by.*	They *gave up.*

For agreement of subject and verb, see **U3a.**

EXERCISE 1

Find the *complete verbs* in the following paragraph from John Steinbeck's short story "The Snake." Write *Yes* after the number of each item that is a complete verb. Write *No* after the number of each item that is not. (Be prepared to point out in class the features that guided your decision.)

He (1) *got up* and (2) *walked* to the case by the (3) *window.* On the sand bottom the (4) *knot* of rattlesnakes (5) *lay* entwined, but their (6) *heads* were clear. The tongues (7) *came out* and (8) *flickered* a moment and then (9) *waved* up and down (10) *feeling* the air for (11) *vibrations.* Dr. Phillips nervously (12) *turned* his head. The woman (13) *was standing* beside him. He (14) *had not heard* her get up from the (15) *chair.* He (16) *had heard* only the (17) *splash* of water among the (18) *piles* and the (19) *scampering* of the rats on the (20) *wire* screen.

EXERCISE 2

Many English words can be used either as nouns or as verbs. Which is which in the following pairs? Put *N* after the number of the sentence if the italicized word is used as a noun. Put *V* if it is used as a verb, or as part of a verb. (Be prepared to explain in class what guided your choice.) Write on a separate sheet of paper.

1. My *shoulder* was bruised.
2. I *shouldered* his burden.
3. The member *voices* an objection.

4. Their *voices* were keeping me awake.
5. The agent will *book* our passage.
6. The *books* were lost in transit.
7. The patient's *eyes* were closed.
8. The patient *eyed* me cautiously.
9. I *elbowed* my way through the crowd.
10. My *elbow* no longer hurt.
11. They will *tailor* the program to our needs.
12. The new *tailor* does his work well.
13. A *test* is scheduled for Monday.
14. We are going to *test* your plan.
15. The slightest *motion* could have betrayed us.
16. The referee *motioned* to me.
17. We ought to *table* the motion.
18. At last a *table* was cleared for us.
19. The lovely *drive* came to an end.
20. My brother is going to *drive*.

Review the features that help us recognize adjectives.

Adjectives are words like *new, old, sharp, strong, hopeful, unusual, possible,* and *penniless.* They answer questions like "what kind?" or "which one?" When we use a noun like *car,* we often fill in other words that help explain what kind of car it is, or which car we mean:

an *old* car	an *expensive* model
a *new* model	a *second* car
the *big* car	the *red* Buick
a *foreign* car	an *antique* Studebaker

Words that provide this kind of additional information are called **modifiers.** Adjectives modify nouns. Their most common position is immediately before a noun to tell us what kind or which one.

The following features help us recognize adjectives:

(1) Most adjectives can be used in ways that show degree. We can use them after **intensifiers** like *very, fairly,* or *extremely.* We use adjectives in comparisons, attaching the endings *-er* and *-est,* or using *more* and *most:*

Sigrid is a *thin girl.*
Sigrid is a very thin girl.
Sigrid is a *thinner* girl than her sister.
Sigrid is the *thinnest* girl of them all.

Adjectives that are "degree words" have two additional forms other than the plain form: the **comparative** (used in comparisons to show that something is "more so"); and the **superlative** (used to show that something stands out from all the rest):

PLAIN:	smart	warm	famous
COMPARATIVE:	smarter	warmer	more famous
SUPERLATIVE:	smartest	warmest	most famous

NOTE: With a few adjectives, we change the whole word:

PLAIN:	good	bad	little
COMPARATIVE:	better	worse	less
SUPERLATIVE:	best	worst	least

(2) Some adjectives cannot show degree but instead have to do with number. Such **number adjectives** are *some, few, much, many, several, any, both, every, each, no, either, neither.* Others are the regular number words such as *one, two, three; first, second, third,* and so on. These number adjectives *come before* any other adjective that might modify the same noun:

some old rags	*both* identical twins
several young men	*three* blind mice
no Canadian coins	the *third* flat tire

MODIFIERS COMPLETE THE PICTURE:

BARE: The tree had branches.

FILLED IN: The apple tree had many leafy branches.

(3) Other words may take the place of an adjective and serve the same function. For instance, a second noun may replace an adjective immediately before a noun. The **modifying noun** always comes after any true adjective that might modify the same noun. We can say "her new *winter* coat" but not "her *winter* new coat." Here are typical uses of modifying nouns:

a *brick* house	a *dunce* cap
my *history* teacher	a *can* opener
apple pie	the *refrigerator* door
a *child* prodigy	a *police* officer

(4) The most typical position for the adjective is before a noun. However, the adjective may also follow the noun it modifies. This happens in a number of set expressions and in cases where more than one adjective modifies the same noun:

God *Almighty*	the members *present*
notary *public*	the money *available*

Her eyes, *quiet and gentle,* followed him around the room.

(5) Many adjectives use typical suffixes that can help us make new adjectives. We can turn nouns like *sheep* and *metal* into adjectives like *sheepish* and *metallic.* Here are some typical adjective endings:

–ous: courageous, famous, mysterious
–ful: wonderful, peaceful, hopeful
–less: hopeless, penniless, luckless
–like: warlike, childlike, lifelike
–some: handsome, burdensome, gruesome
–able: washable, forgivable, unforgettable
–ible: possible, audible, incredible
–al: occasional, exceptional, original
–ive: aggressive, massive, impressive

See **S2b** for adjectives used after linking verbs.

After the number of each sentence, write down every modifier that *modifies one of its nouns.* After the modifier, put the appropriate abbreviation in parentheses: *A* for typical adjective; *NA* for number adjective; *MN* for modifying noun. (Do *not* write down noun markers: articles and possessive or demonstrative pronouns.) Write on a separate sheet of paper.

EXERCISE 1

EXAMPLE: The old city jail housed several offenders.
(Answer) *old (A), city (MN), several (NA)*

Sentences

1. My hometown has a <u>colorful</u> festival every year.
2. Large crowds attend the Orange Fiesta.
3. Different organizations prepare floats for the parade.
4. Many floats use beautiful flowers.
5. Several floats carry groups in traditional Mexican costumes.
6. After the parade, the second important attraction is the talent contest.
7. Each contestant must pass several tests.
8. Three prominent citizens screen the applicants.
9. These lenient judges eliminate few contestants.
10. Every contestant sings a recent popular song.
11. These amateurish performances get much applause.
12. Ambitious performers do a dance number.
13. Some participants play the inadequate fairgrounds piano.
14. The final vote follows the endless performances.
15. Our energetic young mayor congratulates the happy winners.
16. The two runners-up give the first prize envious looks.
17. The golden trophy resembles a large shiny orange.
18. Each visitor finds a choice of favorite foods.
19. The town marshal keeps a watchful eye on any troublemakers.
20. A quiet cool evening concludes a hot noisy day.

EXERCISE 2

In each of the following, the italicized word modifies a noun. Each italicized word is an adjective that shows a typical or common adjective ending. Give the meaning of each adjective in your own words.

1. her *native* city
2. a *mutual* friend
3. an *unfortunate* remark
4. *respectable* merchants
5. the *ancestral* mansion
6. a *conspicuous* gap
7. an *elaborate* system
8. our *previous* visit
9. an *unintelligible* shout
10. a *private* conversation
11. *ornamental* plants
12. an *incredible* story
13. an *essential* requirement
14. their *immediate* reply
15. the *obvious* answer
16. a *mechanical* smile
17. an *undeniable* truth
18. a *permanent* job
19. a *generous* allowance
20. *malicious* intent

Use adjectives to fill the blanks in the following frame sentences. (Make some use of modifying nouns if you wish.) Use more than one adjective in at least some of the blanks. Write the completed sentences on a separate sheet.

EXERCISE 3

EXAMPLE: The _____ rider mounted the _____ horse.
(Answer)   The *dirty little* rider mounted the *wooden toy* horse.

1. The stranger had a (an) _____ face, _____ eyes, and _____ hair.
2. The _____ traveler asked the _____ guide _____ questions.
3. _____ viewers watch _____ shows.
4. The _____ author wrote _____ stories for _____ readers.
5. _____ mechanics repair _____ cars for _____ customers.
6. In _____ movies, _____ police chase _____ criminals.
7. _____ citizens need _____ air, _____ water, and also _____ space.
8. The _____ city has _____ buildings and _____ streets.
9. The _____ guests ate a _____ dinner.
10. The _____ youngster dreamed of a _____ house with a _____ garden.

Review the features that help us recognize adverbs.

S1e

Reviewing Adverbs

Adverbs are words like *now, soon, slowly, cautiously, suddenly,* and *everywhere.* They typically modify verbs. They go with a verb to answer such questions as "How?" "When?" or "Where?" Many adverbs (but *not all*) are made up of an adjective followed by the ending *–ly: fresh / freshly, tender / tenderly, serious / seriously, odd / oddly.*

How?	The wheel spun *quickly.* We approached the clearing *cautiously.* The boat turned *sharply.* I disagreed *strongly.* We bought it *cheaply.* She persuaded us *easily.* They solved the problem *intelligently.*
When?	Hubert is studying *now.* The guests arrived *late.* You will leave town *immediately.*
Where?	Mark had lived *abroad.* Fate had brought him *here.*

To help you recognize adverbs, remember:

(1) When the same *word is used as both adjective and adverb, the adverb is the form with* –ly:

ADJECTIVE: The *silent* stranger nodded.
ADVERB: The stranger nodded *silently.*

ADJECTIVE: The *beautiful* bird sang.
ADVERB: The bird sang *beautifully.*

But remember that many adverbs do not have the *–ly* ending. Many such "unmarked" adverbs tell us about time or place. In turn, there are a few adjectives that already have an *–ly* ending when used as adjectives:

ADVERBS: now, soon, tomorrow, yesterday, often, always, together, here, there, nowhere, upstairs, downtown, outside

ADJECTIVES: a *friendly* person, a *leisurely* walk, a *cowardly* act

In a few cases, adjective and adverb have exactly the same form: *fast, early, much.* In one case, adjective and adverb are completely different: *good/well.*

ADJECTIVE: a *fast* train
ADVERB: he talked *fast*

ADJECTIVE: the *early* bus
ADVERB: she left *early*

ADJECTIVE: a *good* run
ADVERB: she ran *well*

See **U2c** for adverb forms required in written English.

(2) Adverbs can often move more easily in a sentence than other sentence parts.   Their position is not as fixed as that of adjectives:

We *quickly* checked our supplies.
Quickly we checked our supplies.
We checked our supplies *quickly.*

(3) Many adverbs modify adjectives or other adverbs.   These are typically **intensifiers,** showing degree:

WITH ADJECTIVE: The sale was *fairly* successful.
                             We have had an *extremely* dry season.
                             The water was *quite* cold.

WITH ADVERB: The guests left *too* late.
                             She spoke Japanese *amazingly* well.
                             The hall emptied *incredibly* fast.

(4) Like adjectives, many adverbs change their form to show degree. We have forms like *soon, sooner, soonest;* or *easily, more easily, most easily.*

PLAIN: She judged everyone *fairly.*
COMPARATIVE: They judged others *more fairly* than us.
SUPERLATIVE: He judged *most fairly* of them all.

NOTE: Even when an adjective comes next to a verb, it points back to something else and tells us "what kind?" When an adverb comes next to a verb, it modifies the verb and *tells us how* (or where or when) something is done:

ADJECTIVE: The stranger was *generous.*
ADVERB: The stranger acted *generously.*

ADJECTIVE: The boy seemed *intelligent.*
ADVERB: The boy answered *intelligently.*

For more on adjectives with "linking verbs" see **S2b.**

After the number of each sentence, write down all the adverbs that are used in it. Remember that adverbs may modify verbs, adjectives, or other adverbs.

EXERCISE 1

EXAMPLE: We usually meet downstairs.
(Answer) *usually, downstairs*

1. Authors are always discussing teenagers.
2. Sometimes the author has studied them carefully.
3. Often a book treats the subject superficially.
4. Some writers know young people fairly well.
5. Few adults understand them completely.
6. Teenagers seldom accept adult standards easily.
7. Many teenagers meet their friends frequently.
8. They meet them somewhere outside.
9. They may go downtown together.
10. Today young people usually dress casually.
11. Fashions change fairly fast.
12. Suddenly everyone dresses differently.
13. Young people are extremely sensitive to ridicule.
14. They listen seriously to their friends.
15. Occasionally they conform too eagerly.
16. Teenage humor is popular everywhere.
17. Teenage jokes sometimes exaggerate something wildly.
18. Some young people read *Mad* magazine faithfully.
19. Often it cleverly spoofs current movies.
20. It rarely treats a subject respectfully.

Sentences

In some ways, adjectives and adverbs overlap. Sometimes, two different adverbs have been made from the same word. Can you still tell adjectives and adverbs apart? Look at the italicized word in each of the following sentences. After the number of the sentence, write *Adj* if the word is used as an adjective. Write *Adv* if the word is used as an adverb.

1. The letter had been mailed *late*.
2. Marvin had been a *lonely* boy.
3. Have you seen Marvin *lately*?
4. Time went *fast*.
5. Few things in the town had changed *much*.
6. *Late* applications were rejected.
7. Job seekers were getting in line *early*.
8. The students in her class worked *hard*.
9. Sue *eagerly* opened the letter.
10. The neighbors *hardly* knew the girl.
11. The travelers met a *cowardly* lion.
12. Ann had copied the number *right*.
13. We were returning from a *leisurely* trip.
14. A relative had been *wrongly* accused of the crime.
15. Fred was *rightly* rewarded for his efforts.
16. My friends caught a *late* bus.
17. The principal had handled the matter *wrong*.
18. The guide *carefully* answered my question.
19. The *early* bird gets the worm.
20. We stayed in the *fast* lane.

For the blank in each of the following sentences, write down four or five different adverbs that would tell us *how*. Use different adverbs each time. Write on a separate sheet. (Be prepared to compare your answers with those of your classmates.)

EXAMPLE: The burglar opened the door _____ .
(Answer)   *quickly, slowly, cautiously, stealthily, carefully*

1. She ran the last fifty yards _____ .
2. The bomb squad took the device apart _____ .
3. Some parents treat their children _____ .
4. The audience applauded _____ .
5. The defenders fought _____ for their freedom.
6. My friends _____ lent me the money.
7. Her friends _____ turned her down.
8. The auditors checked all records _____ .
9. The applicant answered all questions _____ .
10. They _____ defended their actions.

Review the connectives and prepositions that we use as links in a sentence.

There are several kinds of words that help us provide links between the major building blocks of a sentence. The most important of these words are connectives and prepositions. Even in a short sentence, **connectives** like *and* and *or* help us join two or more things of the same kind:

Immigrants came to our town from *Sweden* and *Germany*.
Someone was always *borrowing* or *stealing* our tools.
Sue and *her sister* mailed the letters.
I prefer *movies* or *concerts* to lectures.

Connectives do their most important work when they help us join short sentences as part of a longer combined sentence.

See **S4** for a review of different kinds of connectives.

Prepositions are words like *at, in, on, of, to, between, into, by, through, for, about, until, like, with,* and *without*. Among the many other words that are used as prepositions are *after, against, along, among, as, before, behind, below, beyond, during, except, off, on, since, toward,* and *upon*. Combinations of several words like *as well as, because of, instead of, in spite of, on account of,* and *out of* are also used as prepositions.

Look at the way prepositions link different parts of a sentence in the following examples:

It is *about* a mile *from* the house *to* the school.
The waves washed *against* the piles *under* the floor.
He took an eyedropper *from* the drawer and bent *over* the starfish.

At the head *of* the gulch, they found the deuce *of* clubs pinned *to* the bark
   with a bowie knife. (Bret Harte)

PREPOSITIONS AT WORK:

Study Law at Home

Order by Mail   **REDUCTION IN PRICE**

A NEWSPAPER FOR THE PEOPLE

PREPOSITIONS

A Checklist

The following words may all be used as prepositions. Note that many point out relationships in *time* or in *space*:

about	behind	from	since
above	below	in	through
across	beneath	inside	to
after	beside	into	toward
against	between	like	under
along	beyond	near	until
among	by	of	up
around	despite	off	upon
as	during	on	with
at	except	outside	within
before	for	over	without

The following *combinations* are also used as prepositions:

aside from	instead of
as to	in view of
as well as	on account of
because of	on behalf of
due to	out of
in spite of	regardless of

Prepositions are often the first part of a prepositional phrase. A **phrase** is made up of several words that work together as a unit. In a prepositional phrase, the first word is the preposition itself. The rest of the phrase is the noun that the preposition ties to the sentence: *by mistake, on the roof, from a friend.* Here as elsewhere, the place of a noun may be taken by a noun substitute, such as a pronoun: *with him, for me, against everybody.*

Remember the following points about prepositions and prepositional phrases:

(1) Prepositional phrases may modify different parts of a sentence. In the following examples, the prepositional phrase modifies *a noun:*

the town *above the river*	the man *in the middle*
the group *around the fire*	a letter *from my mother*
boys *without shoes*	a service *at sunrise*

In the following examples, the prepositional phrase modifies *a verb:*

ran *across the street*	left *for lunch*
was born *in Ohio*	squeezed *through the window*
had climbed *over the fence*	was thrown *into the pool*

In the following examples, the prepositional phrase modifies *an adjective:*

angry *at me*	rich *in resources*
aware *of the problem*	indifferent *to praise*
short *of cash*	satisfied *with the service*

(2) Prepositional phrases often carry along modifiers of their own. Often, the noun in a prepositional phrase is itself further modified— by adjectives, for instance, or by additional prepositional phrases:

Elmer	trudged	through the *quiet* streets.
The door	was opened	by the *polite young* man *in shorts.*
The wind	whistled	around the *lonely* tent *among the giant trees.*

What prepositions are missing in the following sentences? After the number of each blank space, write the preposition that you think would fit best.

EXERCISE 1

A. "The Veldt" is a science-fiction story (1) _____ a family (2) _____ the future.
B. The story was written (3) _____ Ray Bradbury.
C. Everything (4) _____ the house is automated (5) _____ the convenience (6) _____ the family.
D. Most housework is done (7) _____ help (8) _____ human beings.
E. People travel (9) _____ their jobs and businesses (10) _____ helicopter.
F. Trouble starts (11) _____ the installation (12) _____ a playroom (13) _____ the two children.
G. (14) _____ playtime, the room turns (15) _____ a completely realistic foreign setting.
H. The family can travel (16) _____ the ocean and (17) _____ the world (18) _____ leaving the house.
I. The children fall (19) _____ love (20) _____ the African veldt and the animals there.
J. They play (21) _____ roaring lions (22) _____ the hot African sun.
K. The parents cannot sleep (23) _____ the frightening noises (24) _____ the playroom (25) _____ the night.

EXERCISE 2

After the number of each of the following sentences, write down all prepositional phrases in it. Write on a separate sheet of paper.

(Be prepared to explain in class what each prepositional phrase modifies.)

EXAMPLE: Readers with problems write to the newspaper.
(Answer)   *with problems, to the newspaper*

1. Some columns in the newspaper give free advice.
2. Readers with termites in their houses ask the paper for help.
3. Homeowners want advice about the uses of crabgrass killer.
4. During the summer, poison oak remedies are described.
5. Readers are searching for the road to success.
6. People angry with their neighbors are looking for comfort.
7. Young people dissatisfied with life ask questions.
8. The answers often leave them without a definite course of action.
9. My favorite columnist likes answers with a sarcastic twist.
10. In spite of their defects, these columns are widely read.

EXERCISE 3

Complete each of the frame sentences listed below. Each time work prepositional phrases into the sentence as modifiers. Write on a separate sheet of paper.

EXAMPLE: The stranger _____ approached the gate _____ .
(Possible   The stranger *in the green convertible* approached the gate *at a*
Answers)   *very high speed.*
            The stranger *in the shabby coat* approached the gate *at the end of*
               the park.
            The stranger *with the kangaroo* approached the gate *in a devil-*
               may-care mood.

1. The stranger _____ opened the suitcase
_____ .

2. The judge _____ sentenced the prisoner
_____ .

3. The news _____ brought panic _____ .
4. The girls _____ stared _____
and then they ran _____ .
5. The space traveler _____ called the landing
_____ a case _____ .
6. _____ King Kong goes on a rampage _____ .
7. _____ , Dorothy sets out to find the Wizard _____ .
8. _____ , Dr. Frankenstein creates a monster _____
and _____ .
9. Immigrants _____ came _____ .
10. People _____ like people _____ .

In each of the following sentences, one word has been italicized. After the number of the sentence, put an abbreviation:

N   for noun;
Pro   for pronoun;
V   for verb (or part of a complete verb);
Adj   for adjective;
Adv   for adverb;
Prep   for preposition.

EXAMPLE: *Tourists* were crowding the beaches.   (Answer)   *N*

1. The fans were *cheering* the victory of their team.
2. *Everyone* was waiting for rain.
3. He went to the hospital for a *serious* operation.
4. Many *nations* send soccer teams for the World Cup.
5. The reservoirs were empty *after* years of drought.
6. She ran *faster* than any of her competitors.
7. Large clouds of dust *rose* from the dry fields.
8. Children were vaccinated *against* measles.
9. Many applicants had arranged *their* interviews in advance.
10. We missed our long *walks* in the country.
11. The *government* furnished free information to farmers.
12. Someone had made a very *costly* mistake.
13. *Without* a reservation it was hard to find a room.
14. *These* schedules have all been changed.
15. Someone had *deliberately* started the fire.
16. Our office will *notify* you of any changes.
17. Yours was the *third* complaint in two days.
18. Everyone was talking *during* the intermission.
19. The contestant had *broken* several rules.
20. The new team worked together *well*.
21. The magazine featured two articles on the *problem*.
22. *Nobody* had been informed.
23. We *were* eating dinner when the phone rang.
24. He did the dishes *cheerfully*, without complaints.
25. He had a *cheerful* manner as he did the dishes.

Recognize the basic parts of a complete English sentence.

Though motor vehicles come in every size and shape, we easily recognize a few basic types: the two-wheeled motorcycle; the ordinary four-wheeled car or truck; the truck-trailer with a two-wheeled trailer and its four-wheeled cab. Similarly, sentences of every size and shape are variations of a few basic types. Just as we may classify motor vehicles according to number of wheels, so we may classify sentences according to number and kind of basic parts.

S2a

**Subject and
Predicate**

Recognize the subject and the predicate of a sentence.

What makes a complete English sentence?

The normal English sentence has at least two basic parts. First, there is a part that makes us focus on a thing, a person, an idea. This part we call the **subject.** Second, there is a part that *makes a statement* about the subject. This part we call the **predicate:**

SUBJECT	PREDICATE
Dogs	bark.
The helicopter	hovered.
An ambulance	was waiting.
This program	has been discontinued.
Her arrival	was unexpected.
Your invitations	have arrived.
Your kindness	will be remembered.
These disturbances	must stop.

Remember:

(1) Normally, the subject is the first of the two basic sentence parts. The core of the subject is usually a noun: *dog, helicopter, ambulance, program, arrival, invitation, kindness, disturbance.* This is the part that actually names something, or points it out, or calls it to our attention. Often the place of a noun is taken by a pronoun. The pronoun substitutes for a noun:

NOUN:	*Dogs* bark.	NOUN:	*A friend* was waiting.
PRONOUN:	*They* bark.	PRONOUN:	*Someone* was waiting.

(2) Normally, the predicate is the second of the two basic sentence parts. The core of the predicate is the verb: *fly, wait, come, stop.* Often an auxiliary is needed as part of the complete verb:

SUBJECT	PREDICATE
(Planes)	fly.
(Your friend)	is waiting.
(A year)	had passed.
(Our turn)	will come.
(The shouting)	stopped.
(A new search)	has been authorized.
(Her expression)	softened.

(3) Each of the basic sentence parts may carry along modifiers. Sometimes, a single noun serves as the subject of the sentence. More typically the noun carries along other material:

BARE: *Friends* dropped in.
MODIFIED: *Her various friends* dropped in.

BARE: *Honesty* paid off.
MODIFIED: *This remarkable honesty* paid off.

In the following examples, prepositions help us work in added material after the verb:

Our quarrel / had continued *for months.*
His attitude / will change *in the near future.*
All truths / wait *in all things.*
The machine/worked *until yesterday.*

(4) The same sentence may have more than one subject or predi-cate. Typically, several nouns serving as subjects for the same predicate are linked by *and* or *or:*

SINGLE SUBJECT: *High taxes* had driven them out of business.
COMPOUND SUBJECT: *High taxes* and *a bad location* had driven them out of business.

Several verbs, linked by *and* or *or,* may combine as a compound predicate:

SINGLE PREDICATE: She *reached* into the cage.
COMPOUND PREDICATE: She *reached* into the cage and *picked up* the animal.

NOTE: The following pointers will help you recognize the subject and predicate in actual sentences:

• The subject *cannot* be a noun linked to the rest of the sentence by a preposition:

The *driver* (of the sports car) has left.

Car is not the subject. It is linked to the subject, *driver,* by the preposition *of.*

• When the subject changes in **number,** the predicate frequently changes along with it:

The boy selected by the group *has left.*
The boys selected by the group *have left.*
The parts stolen from the car *are* valuable.
The part stolen from the car *is* valuable.

See **U3a** for agreement of subject and verb.

Sentences

EXERCISE 1
Strip down each of the following to the minimum that would still be a complete English sentence. Remove all modifiers. Keep any noun markers or auxiliaries. Make sure your "minimum sentence" has a subject and a predicate.

EXAMPLE: Lazy dogs were dozing in the sun.
(Answer) *Dogs were dozing.*

1. The door of the lunchroom opened.
2. Two customers were talking at the counter.
3. The silent strangers ate with their gloves on.
4. Tarzan often fights for justice.
5. The people in the story traveled back in time.
6. A winter carnival will start soon.
7. A mad scientist was experimenting with deadly rays.
8. Prehistoric monsters were lurking in the lagoon.
9. Millions of people watched during the first trip to the moon.
10. The neighborhood children had always played in the empty lot.
11. The Marx Brothers' movie ended in a wild-goose chase.
12. Robinson survived on a desert island.
13. The Brontë sisters wrote about life in the moorlands.
14. They went on a joyride in a stolen car.
15. The two famous comedians starred in dozens of movies.
16. Everything in our town has changed over the years.
17. The friends of Doctor Doolittle looked for the great pink snail.
18. This flower girl talked like a duchess.
19. Sometimes nobody cares.
20. The Queen of Scotland was accused of treason.

EXERCISE 2
Which of the following is a complete verb that could serve as the predicate of a sentence? For each such verb, add a subject and write down the complete sentence. (Add no other parts.) Write *No* after the number of each item that provides only *part* of a complete verb or that provides a completely different sentence part. Write on a separate sheet of paper.

1. leaks
2. had surfaced
3. an old hydroplane
4. has improved
5. may explode
6. your record
7. was shivering
8. had given up
9. a chance
10. could have succeeded
11. cruising
12. seen again
13. will return
14. very true
15. descended
16. my word
17. broken
18. wept
19. might be waiting
20. has arrived

Know the four most common short sentence patterns.

In the "bare-minimum" sentence, the subject and the verb alone complete the basic structure. In other sentences, a third (and sometimes a fourth) part is necessary. These parts are not hooked onto the sentence by a preposition or other connecting word. They are *built into* the basic structure. Removing them would be like removing the third and fourth wheel of a truck. We call such sentence parts completers, or **complements.** They become part of the basic structure by completing the predicate:

SUBJECT	VERB	COMPLETER	COMPLETER
My cousin	wrote.		
My cousin	wrote	a letter.	
My cousin	wrote	her mother	a letter.
Fred	called.		
Fred	called	Michael.	
Fred	called	Michael	his friend.

To recognize the most common sentence types in English, we have to ask: How many slots are there in the basic structure of the sentence? And, what kind of word fills the different slots?

(1) PATTERN ONE: SUBJECT–VERB *(S–V)*

In the "bare-minimum" sentence, the *verb alone* serves as the complete predicate. Verbs that do not need a complement are called **intransitive** verbs. They are "not going any further." They do not *lead* to anything.

SUBJECT	VERB	
The flies	buzzed.	
The time	has come.	S–V
His attitude	will change	
The champion	was resting.	
Our scheme	would have failed.	

(2) PATTERN TWO: SUBJECT–VERB–OBJECT *(S–V–O)*

In the second type of sentence, the verb carries the action of the subject across to the **object.** The object then is the *second noun* (or noun substitute) that becomes part of the basic structure. Often this second noun fills in the target of an action, the result of a performance. Verbs that "go on" to an object are **transitive** verbs:

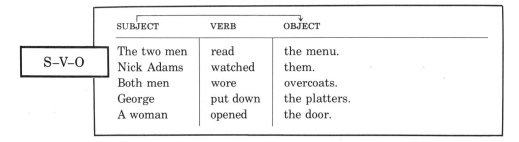

	SUBJECT	VERB	OBJECT
S–V–O	The two men	read	the menu.
	Nick Adams	watched	them.
	Both men	wore	overcoats.
	George	put down	the platters.
	A woman	opened	the door.

Many verbs have both transitive and intransitive uses. Thus they may appear in either of the first two patterns:

INTRANSITIVE: The search *continued*.
TRANSITIVE: The inspector *continued* the search.

INTRANSITIVE: Mr. Smothers *walked*.
TRANSITIVE: Mr. Smothers *walked* his dog.

When we encounter the "subject–verb–object" pattern in sentences, pronouns may take the place of one or both of the nouns. Modifiers may have been added to the sentence:

They had invited *us*.
She knew *everything*.

Harriet Tubman led slaves *to freedom*.
Death devours *all lovely* things. (Edna St. Vincent Millay)

(3) PATTERN THREE: SUBJECT–LINKING VERB–NOUN (S–LV–N)

In the third type of sentence, the verb is again followed by a second noun. But here the pattern is not "one thing affects something *else*." Instead, the second noun provides a *description* of the first, naming it over again. The verb in this pattern pins a label on the subject. We call such verbs **linking verbs.** The noun after the linking verb is sometimes called a "predicate noun."

	SUBJECT	LINKING VERB	NOUN
S–LV–N	The girl	was	her cousin.
	The location	remained	a secret.
	The stranger	became	her husband.
	The mission	has been	a success.

The most common linking verb is *be* (*is, are, was, were, has been,* and so on). Here it is used as a verb in its own right. Remember that it is *also* used as an auxiliary:

AUXILIARY: Ruth *was* protecting Lydia.
LINKING VERB: Lydia *was* her friend.

AUXILIARY: Jim *will be* working at night.
LINKING VERB: Jim *will be* a guard.

Again, pronouns may take the place of either noun. Modifiers may modify each of the three basic parts. All of the following are S–LV–N sentences:

It remained a secret.
Money was *everything.*

Our *political* constitution is the hope *of the world.* (Emerson)

SO I HAVE HEARD

Many familiar sayings make use of the simple sentence patterns. How many of the following can you complete? Write on a separate sheet of paper.

A. Pattern One *(S–V)*. Fill in a single verb—one word.

   1. Time _____ .
   2. Money _____ .
   3. Beauty _____ .
   4. Speed _____ .
   5. Power _____ .

B. Pattern Two *(S–V–O)*. Fill in a single noun, alone or with its noun marker.

   6. Misery loves _____ .
   7. Might makes _____ .
   8. Clothes make _____ .
   9. Curiosity killed _____ .
  10. Haste makes _____ .

C. Pattern Three *(S–LV–N)*. Fill in a single noun, alone or with its noun marker.

  11. Time is _____ .
  12. Ignorance is _____ .
  13. Knowledge is _____ .
  14. My home is _____ .
  15. The world is _____ .

(4) PATTERN FOUR: SUBJECT–LINKING VERB–ADJECTIVE (*S–LV–Adj*)

In building the first three sentence types, we use words from two major word classes: nouns and verbs. In building the fourth sentence type, we draw on adjectives. Here, the label that the linking verb pins on the subject is a word like *new, great, long, green, colorful, delicious.* Often, these "predicate adjectives" point to qualities that we can see, hear, taste, feel, or smell:

	SUBJECT	LINKING VERB	ADJECTIVE
S–LV–Adj	Her eyes	were	brown.
	The President	looked	tired.
	The speaker	sounds	hoarse.
	The food	tasted	salty.
	His feet	felt	cold.
	The flowers	had smelled	fresh.

Remember that most adjectives can be used in ways that show *degree:*

Phillotson seemed *very tired.*
Blood is *thicker* than water.
Her sister looked *happiest.*

The following are all basically S–LV–Adj sentences. What makes each different from the bare-bones model?

They sounded completely happy.
She was straightforward, loyal, and brave. (Edith Wharton)
A plowman on his legs is higher than a gentleman on his knees.
  (Benjamin Franklin)

EXERCISE 1

Sort the following sentences out into the four major sentence types they illustrate. Put the right abbreviation after the number of each sentence: (1) *S–V;* (2) *S–V–O;* (3) *S–LV–N;* (4) *S–LV–Adj.* (Be prepared to defend your choices in class. Write on a separate sheet of paper.)

EXAMPLE: Dr. Smith is a biologist.
(Answer) *S–LV–N*

1. The messenger shrugged his shoulders.
2. The performance will continue.
3. Her parents had grown very old.

4. Our clothes felt soggy.
5. His word was law.
6. Her voice had become bitter.
7. The roads were impassable.
8. Mike was dissecting a frog.
9. Your friends should cooperate.
10. The story sounded familiar.
11. Joan had been selling encyclopedias.
12. Spring will return.
13. The listeners grew impatient.
14. My friend was feeding our mice.
15. The plumber had finished the work.
16. My cousin is a pilot.
17. Her origins remained a mystery.
18. His condition is improving.
19. Your friends will be expecting a letter.
20. Storage has become a problem.

Follow the instructions for completing each of the following sentences.

EXERCISE 2

A. Each of the following could stand by itself as an *S–V* sentence. But it could also be completed as an *S–V–O* pattern. After the number of the sentence, write a possible object that would complete the sentence. Write a single noun that would fit the blank space in the sentence. Include a noun marker if needed.

1. Angelina changed _____ .
2. The farmers were working _____ .
3. The detectives searched _____ .
4. The choir always sang _____ .
5. The runner in second place tripped _____ .
6. The Germans withdrew _____ .
7. You should try _____ .
8. My cousin has been growing _____ .
9. The device disintegrated _____ .
10. The council may reconsider _____ .

B. Complete each of the following. After the number, write a noun to complete an *S–LV–N* sentence. Include a noun marker if needed.

11. Washington became _____ .
12. The movie was _____ .
13. My family had been _____ .
14. Ants are _____ .
15. My favorite remained _____ .

C. Complete each of the following. After the number, write an adjective to complete an *S–LV–Adj* sentence. (Use only adjectives that would fit in after *very*.)

16. Radioactivity is _____ .
17. A teacher should be _____ .
18. Our cheerleaders were _____ .
19. I should have been _____ .
20. The driver remained _____ .

EXERCISE 3

In the following sentences, the simple sentence patterns have been *expanded*. Modifiers have been added to the basic structure. Can you still recognize the major patterns? After the number of each sentence, put the right abbreviation: *S–V; S–V–O; S–LV–N;* or *S–LV–Adj*. Write on a separate sheet.

1. Visitors are enthusiastic about our colonial architecture.
2. Large holiday crowds lined the streets.
3. The field had been a training area for the militia.
4. A girl in a flag-draped booth sold balloons.
5. Dickie Chapelle had been a photographer in World War II.
6. Tired travelers were resting on the benches.
7. Self-confidence is the secret of success.
8. Golda Meir became the prime minister of Israel.
9. Millions of people read newspapers in the morning.
10. The heavy rain had started again.
11. They had traveled to Africa as a team.
12. Muhammad Ali remained the champion for many years.
13. My aunt was always suspicious of strangers.
14. The stage was ideal for a musical.
15. The police questioned everybody carefully.
16. Many people were waiting in line.
17. The railroad barons accumulated huge fortunes.
18. My grandmother remained perfectly calm.
19. We found the picture in an old newspaper.
20. Shirley Temple later became an ambassador.

S2c

Longer Sentence Patterns

Know the sentence patterns that use four basic parts.

There are several common sentence patterns that have four basic parts. They need *two* completers before they make a complete statement:

INCOMPLETE: The news made _____ .
STILL INCOMPLETE: The news made *my friends* _____ .
COMPLETE: The news made *my friends happy.*

The following sentence patterns use four basic parts to make a complete statement:

(1) PATTERN FIVE: SUBJECT–VERB–INDIRECT OBJECT–OBJECT *(S–V–IO–O)*

With Pattern Five, we use a transitive verb, a verb that "goes on." However, this time we do not head directly for the object. Instead we make a *detour* through another complement—another noun (or noun substitute). This additional noun is inserted between the verb and its object. The added noun is called the **indirect object.**

The verbs that fit this pattern typically pass *something* on *to somebody: give, send, teach, write, buy, lend, offer.* Other verbs that fit this pattern are *ask* and *show*:

SUBJECT	VERB	INDIRECT OBJECT	OBJECT
Her parents	gave	*the couple*	a car.
Grandmother	had sent	*the children*	a parcel.
Mr. Smith	teaches	*our class*	Latin.
The aunt	bought	*Susan*	some clothes.
Myra	offered	*the guests*	candy.
The reporters	will ask	*the governor*	questions.

S–V–IO–O

Again, pronouns may take the place of one or more of the nouns. Modifiers may modify any of the four basic parts—subject, verb, indirect object, object. The following expanded sentences all show the *S–V–IO–O* pattern:

Dolores showed us her conch shell.
I can give you any kind of sandwich.
The stranger poured himself a drink from the jug.
A jury from hell granted Jabez Stone his freedom.
His parents wrote him a long letter about their trip.

(2) PATTERN SIX: SUBJECT–VERB–OBJECT–OBJECT COMPLEMENT *(S–V–O–OC)*

This pattern can be explained as a combination of Pattern Two *(S–V–O)* and Pattern Three *(S–LV–N)*. We first have a transitive verb carry the action or process across to the object. We then go on to another noun that *pins a label on the object.* This last noun in the four-part structure of the sentence is called an **object complement.**

The verbs that fit this pattern are words like *make, call, elect, appoint, name, consider:*

	SUBJECT	VERB	OBJECT	OBJECT COMPLEMENT
S–V–O–OC	Timothy	called	his uncle	*a miser.*
	Jabez	made	Daniel Webster	*his lawyer.*
	Her parents	considered	the engagement	*a mistake.*
	The Smiths	had named	the camp	*Nirvana.*
	The class	elected	the newcomer	*secretary.*

In Pattern Six, the last two basic parts point to the same person or thing. Can you still recognize this underlying pattern in the following sentences?

His friends were going to elect Jabez governor.
The devil called his bargain with Jabez a mortgage.
Walter Butler had made himself head of the jury.
He wanted to appoint himself commissioner.

(3) PATTERN SEVEN: SUBJECT–VERB–OBJECT–ADJECTIVE $(S–V–O–Adj)$

This pattern can be explained as a combination of Pattern Two $(S–V–O)$ and Pattern Four $(S–LV–Adj)$. Again we have a transitive verb carry the action across to an object. Again we proceed to pin a label on the object. Here, however, the label is not a noun but an *adjective.*

Note that most of the adjectives that fill the fourth slot in the sentence can appear with endings or intensifiers that indicate *degree:*

	SUBJECT	VERB	OBJECT	ADJECTIVE
S–V–O–Adj	Her speech	had made	the audience	*angry.*
	The shoes	made	Betty	*taller.*
	Jim	considered	our plans	*very foolish.*
	Her friends	were painting	the house	*blue.*
	The report	called	the company	*negligent.*

Can you still recognize this basic pattern in the expanded sentences that follow?

These constant threats were making us nervous.
A friendly word can make a sad person happy.
His apology left the angry crowd speechless.
The grueling work leaves her exhausted.

In each of the following pairs, which sentence takes the detour through the indirect object? (Pattern Five: *S–V–IO–O*) Put *IO* after the number of this sentence. In which sentence does the object complement pin a label on the object? (Pattern Six: *S–V–O–OC*) Put *OC* after the number of this sentence.

EXERCISE 1

1. Aunt Linda found her daughter a job.
2. The boss considered the offer a joke.

3. Grandfather left me his watch.
4. His death left her a widow.

5. The emperor made him a duke.
6. They made the bird a cage.

7. The dying man left the rescuers a message.
8. The rescuers considered her survival a miracle.

9. The doctor called the operation a success.
10. The Pope granted the ambassador an audience.

Each of the following sentences illustrates a sentence pattern that has four basic parts. After the number of each sentence, write the appropriate abbreviation: Pattern Five: *S–V–IO–O;* Pattern Six: *S–V–O–OC;* or Pattern Seven: *S–V–O–Adj.* (Be prepared to point out in class the features that guided your choices.)

EXERCISE 2

1. Upton Sinclair gave America a classic.
2. He called his novel *The Jungle.*
3. The book showed people the slaughterhouses of Chicago.
4. Many readers found this picture unforgettable.
5. The meat-packing industry had made Chicago its center.
6. The slaughterhouses gave immigrants work.
7. Employers kept wages low.
8. Poverty made people desperate.
9. Sinclair considered the conditions very bad.
10. He found safety precautions nonexistent.
11. His charges gained him a large audience.
12. The voters had elected Theodore Roosevelt President.
13. Some people might have thought these criticisms unpatriotic.
14. Roosevelt considered the charges serious.
15. Congress gave him new laws.
16. Supervision made the plants safer.
17. Technology made the work easier.
18. Unions gave the workers security.
19. These changes made the jobs more attractive.
20. A book had taught the country compassion.

Sentences

EXERCISE 3

The following sentences illustrate all seven basic sentence patterns. They are taken from the "Sayings of Poor Richard" by Benjamin Franklin. For each pattern, write a saying of your own. Make sure it follows the same basic pattern as the original.

EXAMPLE: The cat in gloves catches no mice. *(S–V–O)*
(Imitation)   *The driver of the safe car gets no citations.*

1. Little boats should keep near shore.
2. The sleeping fox catches no poultry.
3. Diligence is the mother of good luck.
4. The used key is always bright.
5. A dry well teaches us the worth of water.
6. Debt makes another person your master.
7. The misfortunes of others should make us cautious.

UNIT REVIEW EXERCISE

Look at the following folk sayings from around the world. What is the basic sentence pattern in each? Put the right abbreviation after the number of the sentence:

S–V	*S–V–IO–O*
S–V–O	*S–V–O–OC*
S–LV–N	*S–V–O–Adj*
S–LV–Adj	

1. Misery loves company.
2. A sleeping fox counts chickens in its dreams.
3. People are the architects of their own fortunes.
4. The borrower is a slave to the lender.
5. Wise people learn from the misfortunes of others.
6. Little strokes fell great oaks.
7. We should call a spade a spade.
8. People must go to heaven in their own way.
9. A small leak will sink a great ship.
10. Laziness makes all things difficult.
11. A friend in need is a friend indeed.
12. You should give the devil his due.
13. Brevity is the soul of wit.
14. The trodden path is safest.
15. Birds of a feather flock together.
16. All cats look gray in the dark.
17. Gratitude is the memory of the heart.
18. You cannot teach an old dog new tricks.
19. A cheerful look makes a dish a feast.
20. Haste makes waste.

Know the most common ways of adapting simple sentences for special uses.

Many sentences are simple statements. They often start with the subject. Then the verb makes a statement about the subject. However, many other sentences are not statements but questions or requests. In questions and requests, the material in the simple sentence is reshuffled or rearranged. We still recognize some of the basic parts. But they have been adjusted and fitted together in a different way. We call such readjustments and rearrangements **transformations.**

Study some common ways we adapt simple sentences.

Know how we turn statements into questions and requests.

We can turn a statement into a question or a request by changing or rearranging some of the basic sentence parts:

(1) To turn a statement into a question, put all or part of the verb in front of the subject. "He is ill" is a statement. *"Is he ill?"* is a question. Here we have moved the whole verb in front of the subject. This works whenever the complete verb is a single form of the verb *be*:

Is the package ready?
Are cats good pets?
Was the delay necessary?

If the verb includes one or more auxiliaries, we *switch the first auxiliary* so that it comes before the subject. The subject then splits up the verb:

STATEMENT: George *has been* absent.
QUESTION: *Has* George *been* absent?

STATEMENT: Your friend *could be* right.
QUESTION: *Could* your friend *be* right?

STATEMENT: Her predictions *have come* true.
QUESTION: *Have* her predictions *come* true?

If there is no auxiliary that could be moved, we put a form of *do* in front of the subject:

STATEMENT: Your parents *know* him.
QUESTION: *Do* your parents *know* him?

STATEMENT: The price *sounds* right.
QUESTION: *Does* the price *sound* right?

STATEMENT: The Aztecs *worshiped* the sun.
QUESTION: *Did* the Aztecs *worship* the sun?

THREE KINDS OF
SENTENCES

STATEMENTS:

People start pollution.

We have made dieting easier.

A new process converts animal waste.

QUESTIONS:

Are you troubled with CAR SICKNESS?
Does your HEAD ACHE?
Are you sometimes FAINT?

ARE YOU GETTING WRINKLES?

REQUESTS:

SEND IN THE COUPON.

BE YOUR OWN BARBER!!

Become a
TRAFFIC EXPERT.

Adorn Your Home.

The same rules hold true after question words like *why, how, when, where,* and *what.* They do *not* apply when *who, what,* or *which* asks a question about the subject:

How *have* you *solved* the problem?
When *will* the bridge *be* ready?
What *does* his lawyer *say?*

What *has caused* the delay?
Who *talked* him out of it?

NOTE: *Do* is also used in negative statements with *not*. Here, however, the subject does not change its position:

STATEMENT: Teenagers *need* supervision.
NEGATIVE: Teenagers *do* not *need* supervision.

STATEMENT: The rancher *welcomes* visitors.
NEGATIVE: The rancher *does* not *welcome* visitors.

In questions and negative statements with *not,* the word *do* is used as an auxiliary. It adds the auxiliary missing from the basic pattern. A third use of *do* as an auxiliary is its use in the **emphatic** form of a verb: "I *do* believe you." "That *does* make sense."

(2) To turn a statement into a request, leave out the subject and change the verb to the request form (or **imperative**).   The result serves us both for polite requests and strong orders: "Please leave the room." "Leave this house at once!" In all of these, we are using only the verb, *without a subject.* We can usually tell from the situation who is being asked or who is being ordered. We say that in such cases the subject is "understood."

STATEMENT: Margot closed the door.
REQUEST: Close the door!

STATEMENT: The citizens kept the city clean.
REQUEST: Keep the city clean.

STATEMENT: The teacher gives the boy a chance.
REQUEST: Give the boy a chance!

STATEMENT: The spectators were quiet.
REQUEST: Be quiet!

NOTE: Request sentences are the major exception to the rule that the typical English sentence has at least a subject and predicate. The subject of a request sentence is *you* "understood."

Turn each of the following statements into a question by switching the verb or splitting the verb. Use simple *Yes*–or–*No* questions ("Has he *called?*"). Use all parts of the original sentence. Change only the verb or its position as necessary.

EXERCISE 1

1. Eisenstein was Russian.
2. Eisenstein filmed *Battleship Potemkin.*
3. This movie has become a classic.
4. It made its director famous.
5. Its most famous scene takes place in Odessa.

6. Odessa is a port on the Black Sea.
7. Russia is heading for revolution.
8. Angry demonstrators are gathering on the famous steps.
9. The czar's soldiers fire into the crowd.
10. Eisenstein shows women and children being killed.

EXERCISE 2

Rewrite each of the following sentences to turn it into a request. Leave out the subject and change the verb to the request form.

1. The voters elected Thatcher mayor.
2. The Smiths always keep the garage clean.
3. Everybody was watching out for snakes.
4. Both parties were reasonable.
5. You should know your rights as a citizen.
6. Viewer contributions support public television.
7. You should listen to my side of the story.
8. The loser was a good sport.
9. You should have asked for a refund.
10. The patient was breathing normally.

EXERCISE 3

Which uses of *do* are illustrated below? After the number of each sentence, put the right abbreviation: *Ques* if the word is brought into the sentence as part of a question; *Neg* if it is brought in as part of a negative statement with *not*; *Emp* if it is used as part of the emphatic form of a verb; *V* if it is used as a verb in its own right.

1. Why do we call Samuel Clemens "Mark Twain"?
2. Young Eva did her homework during the lunch hour.
3. Emily Dickinson does not use traditional verse forms.
4. Eleanor Roosevelt did much for her country.
5. Do you like the horror stories of Edgar Allan Poe?
6. Poe did terrify generations of readers.
7. Who did an English translation of the novel?
8. Longfellow does seem old-fashioned to modern readers.
9. Where does Eudora Welty locate many of her stories?
10. Cooper's Indians did not seem real to Mark Twain.
11. The victims in Shirley Jackson's "The Lottery" had done no harm.
12. Richard Wright did not stay in America.
13. Why did she call the book *Vein of Iron*?
14. What was he doing for a living?
15. Many readers do like sentimental stories.
16. Did you ever read the story of Anne Frank?
17. Many early American writers did write about New England.
18. A poet does not often become rich and famous.
19. How does the story end?
20. Huck did Tom a favor.

Know how we change sentences from active to passive.

When we describe an action, we usually go from the "doer" to the action and from there to the target. In such sentences, the subject *does* something. We call such sentences **active** sentences:

ACTIVE: The crew cleaned the ship.
ACTIVE: The assistant coach was teaching the newcomers.

Sometimes, however, we start a sentence with the target, or the receiver. The subject has something *done* to it. We call such sentences **passive** sentences:

PASSIVE: The ship was battered by huge waves.
PASSIVE: Whole city blocks were torn down.

Here is how we adapt active sentences to turn them into passive sentences:

(1) To produce a passive sentence, we move the original object in front of the verb.   There it becomes the subject of the new sentence. Then we change the verb to a passive form, using the auxiliary *be* (*is, was, has been, will be*). Third, we move the original subject to a place after the verb and introduce it with the preposition *by:*

ACTIVE: Rain *damaged* the buildings.
PASSIVE: The buildings *were damaged* by rain.

ACTIVE: Her classmates *elected* Judy president.
PASSIVE: Judy *was elected* president by her classmates.

ACTIVE: His teachers *had called* the boy brilliant.
PASSIVE: The boy *had been called* brilliant by his teachers.

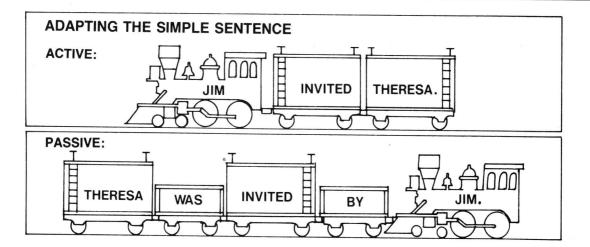

ADAPTING THE SIMPLE SENTENCE

ACTIVE: JIM INVITED THERESA.

PASSIVE: THERESA WAS INVITED BY JIM.

(2) The original subject often disappears from the sentence. This happens when our interest is not in who started an action but in what *result* the action produced:

ACTIVE: *Officials* had declared the building unsafe.
SHORT PASSIVE: The building had been declared unsafe.

ACTIVE: *Applicants* must submit applications on time.
SHORT PASSIVE: Applications must be submitted on time.

(3) When there are two objects, two different passives are possible:

ACTIVE: The official gave *the drivers* last-minute *instructions.*
FIRST PASSIVE: Last-minute *instructions* were given the drivers.
SECOND PASSIVE: *The drivers* were given last-minute instructions.

NOTE: In some sentences the subject moves toward the end of the sentence but *remains* the subject of the sentence. We often use the word *there* as a sentence opener, followed by a form of *be:* "There is . . ."; "There was . . ."; and the like. *There* is not the subject in such a sentence. The subject is *whatever it is* that is "there":

	VERB	SUBJECT
There	is	little time.
There	are	three possibilities.
There	was	no hope.
There	has been	a fire.

See **U4a** on avoiding the awkward passive.

EXERCISE 1

A. Change the following sentences from active to passive. Make the original object the subject of the new sentence. Change the verb to the passive form. Put the original subject after the verb, introduced by the preposition *by.*

EXAMPLE: The rain damaged the roof.
(Answer) *The roof was damaged by the rain.*

1. The coach offered the players a ride.
2. The cook kept my dinner in the oven.
3. Bret Harte gave the story a trick ending.
4. My friends call me Ishmael.
5. My father considered education an investment.
6. A spectacular fire destroyed the old hotel.
7. The new law excluded Chinese immigrants.
8. Thousands of people will visit the new trade center.
9. Grim-faced customs officials checked all baggage.
10. Specially trained agents report violations.

B. Change the following sentences from active to passive. Leave out the original subject.

EXAMPLE: A mechanic has tuned the engine.
(Answer) *The engine has been tuned.*

11. The builders will build the new school on a different site.
12. Modern research had almost wiped out malaria.
13. The voters elected Charlotte Witton mayor of Ottawa in 1963.
14. The post office should forward all mail to our new address.
15. The judges awarded Boris Pasternak the Nobel Prize in literature.

After the number of each sentence, write *A* for active, or *P* for passive. Write on a separate sheet of paper.

EXERCISE 2

1. Bret Harte wrote bittersweet stories about the Old West.
2. He had been taught Greek as a young boy.
3. He had read the great writers of England and America.
4. His education was interrupted at the age of thirteen.
5. At eighteen he accompanied his mother to California.
6. For a time he was employed as a typesetter.
7. He gradually became famous as a writer.
8. Harte was dismissed by one newspaper for his protests against the murder of Indians.
9. Later he was made secretary of the California mint.
10. His first books had been published around 1867.
11. He was appointed editor of the *Overland Monthly*.
12. This magazine printed his best stories.
13. Tales like "The Luck of Roaring Camp" were very popular.
14. Readers shed tears over "The Outcasts of Poker Flat."
15. Bret Harte was praised on both seaboards.
16. He has been called the father of the "human interest" story.
17. His stories of the West are still read.
18. In 1878 Harte was appointed consul in Germany.
19. Later he was transferred to Glasgow.
20. His work shows us a period in American history.

Use each of the following sayings as a *model sentence*. For each, write a modern or updated saying of your own.

EXERCISE 3

1. Handle your tools without mittens.

   (Sample imitation: Do your work without complaints.)

2. Keep your shop, and your shop will keep you.
3. Lost time is never found again.
4. There are no gains without pains.
5. There will be sleeping enough in the grave.

After the number of each sentence, put in parentheses the basic pattern from which it was adapted. Then put the right abbreviation to show *how* it was adapted:

Ques for questions;
Imp for requests (imperative);
Neg for negative statements with *not;*
Pass for passive;
There for *There-is* sentences.

EXAMPLES: Does Bert know Spanish?
  Give the handicapped a break.
(Answers) *(S–V–O) Ques*
  (S–V–IO–O) Imp

1. Must television programs be predictable?
2. Television does not encourage experiments.
3. When do the critics call a program exceptional?
4. Must the performers be famous?
5. Do the sets cost a fortune?
6. Money is not the answer.
7. Programs are produced by people.
8. These people must be given elbowroom by the networks.
9. Artists do not enjoy close supervision.
10. The networks must be told these things by the public.
11. Give your artists freedom.
12. Take risks.
13. Be creative.
14. The audience does not expect perfection.
15. There will be successes.
16. There may be failures.
17. What can the viewers do?
18. How can your opinions influence these programs?
19. Tell the station your reactions.
20. Write the manager a letter.

S4

**WRITING
COMBINED
SENTENCES**

Make several related ideas part of a combined sentence.

Often we take several sentences, each with its own subject and verb, and work them into larger combinations. Sometimes we join the smaller units very loosely, so that they can easily be separated again, like the freight cars that make up a train. Sometimes we join the units more permanently, like the different stories of a building. When we use a unit with its own subject and verb as *part of a larger sentence,* we call it a **clause.** Look at the following sentences. Each combines several ideas that could have appeared in separate sentences:

Coordinating Connectives:	and, but, for, or, nor, yet, so	KINDS OF CONNECTIVES
Adverbial Connectives:	however, therefore, moreover, furthermore, nevertheless, besides, indeed, consequently, in fact	
Subordinating Connectives:	when, whenever, while, before, after, since, until, as, if, because, unless, provided, though, although, whereas; so that, no matter how, no matter what	
Relative Pronouns:	who, whom, whose; which, that	
Special Connectives:	that, why, whether, how, who, what, whoever, whatever	

Sharks are fish, but dolphins are mammals.
Jim lived with another family until his mother returned.
His niece was driving, although her license had expired.
We bought a whole salmon, which had been caught the same day.
Few people in the town knew who he really was.

To make several clauses part of a larger combined sentence, we use words like *and, but, until, although, who, which,* and *that.* These serve as connecting links, or **connectives.** There are five major kinds of connectives. Each group works in a somewhat different way. Each gives us a different way of joining one idea to another.

Use coordination to join two independent clauses.

S4a

Coordination

The most simple way to join two related ideas is to coordinate them. We simply put them next to each other, with a link that seems to say: "Both of these things are true, and neither is more important than the other." We call the process coordination if we can easily unhitch or uncouple the two joined clauses again. The two clauses remain on an equal footing. We call them **independent** clauses:

INDEPENDENT: The hours were long, and *(equally important)* the pay was low.

Two major kinds of connectives coordinate independent clauses:

(1) We can join two clauses by familiar coordinating connectives. The true **coordinators,** or coordinating connectives, are *and, but, or, for, so, yet,* and *nor.* In writing, a comma usually shows the slight break between the two clauses:

The stars were gone, *and* the night was completely dark.
We rushed to the station, *but* the train had left.
The tombs were unmarked, *for* grave robbers would plunder them.
My uncle would tell stories, *or* a neighbor would drop in for a chat.
The building had been condemned, *so* the tenants moved.
We were promised prompt service, *yet* nobody came.

The connective *nor* causes the subject and the first part of the verb in the second clause to trade places:

They were not at their old address, *nor* was their name in the phone book.

NOTE: In each of these examples, the connective links two clauses that could appear as separate sentences. Each clause has its own subject and predicate. The same connectives may merely link words *within* a clause. *For* is also used as a preposition. *So* and *yet* have various other uses:

spick *and* span	a penny *for* your thoughts	double *or* nothing
tired *but* game	not *so* fast	not *yet*

(2) We can join two clauses by more formal adverbial connectives. Instead of *and, but,* and *so,* we can use *furthermore, moreover, however, nevertheless, therefore, consequently, besides, indeed,* or *in fact.* The most typical punctuation with these **adverbial connectives** is the semicolon:

There are miles of desert ahead; *therefore,* all cars should carry water.
Sarah likes books; *in fact,* she reads all the time.
There are hundreds of languages; each language, *furthermore,* has many dialects.
Tariffs hinder trade; they are *nevertheless* necessary.

Coordinators *must* appear at the point where the two clauses join. But, like adverbs, words like *however* may change their position in the second clause:

His ancestors were fighters; *however,* Rip lacked their spirit.
His ancestors were fighters; Rip, *however,* lacked their spirit.
His ancestors were fighters; Rip lacked their spirit, *however.*

See **M4a** for punctuation with coordinators and connectives.

EXERCISE 1

In which of the following sentences does a coordinator join two independent clauses? After the number of each such sentence, write the subject and complete verb of each clause, joined by the connective. (Omit all modifiers, but include noun markers and auxiliaries.) If a sentence does *not* contain two clauses, write *No.*

EXAMPLE: The dogs throughout the neighborhood barked, for Richard was starting on his evening walk.
(Answer) *The dogs barked,* for *Richard was starting.*

1. I hate cereal, but I like cereal commercials.
2. My sister and I root for the underdog.
3. In the commercials, the good people eat cereal, so they grow very strong.
4. They can then beat the underdog, for the underdog does not like cereal.
5. The viewer can tell the underdog not only by his tastes but also by his looks.
6. Either he is an ugly fat giant, or he has not shaved in years.
7. The champion may look small, but goodness triumphs in the end.
8. The champion has an unfair advantage, for cereal builds muscles.
9. Admirers of the underdog need patience, so we do not give up hope.
10. One day a fat giant will take on the champion and win the fight.

In each of the following sentences, an *adverbial connective* helps tie together two independent clauses. After the number of each sentence, write down the subject and verb of each clause along with the connective. (Omit all modifiers but include noun markers and auxiliaries.)

EXERCISE 2

EXAMPLE: City planners worry about the future; their advice, however, is often ignored.
(Answer) *Planners worry; their advice, however, is ignored.*

1. America was the land of open spaces; now, however, many cities are crowded.
2. Tall office buildings have risen downtown; single homes, furthermore, are giving way to apartment buildings.
3. In the morning, commuters pour into the city; however, public transportation is often inadequate.
4. Freeways are built; nevertheless, they hardly keep pace with the stream of cars.
5. The trip into the city takes much time; besides, the commuter must then find a parking space.
6. Few commuters belong to car pools; most cars, in fact, take only one person to work.
7. Few commuters move back into the city; indeed, the flight to the suburbs continues.
8. Small-scale remedies are useless; therefore, many cities are taking drastic action.
9. Cars cause much of the trouble; new shopping malls, therefore, allow pedestrians only.
10. The city of today will soon be gone; indeed, it will join the covered wagon.

EXERCISE 3

Use each of the following as a *model sentence*. For each, write a very similar sentence of your own. Use the same connective.

1. You can lead a horse to water, but you can't make it drink.

   (Sample Imitation: You can send a child to school, but you can't make it learn.)

2. Do not squander time, for it is the stuff of life.
3. You may encounter many defeats, but you must not be defeated. (Maya Angelou)
4. We can give advice, but we cannot give conduct.
5. Take care of today, and tomorrow will take care of itself.
6. He was a simple, honest man; he was, moreover, a good neighbor and a thoughtful friend.
7. She tramped across the New Mexico landscape, and her camera found beauty in the bleached skulls of long-dead animals.
8. He was horribly afraid of rats, so he did not try to sleep. (Willa Cather)
9. Words are cheap; most people, therefore, judge us by our actions.
10. Most Americans believe in progress; however, progress has its price.

EXERCISE 4

Often we join three or more related ideas in a larger combined sentence. The following example joins three independent clauses, each with its own subject and verb:

His meetings with Beatrice were short, *but* they filled his whole life, *for* her memory stayed with him all day.

The following sentence frames use coordinators and adverbial connectives. In each case, fill in material of your own.

1. _____ was a great _____,
   but _____,
   for _____ .
2. The _____ were _____,
   and the _____;
   nevertheless, _____ .
3. The _____ started _____,
   yet _____;
   therefore, _____ .

S4b

Subordination

Use subordination to link a dependent clause to the main clause.

A clause may be joined to another permanently by means of a word like *if* or *because*. Like a shelf attached to a wall, such a clause becomes **dependent** on the main structure. We no longer treat it as a self-sufficient unit that could stand by itself. When someone says, "If it had rained," we ask, "If it had rained, *then what?*" We look for a **main clause** to which we can attach the *if* clause:

MAIN CLAUSE	DEPENDENT CLAUSE
The crowd would have left	*if it had rained.*
Her car stalled	*when she reached the corner.*
The crop will be poor	*unless the weather improves.*

Words like *if, when, as, while, where, whereas,* and *although* are subordinating connectives, or **subordinators.**

Remember:

(1) Subordinators give us many different links between two ideas. Subordinating connectives express some of the following relationships:

TIME AND PLACE: *when, whenever, while, before, after, since, until, as, as if, as long as, where, wherever*

REASON OR CONDITION: *if, because, unless, provided, so that*

CONTRAST: *though, although, whereas, no matter how*

Like adverbs, subordinators often help us find out how, when, or where. The kind of dependent clause they introduce is therefore often called an **adverbial** clause.

(2) Subordinators make possible great variety in sentence building. They may attach a dependent clause to the main clause *at several different points.* A coordinator like *and* or *but* brings in a second clause that *follows* the first. A subordinator brings in a dependent clause that *may* follow the main clause (but does not have to):

They will leave *when you are ready.*
The company will repossess the car *unless you pay the difference.*

But often the dependent clause *comes before* the main clause:

If you have changed your mind, you should say so.
When the symphony began, Paul sank into one of the rear seats with a long sigh of relief. (Willa Cather)
If the moon smiled, she would resemble you. (Sylvia Plath)

Sometimes the dependent clause *interrupts* the main clause:

I wear my hat *as I please* indoors or out. (Walt Whitman)

Several dependent clauses may be attached to the same main clause:

> *After a concert was over,* Paul was often irritable and wretched *until he got to sleep.* (Willa Cather)

(3) Some subordinators are combinations of two or more words. With *paired* connectives like *so that, as . . . as, so . . . as,* or *more . . . than,* the first part of the combination often hooks back into the main clause:

> Laziness travels *so* slowly *that* Poverty soon overtakes it.
> Piloting was not quite *so* romantic *as* I had imagined. (Mark Twain)

NOTE: *Before, after, since, until,* and *as* double as prepositions. They then introduce a noun, rather than a clause with its own subject and verb:

CONNECTIVE: *After winter came,* he always started back for Gold Rock.

PREPOSITION: From March or April *until winter* he wandered slowly among the mountains.

See **M4b** for punctuation of adverbial clauses.

EXERCISE 1

In which of the following sentences does a subordinator join a dependent clause to the main clause? Write the subordinator after the number of each such sentence. Write *No* after the number of all others. (Be prepared to identify the subject and verb of each clause.) Write on a separate sheet of paper.

EXAMPLE: People often visit a place after a writer makes it famous.
(Answer) *after*

(A) 1. Authors often write about their own part of the country, because they know it best.
2. When they write about a place, we often recognize the local customs and traditions.
3. Eudora Welty wrote about Mississippi, where she was born.
4. While she studied journalism in New York, she wrote news and publicity.
5. After her return to Mississippi, she wrote short stories.
6. She described people as she saw them.
7. She did not close her eyes when people did cruel or callous things to each other.
8. One of her characters visits old people because it is her good deed as a scout.
9. Before she enters the home, she hides a beautiful red apple.
10. She eats the apple after she leaves.

(B) 11. Although Ben Franklin is best known as a public figure, he played other roles.

12. He was a printer before he went into business for himself.

13. After some years in his father's shop, he was apprenticed to his brother.

14. When the brother was jailed, Benjamin edited his brother's newspaper.

15. Because of a quarrel, Ben left Boston for Philadelphia.

16. Until his retirement, Franklin published America's first major weekly.

17. Franklin retired from business when he was only forty-two years old.

18. He was always dissatisfied unless he could use his time well.

19. He busied himself with experiments whenever he could find the time.

20. He badgered his fellow citizens until they supported his projects.

After the number of each sentence, write an adverbial clause that would fill the blank. Use as many different subordinators as you can. Make sure the clause you write has its own subject and verb. (Write on a separate sheet.)

EXERCISE 2

EXAMPLE: A car has the right-of-way _____ .
(Answer)   *if it approaches the intersection from your right.*

1. Your car must come to a complete stop _____ .
2. Some drivers increase their speed _____ .
3. A car stopped for a red light should not start moving _____ .
4. Bicycles are forbidden on freeways _____ .
5. Teenagers are allowed to drive _____ .
6. Fog is dangerous _____ .
7. _____ , you should stop for a rest.
8. The accident rate goes down _____ .
9. The state will renew your license _____ .
10. A driver should not change lanes _____ .
11. A warning sign is often posted _____ .
12. Many roads turn slippery _____ .
13. _____ , a police officer will give you a ticket.
14. You may have to appear in court _____ .
15. Signaling early _____ helps prevent accidents.
16. Cars have changed a great deal _____ .
17. Drivers must pass a test _____ .
18. Their eyes are tested _____ .
19. _____ , keep your mind on your driving.
20. Always drive carefully _____ .

Sentences

Point out the subordinator used in each of the following sayings. Use the sayings as *model sentences*. Write five modern proverbs each of which uses a pattern very similar to that of one of the original sentences.

1. Plow deep while sluggards sleep.

   (Sample Imitation: Sit tight while rowdies fight.)

2. If you will not hear Reason, she'll surely rap your knuckles.
3. Laziness travels so slowly that Poverty soon overtakes it.
4. Nobody loves you when you are down and out.
5. Do not lock the barn after the horse has been stolen.
6. When you drink the water, think of the source. (Chinese proverb)

Each of the following model sentences combines *several* clauses in a larger combined sentence. Read each sentence aloud. Then write a similar sentence of your own. Fill in the blanks in the frame sentence that follows each model, using material of your own. (Write on a separate sheet.)

1. Model: *I* always *go* to sea as a sailor,
because *they make* a point of paying me for my trouble,
whereas *they* never *pay* passengers a single penny. (Herman Melville)

Your Turn: I always _____ ,
because _____ ,
whereas _____ .

2. Model: *I* dreadfully *wanted* to ask a question,
but *I was carrying* about as many short answers
as *my cargo-room would admit* of,
so *I held* my peace. (Mark Twain)

Your Turn: _____ wanted to _____ ,
but _____
as _____ ,
so _____ .

3. Model: When *I heard* the nurse knock with my tray,
an immense *relief flooded* through me,
because *I knew* I was out of danger for that day. (Sylvia Plath)

Your Turn: When I _____ ,
a (an) (the) _____ ,
because _____ .

Use relative pronouns to join a relative clause to the main clause.

S4c
Relative Clauses

Who, which, and *that* join a dependent clause to the main clause. They often modify a *noun:* "the man *who called,*" "in the book *that you mentioned.*" The dependent clause that modifies a noun is called a **relative** clause. The *who, which,* or *that* at the beginning of a relative clause is called a **relative pronoun.** These words have a double function: Like a connective, they join one clause to another. Like a pronoun, they take the place of a noun *in the dependent clause:*

STATEMENT:	I could hardly hear the woman.
ADDED SOURCE:	*The woman* answered the phone.
RESULT:	I could hardly hear the woman *who* answered the phone.

STATEMENT:	Jim stared at the ticket.
ADDED SOURCE:	I handed him *the ticket.*
RESULT:	Jim stared at the ticket *that* I handed him.

Remember:

(1) A relative clause may modify a noun at different points in a sentence:

An applicant *who had applied earlier* got the job.
The mayor promised help to the workers *who were laid off.*
The party *to which we were asked* was called off.

Several relative clauses may modify different nouns in the same sentence:

The clouds, *which were getting darker,* reminded us of the umbrella *that we had left behind.*

RELATIVE CLAUSES TELL US WHAT KIND:

**All That You
Like in a Hat**

**The Car That Meets
Requirements of Economy**

**The one toy that holds
fun for years**

(2) The complete list of relative pronouns includes who, whom, whose, which, *and* that. We use *who* when the pronoun refers to persons. We use *which* when it refers to things or ideas. We use *that* for either. (*Whose* also is now acceptable for both persons and things.)

> She wrote to the mayor, *who* agreed to her request.
> We went to her office, *which* was in the old courthouse.
> We bought a car *whose* owner had taken good care of it.

See **U2b** for *who* and *whom*.

(3) In many relative clauses (especially in spoken *English), the relative pronoun has been omitted.* This typically happens when *that* would have been the object of the clause:

> We stared at the sheets *that she had distributed.*
> We stared at the sheets *she had distributed.*
>
> The ticket *that you bought* expires in two weeks.
> The ticket *you bought* expires in two weeks.

(4) A relative clause may modify a sentence part that has taken the place of a noun. In the following example, the relative clause modifies the pronoun *those:*

> God helps those *who help themselves.*

NOTE: Relative clauses are sometimes separated from the rest of the sentence by commas. These commas show that the relative clause is not part of the main point. It merely adds information.

See **M4c** for punctuation of relative clauses.

EXERCISE 1

Find the relative clause in each of the following capsule plots of old movies. Write the whole relative clause after the number of the sentence.

EXAMPLE: Four travelers who need help visit a wizard.
(Answer) *who need help*

1. *Heidi* is the classic about the Swiss girl who loves her grandfather.
2. A flier whose plane has crashed returns to civilization.
3. A submarine sights a giant octopus that was created by radiation.
4. A doctor heals a patient whom she has rescued.
5. Before the wedding, the bride learns things that raise doubts about the marriage.
6. An advertising executive who steals customers from other agencies tangles with a competitor.

7. An old man who refuses to die chases Death up a tree.
8. A nun and a priest save a parochial school that is in money trouble.
9. Scientists battle a giant tarantula which seems indestructible.
10. A veteran flier takes over a plane whose pilot and copilot have become ill.
11. An American singer whose husband has been killed looks for the murderer.
12. A master thief plays cat and mouse with Scotland Yard, which finally captures her.
13. A recently widowed American who lives in the Far East falls in love with a missionary.
14. The heroine works with a group who smuggle weapons into an occupied country.
15. Poker Flat, which practices vigilante justice, exiles a gambler and other shady characters.
16. A young woman who loves horses trains for an Olympic gold medal.
17. A tough-talking American who lives in Casablanca helps the French Resistance movement.
18. Dedicated performers save a circus that is the greatest show on earth.
19. A frontier town is saved by a sheriff who really died many years ago.
20. In prehistoric times, a boy falls in love with a girl who belongs to an enemy tribe.

In which of the following sentences does a relative pronoun join a dependent clause to the main clause? Write *Yes* after the number of each such sentence. Write *O* if there is a relative clause from which the relative pronoun has been omitted. Write *No* if there is no relative clause. (Remember that the words we use as relative pronouns also have other uses.)

EXERCISE 2

1. Last summer I visited my Uncle Simon, who remembers the lore of of the Old West.
2. As a child, Aunt Sue had relatives that had come West in covered wagons.
3. The stories they told of the early days have many familiar features.
4. Who has not read tales about the travelers to Oregon or California?
5. The routes they traveled were often uncertain.
6. Sometimes they merely followed the wheel tracks that were left by other parties.
7. In later years, good maps made that procedure unnecessary.
8. The early settlers described the hardships they had suffered.
9. They wrote of people who ferried their belongings across swollen rivers.
10. The deserts they crossed drove their cattle mad with thirst.
11. The heavy wagons were dragged up riverbeds that wound up into the mountains.

12. Trails that would discourage a sturdy hiker were traveled even by children.
13. Often the slowly traveling parties were caught by early snow.
14. That emergency required of these pioneers all the courage they could muster.
15. The parties that were snowed in sometimes spent a whole winter in improvised cabins.
16. The lucky ones escaped the starvation and disease that threatened them.
17. For food, they trapped the foxes and coyotes that roamed the mountain forests.
18. Some who were not so lucky perished.
19. Many writers have retold the hardships to which these trailbreakers were exposed.
20. Which of these stories have you read?

EXERCISE 3

Each of the following sentences has several nouns. Rewrite each sentence *twice*. Each time add a relative clause to modify a different noun in the sentence.

EXAMPLE: The witness talked to the police.
(Answer)   The witness *who had seen the accident* talked to the police.
           The witness talked to the police, *who listened politely.*

1. The performer smiled at the crowd.
2. In the movies, the boy used to get the girl.
3. Animals are threatened by progress.
4. Ships sailed to the new continent.
5. People cause accidents.
6. Young people look for friends.
7. Teenagers read books.
8. Maps guide drivers.
9. Roads take tourists to remote areas.
10. Immigrants came to the country.

EXERCISE 4

Find the relative clauses in the following sayings. Then use three or more of these as *model sentences*. For each, write an updated saying that is very similar in structure to the original.

1. People who rise late must trot all day.
2. They that won't be counseled can't be helped.
3. God helps those that help themselves.
4. Do not hire someone who does your work for money, but someone who does it for the love of it.
5. It all depends on whose ox is being gored.

Use a noun clause to replace one of the nouns in the main clause.

A special type of dependent clause is not really *joined* to another clause. It is not like an added link in a chain. Instead, it replaces a basic part. Special connectives like *that, how, why,* and *whether* introduce dependent clauses that we can substitute for one of the nouns in the main clause. Such dependent clauses are called **noun clauses.**

In all of the following pairs a noun clause replaces one of the original nouns in the main clause:

NOUN: He denied *the accusation.*
NOUN CLAUSE: He denied *that he was guilty.*

NOUN: Jim asked me *a question.*
NOUN CLAUSE: Jim asked me *how I felt.*

NOUN: My parents never learned *the truth.*
NOUN CLAUSE: My parents never learned *why he had resigned.*

NOUN: We were saddened by *the news.*
NOUN CLAUSE: We were saddened by *what we had heard.*

Remember:

(1) The most common type of noun clause takes the place of the object after verbs like say, tell, know, ask, *and* deny. The noun clause then tells us what was said, asked, or denied:

NOUN: Ann told us *the story.*
NOUN CLAUSE: Ann told us *what she remembered.*

NOUN: Mario knew *the street.*
NOUN CLAUSE: Mario knew *where the family lived.*

(2) Most of the words that can introduce a noun clause have other possible uses. Many noun clauses start with *that,* used as a special kind of connective. Other words used as **special connectives** for this purpose are question words like *who, whoever, which, what, why, where, when,* and *how.* The words *that, who,* and *which* are also used as relative pronouns. *When, where,* and *if* are also used as subordinators. To recognize them in their special use at the beginning of a noun clause, ask: Can I put "the fact" or "the person" or "the object" in place of this clause?

NOUN: He forgot *the fact.*
NOUN CLAUSE: He forgot *that the store was closed.*

NOUN: She remembered *the person.*
NOUN CLAUSE: She remembered *who told her.*

NOTE: No comma separates the noun clause from its main clause.

EXERCISE 1

Can you tell relative clauses and noun clauses apart? Put the right abbreviation after the number of each sentence: *RC* for relative clause; *NC* for noun clause. Put *None* if the sentence does not contain any dependent clause of either kind. (Be prepared to explain in class how each dependent clause fits into the sentence.)

1. The biggest international sports event is the Olympic Games, which take place every four years.
2. We all know that the Games started in ancient Greece.
3. Tourists can still see where the athletes competed.
4. Ancient Greek vases show how the participants looked.
5. Greek poets praised the athletes that were victorious.
6. The modern Games have become costly affairs.
7. The host country feels that it must put its best foot forward.
8. Often it builds a huge new stadium, which can accommodate the events.
9. It may build an Olympic village that houses thousands of athletes.
10. The countries that send teams make elaborate preparations.
11. They know that their national prestige is at stake.
12. We can see why major countries send big teams.
13. Each country hopes that its athletes will triumph over its rivals.
14. The rule requires that all participants must be amateurs.
15. This rule explains the absence of great names from professional sports.
16. Nevertheless, most countries support the athletes who represent them.
17. In the opinion of many observers, many participants are really professionals.
18. The crowds early decide who is going to be their favorite.
19. A gymnast may capture the heart of everyone who watches her.
20. Whoever wins the big skiing or swimming events is admired by millions.

EXERCISE 2

Each of the following sentences includes several nouns. Rewrite each sentence, replacing one noun with a noun clause.

EXAMPLE: The thief knew his business.
(Possible   The thief knew *what he was doing.*
Answers)   *Whoever stole the painting* knew his business.

1. The headlines announced the fact.
2. Alice asked a question.
3. No grown-ups ever told me a secret.
4. The instructor will explain the process.
5. The place was quite different from our dream.
6. Historians still do not know the truth.
7. The mechanic knew the reason.
8. The official denied the rumor.
9. My friend could not remember the person.
10. The people must have been well prepared for the job.

What kind of connective joins the two clauses in each of the following combined sentences? After the number of the sentence, put the right abbreviation. (Do not include any connective that merely joins individual words or phrases.)

Co   for coordinating connective;
Adv   for adverbial connective;
Sub   for subordinating connective;
Pro   for relative pronoun;
Spec for a special connective used to start a noun clause.

1. My sister and I went to horror movies when we were younger.
2. These movies frightened us; nevertheless, we always came back.
3. Although there were many kinds, we had some favorite plots.
4. The story may take place in a Scottish castle, where at midnight a ghost plays the bagpipes.
5. Sometimes there is a ghost in rusty armor who haunts the halls.
6. Some tricks were repeated many times, but they frightened us anyway.
7. Someone knocks on the door on a dark night; it is only a neighbor, however.
8. Candles suddenly go out because wind blows through an open window.
9. As you might expect, creaking doors suddenly open.
10. We knew that a story by Edgar Allan Poe promised chilling terrors.
11. One tale that he wrote is about a person's relative buried alive.
12. She returns from the vault while ominous noises fill the night.
13. She has been in the vault two weeks, and she looks it.
14. Her brother goes mad with terror when he sees her shrouded figure.
15. In some stories death is a blessing that the victims would welcome.
16. In later years, the horror movies featured mechanical monsters that turn against their creators.
17. Mad doctors misuse what they have learned.
18. Machines learn how they can run our planet.
19. These robots did not impress me, so I stopped going to horror movies.
20. Poe made his monsters believable; besides, they were at least human.

Know and use special sentence resources.

S5

Many of the building blocks we use in an English sentence do double duty. We do not always put familiar sentence parts to their simple and ordinary uses. We may use them for special purposes, thus adding to our sentence resources.

In the following examples, nouns are put to special uses:

Emily Brontë, *Charlotte's sister,* was also a famous novelist.
Indira Gandhi, *member of a famous family,* became prime minister of India.

In the following examples, verb forms are put to special uses:

Going on this *whaling* voyage was a *fascinating* experience.
I love *to sail forbidden* seas and *land* on barbarous coasts. (Herman Melville)

Study these special uses of words. They give us many new ways of expanding a sentence. Make use of them to stretch your own sentence resources.

S5a
Using Appositives

Use appositives to work added information into a sentence.

An **appositive** is a second noun "put next to" another noun. An appositive is simply *put there,* without a linking verb or a preposition to tie it to the noun to which it belongs. The appositive often carries its own noun markers with it. It may in turn have its own modifiers:

His friend, *a sophomore,* drove the car.
Peter, *his pet alligator,* had escaped from the cage.
Her husband, *a former prizefighter,* opened the door.
We called on Mrs. Smith, *our new neighbor.*

(1) We typically set off appositives by commas in writing. It is as if we were interrupting the sentence in order to bring in information from a different source:

STATEMENT:	The sports arena burned to the ground.
ADDED SOURCE:	The sports arena was a "fireproof" multimillion-dollar structure.
RESULT:	The sports arena, *"fireproof" multimillion-dollar structure,* burned to the ground.

STATEMENT:	The police found the murder weapon.
ADDED SOURCE:	The murder weapon was an Italian mail-order rifle.
RESULT:	The police found the murder weapon, *an Italian mail-order rifle.*

(2) More than one appositive may modify the same noun:

She had her own bicycle now, *a shiny new import, a Christmas gift.*
She was a famous photographer, *author of several books, winner of many awards.*

EXERCISE 1

Each of the following pairs gives you an original statement and further information from an *additional source.* Work the additional information into the original statement as an appositive. Write on a separate sheet of paper.

EXAMPLE: Mahalia Jackson sang many traditional songs.
            She was a gospel singer.
(Answer)   Mahalia Jackson, *a gospel singer,* sang many traditional songs.

 1. The Siberian tiger may survive only in zoos.
    It is an endangered species.

 2. Teddy Roosevelt preached a rugged outdoor life.
    He was our twenty-sixth President.

 3. Science fiction often deals with telepathy.
    It is a kind of mind reading.

 4. The city park included a menagerie.
    It was a small zoo.

 5. Elizabeth Blackwell encountered much prejudice.
    She was a nineteenth-century physician.

 6. *Leaves of Grass* is by Walt Whitman.
    Whitman is America's best-known poet.

 7. His most famous poem mourns a tragic event.
    The event is the death of Lincoln.

 8. Amsterdam has many picturesque canals.
    It is a city in Holland.

 9. Margaret Truman wrote *Women of Courage.*
    She was daughter of a President.

10. Austin was named after an early settler.
    It is the capital of Texas.

EXERCISE 2

In each of the following sentences, a noun is followed and modified either by an adjective or by an appositive. After the number of the sentence, write the appropriate abbreviation: *Adj* for adjective; *App* for appositive. (Either kind of modifier may in turn be modified by other material.) Write on a separate sheet of paper.

 1. The best-known American poet is Walt Whitman, the poet of democracy.
 2. Whitman, son of a carpenter, worked as a journalist.
 3. He loved the big cities, full of varied life.
 4. Manhattan, city of crowds and ferries, was his favorite.
 5. He wrote about steamers and railroads, symbols of the new America.
 6. To him America was a New World, free of traditional barriers.
 7. In 1855 he published *Leaves of Grass,* a long collection of poems.
 8. Whitman's writing, frank for its time, caused much controversy.
 9. Later he wrote about America's national tragedy, the Civil War.
10. Whitman, famous in America and Europe, died in 1892.

EXERCISE 3

After the number of each sentence, write an appositive that could fill the blank. Add other material to the appositive as needed.

EXAMPLE: Censorship, _____, exists in many countries.
(Answer) *the control of books or news*

1. The shark, _____, frightens swimmers in warm waters.
2. Scrooge, _____, changed his mind about Christmas.
3. Alaska, _____, has many natural resources.
4. Atlanta, _____, grew by leaps and bounds.
5. George Washington, _____, had many friends and enemies.
6. The theater was showing *Gone with the Wind*, _____.
7. City squares attract thousands of pigeons, _____.
8. On Sundays she read *The New York Times*, _____.
9. The program was about Elizabeth, _____.
10. The Cherokees, _____, were moved from their homes.
11. William Shakespeare, _____, wrote *Julius Caesar*.
12. My sister likes geography, _____.
13. Huck Finn, _____, traveled down the Mississippi on a raft.
14. Heidi, _____, went to live in the Alps.
15. Many pilgrims travel to Jerusalem, _____.
16. Lamps used to burn kerosene, _____.
17. The pyramids were tombs for the pharaohs, _____.
18. The swamps were full of alligators, _____.
19. The Spaniards sailed to the New World in galleons, _____.
20. The blues, _____, was their favorite kind of music.

S5b
Using Participles

Use participles to help build up detail in a sentence.

One way we stretch our sentence resources is to use the full range of English **verbals.** These are forms like *writing, written,* and *to write;* or *changing, changed,* and *to change.* These forms also appear as verbs or parts of verbs. But when we use them as verbals, we use them for other purposes. In each of the following sentences, verbals —either alone or with material they carry along—have taken the place of other sentence parts:

The *printed* map showed trails open for *hiking.*
Climbing monkeys like *to have* places *to climb* to.
Not *to watch* workers is *to leave* them your purse open. (Ben Franklin)

The first major kind of verbals are the **participles.** We first find them as parts of a complete verb. They are the two forms of a verb that combine with the auxiliaries *be (am, was)* and *have:*

am *writing*	have *written*
was *writing*	was *written*
had been *writing*	had been *written*

• *Writing* occurs in many forms showing action now in progress. It is called the **present** participle. All present participles end in *–ing* and are often simply called *–ing* forms: *asking, writing, loving, complaining, analyzing.*

• *Written* occurs in many forms showing action completed in the past. It is called the **past** participle. A number of past participles end in *–en: broken, given, taken, bitten.* By way of analogy, all past participles are sometimes called *–en* forms. But many of them actually have other endings.

Remember:

(1) We can use participles as modifiers. We can lift forms like *writing* and *written* out of their usual place after an auxiliary and instead use them to modify a noun. They are then used as verbals— words derived from verbs but serving a different function:

STATEMENT: Bees surrounded him.
ADDED SOURCE: The bees were *buzzing.*
RESULT: *Buzzing* bees surrounded him.

STATEMENT: The archeologist studied the vase.
ADDED SOURCE: The vase had been *broken.*
RESULT: The archeologist studied the *broken* vase.

(2) Participles may carry with them the objects and modifiers that went with the original verb. The verbal, together with the material it carries along, makes up a **verbal phrase.**

STATEMENT: The tremors subsided.
ADDED SOURCE: The tremors were *shaking the building.*
RESULT: The tremors *shaking the building* subsided.

STATEMENT: Agnes made friends with our neighbors.
ADDED SOURCE: Our neighbors were *speaking Spanish.*
RESULT: Agnes made friends with our *Spanish-speaking* neighbors.

STATEMENT: Fred approached.
ADDED SOURCE: Fred *was holding the dead snake gingerly in one hand.*
RESULT: Fred approached, *holding the dead snake gingerly in one hand.*

(3) Participles help us make our sentences more varied. One or more such verbals may *introduce* a sentence:

The path no longer looked the same. *Coming,* they had watched another face of it. Now, *retreating,* they hardly recognized their course.

• One or more verbals may *interrupt* the sentence, breaking up its basic rhythm:

His big yellow eyes, *narrowed with hate,* looked straight ahead. (Ernest Hemingway)

- *More than one verbal phrase* may appear in the same sentence:

The *wildly careening* bus hurtled the *badly shaken* passengers down the narrow mountain road.

- One or more verbals may *conclude* the sentence:

Sam was waiting, *wrapped in a quilt on the wagon seat.* (William Faulkner)

We sat together, *holding our lunch buckets on our knees, looking out at the trees beside the roads.* (Lois Phillips Hudson)

It snowed furiously for days, *covering all known landmarks, closing airports and schools, altering our plans and commitments.*

NOTE: The verbal or verbal phrase comes into the sentence without commas when it is needed to tell us which one or what kind. It is often set off by commas when it is merely added to round out the picture.

See **M5a** for more information on how to punctuate verbals.

EXERCISE 1

In the following sentences, participles are used both as parts of complete verbs and as modifiers taking the place of adjectives. After the number of each sentence, write down any *participle used as a modifier*. If no participle is used as a modifier, write *None*.

1. We all have known people pursued by bad luck.
2. Gadgets just bought break down.
3. A neighbor is injured by a lawn mower running wild.
4. A floor freshly polished is ruined by muddy feet.
5. Wallpaper just pasted drops on top of the paperhanger.
6. Some people are not satisfied with such real problems.
7. Lacking real problems, they exaggerate minor disasters.
8. My friend Henry is such a worrier, fighting unnecessary battles.
9. He is now worrying over a rabbit given to him by his parents.
10. This rabbit, called Peter by his owner, has buckteeth.
11. Knowing little about rabbits, I had considered them natural rabbit teeth.
12. In reality these teeth are a hereditary defect.
13. Normal teeth, meeting perfectly, are ground down by normal wear.
14. The constantly growing buckteeth must be trimmed back.
15. With his fully grown teeth, Peter literally cannot shut his mouth.
16. I daily hear the latest news about this suffering rabbit.
17. Last year Henry had a mynah bird causing problems.
18. Spoiled by its master, the bird refused ordinary bird food.
19. It preferred delicacies brought from the far corners of the globe.
20. Dates were the favorite food of this sulking creature.

Each of the following pairs give you an original statement and then added information from an additional source. Work the added information into the first statement as a verbal or verbal phrase. (Try out different positions for the verbal or verbal phrase.)

EXERCISE 2

EXAMPLE: We looked up at the giant redwoods.
         They were almost touching the sky.
(Answer)   We looked up at the giant redwoods, *almost touching the sky.*

1. The dogs were barking outside.
   They had been wakened by the smell of frying meat.

2. Pioneer fliers often got lost.
   They were flying without a radio.

3. The deck of the boat was covered with fish.
   They were heaped one on top of the other.

4. Everyone was hard at work on the boat.
   It was tossing wildly.

5. Two women were processing the fish.
   They were standing side by side.

6. The lion watched.
   It was moving its great head from side to side.

7. Many people in the line gave up.
   They were discouraged by the long wait.

8. We scrambled across the field.
   We were running for dear life.

9. The service academies admit candidates.
   They have been carefully selected.

10. The water burst through the dam.
    It was sweeping everything away in its path.

The following sentences use the full range of possibilities for the use of participles in the English sentence. Read each sentence aloud. Then choose *five* of these as model sentences. For each model sentence, fill in the sentence frame that follows it with material of your own.

EXERCISE 3

1. Time is a dressmaker *specializing* in alterations.   (Faith Baldwin)
FRAME: _____ is a _____ing _____ .

2. *Opening* the trap, he dropped the noose over the big snake's head and tightened the thong.   (John Steinbeck)
FRAME: _____ing the _____ , he (she) _____ and _____ .

3. Margaret listened intently, *encouraging* her with *searching* questions.
   (Jean Houston)
   FRAME: _____ , _____ing _____ with _____ing
   _____ .

4. *Wandering* among the shoppers, *standing* on O'Connell Bridge, *walking*
   the quays, I turned the past and the present over and over in my mind.
   (Elizabeth Cullinan)
   FRAME: _____ing _____ , _____ing _____ ,
   _____ing _____ , I _____ .

5. The children, *running* from room to room, found the piano and began to
   bang on the keyboard.
   FRAME: The _____ , _____ing _____ , _____ and
   _____ .

6. Mr. Oakhurst alone remained erect, *leaning* against a rock, calmly
   surveying them. (Bret Harte)
   FRAME: _____ alone remained _____ , _____ ing _____ ,
   _____ing _____ .

7. The little boat, *lifted* by each towering wave, and *splashed* viciously
   by the crests, made progress that was not apparent to those in her.
   (Stephen Crane)
   FRAME: The _____ , _____ed by _____ , and _____ed
   by _____ , made _____ that _____ .

S5c

Verbal Nouns and Infinitives

Make verbal nouns and infinitives take the place of nouns and other sentence parts.

Verbals often take the place of nouns. One verbal that may replace a noun is the familiar *–ing* form: *asking, leaving, writing.* When this form trades places with a noun, we call it a **verbal noun.** Another verbal that may replace a noun is the *to* form: *to ask, to leave, to write.* We call this form the **infinitive.**

VERBAL NOUN: *Swimming* builds muscles.
   Seeing is *believing.*
   My friends kept me from *studying.*

INFINITIVE: *To err* is human.
   To give is more blessed than *to receive.*
   My uncle taught me *to think.*

Often such verbals carry *their own objects and modifiers:*

We should stop *wasting time.*
To admit mistakes requires courage.
Robert had learned *to speak French fluently.*

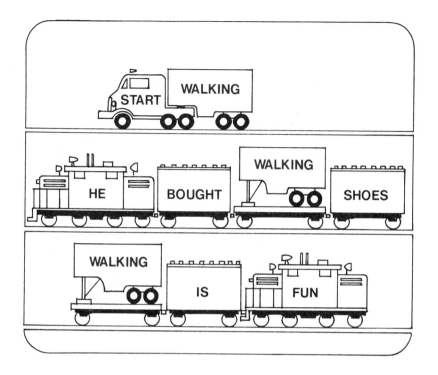

Here are additional uses of infinitives:

(1) In many two-verb combinations, the second verb appears as an infinitive. For instance, we use the infinitive in combinations using *have to, am going to, ought to, used to:*

> Your friend will *have to leave.*
> The chain is *going to break.*
> You *ought to be* glad.
> I *used to know* his sister.

Very similar is the use of the infinitive after verbs like *happen, seem, need, hesitate:*

> A neighbor *happened to pass by.*
> His gestures *seem to annoy* you.
> We *need to study* this proposal carefully.

An infinitive follows the *object* of the first verb after verbs like *want, permit, allow, enable, order, like, ask:*

> Henry *wants* me *to go.*
> The guard *allowed* the visitors *to pass.*
> The loan *enabled* him *to stay* in business.

(2) Infinitives can substitute for many different modifiers. An infinitive may modify a *noun:*

a place *to sit*	time *to leave*
a speech *to remember*	a thought *to keep in mind*

An infinitive may modify a *verb:*

paused *to think*	came *to repair the heater*
called *to let us know*	resigned *to prove a point*

An infinitive may modify an *adjective:*

eager *to serve*	hard *to believe*
ashamed *to admit his guilt*	impossible *to forget*

(3) Infinitives often appear in sentences that start with the pronoun it. The verbal then fills in the details later, as in the following "Poor Richard" examples:

It is cheap and easy *to destroy.*
It is hard for an empty bag *to stand upright.*
It is easier *to build two chimneys than to keep one in fuel.*

EXERCISE 1

After the number of each sentence, write down every verbal noun and infinitive in the sentence. Write down only the verbal— do not include any other part of a verbal phrase. (Do not include verb forms that are part of a complete verb.)

EXAMPLE: He started to thank her for helping them.
(Answer) *to thank, helping*

1. All she wanted was the right to watch the pageant.
2. He was bursting to talk to someone about the lucky turn of events.
3. He began pacing up and down as he waited for her to return.
4. Paul dashed out to the front of the house to seat the early comers. (Willa Cather)
5. He felt no necessity to do any of these things; what he wanted was to see, to be in the atmosphere. (Willa Cather)
6. Their constant complaining began to spoil his vacation.
7. Reading the want ads convinced him that now was the time to apply.
8. You ought to know that they want me to leave.
9. Boating and hiking were her favorite sports.
10. You did the right thing by asking them to apologize.
11. She wants to leave early to avoid the rush-hour traffic.
12. Talking loudly is frowned upon in the library.
13. Events seemed to happen quickly after that first day.
14. His father permitted him to use the car Saturday nights.
15. The most popular sport today is jogging.

The *–ing* form is one of the verbals we use to stretch our sentence resources. Can you tell apart the different jobs it can do in a sentence? After the number of each sentence, write *V* if the *–ing* form is used as part of a complete verb. Write *P* if it is used as a participle, modifying a noun. Write *VN* if it is used as a verbal noun. (Write on a separate sheet of paper.)

EXERCISE 2

1. Reviewing television shows is a hard job.
2. The reviewer is watching shows all the time.
3. Watching so many programs has soured many reviewers.
4. They object to shows using the same tired plots.
5. Being fair is not easy for the tired critic.
6. The quality of the typical program is not improving.
7. Network executives are not paying attention to negative criticism.
8. They may listen to a critic mixing praise with blame.
9. Finding something praiseworthy is often difficult.
10. One reviewer discussed a program using a boy superman.
11. Usually the hero is shooting at people with atomic guns.
12. His favorite pastime is hunting foreign agents.
13. He keeps them from stealing a death-ray machine.
14. Or he foils them by freeing a kidnapped scientist.
15. Children watching such programs are used to violence.
16. The reviewer did not enjoy watching all this mayhem.
17. In her opinion, television violence is getting worse.
18. Praising any part of this show was difficult for her.
19. Looking for good features, the reviewer noticed the color.
20. She compromised by praising the color.

Look at the way the following sentences use verbal nouns and infinitives. Use each as a *model sentence*. Fill in each sentence frame with material of your own. Write on a separate sheet of paper.

EXERCISE 3

1. To conquer fear is the beginning of wisdom. (Bertrand Russell)
FRAME: To _____ is the beginning of _____ .

2. A fool's tongue is long enough to cut his throat.
FRAME: A _____ is _____ enough to _____ .

3. Blowing out the other fellow's candle won't make yours shine any brighter.
FRAME: _____ing _____ won't make _____ .

4. We in America have always believed in hitching our wagon to a star.
   (Margaret Mead)
FRAME: We in _____ have always believed in _____ing _____ .

5. No one is exempt from talking nonsense. (Montaigne)
FRAME: No one is exempt from _____ing _____ .

S5d

**Absolute
Constructions**

Use verbals that carry along their own subjects.

When we work a verbal from an added source into a sentence, it sometimes carries the *subject* of the source statement along with it. The resulting combination seems less closely tied to any one part of the sentence than normal modifiers. Such a group of words is called an **absolute** construction:

STATEMENT:	We stood absolutely still.
ADDED SOURCE:	Our eyes were fixed on the snake.
RESULT:	We stood absolutely still, *our eyes fixed on the snake.*

STATEMENT:	He sprinted across the field.
ADDED SOURCE:	His cleats were biting into the turf.
RESULT:	He sprinted across the field, *his cleats biting into the turf.*

STATEMENT:	The driver headed home.
ADDED SOURCE:	Her car was piled with furniture.
RESULT:	The driver headed home, *her car piled with furniture.*

Remember:

(1) Absolute constructions may appear in a variety of positions. They may appear at the beginning or in the middle of a sentence:

The preparations being complete, the two soldiers stepped aside.
The truck, *its radiator steaming,* came to a rumbling halt.

(2) Several absolute constructions may appear together. Read the following sentence out loud:

It was the thunder of a great bald eagle who beat his way off the rocks
   and straight up over them,
     his claws hanging down,
     his hot red eyes sparkling for one second in the light of the sky.
   (Walter Van Tilburg Clark)

(3) Absolute constructions sometimes appear in a shortened form. When the verb in the source statement is a form of *be,* the verbal is often *omitted:*

STATEMENT:	The old guard sat in the corner.
ADDED SOURCE:	A newspaper *was* on his knee.
ADDED SOURCE:	A black patch *was* over one eye.
RESULT:	The old guard sat in the corner, *a newspaper on his knee, a black patch over one eye.*

STATEMENT:	The alert reporter was on hand.
ADDED SOURCE:	Her notepad was open.
ADDED SOURCE:	Her camera was around her neck.
RESULT:	The alert reporter was on hand, *her notepad open, her camera around her neck.*

THE EIGHTY-YARD RUN

Here are three sentences from a story by Irwin Shaw. Read the sentences aloud. Study the use made in them of *ordinary verbal phrases* and of *absolute constructions*. Then use each of these examples as a *model sentence*. Fill in your own words but preserve, as far as possible, the structure of the original.

1. Darling tucked the ball in, spurted at him,
   driving hard,
   hurling himself along,
   all two hundred pounds bunched into controlled attack.

(Imitation):   Stephen took his coin back, looked at it,
   swallowing hard,
   pulling himself up,
   all his dreams shattered by the unexpected rebuff.

2. There was only the safety man now,
   coming warily at him,
   his arms crooked,
   hands spread.

3. He smiled a little to himself as he ran,
   holding the ball lightly in front of him with his two hands,
   his knees pumping high,
   his hips twisting in the almost girlish run of a back in a broken field.

Use the following for a sentence-combining exercise. Work the material from the added source sentences into the main statements as absolute constructions.

EXAMPLE: He sat on a log.
   The invisible compass was in his hand.
(Result)   He sat on a log, *the invisible compass in his hand.* (William Faulkner)

1. The car stood by the side of the road.
   Its radiator was dripping water.

2. He stood watching the approaching locomotive.
   His teeth were chattering.

3. She kept up the speed.
   Her hands were gripping the wheel.

4. They lived in a big mansion.
   A black limousine was parked outside.

5. The owner was sitting on the porch.
   A big mean dog was lying at her feet.
   A shotgun was across her knees.

6. She crossed the finish line.
   Her heart was pounding wildly.
   Her legs were trembling with exhaustion.

7. He headed right for the safety man.
   His arms and legs were working beautifully together.

8. The boat came around the corner.
   Its white sail was glistening in the sun.

9. A lieutenant stood at the right of the line.
   The point of his sword was upon the ground.
   His left hand was resting upon his right.

10. He could imagine his father at the top of the stairs.
    His legs were sticking out from under his night shirt.
    His feet were in carpet slippers.

EXERCISE 2

Can you find the absolute constructions in the following sample sentences? After the number of each sentence, write down any absolute constructions that the sentence contains. Write *No* if there is no such construction in the sentence. (Be prepared to point out other, more ordinary uses of verbals in class.)

EXAMPLE: The dispatcher repeated the instructions, her voice becoming impatient.

(Answer) *her voice becoming impatient*

1. Sue greeted us at the door, a smile on her face.
2. There he stood, holding his breath, terrified by the noise.
3. An old lady appeared, eyes bright and arms filled with flowers. (Jean Houston)
4. The family slowly made its way back, the children crying, the adults grumbling.
5. He sat on the lowest step, staring into the street.
6. Pencil ready, the detective waited for me to start talking.
7. Our cameras ready, our guide moving a few steps ahead, we cautiously entered the high grass.
8. Paul dismissed the carriage and walked, floundering along the tracks, his mind a medley of irrelevant things. (Willa Cather)
9. Their guns blazing, the desperadoes careened down the street in their getaway car.
10. His feet propped up on the table, his hat low over the eyes, the visitor did not inspire confidence.

Expand each of the following sentences. Rewrite each sentence *twice*. Each time add one or more absolute constructions.

EXAMPLE: Fred came into my office.
(Possible
Answers)   *His funds running low,* Fred came into my office.
            Fred came into my office, *his hands in his pockets.*
            Fred came into my office, *a sick-looking puppy cuddled in his arms.*

1. The police car took off in pursuit.
2. We returned to our camp.
3. The horses were coming down the homestretch.
4. The teacher explained the problem.
5. The dancers performed their traditional dances.

Study the use of special sentence resources in the following sentences. After the number of each sentence, put one of the following abbreviations:

App   for appositive;
Part for participle;
VN   for verbal noun;
Inf   for infinitive;
Abs   for absolute construction.
(Do not include any forms used as parts of a complete verb.)

1. Losing this game would have ruined our season.
2. They sent us a chatty letter to report on their travels.
3. Przewalski's horses, the only true wild horses, live in Asia.
4. In the old days, Masai warriors used to fight lions.
5. Shy zoo animals need protection from prying human eyes.
6. Zoos filled up their stock by catching new specimens in the wild.
7. Its peak covered with snow, stately Mount Hood looms over the city.
8. The city was building malls, spacious areas for pedestrians only.
9. King Kong, the giant ape, has appeared in several movies.
10. The beaches along the northern coast were too cold for swimming.
11. Its lights blazing, the big ship looked like a palace.
12. Part of her job was to talk to unhappy passengers.
13. We visited the estate, its mansion beautifully restored.
14. Visitors to Vicksburg can see trenches and bunkers made a century ago.
15. Her passengers waving happily, my aunt backed out of the driveway.
16. We sat on the deck, listening to announcements by the captain.
17. The *Delta Queen*, our sister ship, had tied up at the pier.
18. My uncle started blaming us for the accident.
19. We were looking for a sheltered place for our camp.
20. They were finally leaving for good, their debts paid.

FOR FURTHER STUDY

LANGUAGE IN ACTION

When we study our language, we usually learn about one thing at a time. We try to learn first the most basic rules—the way things are *usually* done. But when we see language in action, we are always reminded of its richness and variety. There is always something new and different to keep us interested. The following activities give you a chance to explore some of the richness and variety of our language.

ACTIVITY 1

A well-built sentence "follows the rules" even when the message it carries goes far beyond what we usually hear or read. Each of the following messages is quite unusual. Would you agree that nevertheless each follows the rules for how to put sentences together in English?

> I snore in code.
> Bowler hats should no longer be filled with spaghetti.
> Siberian seals blew trombones.
> Coins for the blind ran down alleys.—Ted Joans, *Afrodisia*

Write four "far-out" sentences of your own. Make sure they follow the rules for sentence building in English. But make them sound as if they had been written by someone with a wild imagination.

ACTIVITY 2

Great writers are often people who know and love our language. Often, they use *more* of it than ordinary people do. Study the way two well-known writers use language resources in the following sample passages:

A. In *Life on the Mississippi* and other books, Mark Twain wrote about his work as a river pilot when the river was a major artery of trade. Write down *all adjectives* that you can find in the following sentence. How many are there? Be prepared to show in class what tests you applied to tell adjectives apart from other kinds of words.

> In time this commerce . . . gave employment to hordes of rough and hardy men; rude, uneducated, brave . . . heavy drinkers, coarse frolickers, heavy fighters, reckless fellows . . . elephantinely jolly, foul-witted, profane, prodigal of their money, bankrupt at the end of the trip, fond of barbaric finery, prodigious braggarts; yet, in the main, honest, trustworthy, faithful to promises and duty, and often picturesquely magnanimous.

B. Write down *all prepositional phrases* that you can find in the following passage. How many are there? Discuss in class any problems or complications you may have encountered.

Canton-flannel gulls flew near and far. Sometimes they sat down on the sea, near patches of brown seaweed that rolled on the waves with a movement like carpets on a line in a gale. The birds sat comfortably in groups, and they were envied by some in the dinghy, for the wrath of the sea was no more to them than it was to a covey of prairie chickens a thousand miles inland. Often they came very close and stared at the men with black bead-like eyes.—Stephen Crane, "The Open Boat"

A single sentence can carry much freight. Look at the following capsule plots for old movies. Each is just one single sentence. Can you see how the writer tried to cram each with all the essential details? Read each of them aloud. Can you do it in one breath?

ACTIVITY 3

***Zero Hour** (1957). A war veteran flyer whose experiences have left him mentally shattered is aboard a commercial plane when the pilot and co-pilot become ill and he is forced to take over the controls.

***Tarantula** (1956). Giant tarantula escapes from a laboratory and a series of mysterious killings of sheep, cattle and men start an extensive battle to stop the creature which seems indestructible.

***The Trap** (1959). A notorious head of a crime syndicate, using violence, isolates a small town in Southern California in his attempt to flee the country.

***High Society** (1956). A reporter and a photographer for a magazine cover a fashionable Philadelphia wedding and their presence in the household causes a series of events that make the prospective bride question the rightness of making a stuffed shirt her second husband.

Your Turn: Write a similar capsule plot for several movies you know well. Make sure your capsule plot fits into one complete sentence. (Try to include one of the great movie classics.)

There are many ways to modify the parts of an English sentence. The number and variety of the modifiers that we can work into a sentence are truly amazing. Notice what Bret Harte could do with as simple a basic sentence as "He lay":

Pulseless and cold,
with a Derringer by his side and a bullet in his heart,
though still calm as in life,
beneath the snow
    lay he
        who was at once the strongest and yet the
        weakest of the outcasts of Poker Flat.

Note what Thoreau could do with the simple sentence "I observed ants":

One day when I went out to my woodpile,
or rather my pile of stumps,
    I observed two large ants,
      the one red,
      the other much larger,
      nearly half an inch long,
      and black,
      fiercely contending with one another.

Read each of these sentences out loud. How close could you come to this kind of sentence in a sentence of your own? Fill in your own material in the two sentence frames below. See how much information you can make each sentence carry. (Write on a separate sheet of paper.)

1. _____ ,
  with a _____ ,
  _____ ,
    (lay he) (stood he) (stood she)
      who was _____ .
2. One day when _____ ,
  I observed _____ ,
    _____ ,
    _____ ,
    _____ .

When we study language, we often look at *written* sentences. But not everything in our spoken language shows when we write something down. For instance, writing does not usually show differences in **stress.** We pronounce some syllables with greater force than others. Can you hear the basic difference between *stressed* and *unstressed* syllables in the following?

the tăll mán wĭth thĕ gréen hát

To get the rhythm of a phrase or sentence right, we must at least distinguish between stressed and unstressed syllables, without necessarily pinning down *degrees* of stress. Copy the following, putting ' over all stressed syllables. If your classmates have marked any passage differently, read the different versions out loud. For any of these, is more than one version possible in normal English?

1. a wonderful day at the beach
2. a girl in a blue sports car
3. the wise-looking elephants in the city zoo
4. He was known as a good-for-nothing.
5. The ruler had been broken in half.
6. Visiting the cathedral is an absolute must.
7. The biology teacher broke off the experiment.
8. John Henry had lost his copy of the textbook.
9. The band reached its peak in the spring of that year.
10. We went to an exhibition of artistic photographs.

ACTIVITY 5

How is stress used to *signal meaning?* Look at the words repeated in each of the following pairs. Where would you put the stress mark for the first version? Where for the second? What is the difference? (Can you sort out these pairs into major categories and describe the major possibilities they illustrate?)

1. She has a sour face but a *sweet heart.*
   She had been his childhood *sweetheart.*

2. Mr. Ruckner will *conduct* the orchestra.
   She earned a medal for good *conduct.*

3. Jim had always been a *rebel.*
   People should *rebel* against injustice.

4. No one saw the burglars *get away.*
   Her friend drove the *getaway* car.

5. His friends were living in a *round house.*
   The engine was taken to the *roundhouse.*

ACTIVITY 6

6. The raven is a *black bird*.
   The first arrival was a *blackbird*.

7. Hunters need a *permit*.
   The commission does not *permit* fishing in the river.

8. The secretary will *record* our conversations.
   We should send him a *record* of the proceedings.

9. He knew the restaurant from *frequent* visits.
   Her habit was to *frequent* only first-class restaurants.

10. The president will *present* the gift.
    We tried to find a suitable *present*.

11. My aunt lived in a little *white house*.
    The President's family moved into the *White House*.

12. *Look out* for snakes.
    Be on the *lookout* for snakes.

13. Sue painted a cow with blue legs and a *red head*.
    Jim went for a walk with a *redhead*.

14. He *cast off* his clothes.
    He wore *cast-off* clothes.

15. Surrey Lane is certainly not a *main street*.
    He had a shop on *Main Street*.

Chapter 3

Composition
Writing for a Purpose

Chapter
Preview 3

IN THIS CHAPTER:

- How to handle the major steps in the process of writing a paper.

- How to attract and hold your readers' attention and guide them from point to point.

- How to improve your writing by becoming a careful observer.

- How to write papers that define a term, weigh the pro and con on an issue, or persuade an audience.

- How to handle the research and documentation for a short research paper.

- How to write an effective business letter.

Make your writing serve your purpose.

The difference between casual talk and a written composition is that the composition is *put together for a purpose*. It has a job to do: It tries to describe a product, explain a process, or defend a point of view.

Here are some of the major purposes writing may serve:

● *Writing to inform.* In much writing, our main purpose is to record, to report, to inform. We describe the actual shapes, sounds, or colors. We report processes and events as they actually take place. The key questions in this kind of writing are:

> What do you see?
> What actually is happening?
> What are the facts?

● *Writing to interpret.* In much writing, our main purpose is to explain something. We weigh the evidence and evaluate information. The reader may not be satisfied. He or she will ask:

> Can you make any sense of it?
> What does it all mean?

● *Writing to persuade.* In some of our writing, our main purpose is to persuade. We want to influence what people think and do. We want them to change their attitudes, to support a program, to vote for a party. The key question in the reader's mind is:

> What do you want me to do?

Suppose you are helping to select material for a publication that collects and prints student writing. How do you react to the following examples of student writing? Which do you like best? Which do you like least? What purpose does each piece serve—is it writing to inform, to interpret, or to persuade?

Explain the reasons for your preferences in class discussion.

The Accident by the Seaside

As we eased up the beach, I noticed a pelican on the sand, huddled and motionless. It watched us as we approached but made no attempt to fly.

I looked at the bird, which was as large as a graceful swan. It had a moderate wingspread and a rounded tail. It was creamy white with slight tints of flesh. I peered at the great bill with a hook at the end, so light yet so strong, and thought, not for the first time, how strange and beautiful it must be that a creature so grotesque could know one complete moment of flashing beauty. At the very last split second of its dive, a fishing pelican folds its clumsy wings and cleaves the water like a hurled arrow, all grace, power, and precision. But at this particular moment I had a feeling that this bird would know no more such moments.

I ran my fingers along its fine, silky, almost naked throat feathers. I could feel no obstructions. The bird flinched a little, took a few steps and then grew still.

The sun went down in a smear of crimson. We carried the bird to the sea, through the dunes and across the deserted beach. The tide was ebbing; the waves were steel-colored in the soft dying light. We set the bird down in the water; something happened. It had ended. Silently, the great head fell forward into the waves.

We buried it at the foot of the dunes where the sea could watch over it. The tides would never reach this far.

Small American Cities

A small city has a few disadvantages, one of which is major. When you need a part for something, whether it be for the household appliance, the automobile, or the tractor, it is usually not in stock. This means that the store will have to order it for you, or else you must make a trip to a large city where the distributing house is located. Some other disadvantages are that the highest quality doctors, lawyers, and professional people are in the large cities where they can receive a larger income for their services.

The advantages of small cities far outnumber the disadvantages. First of all, everyone knows almost everyone else. This helps bring the town closer together and function as a whole unit. When something happens to someone, everyone helps the friend. Another advantage is attending a small school. Every student knows every other student, which in turn brings the student body and also teachers closer together. The teachers seem to want to help you more when you do not understand a course, because they have more time. Still another advantage is that business can be conducted without lawyers drawing up all kinds of legal papers, because all know how far they can trust another person. In my opinion, there are many advantages, as compared with the disadvantages. For this reason, I would rather live in the interesting, but still busy small city.

Bike Bigotry

Because of the lack of responsibility on the part of a few motorcyclists, all cyclists are downgraded. They are discriminated against in many different ways, but who ever heard of civil rights for motorcyclists?

At one drive-in I know, cyclists are not allowed to see the movies. The manager says they always cause trouble. Speak of a glittering generality—this one is! At a nearby restaurant, the people refuse to serve anyone on a motorcycle. If one misses seeing the signs saying, "Motorcycles Prohibited," the local rent-a-cop quickly makes it clear that he or she is not welcome.

This is wrong! People should be able to eat where they want or see any movie, regardless of what they are driving. The vast silent majority, consisting mostly of parents, stereotype anyone who rides a cycle as a bum, nut, hippy, or welfare case. People get these impressions through television, newspapers, and a few movies like "Hell's Angels."

Some people believe only what they want to, but I just wish they would go out and get to know a few of us cyclists, or for that matter, a whole lot of us. If they would, they might realize we are not all that bad.

My own high school developed a motorcycle club to teach proper use of a bike. I myself try to hold to a reasonable rate of speed while on the road, and if I want to race I go to the track to do it. The same holds true for most of my friends. We do not carry chains, knives, or guns. We don't even carry stones.

The reasons most of us ride cycles are the feeling of freedom and the low cost of upkeep that we just can't get in a car. I don't cycle just to look tough.

A Day on the Lake

Our family had a summer cottage up in the northern part of Vermont. It was a nice little cottage, and it was right on a lake. I remember spending two summers at that cottage. I can recall the one day in my whole life that I ever did something peaceful with my father. It was one warm morning. I went to my mother's room and asked her if she would come out into the water with me. I figured that she and my father must have just finished one of their fights, because she was rather upset. I left her room, and my father saw me. He didn't say anything to me, but when I went into the water by myself, he came in with me. He talked to me, and he let me go out deeper than Mommy ever had. At the time this meant a lot to me. Things were quiet, and for the first time in my life my father was doing something with me.

PREVIEW EXERCISE 2

Have you recently felt like *talking back* as someone was making unfair accusations? Do you have a *complaint* concerning something that people are very insensitive about? Have you recently felt like *defending* a place or a type of person against unjust criticism? Write a short paper that serves one of these purposes.

Use a well-developed paragraph to do justice to one major point at a time.

Paragraphs come in many shapes and sizes. The most basic kind of paragraph, however, is one in which a writer uses five or six sentences to *present, explain, and support one major point.*

Write a topic sentence that sums up the key point of your paragraph.

A well-written paragraph has a point. Often the very first sentence sums up the key idea. When the central point is clearly stated, we call it the **topic sentence.** When the details that follow clearly explain and support it, we say that the details are **relevant.** They do a necessary job: to show that there is something to what you say.

A good topic sentence is like a conclusion that the readers themselves could reach after studying the material in the rest of the paragraph. In the following example, read the supporting material first. What conclusion do you reach? Then read the topic sentence. How close is your conclusion to that of the author?

TOPIC SENTENCE: *Symbols suggesting that the homeowner has ties going far back into American history are growing in popularity . . .*

SUPPORTING
MATERIAL: . . . One of the new vogues is the installation of flickering gaslights outside higher-priced homes. A large development firm in the Detroit area now promotes its new "estates" with expensively printed brochures illustrated with such Early American symbols as hitching posts, spinning wheels, muskets, horseshoes, old lanterns and town crier's bells. It places gray-haired hostesses in period costumes in its model homes and transports prospects about the projected development in horse-drawn carriages.—Vance Packard, "The Status Seekers," *Look*

(1) Use your topic sentence to add up related details. In writing a good paragraph, we funnel related material toward one key idea. Can you see this funneling process at work in the following example?

DETAILS: Arabs are rigging out their camels with phosphorescent harnesses so car drivers can see them in the dark. Finns have done something similar with their reindeer, daubing the antlers with reflective paint. And Navajos in New Mexico have marked their cattle with glowing colors, too.

TOPIC SENTENCE: *Herders in remote parts of the world have had to start protecting their animals against automobile traffic.*

C1

**WRITING A
PARAGRAPH**

C1a

**Writing the
Topic Sentence**

(2) Experiment with ways to strengthen or reinforce your topic sentence. Often the sentence that follows it *explains* the key idea in more detail:

> *The best way to kill a conversation is to have someone start telling funny stories.* Nothing produces an embarrassed silence more quickly than the desperate attempt by everybody to think of another funny tale. . . .

Sometimes we start the paragraph with a *question* to which the topic sentence gives the answer:

> Who is the guest most likely to spoil a party for the other guests? *Surprisingly enough, it is the person who spoils the conversation by telling stories. . . .*

Sometimes we restate the key idea in a **clincher sentence** at the end of the paragraph:

> *The amateur storyteller can easily spoil a party by making the other guests feel like inarticulate dolts. . . .* (Several examples follow) . . . Nothing makes the other guests more uncomfortable than the person who every five minutes "thinks of another" and breaks loose.

(3) Study the way good writers let different words and phrases echo their key ideas. In a good paragraph, a network of related expressions often keeps our attention focused on the main idea stated in the topic sentence. In the following example, look at the different words that keep our minds on the idea of fear:

> *The world of Greek mythology was not a place of terror for the human spirit.* It is true that the gods were *disconcertingly* incalculable. One could never tell where Zeus's *thunderbolt* would strike. Nevertheless, the whole divine company, with a very few and for the most part not important exceptions, were beautiful with a human beauty, and nothing humanly beautiful is really *terrifying*. The early Greek mythologists transformed a world full of *fear* into a world full of beauty. —Edith Hamilton, *Mythology*

EXERCISE 1

Each of the following sample paragraphs starts with a topic sentence. Read each paragraph carefully and do the following:

A. Restate the point made in the topic sentence.

B. Identify briefly the material that has been pulled together in the paragraph.

C. Show briefly that the material in the paragraph is *relevant* —that it is related to the topic sentence.

1. *Africa is a continent of amazing contrasts.* Geographically, it has almost every kind of land one can think of. It has arid desert in the Sahara and Kalahari; swamps near some coasts, and the *sudd* in the southern Sudan—a mass of tangled, reed covered, floating islands in the Nile; vast stretches of savannah land on the borders of deserts, with long "elephant grass" and low trees and bushes. It has fertile soil and meadow lands in parts of South Africa and Rhodesia, and in Kenya and Uganda; mountains, great rivers, and lakes as large as seas; even snow near the Equator, on the peak of Mount Kilimanjaro.
—Margaret Shinnie, *Ancient African Kingdoms*

2. *Today, literally no part of the human body is beyond the reach of the healing knife.* Segments of major arteries, blocked or weakened by disease, can be replaced nearly at will. Removing diseased sections of lung to prevent recurrence of tuberculosis and for other purposes is commonplace. Surgery has developed high skill in treating multiple injuries of appalling severity, as well as the major burns from gasoline that the automobile age has so sharply increased. Even the liver and pancreas, two organs that have been particularly resistant to surgery, can now be operated on successfully.—Leonard Engel, "The Healing Knife," *The New York Times Magazine*

3. *For hundreds of years now, many tasks have been passing from what the economists call "customary" work, done without pay, to wage work.* Canning, clothes-making, and the care of the sick are now jobs, not unpaid chores. The hired help has replaced the farmer's children. The paid baby-sitter has replaced neighborly child-watching. Young people learn to drive, skate, ski, and swim from paid instructors, rather than older relatives.—Caroline Bird, *Born Female*

4. *The observation that Americans work at their play and play at their work has become one of the clichés of our society.* Every weekend, some 20 million pale pencil-pushers turn into red-necked and blistered boaters. The flabby office worker becomes a compulsive athlete, driving ten hours in a blizzard in order to spend half of that length of time skiing. People eagerly leave a warm bed in order to spend the small hours up to their hips in a freezing stream, matching their wits against a fish. The number of people who spend their weekends pounding around tennis courts is growing all the time.

5. *When I was a child, New York was the natural Mecca for the immigrants coming to the New World.* Every letter to my father, written in Russian, Polish, or Hebrew, from some relative in our Ukrainian town, Zareby Koscielne, usually ended with the question, "When will you send money for a *shifskart?*" The ship's ticket was a passport to Cherry Street, East Broadway, Delancey Street, night school—to the United States taking in the huddled masses. It was a ticket to

family honor—redeemed at Ellis Island by brothers, sisters, cousins, uncles, and friends. It was money given like a grant-in-aid, rather than as a returnable loan. It was blood money in its most honorable sense—money given so that others of one's clan could get to Ellis Island, to the hustling, emerging United States of America.—Harry Roskolenko, "A Jewish Search for Freedom," in *The Immigrant Experience*

EXERCISE 2

In each of the following sample paragraphs, the topic sentence has been left out. What general conclusion does the rest of the paragraph point to? In your own words, state the key idea of the paragraph. Write it as a possible topic sentence after the number of the paragraph. (Write on a separate sheet.)

1. _____

   _____. There was always danger of fire on a riverboat. Sparks flew out of the tall chimneys and fell down on the decks piled with bales of cotton or with boxes of cargo. There were snags and sandbars in the river, and every year boats hit them and sank. A tree snag could tear the bottom out of a steamboat, and the Mississippi was full of snags. The worst danger of all was an exploding boiler. Boilers were made of iron, and they could explode if the fires were too high. Too much steam could blow them to pieces.

2. _____

   _____. In the early days of our country, only men who owned property or paid taxes were allowed to vote. Gradually, the right to vote was given to all adult men. Freed former slaves and their descendants struggled for many years for full voting rights. American women had to wait until 1920, when the Nineteenth Amendment gave them the right to vote in every state. Recently, the voting age has been lowered from twenty-one to eighteen.

3. _____

   _____. We frequently see newspaper articles or letters to the editor that protest against crowded or unhealthy conditions in some menagerie or small zoo. Antizoo organizations publish reports that call for the liberation of zoo animals. Animal psychologists tell us about the abnormal lives most animals live in traditional zoos. Modern zoos try to substitute open spaces for the cramped, depressing cages of the past.

4. _____

   _____. Some years ago, while developing new teaching methods for "minority group learners," I asked an eight-year-old black boy, "Tommy, how much is this—five plus three plus two?"

Tommy made a face indicating boredom. I then upended the chair I was sitting on and began to drum on it, asking, "Tommy, how much is this: bump bump bump bump bump—bump bump bump—bump bump?" Tommy grinned and said, "That's ten, man." "Why didn't you tell me before?" I asked. "'Cause you didn't ask me before," he replied.—Jean Houston, "The Mind of Margaret Mead," *Quest*

5. _____

_____. It ought not to be funny to see a man, especially a fat and pompous man, slip suddenly on a banana skin. But it is. When a skater on a pond who is describing graceful circles and showing off before the crowd, breaks through the ice and gets a ducking, everybody shouts with joy. To the original savage, the cream of the joke in such cases was found if the person who went through the ice never came up again. I can imagine a group of prehistoric men standing round the ice-hole and laughing till their sides split. If there had been such a thing as a prehistoric newspaper, the affair would have been headed up: "*Amusing Incident. Unknown Gentleman Breaks Through Ice and Is Drowned.*"—Stephen Leacock, *Further Foolishness*

Study the way the key idea is echoed in the following sample paragraph. Write down *six words or expressions* used in it to point in some way to the taking in and mixing of many nationalities in our country.

EXERCISE 3

America has been a melting pot in the best sense of the term. Each ingredient has added its own element of strength. The constant infusion of new blood has enriched our cultural life and speeded our material growth. Many other peoples, it is true, are also of mixed origin. But this country has blended different people faster and more thoroughly than any other. The result has been not a forced merging but peaceful absorption. The same nationalities that used to war in the Old World have lived together in harmony in the New.

Select *five* of the following groups. What statement could you make about each that you could support well in a paragraph? Write the statement down as a possible topic sentence. (Your teacher may ask you to write a paragraph to follow up one topic sentence.)

EXERCISE 4

1. Baseball fans
2. Motorcycle riders
3. Teenage drivers
4. Celebrities on talk shows
5. First-year high school students
6. High school athletes
7. Parents
8. Old horror movies
9. Disaster movies
10. Amateur theatricals

C1b
Giving Examples

Follow up a topic sentence with well-chosen examples.

The most useful all-purpose paragraph first gives the topic sentence. It then follows with several convincing examples. It moves from the key idea to the "for example" or "for instance":

(Topic Sentence)	*At high school I was never comfortable for a minute.*
(First Example)	. . . When I was asked a question in class, any simple little question at all, my voice was apt to come out squeaky, or else hoarse and trembling.
(Second Example)	. . . I could not hit the ball in volleyball; being called upon to perform an action in front of others made all my reflexes come undone.
(Third Example)	. . . I hated Business Practice because you had to rule pages for an account book, using a straight pen, and when the teacher looked over my shoulder all the delicate lines wobbled and ran together.—Alice Munro, *Dance of the Happy Shades*

Remember:

(1) Whenever you can, choose factual examples; include facts and figures. Include examples that readers can check by comparing them with their own experience. Most of the statements backing up the key idea in the following paragraph would probably be confirmed by older people:

Really good education for every child is a new concept, one of which the United States can be justifiably proud. Anyone who doesn't believe this should go to the trouble of consulting records to find just what kind of public schools existed in his own town fifty years ago. What most people would discover is that fifty years ago, city schools were dull and dingy buildings, with classes of forty or more pupils common. County schools were usually one-room affairs, with children of widely varying age and ability taught at the same time. Few of the teachers fifty years ago had anywhere near as much education of any kind as most teachers today. The elementary school curriculum was pretty much limited to the Three R's. . . . The vast majority of the students never went to high school.—Sloan Wilson, "Public Schools Are Better Than You Think," *Harper's*

(2) If you use one main example, develop it in detail. Often good writers will pile up half a dozen or more examples to support a point. Sometimes they will use *one* typical example and discuss it at greater length:

(Topic Sentence)	*Some symbols differ in meaning according to the difference in their realistic significance in various cultures.*

(Support)   For instance, the function and consequently the meaning of the sun is different in northern countries than in
tropical countries. In northern countries, where water is
plentiful, all growth depends on sufficient sunshine. The
sun is the warm, life-giving, protecting, loving power. In
the Near East, where the heat of the sun is much more
powerful, the sun is a dangerous and even threatening
power from which man must protect himself, while water
is felt to be the source of all life and the main condition for
growth.—Erich Fromm, *The Forgotten Language*

*(3) Use the directional signals that help readers see where they
are going.*   The following **transitional expressions** are common in
paragraphs that give examples:

for example, for instance, to illustrate; moreover, similarly, furthermore;
also, besides

Each of the following is the beginning of a paragraph that gives
examples. Each starts with a topic sentence and then gives the first
example. Choose *five* of these. For each, write the next sentence in
the paragraph. Use it to give *a second example*.

EXERCISE 1

1. *In earlier days, several members of the same family would often share in
the work that supported the family.* In the old-fashioned corner grocery
store, husband and wife may still take turns minding the store. _____
_____ .

2. *Many jobs that were once done by hand are now done by machines.* Automatic crop pickers now pick grapes and tomatoes. _____
_____ .

3. *The great colonial empires built by European nations have almost completely disappeared.* England, which used to rule much of Asia and Africa,
finally had only a few colonial outposts like Hong Kong. _____
_____ .

4. *During our history, several major modes of transportation have gradually
become old-fashioned and given way to something else.* The horse, once
the basic means of moving people, is now used only for pleasure riding
or for racing. _____
_____ .

5. *In the modern world, different groups have begun to object to traditional
names by which they used to be called.* Some young Eskimos explain that
their name originally meant "raw meat eater" and prefer the name *Inuit.*
_____ .

6. *Parents find different reasons for objecting to the marriage of their daughter or son.* Some parents worry about the religion of the intended partner and insist that the person adopt the parents' faith. _____

_____ .

7. *Some of the most familiar forms of American popular music have been around for many years.* Country music lived in small towns and in the countryside for many years before radio and television discovered it, and much of it goes back to the folk music of England and Scotland. ____

_____ .

8. *Public opinion has only slowly accepted women in positions that were once reserved for men.* Much prejudice and hostility hampered the work of Elizabeth Blackwell, the first American woman who became a physician.

_____

_____ .

EXERCISE 2

Which of the following statements could you best follow up? Which would you have a hard time supporting? (Why?) On a separate sheet, write down several different examples to support each statement. (Your teacher may ask you to write one or more sample paragraphs using one of these statements as a topic sentence.)

1. Throughout history, many different societies have kept slaves.
2. Many animal species that used to roam the wilds in large numbers have become very rare.
3. Modern Americans use countless gadgets that are not really essential to their well-being.
4. Over the years, cars have become loaded down with many added features not really needed to move the car from here to there.
5. Each year brings a new supply of passing fads.
6. Wild animals often travel large distances.
7. The United States has bought several large chunks of territory from other countries.
8. Everyone knows different kinds of ethnic food brought to this country by different nationalities.
9. A big new dam can change the area where it is built in many ways.
10. Newspaper readers seem to be fascinated by sightings of mysterious creatures or by unexplained phenomena.

EXERCISE 3

The need to give convincing examples is especially strong when we take an *unpopular* point of view. When we go counter to public opinion, we have a job to do: We have to show why everyone else is wrong. Study the following sample paragraph. Do two things:

1. Explain what makes the writer's point of view different. Then point out the examples used in the paragraph.

2. Write a paragraph in which *you* support a point of view that is different from what many other people think. Make a special effort to give convincing examples.

In Defense of Snakes

In the end, humans do far more damage to snakes than snakes do to *humans*. Indian snake charmers often rip out the fangs of cobras or sew their lips shut to make them safe to "charm." (Cobras are totally deaf to music and the charmer's toots on his recorder are purely for the *public's* ears; the reason the poor snake is swaying and spreading his hood like that is because the basket is his *home* and he is trying to protect his territory.) Cobras treated so brutally soon die of starvation or sheer exhaustion. Snake meat is standard fare in Southeast Asia, and snakeskin, though its popularity has been diminished by synthetic fabrics and leathers, is still a fashionable luxury. In this country, we shoot snakes, run over them with automobiles, and bash in their heads, and, for years, snake oil (a product extracted from certain glands of dead snakes) was a staple remedy for rheumatism.

Write a paragraph that gives convincing reasons.

C1c
Giving Reasons

Often when we state a key idea, the reader's question is "Why?" Whenever we suggest a change or recommend a program, the reader expects us to present convincing *reasons*. What makes the new approach preferable? What was wrong with the old way? What difference would the change make to the reader?

Here are some familiar uses of the paragraph that gives reasons:

(1) We give reasons to help people see the point of practical advice. Guidelines of all kinds begin to make sense when the reader can see the reasons behind them. Here is a sample paragraph from an article about how to arrange for a job interview:

(Topic Sentence)   *Often you have no control over the time of your interview, but if you can arrange it, try not to be the last interview of the day.* Morning is generally best because your

(Reasons)   interviewer will be more alert. Interviewing is a tedious, wearing task, and after seeing four or five applicants for the same job the interviewer may be groggy. If yours is the last interview of the day—or of the week—your interviewer could be thinking about getting home through the traffic. . . .—Karin Abarbanel and Gonnie McClung Siegel, *Woman's Work Book*

(2) We give reasons to add force to warnings and the like. Restate the key idea of the following paragraph in your own words. Then explain the reasons that back it up:

(Topic Sentence) *An average driver in an average car who is mad enough to touch an indicated 100 mph on a public highway should*

(Reasons) *get six months.* The ordinary U.S. automobile, softly sprung, slow steering, is relatively safe at such a reading only in the hands of an expert of the first order. The average driver, who wouldn't even know it when the back end started to break away, unable to sense a front-wheel slide in time to do anything about it, unskilled in the business of steering on the throttle, is perfectly helpless if the car deviates from a straight line at high speeds. Because he can run up and down the Pennsylvania Turnpike all day as fast as he can go—if his luck holds—he's apt to think he's a safe high-speed driver. But what happens if he blows a tire, hits a slippery place, or comes around a bend to find a wreck in front of him? The difference between the expert and the novice is then decided, usually with a mortician in ultimate attendance. —Ken W. Purdy, *The Kings of the Road*

(3) We give reasons to explain a feeling or decision. People respect our point of view if we explain why we feel the way we do. Explain the reasons given in the following paragraph:

(Topic Sentence) *In my own school days, a class devoted to the history of black people in the United States always caused me pain-*

(Reasons) *ful embarrassment.* This would not have been so if that history had been presented truly, showing the accomplishments of the black race both in Africa and in this hemisphere. But as it was, the indictment of slavery was also an indictment of the people who were enslaved— a people who, according to the texts, were docile and child-like, accepting their fate without once attempting to free themselves. To me, this lackluster history of black people, devoid of any heroic or pride-building qualities, was as much a condemnation of myself as it was of my ancestors. I used to sit tensely waiting out those class hours, trying to think of ways to repudiate what the textbooks said, for I recognized that there was a terrible contradiction between what was in them and what I learned at home. —Mildred Taylor, "First Person," *Working Woman*

NOTE: The **transitional expressions** that lead the reader from one reason to the next are often similar to those that appear in paragraphs giving several examples. Look at the links in the following skeleton outline:

I feel that high schools should de-emphasize contact sports. In the first place, _____
_____ *. Also,* _____
_____ *. Besides,* _____
_____ *. Therefore,* most people would agree that _____ *.*

Choose *five* of the following topic sentences. Write down each in the version that comes closest to your own opinion. Then go on to give *one good reason*. Write it down as a sentence or two that would complete the first part of a paragraph giving reasons.

EXERCISE 1

1. The government should see to it that more (fewer) people come to our national parks. _____
_____ .

2. High schools should (should not) de-emphasize contact sports. _____
_____ .

3. Millions of people from all over the world came as immigrants to America.
_____ .

4. Drivers should be asked to pass stricter (less strict) tests before they are allowed to drive a car. _____
_____ .

5. The government should (should not) require everyone in a car to use safety belts. _____
_____ .

6. (Math) (English) (your choice) is one of the least popular subjects among high school students. _____
_____ .

7. The government should (should not) support free public television.
_____ .

8. People should (should not) be allowed to decide for themselves when and where they want to smoke _____
_____ .

9. Members of minority groups have often felt misrepresented or left out when watching a movie or television program. _____
_____ .

10. The system of rating films for different ages is useful (useless). _____
_____ .

Composition

EXERCISE 2

On a separate sheet of paper, write a paragraph that serves one of the following purposes:

1. Give reasons why high school students should (should not) learn how to cook;
2. Give reasons why you like a big (small) car;
3. Give reasons why members of your (sex) (race) (ethnic group) (religious group) should get more (less) attention in the news media;
4. Give reasons why the authorities should treat juvenile offenders more (less) strictly;
5. Give reasons why (some) (no) group of students should receive special treatment.

C1d

Process, Comparison, Argument

Write the kind of paragraph that takes the reader along from one step to the next.

Not every paragraph starts with a topic sentence and then goes on to give examples or reasons. In some paragraphs, we follow along as the writer moves from one point to the next. Sometimes, the writer leads us up to a conclusion at the end.

Each of the following kinds of paragraphs serves a different, specific purpose:

(1) A paragraph may trace a process or event as it happened in time. Directional signals like *now, then, next, later, finally,* and *meanwhile* may help the reader move forward in the right direction. Such a paragraph follows **chronological** order. In the following sample paragraph, point out all signals that help keep the time sequence straight:

> I opened the door of its cage and threw the snake in. The shrew approached it, preceded by his quivering mass of whiskers. The snake made a slight movement, the shrew sniffed and then backed rapidly away, hissing furiously in the same way I had noticed before. I removed the snake and tried a frog, with the same results. Then I tried a fish, which according to the earliest reports on this animal is its only food, and the shrew refused that as well. He was rapidly getting bored with these proceedings and was casting hopeful looks at his bedroom, when I threw in a large crab. He approached, sniffed, and then, before the crab had time to get its pincers ready, the shrew had overturned it and delivered a sharp bite through the underside, almost cutting the crab in two with one bite. Having done this, he then settled down and finished off his meal with great rapidity, scrunching loudly and quivering his whiskers. Within half an hour he had polished off four crabs, and so his feeding problem was settled for the moment.—Gerald M. Durrell, *The Overloaded Ark*

(2) A paragraph may trace a comparison or contrast.   Sometimes a topic sentence sums up the main point of the comparison or of the contrast. But often we see the comparison take shape as we read along. The first part of the paragraph may show how two things are similar. The second part of the paragraph may show how they are different. In the following sample paragraph, we see a contrast take shape between two sides of police work. What specific contrasts does the author present?

(First Side)   Like any other job, police work falls into set patterns: patrol this sector, cover this assignment, check this complaint, interview this man, this woman, this child, investi-
(Second Side)   gate this company, work on this case. But you are always conscious that the unexpected, the sudden violent event, is also part of the routine. If there is an undue hardness in the voice of the traffic cop stopping an offender for a minor violation, it might be because he remembers, in some deep part of his brain, hearing or reading of some cop, somewhere— stopping a light-jumper, a speeder, an improper turner—a cop who, summons book in hand, was shot dead. For no reason. If there is a dictatorial tone in the command of a policeman who tells a group of curious onlookers at some unusual event to move on, it might be because he has seen a curious crowd grow into a menacing mob.—Dorothy Uhnak, *Policewoman*

(3) A paragraph may examine an idea and then change or correct it as needed.   This kind of **Yes, but** paragraph typically starts with something that has often been said or something that someone else has claimed. It then works around to the writer's objections or to the writer's contrasting point of view. The typical signal for the writer's attack on the original idea is a transitional expression like *but, however, on the other hand,* or *nevertheless:*

(Yes)   Many students feel that a truly popular teacher must be tolerant and easygoing. Preferably, he or she would be someone who puts
(But)   the class at ease, joking with the students. *However,* the truly popular teacher is at the same time often the one who maintains good discipline. Last year, the one of my teachers who proved most popular with her students was my tenth-grade English teacher. She was always patient with students and never embarrassed them in front of the class. Yet she always stayed in full control of the situation. She saw to it that assignments were finished on time, and she graded strictly on the student's actual performance.

(4) A paragraph may look at examples or details first and then draw a conclusion at the end.   The writer looks at the record, or

presents the facts, and then moves **from fact to conclusion.** The topic sentence *follows* the relevant details. Two kinds of directional signals appear in this kind of paragraph. Words like *also, another, furthermore, besides,* and *moreover* may take us from one example, or one piece of evidence, to the next. Expressions like *therefore, consequently, obviously, we can see that,* and *we must conclude that* show that the writer is ready for the general statement at the end.

Can you find any such traffic signals in the following sample paragraph?

(Examples First) One of the best-remembered characters in all literature is Tiny Tim in Charles Dickens's *A Christmas Carol.* Another unforgettable child character is Dickens's Oliver Twist, asking for a second helping of gruel in the dreary orphanage, or trying to survive among thieves and crooks. Furthermore, the most vivid scenes in several of Dickens's other books are episodes from the hero's childhood. Who can forget David Copperfield's feelings about his stepfather or about being sent to work in the factory? In another of Dickens's most widely read books, *Great Expectations,* the childhood scenes are also (Conclusion) the most memorable. *Charles Dickens had an uncanny ability to re-create in writing the observations, feelings, and attitudes of a child.*

A paragraph of this kind has a shape like a funnel—wide at the top to catch all relevant material, narrow at the end to channel it in the right direction. Writing this kind of paragraph is good training because it forces the writer to collect evidence *before* stating an opinion.

EXERCISE 1

Study the following sample paragraphs. About each paragraph, answer the following questions:

A. What is the major purpose of the writer?

B. How is the paragraph organized?

C. Is the main idea summed up in a topic sentence, and where does it appear?

D. Where are transitional expressions used?

1. Huckleberry Finn just barely manages to escape real harm at the hands of his drunken, violent father. Every time he steps off his raft he is menaced by people. He sees an old man shot down in a public street. He sees two young boys hunted down and shot in a family feud. Moreover, some of his own traveling companions—the Duke and the Dauphin—become the victims of crude violence. We can see that much of Huck's experience is concerned with a callous and violent adult world.

2.   Garbage being unglamorous, nobody spends much money on research about it, which is too bad. I have clippings on at least two dozen processes for using it as an energy source. Here's one: The garbage is pounded into four-inch chunks and run over a magnet, which takes out ferrous metals. It's then pounded into tiny particles, and an air blast separates them by weight. Dirt and glass are taken out; the rest is pressed into burnable pellets. Overall, the system recovers 95 percent of the garbage, with an overall 60 percent going into the pellets. The other 35 percent is reusable material, and is sold as such. The pellets (at today's figures, there is a plant that really does this) sell for less than half the price of coal, and burn with slightly more than half the heat energy of coal. Transportation costs would run it up a little, but we wouldn't have to fill holes with 95 percent of our garbage.—Gene Marine, "Here Comes the Sun," *Ramparts*

3.   It is odd that American men are so frequently presented in European caricatures of the type, in fiction, plays, and films, as being extremely ill-mannered, loud, rough customers. Such Americans exist, of course, just as sneering Englishmen, bullying Teutons, insolent Latins also exist. But it has always seemed to me that American manners in general tend to err on the side of formality and solemnity. They are rather like those of elderly English dons and clergymen. The ordinary English are much more casual. We do not take enough trouble, for example, with our introductions. Terrified of appearing pompous, we hastily mumble names, or hastily accept a mumble instead of names, so that our introductions do not serve their purpose, and often, not knowing to whom we are talking, we saunter into the most dreadful traps. The deliberate ceremony that most Americans make of introductions protects them from these dangers and errors.—J. B. Priestley, *Midnight in the Desert*

4.   Charity is not simply a donation to the community chest and a gift to the Hundred Neediest Cases at Christmastime. It is not merely giving one's hours as a volunteer in a hospital or subscribing to the relief of flood victims a hemisphere away. It is both larger and smaller than those things, at once easier and harder, and it does, indeed, begin at home. Charity is graciousness and tact. Charity is a guarded tongue. It is picking up one's toys, giving a hand with the dinner dishes, writing a bread-and-butter letter to one's hosts. It is turning off television at a respectable hour so one's neighbor can sleep in peace, and being patient with bores. It is thanking sales clerks in shops, forbearing to pass on the bit of malicious gossip so tempting to tell, wielding knife and fork so that we do not offend.—Phyllis McGinley, *Sixpence in Her Shoe*

5.   Like pigeons, dogs are thought to have a supernatural ability to find their way home across hundreds, even thousands, of miles of

strange terrain. The newspapers are full of stories of dogs who have miraculously turned up at the doorsteps of baffled masters who had abandoned them afar. Against these stories, however, can be set the lost and found columns of the same papers, which in almost every issue carry offers of rewards for the recovery of dogs that, apparently, couldn't find their way back from the next block. Stefansson, who has had a great deal to do with dogs—sled dogs and huskies, dogs right in a state of nature if ever dogs were—says that a lost dog "rarely finds his way back." One of his Eskimos, Emiu, a young hunter, almost lost his life in a blizzard, through his "foolishness in trusting his dogs to find the way back to camp"—Emiu's idea that they would do so being, amusingly enough, a belief he had picked up from white men during a visit to Nome.—Bergen Evans, *The Natural History of Nonsense*

EXERCISE 2   Have you recently learned about some new technical or scientific procedure? Have you recently learned a skill that involves following several steps in the right order? Write a detailed paragraph that traces the process or the procedure.

EXERCISE 3   Write a paragraph that shows a *contrast* between two ways of looking at something. Write about an important trait that is sometimes misunderstood. Use the following outline as a rough model:

Charity is not simply _____ . It is not merely _____ . Charity is _____ _____ . Charity is _____ . It is _____ . It is _____ .

EXERCISE 4   Choose a subject on which your opinion differs from that held by the majority. For instance, do you disagree with your friends on rules your school has for student conduct? Do you have an unpopular opinion on some current community issue? Present your opinion in a well-developed *"yes, but"* paragraph. Choose a limited issue on which you can bring in convincing details or examples.

EXERCISE 5   Choose one of the following topics. Write a one-paragraph theme in which you present details or examples first. Then state your *general conclusion at the end*. Choose *one:*

- A character trait you *dis*liked in someone you otherwise liked or admired.

- The most likable trait of a character in a current television program.
- An unusual character trait of a character in a book or play.
- The most important feature that a girl (boy) should look for in a future husband (wife).
- A personality trait often seen in political candidates (television announcers) (police officers).

In each of the following paragraphs, one sentence has been left out. In some cases, the sentence left out is the topic sentence. Sometimes, it is an important link, or an additional example, or the like. Among the three choices that follow the paragraph, find the one that would best fill the blank and complete the paragraph. Write the letter for the right choice after the number of the paragraph.

1. Rare coins often keep gaining in value. A 50-cent piece minted in 1964 in honor of President John F. Kennedy has since doubled its value several times. _____ _____. Some silver quarters that were minted in 1940 and never circulated have jumped in price to many times their face value. For many people, a coin collection started as a hobby has proved a good investment.

    a. Under no circumstances try to clean the coins.
    b. A 1950 Jefferson nickle minted in Denver has come to be worth a stack of silver dollars.
    c. However, you should have a dealer check the pieces in your collection.

2. _____ _____. By the turn of the century, only a few buffalo were left, kept in zoos or on ranches. In 1902, twenty-one buffalo were brought to Yellowstone Park. President Theodore Roosevelt helped establish a game preserve for buffalo in southwestern Oklahoma. Other sanctuaries were created: the Montana Bison Range and the Pisgah Game Preserve in North Carolina. By 1950, there were almost ten thousand buffalo in national herds and private ranches.

    a. The Alaskan herd was established in 1928 with twenty-four buffalo.
    b. Americans waged a merciless war of extermination against the buffalo.
    c. During our century, an effort was made to save the American buffalo.

3. The United States and Britain were for a time bitter enemies. American writers during the War of Independence denounced the English as robbers and murderers. The Americans and the British fought each other again in the War of 1812. _____ _____. The United States came to the support of Britain and France late in World War I. In World War II,

Americans again fought side by side with the British in Europe and in the Pacific.

    a. In modern times, however, England and America became faithful allies.
    b. Americans were hoping to take over much of Canada.
    c. Americans of Irish descent were often hostile to the English.

    4. Families move to the suburbs in search of greenery and fresh air. Retired people move to Florida or California in search of the sun. Factories move south looking for lower taxes or cheap labor. Truckers and laborers follow the oil drillers and mining engineers to Alaska. _____ _____ .

    a. Even the most faraway place in the country can be easily reached by telephone.
    b. For many Americans, America is still a nation on the move.
    c. Most people move for economic reasons.

    5. _____

_____ . Reformers persuaded legislators to outlaw some of the worst tenements as fire and health hazards. Standards for ventilation and sanitation were set. Social workers like Jane Addams and Lillian Wald established settlement houses in the heart of the slums of the great cities. These carried on a varied program of relief and public education. Playgrounds were built to take children off the streets and away from gangs. Fresh-air funds provided vacations to the country. Day nurseries relieved working mothers of anxiety for their children.

    a. The contrast between rich and poor was strongest in the cities.
    b. The most serious problem facing reformers was juvenile delinquency.
    c. The "battle against the slums" was waged on many fronts.

C2

WRITING A PAPER

Learn to handle the major steps in the writing process.

As you study the work of good writers, you should ask yourself: "How was this piece of writing *produced?* What *steps* did the writer go through to produce the finished result? What is the *process* that experienced writers go through as they work on a typical assignment?"

C2a

The Writing Process

Know how to gather and organize material on a limited subject.

In writing a paper, you often have to do several things at the same time. Nevertheless, to get a clear picture of the whole process, think of it as *five* major steps:

(1) Limit your subject. If you treat a large subject in a short paper, you cannot be specific enough to be clear. You cannot come to grips with problems that will seem real to your reader. Freedom of speech becomes real when you *narrow it down* to a real situation: What ideas about government is a teacher free to express in class? What ideas about the school is a student newspaper free to print?

Here are some very large subjects narrowed down:

VERY LARGE:	American Television
MORE LIMITED:	Daytime Television Drama
STILL MORE LIMITED:	Characters in Daytime TV Serials
VERY LARGE:	America the Beautiful
MORE LIMITED:	Scenic California
STILL MORE LIMITED:	The Vanishing Redwoods
VERY LARGE:	The Dangers to Wildlife
MORE LIMITED:	Endangered Species in the U.S.
STILL MORE LIMITED:	The Endangered American Eagle

(2) Gather material. Bring together all the material that seems relevant to your topic. Sometimes you will draw mainly on your *memory*. You will call to mind events and experiences that are related to your topic. Sometimes you will have a chance to take a good look at what you are writing about: You will be writing from close *observation*. Sometimes you will be bringing material together from your *reading*. Take time for this essential material-gathering stage. Get as familiar with your subject as you can. Whenever you can, think and read and talk about it before you start writing.

Make it a habit to *take notes*. The experienced writer is a person who is constantly jotting things down on little scraps of paper. The best way to start your actual writing of a paper is to look over notes that you have collected over a period of time. Here are some notes for a paper on characters in daytime television drama:

1. The central character is a woman that other people come to for advice. She worries about the problems of other people in the family. Husband is scheduled for a serious operation. Daughter has serious career problems. Long discussions of husband's operation over cups of coffee . . .
2. Can't decide whether artists are generally supposed to be suspect because too bohemian. One son-in-law is a painter and in bad financial trouble . . .
3. Several grandparents are lovable, talkative busybodies. Old Pa Gruber always giving advice about what he did in same situation when he was young . . .

(3) Work toward a central idea. When all or most of your paper helps to prove one major point, that point becomes the **thesis** of your paper. It becomes the central idea that helps keep your paper to-

gether. Even while you are collecting your material, start asking yourself: "How does this add up? What general idea emerges that I might follow up? What would hold this material together?"

Here are possible central ideas for the paper on daytime TV:

SUBJECT: Characters in Daytime TV Serials
CENTRAL IDEA: The family in the typical daytime TV serial is composed of predictable types.

SUBJECT: Characters in Daytime TV Serials
CENTRAL IDEA: The people in daytime TV serials are an accident-prone lot; "Trouble" is their middle name.

The central idea helps writers select those details that are most **relevant** to their major point. They can *put aside* details that are not directly related. For instance, the paper about characters in television drama may focus on family types. The writer will then put aside material on how these serials treat doctors, artists, or the like.

(4) *Organize your material.* As you look over the material that is relevant to your central idea, sort it out under several major headings, or break it up into several major steps. Often a subject naturally breaks up into major subdivisions:

The Television Family

CENTRAL IDEA:
First Major
Category:
(Parents)

The family in the typical daytime television drama is composed of predictable, easily recognized types. *The center of the family, and its pillar of strength, is the Worried Mother. . . .*

Second Major
Category:
(Children)

One of the people that the Mother worries about is the Difficult Daughter or the Difficult Son. Their problems at work or in their marriages. . . .

Third Major
Category:
(Older relatives)

Nearly every daytime serial has its Lovable Grandfather. . . .

(5) *Develop each point.* Your scheme of organization provides the paper with its skeleton. By developing each point, you put flesh on the bare bones. In the paper on the television family, the reader expects two or three **examples** of the "Lovable Grandfather." The paragraph in the finished paper might look like this:

Nearly every daytime serial has its Lovable Grandfather, a talkative busybody, hiding under a grouchy exterior a heart of gold. In "This Changing World," there is Old Pa Gruber, walking around his son's house in suspenders and old sweaters. He is always giving advice about what he did in a similar situation thirty years ago. He first hints that there is something wrong with the intended son-in-law, because he doesn't "like the looks of the fellow." In his folksy way, he convinces the daughter that life is not over after the first disappointment in love at age eighteen. In "The Light that Shines," there is a grandfather who could be Pa Gruber's cousin. Untouched by "book learning," he speaks with a heavy German accent and out of his simple wisdom knows the score.

Study the three topics in each set as possible topics for a short paper. After the number of the set, write the letter for the most clearly *limited* topic.

EXERCISE 1

1. (a) Old movies
   (b) Hollywood's dream factory
   (c) Musicals of the golden years

2. (a) Vacations
   (b) Simple rules for campers
   (c) How to have a good vacation

3. (a) My lost home
   (b) The American family
   (c) Children of divorce

4. (a) Stereotypes
   (b) Not all Texans are alike
   (c) Regional types in America

5. (a) Child stars in commercials
   (b) American advertising
   (c) People who help TV sell

6. (a) Career training
   (b) On-the-job training
   (c) My year as an apprentice

7. (a) Leisure-time activities
   (b) Caring for tropical fish
   (c) Taking better care of pets.

8. (a) Crime shows on television
   (b) The TV detective as superman
   (c) Popular television shows

9. (a) Driving: the first year
   (b) A nation of motorists
   (c) Teenage drivers

10. (a) The great outdoors
    (b) Unusual outdoor settings
    (c) The living desert

Over a period of days, *take notes* on one of the following subjects. Do only a rough sorting as you write things down. Gather material for a paper of several paragraphs. At the end of your notes, write down a *possible central idea* for a paper on the subject. Choose one:

EXERCISE 2

A. How do Americans *behave toward each other* in public? How friendly or unfriendly are people at school? How polite or impolite are people in stores? Note typical greetings and incidents. Jot down what people say and do.

B. How are people presented on television? Keep a *TV log* in which you write down your observations under a heading like the following:

- family types in daytime television drama (or soap operas);
- treatment of different occupations (workers, teachers, doctors, truckers, and the like) in comedies;
- treatment of lawbreakers in Western or in crime shows.

C2b

Patterns of Organization

Work out a clear plan of organization for your paper.

The longer a piece of writing becomes, the greater is the need for a clear basic plan of organization. Study the following sample patterns of organization:

(1) **Thesis and support**—*developing a general statement by filling in the examples or reasons on which it is based.* The thesis is the central idea that the writer sets out to develop or support. The more solid the supporting examples or reasons, the better the chance that the reader will take the central idea seriously.

Here is a paper presenting a thesis and several major examples that support the central idea:

Beginnings

(Thesis)   In beginning a story, the writer working for a news-magazine often uses techniques that are familiar to every reader of *Time*. The typical "leads," designed to take the reader into the story, change little from story to story, or from year to year.

(First Example)   The weather lead is always a favorite because it creates a dramatic tone. "Flowers were in bloom on the crumbling towers of St. Hilarion, and hawks turned soundlessly high above Kyrenia." This would be a typical beginning for a story on a Mediterranean island. . . .

(Second Example)   Used over and over in *Time* is the moving-vehicle lead: "One foggy morning in Berlin, a yellow Mercedes drew up at the concrete barrier of the crossing point. . . ."

(Third Example)   Another favorite opening describes an unidentified well-known person whose name is not revealed until later. . . .

There are several familiar ways of arranging the examples or reasons in such a paper:

• *familiar to unfamiliar.* It is often reassuring for a reader to see first some examples that look familiar. Suppose you are writing a paper about how scientists have improved or changed crops. You might start describing such familiar examples as seedless oranges or seedless grapes. The reader might then be more willing to believe your description of square tomatoes (more easily packed).

• *simple to difficult.* We often go from the simple to the more complicated, or from the safe to the more controversial. Suppose you are writing to show that schools should do more to keep *all* students in school—including many that were formerly often excluded. Can you explain why the following order would lead the reader up to the most difficult point last?

 I. Married Students
 II. The Handicapped
 III. Students with Serious Behavior Problems

● *humorous to serious.* We often start with the more entertaining or amusing examples. These can help win the reader over to our side. We can then lead up to some of the more serious examples.

(2) **Classification**—*sorting material out into major categories.* Classification helps us subdivide a sizeable collection of material. It is hard to write clearly unless you group together things that *belong together.* Many different things can happen to spoil a vacation. In a paper, you might want to set up three major categories:

 I. Things to Expect
 II. Freak Accidents
 III. Problems Caused by Thoughtless People

Study the way the author of the following paper has sorted out changes in warfare under four major headings:

The Obsolete Hero

(Key Idea)

(First Category)

Modern warfare leaves little room for the outstanding hero of the Germanic epic or the medieval romance. The individual's exploits in battle are dwarfed by the *statistics* of casualties and losses of today's huge armed forces. In World War I . . . In World War II . . .

(Second Category)

The importance of the individual warrior has been lessened by *weapons* that kill without regard for courage, skill, or strength. Modern artillery . . .

(Third Category)

The most important people in a modern war do not ride to battle on splendid chargers but sit at elaborate panels checking *computations* and pushing buttons. Even operating an antiaircraft gun . . .

(Fourth Category)

The elaborate arrangements made to *supply* a modern army with gear, ammunition, and food are as important as the individual's cowardice or courage. . . .

(3) **Chronological order**—*tracing a process or series of events through major stages.* Chronological order soon becomes tiring if it merely mirrors how events follow each other in time ("and then . . . and then"). By breaking a series of events up into major stages, you can show the reader that *progress* is being made.

Composition

Does the following sample outline give you the feeling that everything is clearly in its place?

Settling the West

    I.   Native Americans of the West

   II.   The White Settler Arrives
       A.   Early pioneers and explorers
       B.   When the cowboy was king
       C.   How farmers fenced the range

  III.   Remnants of the Old West

(4) **Comparison and contrast**—*lining up related ideas or things for a detailed account of similarities and differences*. Parallels and differences emerge most directly when the comparison moves ahead *point by point*. A paper contrasting the views of father and son in a novel taking place around the end of World War I might proceed like this:

Characters in Conflict

(Key Idea)

    Edgar and his father provided a classic example of the generations in conflict. On several of the major issues of the day, their opinions were opposed and feelings ran high. . . .

(First Point: Father)

(Son)

    The father held firm to the biblical account of creation, taking the literal view of the divine creation of man. . . . *The son* was an equally firm believer in the teachings of modern biology. He imagined our ancestors as crawling out of the ocean onto dry land millions of years ago. . . .

(Second Point: Father)

(Son)

    The father championed the sovereignty of his country and had a profound suspicion of "foreign entanglements." . . . *The son* was a supporter of the League of Nations and plans for general disarmament. . . .

(Third Point: Father)

(Son)

    The father believed in individual responsibility, holding people responsible for their own acts. . . . *The son* believed that the behavior of individuals is shaped by the environment in which they grow up. . . .

COMPARISON AND CONTRAST

What do you see? How does each photograph make you react? Write a two paragraph paper—one paragraph on each of these two contrasting pictures.

EXERCISE 1

What is the *pattern of organization* in each of the following excerpted sample papers? Write down the appropriate label after the number of the paper. *How* does the paper illustrate the pattern?

1.   **The Ingenuity of Per Hansa**

Giants in the Earth, by Ole Rölvaag, is a novel about pioneers in the Dakota Territory during the later nineteenth century. The pioneer life required a great deal of ingenuity, which the principal character, Per Hansa, possessed in abundance.

One example of Per Hansa's ingenuity was the method in which he constructed his house and barn. The other settlers built their houses and barns separately. Per Hansa built his house and barn under one roof. . . .

Another example of Per Hansa's ingenuity was his device for capturing ducks. The swamps near the settlement had many wild ducks, but the gunpowder was too precious to waste hunting game. . . .

One of the most ingenious and profitable things Per Hansa thought of was his buying of furs from the Indians to resell in Minnesota. . . .

2.   **My First Real Job**

My first real job was working behind the lunch counter at Woolworth's Five and Ten. All day I made cokes, sundaes, sodas, malts, and milkshakes. The first few days I was the typical impossible beginner. I could never remember how to do anything right even if I had been shown how for the third time. . . .

By the time the summer was half over, I had become experienced enough to be more of an asset than a liability. I knew just exactly how many dips of ice cream to put in a soda . . . .

When fall came, I had become an old pro. Now I was the one who told the other girls when to use the black dipper or the blue dipper, or maybe the red dipper. . . .

3.   **The City Has Its Points**

For many years, everyone heard about people moving out of the cities into the suburbs. Now we hear about people moving back into the rebuilt and redeveloped cities. As a place to live, the city has many features that few of the suburbs can offer.

In the first place, the city is a going concern. The streets are finished. The stores are already built in convenient locations. Sewers are laid, utilities connected. . . .

In addition to the basic needs for living, the city provides many important public services. City transit systems are often highly developed. Many major colleges are located in urban centers. . . .

Finally, the cultural resources of the great city are often very rich. There are theaters, concert halls, libraries, museums, galleries. . . .

4.   **The Two Souths**

    Readers of Alan Paton's novels may discover important parallels between South Africa and the American South. . . .

    Both societies are only a short time away from the life of the frontier and the pioneer. The Texas prairie brings to mind the legend of the American cowboy, depending for protection on his gun rather than the law. The South African veldt brings to mind the oxcarts of the Afrikaners trekking into the interior. . . .

    In both societies, the rural areas preserve a strong Protestantism centered on the reading of the Bible. The American South is associated with fundamentalism in religion. . . . The older Boers in Paton's novels are stern Calvinists. . . .

    In both societies, the scars of a bitter and bloody war against a wealthy and industrialized rival still remain. For a long time, the "Yankee" was resented as an intruder. . . . To the Afrikaner of the old school, cooperation with the "British" was long equivalent to treason. . . .

Choose five of the following general areas.

For each, list three or four major categories that you could describe in a paper. Explain each category in a sentence or two.

EXERCISE 2

1. Celebrities
2. High school students
3. Favorite books
4. Horrible commercials
5. Changing fashions
6. Hard ways to make a living
7. Kinds of good news
8. Little-known sports
9. Status symbols
10. Familiar types in old movies

(Your teacher may ask you to write one of these papers.)

Attract your readers to your subject and leave them with a strong impression at the end.

C2c

Beginnings and Endings

    Good writers know how to attract the attention of their readers. They use the title and introduction to develop their readers' potential interest in the subject. They use the conclusion to reinforce the impression left by the paper as a whole.

    (1) *A good* **title** *identifies the subject and sets the tone.* The best titles are brief, clear, and striking. Stay aways from titles that are long and clumsy, or too general, or too predictable.

LANGUAGE IN ACTION

WHAT'S IN A TITLE?

Look at the following book titles. What kind of book does each make you expect? Would you want to read it? Why, or why not? Which of these titles do you like best? which least?

THE DAWN'S EARLY LIGHT

THE INVISIBLE IMMIGRANTS

SAFETY LAST 5000 NIGHTS AT THE OPERA

THE IMAGE MAKERS

PLEASE SAY PLEASE

THE POPULATION BOMB

WHY KILL TO EAT A NATION OF STRANGERS

HOW TO MAKE WHIRLYGIGS AND WHIMMY DIDDLES

Bonus Project: Make up three imaginary titles that you would like to see on the paperback rack at a local store.

Some titles merely sketch out the *territory* to be covered:

FRESH WATER FOR THIRSTY CITIES
POLICE WORK AS A CAREER

Other titles at the same time hint at the author's *major point:*

OUR TRAFFIC LAWS ARE OBSOLETE
THE STUDENT'S RIGHT TO READ

Often a title provides clues to the author's *tone* and approach. What kind of tone or what kind of approach would you expect in each of the following articles?

THE CASE FOR MALE DISHWASHING
REPORT FROM THE FUTURE
DON'T BITE THE POLITICIAN
NO LAND TO SPARE
HOOKING UP WITH THE UNIVERSE
THE RISING TIDE OF VIOLENCE

(2) *A good* **introduction** *arouses the readers' interest and leads them into the subject.* In a short paper, reach the core of your subject by the end of the first paragraph. An effective introduction may

- link the subject to the *readers' own problems or interests:*

Buying a New Car

One of the great American dreams is buying a new car. And since it's a not-so-cheap proposition, such an undertaking should require much thought and much homework. First, remember. . . . (Anne K. Dukes)

- tie in the writer's specific subject with a *familiar situation:*

The Unfunny Comedians

Television networks have long been extremely sensitive to criticism from large religious or ethnic groups. Programs are carefully screened to remove possibly offensive references to creed, race, or national origin. Nowhere are the results of this self-imposed censorship more evident than in the carefully laundered jokes of television comedy. . . .

- start with a *striking example:*

The Polite East

On every floor of Tokyo's crowded department stores, near every escalator, a graceful Japanese girl stands and bows to customers. She bows and murmurs polite greetings—several thousand times a day. . . .

- start with a *key quotation:*

The Worship of Facts

"Of course I'm sure—I read it in *Newsweek*." For several years, this slogan appeared in large advertisements all over the country. . . .

- start with *one or more provocative questions:*

Rising to the Bait

Do you know when a clearance sale is really legitimate? Can you spot bait advertising? Do you fall for fictitious pricing? According to the Federal Trade Commission, bait advertising is designed to offer, as bait to the consumer, an attractive bargain with the real intention of selling a different, more expensive item. . . . (Ella Gale)

- set out to correct a *common mistake or misunderstanding:*

The Chosen People

When we speak of Puritanism today, most people think of a very strict and narrow religion. They imagine people dressed in drab clothes, with a frown on their faces. This picture is rather distorted. . . .

- set up a *"then-and-now"* contrast:

The Audience Is Everybody

Only a short while ago, the size of any audience was limited by the size of the hall or the strength of the speaker's voice. Today the audience of a television program can be nearly the whole nation. . . .

(3) *A good* **conclusion** *reinforces the central point of the paper.* An effective conclusion does not merely repeat in order to fill space. Instead, it may

- restate the *central idea* in an emphatic or memorable way:

. . . A letter-perfect prom night is like a well-tuned engine—everything about it is predictable. But a meaningful glance in the street may be a miracle. Genuine contact between human beings must be wayward and unplanned.

- draw a *logical conclusion* that the rest of the paper has led up to:

. . . It is a mistake to think that America's leadership in world affairs can be measured in dollars and cents. We cannot exercise leadership unless people want to follow; and the desire to follow requires at least as much inspiration as it does material assistance.

- use a *key quotation* that sums up the main point or prevailing mood:

. . . what the reader remembers best about the novel is Jane Eyre's independent spirit. She acts on a belief stated by an older friend early in the novel: "If all the world hated you, and believed you wicked, while your own conscience approved you, and absolved you from guilt, you would not be without friends."

- use a *revealing incident* to drive home the central point:

. . . Parents are often unaware of what their children manage to see on television. Walking in the park one day with her six-year-old daughter, one mother was surprised at her daughter's reaction to an old newspaper under a park bench. In a calm, matter-of-fact voice the child said, "That is where the body is." Only looking under the paper would convince the child that this old newspaper did not serve the same ghastly purpose as the one on the television show the child had seen.

- show how the specific subject fits into a *larger picture:*

. . . In big league baseball, a player's success must be determined solely by the skill with which he does the job. Not entirely by accident, baseball is the favorite game of a nation that traditionally believes in the importance of individual effort.

Look at each of the following *beginnings*. How successfully does each introduce the reader to what follows? Which of these make you want to go on reading? Why? (Or why not?) Sum up in a sentence or two what each writer does to attract (and hold) the reader.

1. ### In It Up to Their Eyeballs

At the time it seemed like the right thing to do. What did the man expect anyway? Anybody who leaves a brand-new car just sitting there, lights shining and engine purring, should expect someone to borrow it. But now, as Al watched oil drip from the twisted front end of the car, he had the feeling that nobody would see it that way. . . .

2. ### It Changed My Life

Is it true that sports changes the lives of young people? I know it was true in my own case. I love basketball and I wanted to become a high school star and go on to college and be a star and from there go on to the pros. I knew I could not do any of this if I dropped out of school. . . .

3. ### Thoughts About Divorce

The cases in hand are sad. I remember my uncle, who got married, had children, lived in a nice house, and seemed happy. Then he and his wife broke up. Two of the children were foster children—back to their own wrecked home from another. My uncle was lonely and shocked. All of his belongings fit into the trunk of a car. . . .

4. ### Fresh Water for Tomorrow's Cities

On a muggy morning last May, I took a long cooling drink of tomorrow's water. It tasted like rain water and had a vague, pleasing flavor of the sea without being fishy or salty. It was good. It was the same water many of us will be drinking ten years from now. As the result of new processes, the conversion of sea water to fresh is becoming economically feasible for the first time. . . .

5. ### Are Your Beaches Polluted?

More than one million gallons of sewage oozed onto dozens of Long Island beaches last summer following an explosion at two storage plants. Nassau County health officials ordered 63 of the beaches closed and warned anyone who had had any contact with the water to receive inoculations immediately. . . .

6. ### The Scourge of Forest Fires

In August 1933, a forest fire in western Oregon destroyed thousands upon thousands of acres of trees—trees that had taken centuries to grow, taller than masts, greener than the sea. Starting with a small billow of smoke rolling up out of a canyon, it grew into a roaring inferno that defied all attempts to bring it under control. The great Tilamook Fire was only the worst of the fires that each year bring destruction to our forests and their wildlife. . . .

7. **The Secrets of the Deep**

The mysteriousness of the great depths of the ocean has led many people to suppose that some very old forms of life—some "living fossils"—may lurk undiscovered in the deep sea. The forms that have been brought up by scientists in their nets have been weird enough, but basically they have been modern types, adaptations of creatures found closer to the surface. . . .

EXERCISE 2

How effective would the following *conclusions* be in winding up a paper? State in a sentence or two the function that each conclusion seems to serve.

1. Baseball even in its modern guise has not changed in its essentials. It is a rough, tough game, with rules made to be broken if the breaking can be accomplished smoothly enough, a game in which nobody wants to do anything but win.

2. . . . A well-known road-racing driver was once asked to go for a ride in a 1927 automobile. He looked the car over. "Firestone doesn't make that size tire anymore," he said. "How do they happen to be on the car?" "They came on it," he was told. "They seem as good as new. Of course, they'll be replaced with new ones." "Good," he said. "Call me up when you have them. As the car is now, I wouldn't even sit in it. Forty miles an hour, or ten—I won't get in it." Nor would he.

3. . . . Of all Justice Holmes' eloquent sayings, the one I like best was written at 83 in a letter to a young Chinese law student in Washington: "If I were dying my last words would be, Have faith and pursue the unknown end." No young person could have said that.

4. . . . Soon we all will remember our Social Security numbers as naturally as we remember our names. Perhaps the people who assign these numbers to us think of us really as persons with real faces and real names. But perhaps a mechanized industrial society really needs people who are only interchangeable anonymous numbers.

EXERCISE 3

Study the beginnings of news stories in several recent issues of *Time* or *Newsweek*. Is it true that the newsmagazines tend to use familiar "leads" over and over again? Try to identify *three* typical kinds of introductions. Bring several examples of each to class for discussion and comparison.

Help your readers follow from point to point.

Readers can follow if they understand what the author is trying to do. Remember four major ways you can help your reader see where you are headed:

(1) State your central idea in such a way that the reader can see how your paper is going to develop. Use a **program statement** (or sometimes a "program question") to point the direction in which the paper is going to move. What kind of paper—how organized and how developed—would you expect after reading each of the following statements or program questions?

(Key Question)   What are the major safety devices introduced by the large automobile companies during the last five years? What major new devices were developed but *not* made available to the general public?

(Key Idea)   Shakespeare's Brutus had several qualities of a great and noble man, but he lacked one trait that is indispensable for effective leadership.

(Key Idea)   Students can be divided into three major categories: those eager and able to be model students; those who will always make only a minimum effort; and those whose interest can be stimulated if the material is approached the right way.

(2) Use transitional phrases to link one part of your paper clearly to the next. Adequate **transition** helps readers "move on" smoothly from point to point. It steers their attention in the right direction, prepares them for what is next.

Here are some of the most common transitional phrases and the purposes they serve:

CHRONOLOGY: *at first, now, then, later, at least, soon, in the meantime*

ENUMERATION: *in the first place, in the second place; to begin with, first . . . second . . . third . . .; finally*

ILLUSTRATION: *for example, for instance, to illustrate*

LOGICAL CONCLUSION: *therefore, accordingly, as a result, consequently, hence*

OBJECTION OR CONTRAST: *but, however, on the other hand, nevertheless, on the contrary*

CONCESSION: *it is true that, granted that, no doubt*

SUMMARY: *to conclude, to sum up, in short*

Notice the transitional expressions in the following excerpt:

> An insect, *therefore,* is not afraid of gravity; it can fall without danger. . . . *But* there is a force which is as formidable to an insect as gravitation to a mammal. This is surface tension. . . .
>
> *Of course tall land animals have other difficulties.* They have to pump their blood to greater heights. . . . *But* animals of all kinds find difficulties in size for the following reason. . . .
>
> When a limit is reached to their absorptive powers their surface has to be increased by some special device. *For example,* a part of the skin may be drawn out into tufts to make gills, or pushed in to make lungs. . . . A man, *for example.* . . . *Similarly,* the gut. . . . *Just the same* is true of plants. . . .
>
> Some of the methods of increasing the surface are useful up to a point. . . . *For example.* . . . *But.* . . . *So* the portions of an insect's body more than a quarter of an inch from the air would always be short of oxygen. *In consequence.* . . . *Yet,* like ourselves. . . .
>
> *Exactly the same difficulties attach to flying.* It is an elementary principle of aeronautics. . . . *So* the larger airplane. . . . *Applying the same principles to the birds,* we find. . . .
>
> *But it is time that we passed to some of the advantages of size.* . . . —J. B. S. Haldane, "On Being the Right Size"

(3) Make use of words and phrases that echo key ideas.   Words and phrases pointing to the same (or to closely related) ideas show that the paper has **coherence**—the different parts "go together." Notice the network of words referring to death and corruption in the following excerpt from an article on the "Vulture Country" of Spain:

> The sun, to the vulture, is not just something which makes life easier and pleasanter, a mere matter of preference. His mode of life is impossible without it. Here in Andalusia, the summer sun *dries up* every pond and lake. . . . It *kills the* food plants and *wilts* the trees over the heads of the panting flocks. . . .
>
> All animals, both tame and wild, *weaken* in these circumstances, and the weakest go to the wall and *die*. The unpitying sun glares down on the *corpses* and speeds their *putrefaction, rotting* the hide and softening the sinews. . . .
>
> The vulture must fly high—high enough to command a wide territory, for except at times of catastrophe, *dead animals* are never thick on the ground. . . . —John D. Stewart, *Atlantic*

(4) Use sentences of similar structure for related ideas.   **Parallel structure** underscores the continuity of discussion. Use it when different sentences provide several examples for the same point. The repetition of the same pattern serves as a signal to the reader that the writer is still following up the same point:

The summer sun dries up every pond and lake and almost
every river.
It drives the desperate frogs deep into the mud cracks. . . .
It kills the food plants. . . .

The vulture sits on a crag and waits.
He sees the sun bound up out of the sierra. . . .
He waits until the sunstruck rocks and the hard earth heat
up. . . .

In the following excerpts, note any features that make for
coherence and guide the reader from point to point. For each
excerpt, find the following:

EXERCISE 1

A. any *transitional* expressions used;
B. any network of *related words* echoing a key idea;
C. any program statement or use of parallel structure.

1. Once you are up against the fire, first check its direction so that you never get
    trapped. A fire burns uphill, almost never down—that is one of the most
    important factors to remember. The heat creates an updraft which pushes the
    fire up until it reaches a ridge. Then it will usually run sideways (whichever way
    the wind blows) rather than going down the other side. So, if you are ever
    trapped above a fire, try to get over the ridge and down the other side, angling in
    the direction the fire came from once you are over the ridge, so that it will pass
    behind you. . . .

    —Jeanne Tetrault and Sherry Thomas, *Country Women*

2. Within a century, our present civilization may collapse from a lack of
    natural resources. We are headed for a terrible clash of two
    contradictory needs. The first need is the need for farming, for tilling
    the ground. We must have the corn, wheat, barley, rye, rice, and
    potatoes necessary to feed humankind. We must have hay and
    green pasturage for cattle and hogs. To avoid the leaden diet of serfs,
    we must have figs, grapes, apples, plums, pears, cherries. . . .
    The second need is the need for the minerals and other resources
    that lie underground. Our industries have a constantly growing
    appetite for the substances that lie beneath the grainfields, stock
    ranges, and woodlands. Human beings learned to mine before they
    learned to farm. Our requirements for ore and fossil fuels have grown
    tremendously, but the planet in which we dig has not grown by a
    single yard. . . .

3. Motor courts sprang up during the depression of the 1930's. The earliest tourist cabins were simply a cheaper alternative to the hotel, resembling camping facilities. But within a decade motor courts were improved and standardized. In 1935, the first year for which the Department of Commerce reported statistics, there were about ten thousand motels or tourist courts. After twenty years there were some thirty thousand. The new chains and associations of motels soon enabled a motorist to use the same brand of soap, the same cellophane-covered drinking glasses, and the same "sanitized" toilet seats all the way across the country. The long-distance motorist, usually anxious to avoid the "business route," then needed to wander no more than a few hundred yards off the super highway for food and lodging. What he secures in one place is indistinguishable from that in another. . . .

—Daniel J. Boorstin, *The Image*

EXERCISE 2

Write tentative program statements for papers on three of the following topics. Read your statements to your classmates. See if they can correctly predict how each paper would proceed. Choose three of the following:

1. Your Changing Neighborhood
2. What to Do About Boredom
3. Looking for Something to Admire
4. People I Dislike
5. What Makes People Buy
6. Women (Men) in My Family
7. Vandals
8. Old-fashioned Occupations
9. What to Do in the Summer
10. Public Transportation

(Your teacher may ask you to write one of these papers.)

C2e
Outline and Summary

Use outlines and summaries to help you grasp and strengthen organization.

When you write a paper, you should outline the major points that you are going to cover. By working out an outline, you provide yourself with a plan to follow. You also have a chance to visualize the structure of the paper and to discover possible weaknesses while there is still time for reshuffling and reorganization.

In working with short papers, you may be satisfied with mere mental notes. In working with longer papers, you will often rely on *written* outlines and summaries. Remember the following points:

(1) Use an informal outline to help you work out the structure of a paper. A **working outline** is a tentative jotting down of ideas in their approximate order. It helps the writer visualize how the paper is shaping up. It gives the writer a chance to *shift* things around and to add or leave out points as needed.

Here is a working outline for a paper describing a strong emphasis on formal English in a student's English classes:

```
  I.  ban on informal English in compositions
         slang
         colloquial
 II.  books featuring informal English not to
      be read for credit
         Steinbeck
         Vonnegut
III.  requirement for formality in speech
         class discussion
         conference with teacher
         student conversation
```

(2) Use a formal outline to show the organization of a finished paper or article. When submitted with a long report or research paper, it serves as a guide to the overall plan. It enables the reader to form an estimate of how well and in what order the writer has covered the subject.

Study the way numerals and letters are used to label the entries in the following **topic outline:**

Advertisers' Know-How

Central Idea: Most advertising appeals to a few basic motives, some selfish, and some more idealistic.

I. Selfish motives
   A. Attracting the other sex
      1. Cigarette commercials
      2. Hair cream commercials
   B. Status seeking
      1. Outdoing others
      2. Keeping up with the Joneses
   C. Looking for the easy way
      1. Push-button gadgets
      2. "Miracle" chemicals

II. Idealistic motives
   A. Caring for the family
      1. Insurance ads
      2. Dishwasher ads
   B. Helping other people
      1. CARE ads
      2. March of Dimes

Composition

Remember:

● Make sure each major paragraph, and each major *part of a paragraph,* is represented by a topic or subtopic. But do not try to include every minor point mentioned. The purpose of the outline is to reveal the *overall* plan.

● Use *parallel wording* to show which topics go together. For instance, in the outline above, most subtopics start "Attracting . . ." "Looking . . ." "Caring . . ." "Helping . . . ."

● Avoid *single subdivisions.* If only *one* example follows a general point, do not subdivide that point. Whenever you start "A. . . ." or "1. . . ." there should be at least a "B. . . ." or "2. . . ."

(3) Learn to summarize essential information and to see an argument or a process as a whole.   Often a **summary** of about one-third or one-fourth the original length can preserve the gist of the original. To produce such a summary, proceed as follows:

● Choose *key sentences*. Strip them down to the key point they convey.

● Keep only the most essential or typical *details:* one key example to illustrate a major point; one figure chosen among several provided by the author.

● Omit everything that is only introduction. Screen out casual *comment,* further *explanation,* or repetition.

● Make sure that the summary shortens but does not *misrepresent* the original. Keep in important objections or expressions of doubt.

Study the two following passages carefully to find out how the original has been stripped down in the summary:

ORIGINAL

How many people in the world speak English as a first or native language? Exact information on this point is not available, but an estimate of 230 million cannot be very wide of the mark. Of these, 145 million live in the United States, a little less than fifty-five million in the United Kingdom and Ireland, and something like thirty million in the British dominions and colonial possessions. It is even more difficult to arrive at a figure representing those who speak English as a second or auxiliary language. Here the guesses range from fifty million to 125 million. A reasonably conservative conclusion would thus place the total number of speakers of English between 300 million and 325 million, about one-seventh of the world's population.

If one thinks solely in terms of total numbers of speakers, it must be conceded that some authorities place Chinese, the various Indic languages, and Russian ahead of English; others only Chinese. Both Chinese and Indic, however, are terms covering a large number of mutually unintelligible dialects, and though the numbers of speakers of these languages may seem impressive, communication within the languages is much more restricted than in English.—Albert H. Marckwardt, *American English*

SUMMARY

Perhaps 230 million people speak English as their native language —roughly 145 million in the United States, fifty-five in Britain and Ireland, thirty in British areas overseas. Anywhere from fifty to 125 million speak English as a second language, for a conservative total of 300 to 325 million speakers of English, or one-seventh of the world's population. Chinese, the Indic languages, and Russian may be ahead of English in number of speakers, but Chinese and Indic consist of many mutually unintelligible dialects.

The following student paper has some usable material. However, it would profit from revision aimed at a clearer overall scheme of organization. Study the paper carefully and then do three things:

EXERCISE 1

1. Prepare a *working outline* that shows the organization of the paper in its present rough-draft stage.
2. Prepare a *topic outline* that shows how you would revise the paper for clearer organization. Be ready to explain why you changed the organization the way you did.
3. Write a *one-paragraph summary* of the paper in which you keep essential ideas but eliminate all repetition.

Advertising and American Ideals

The ideals of a nation are revealed in its advertisements. Why is this so? In our nation today, one of the biggest industries is advertisement. People depend on advertisements to tell them which washday detergent is really best or which toothpaste really cleans teeth and leaves your breath fresher. If it wasn't for advertisements, television, radio, and most newspapers would be bankrupt. Everything that is on the market has to be advertised or it won't sell. Practically our whole economy is balanced on advertisements.

With this power, advertising must reflect the ideals of a nation. People have goals they set, and if the advertisement doesn't go along with this goal, then the product is not popular, and it will not sell.

Judging from what products are popular today, I would say one of the ideals we have is violence. On every children's cartoon show there is at least one commercial for a commando war outfit, complete, or a machine gun that carries hand grenades, and a pistol. It seems as if we want to raise a warlike generation, trained in killing by the time they are 15.

A very popular product is makeup. Maybelline, Helena Rubinstein, Max Factor, etc., are always found as sponsors for television shows and usually have a large ad in a magazine. So, another ideal could be beauty, or staying young, which is synonymous with beauty.

These are selfish ideals though and there are one or two charitable goals.

The United Fund reflects the ideal of giving. So does CARE, and the Peace Corps. Their advertisements aren't as plentiful as some of the others, but they're very good.

As far as the international ideal of world peace goes there are quite a few advertisements for the UN and religion, in the area of individual worship, has quite a few billboards and spaces in buses, newspapers, and magazines.

I would say our main ideal, high and above all, is materialism. We want toys galore for the children, and cars for the adults, and a beautiful house for all. The attitude is "we feel sorry for the people who live in the slums, and of course we'll help them if it's deductible." We want all for ourselves and more if we can get it.

Following close behind is the ideal of "stay young forever." This is evidenced by all the makeup advertisements, health salon ads, and even the soap you use for your dishes ads.

Our ideals aren't all this petty. We have fine ones like our basic one of democracy. But things like this aren't advertised. They don't really need any advertisement, because everybody knows and respects them.

EXERCISE 2

Find a short *newspaper article* on some current development in science, technology, or the arts. Prepare a summary of about one-fourth the length of the original.

C3
WRITING AND OBSERVATION

Make your writing real by drawing on authentic firsthand observation.

Good writing is packed with authentic detail. Good writers describe places, people, and events in such a way that we seem to see them with our own eyes. When they write about a ball game, we *see* the action on the field. We *hear* the noises of the crowd, we *smell* the roasted peanuts, we *feel* the excitement.

To make us visualize scenes, people, and events, a writer must be a good observer. A good observer notices things. Make your writing show that you are a good observer. Show that you take in more of what you see than the ordinary hurried passerby.

Make your writing real by putting characters and events in an authentic setting.

Learn how to re-create in words the sights and sounds around us. Make us visualize the background against which people move and events take place. Anyone who wants to write about people must learn to do justice to the **setting.** A good observer knows how to make real the places where people live and think and feel.

In order to do justice to a specific setting, observe the following advice:

(1) Develop the reporter's eye for detail. What do you actually see that you might not see in some other place? Often, first-rate writers carry us along by their ability to "put us in the picture." They put things before us in such **specific** detail that we cannot help seeing what they saw:

> The houses are built every which way, of whatever's available: weathered planking, sheets of plywood, corrugated iron or tin, roofs of tar paper. Where possible, one face of a house or every other picket of slat fence is painted blue, deep red, or ocher, but weather gray and rust brown prevail. Wash flutters on lines, roosters crow.... —Annie Gottlieb, "In the Presence of Whales," *Quest*

(2) Make the reader share in actual sense impressions. Give your readers shapes they can see, sounds they can hear, sensations they can feel. We call words that appeal to our senses **sensory** words. Study the many words for different sounds in the following passage:

> ... As we approach a small cove sheltering a sand beach, faint sounds grow louder and louder: gigantic Bronx cheers, explosive sighs, rebel yells, whoops, barks, honks, cockcrows, snorts, sneezes, and gargles. This astounding medley is coming from a heap of the biggest seals I have ever seen—in fact, the largest in the Northern Hemisphere: the northern elephant seal.—Annie Gottlieb, "In the Presence of Whales"

To help the reader imagine what things look like or feel like, make use of comparisons. How many comparisons can you find in the list of sounds you have just read?

(3) Work toward a unifying overall effect. Select details that strengthen the same mood. What general impression do you want the reader to carry away? The author of the following passage concentrates on the *richness* of jungle life. Everything seems to be on a larger scale than usual:

> This was our first experience of real forest, and we ambled slowly along, drinking in the sights and sounds, captivated by everything, *drugged by so much beauty* and colour. On one side of the road was a

deep ravine, *choked* with undergrowth; on the other the hillside sloped steeply upwards. On both sides rose *tremendous* trees, straddling their huge buttress roots, each with its cloak of *parasitic* plants, ferns, and moss. Through this *tangle* the lianas threaded their way, from base to summit, in *loops and coils and intricate convolutions.* On reaching the top they would drop to the forest floor as straight as a plumb line. In places there were gaps where one of the *giant* trees had been felled or had fallen of its own accord, and here the secondary growth *ran riot* over the carcass, and everything was *hung profusely* with the white and deep yellow flowers of the convolvulus, and with a pink starlike flower.—Gerald M. Durrell, *The Overloaded Ark*

(4) Try to introduce movement into a static scene. Describe a city scene as seen by someone *walking down* a city street. Organize your account of a landscape by following the progress of a hiker through a valley or up a mountain. Or, show first what a place looks like from a distance. Then show what is revealed as the observer comes closer.

Can you see how the account of the sunrise gives life and movement to the following description of the Grand Canyon?

I was standing on the rim of the Grand Canyon waiting for daybreak. *As the sun rose over the horizon,* vibrant reds and oranges appeared in the lower layers of the clouds, but the land below the horizon remained in darkness. *The earth turned toward the sunlight,* and several pinnacles rose out of the darkness. *As the sun rose high in flaming colors,* its light revealed the entire canyon. The far rim of the canyon was level, and its sheets of sandstone, arranged in broken and uneven rows, were blended and hazy because of the distance. Far below, the river looked like a small stream. The sheets of sandstone partially shadowed one another, and the contrast of the black shadows appeared to increase the brightness of the orange, red, and brown of the rocks.—Student Theme

EXERCISE 1

A good observer knows how to fill in the details that make a scene come to life before our eyes. Study the details that have been added to the following capsule description. Then write a similar filled-in version for five of the general statements listed below. Make your added details part of the original sentence, or add them in one or two separate sentences.

GENERAL: The island was exactly what any island should be.

FILLED IN: The island was exactly what any island should be—*lavish green acres covered with woods and orchards and fields of berries, ringed by glistening sandy beaches, richly stocked with driftwood.* (Lois Phillips Hudson)

1. The park was exactly what a popular park on a holiday weekend should be.
2. The office was exactly what one might expect in a big modern office building.
3. The school was exactly what one would expect (in an old downtown school) (in a typical country school) (in a typical suburban school).
4. The hospital was exactly what I always thought a hospital would be like.
5. The dentist's office was much more (modern) (old-fashioned) than I had expected.
6. The scene inside the circus tent was exactly like what I remembered.
7. As we walked in, I saw that nothing much had changed about the typical (county fair) (rodeo).
8. Inside, the theater looked exactly like any other theater where hundreds of young kids go on a Saturday afternoon.
9. The (stream) (lake) (woods) looked exactly like what any hiker dreams of and hopes to see.
10. The main street looked exactly like other downtown sections I have seen.

The author of each of the following descriptive passages was a good observer. In each passage, point out several specific details that the observer had to be *there* to notice. Point out any comparisons that help the reader share in the sights and sounds and feelings.

EXERCISE 2

1. A north gale was blowing down the valley, so hard that the chimney smoke streamed parallel to our farmhouse roof, and the ground under my feet was as hard and granular as pebbles. It has always been on days like this that we have heard the hawks. . . . We are so accustomed here to hearing the thin voices of nuthatches and woodpeckers, and the lusty quarreling voices of starlings, that we pay them no heed; or if momentarily we do, it is to listen as people have ever listened to the customary thing, with half an ear. But the voice of the hawks is not like these. It cuts the bitter winter air, and we always feel somehow—hearing it—as though it were the sharpening of a knife. (Alan Devoe)

2. Tiny and gray, with unblinking black shiny eyes, the mouse is sitting among the cookie crumbs. Its soft fur slants back from a trembling pink nose. The curved ears have pink inner surfaces coated with almost invisible white hairs. . . . He moves swiftly across the floor, his tiny pink feet a blur. He leaps onto the low windowsill, and from there goes up the yellow curtain in a lightning climb. Ten feet in the air now, he slows down and looks down.

3. In and out of these blooms flipped the sunbirds, glinting metallically in the sun, hanging before the flowers for a brief instant on blurred and trembling wings. On the dead trees, bleached white as coral against the green, there were groups of pygmy kingfishers, small as wrens, brilliant in their azure blue, orange, and buff plumage, with their crimson beaks and feet. Flocks of hornbills would be startled at the sight of us as they fed in the treetops, and would fly wildly across the road, uttering loud honkings, their great untidy wings beating the air with a sound like gigantic blacksmith's bellows. (Gerald M. Durrell)

4. Joe's place stood on a cleared bend in the bayou. The weatherboards and shingles were green with age. The house rested on high slender pillars and there were patches of bright red brick where the covering mortar had fallen away. The yard was shaded by two enormous water oaks, hung with gray Spanish moss, and an iron kettle stood beneath the trees. . . . At the bank of the bayou five or six towering cypress trees leaned heavily toward the water, for the slow currents of a century had washed their roots completely bare of soil. To get a new anchorage on the land, the trees had sent out a forest of gnarled roots and stubby knees along the shoreline. (Thomas Sancton)

EXERCISE 3

Write a *one-paragraph* theme describing your school. Use vivid specific details to support your general impression.

PROSE MODEL 1

Some of the most unforgettable descriptions in American literature are those in which Mark Twain recalls the setting of his childhood days. Study the following passage carefully, and write down your answers to the questions that follow it.

MARK TWAIN

"Steamboat a-Coming!"

Once a day a cheap, gaudy packet arrived upward from St. Louis, and another downward from Keokuk. Before these events, the day was glorious with expectancy; after them, the day was a dead and empty thing. Not only the boys, but the whole village, felt this. After all these years I can picture that old time to myself now, just as it was then: the white town drowsing in the sunshine of a summer's morning; the streets empty, or pretty nearly so; one or two clerks sitting in front of the Water Street stores, with their splint-bottomed chairs tilted back against the walls, chins on breasts, hats slouched over their faces, asleep; a sow and a litter of pigs loafing along the sidewalk, doing a good business in watermelon rinds and seeds; two or three lonely little freight piles scattered along the "levee"; a pile of "skids" on the slope of the stone-paved wharf, and the town drunkard asleep in the shadow of them; two or three wood flats at the head of the wharf, but nobody to listen to the peaceful lapping of the wavelets against them; the great Mississippi, the majestic, the magnificent Mississippi, rolling its mile-wide tide along, shining in the sun; the dense forest away on the other side; the "point" above the town, and the "point" below, bounding the river-glimpse and turning it into a sort of sea—a very still and brilliant and lonely one. Presently a film of dark smoke appears above one of those remote "points." Instantly a drayman, famous for his quick eye and prodigious voice, lifts up the cry, "S-t-e-a-m-boat a-comin'!" and the scene changes! The town drunkard stirs, the clerks wake up, a furious clatter of drays follows, every house and store pours out a human contribution, and all in a twinkling the dead town is alive and moving. Drays, carts, men, boys, all go hurrying from many quarters to a common center, the wharf. Assembled there, the people fasten their eyes upon the coming boat as upon a wonder they are seeing for the first time. And the boat *is* rather a handsome sight, too. She is long and sharp and trim and pretty. She has two tall, fancy-topped chimneys, with a gilded device of some kind swung between them; a fanciful pilot-house, all glass and "gingerbread," perched on top of the "texas" deck behind them. The paddle-boxes are gorgeous with a picture or with golded rays above the boat's name. The boiler-deck, the hurricane-deck, and the texas deck are fenced and ornamented with clean white railings. There is a flag gallantly flying from the jack-staff. The furnace doors are open and the fires glaring bravely. The upper decks are black with passengers; the captain stands by the big bell, calm, imposing, the envy of all; great volumes of the blackest smoke are rolling and tumbling out of the chimneys—a grandeur created with a bit of pitch-pine just before arriving at a town. The crew are grouped on the forecastle; the broad stage is run far out over the port bow, and an envied deckhand stands picturesquely on the end of it with a coil of rope in his hand; the pent steam is screaming through the gauge-cocks; the captain lifts his hand, a bell rings, the wheels stop; then they turn back, churning the water to foam, and the steamer is at rest. Then such a scramble as there is to get aboard, and to get ashore, and to take in freight and to discharge freight, all at one and the same time; and such a yelling and cursing as the mates facilitate it all with! Ten minutes later the steamer is under way again, with no flag on the jack-staff and no black smoke issuing from the chimneys. After ten more minutes the town is dead again, and the town drunkard asleep by the skids once more.—from *Life on the Mississippi*

READING QUESTIONS

1. In one sentence each, define or explain: *packet, expectancy, wood flats, withal, prodigious, drayman, dray, jack-staff, pent.*
2. List the three details that are most likely to make readers feel that they are actually watching the scene.
3. List five single words that vividly and concretely call up actual sights and sounds.
4. List three words or expressions that convey a vivid picture through comparison or analogy.
5. List five words or expressions that all mirror the general impression or unifying mood *before* the arrival of the boat. Then list five words that all mirror the changing mood *just after* the boat has been sighted. Then list five words that mirror the overall impression of the *boat.*

WRITING TOPICS

1. Describe a scene as it comes to life during the highlight of a daily routine. You might choose the passing of a school bus on a country road; the arrival of a train or bus at a usually quiet depot; the arrival and departure of a plane at a small quiet airport; or a similar event of your own choice.

2. Describe a *downtown street* in such a way that the reader is left with a unifying overall impression. What are typical sights, noises, odors? Make your account as detailed and concrete as you can. Or, work out the contrast between one of the main business streets of a big city and an adjoining street that is less prosperous or less well kept up.

3. Describe a setting that seems symbolic of a *way of life:* a country club, a camp for migrant farm workers, a convent, a factory town, a waterfront. What details contribute most to the overall picture or atmosphere? Try to make the people who have read your paper feel that they have visited the place themselves.

4. Write a paper in which you take your readers *off the beaten path.* Take them down a road off the main highway, or to a part of the city usually ignored by visitors. Take your readers to the orange orchards of California or the vanishing prairie outside a town in the Middle West. Make the place seem vivid and real to readers who may never have a chance to visit it.

A TRIP INTO AMERICA'S PAST

Pretend you are someone who has moved from the noise and confusion of cities back to the countryside. Describe these rural buildings to a friend who stayed in the city. Or, describe a typical day spent working around farm buildings such as these.

Composition

A WALK DOWN A CITY STREET

Pretend you are walking in a strange city. You come upon this church. Describe the unusual sight in a letter to a friend.

A TRIP INTO THE FUTURE

Pretend that for a long time you have been living in a secluded community in the woods. Now, for the first time, you are flying over these supercities of the twenty-first century. Prepare as full and as vivid a description of these strange sights as you can.

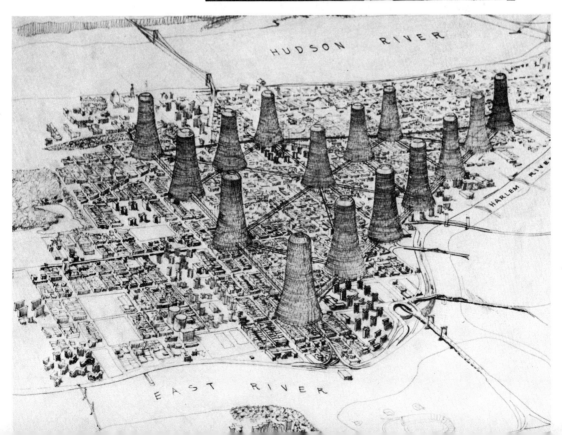

C3b

Writing About People

Give a vivid and fair account of people.

When you write a paper about a person, you want your reader to feel at the end: "I now know this person better than I would on the basis of mere superficial acquaintance. I now understand the kind of person he or she is better than I did. I now can predict this person's behavior in certain situations."

Remember:

(1) Describe appearance and surroundings in a way that shows something about the person. Study the following passage by a famous biographer. How do the details about the setting and physical appearance prepare us for her general impression of the man's character?

> Justice Brandeis I saw when he was eighty-five the year before he died. His Washington apartment was bleak, entirely undistinguished, bare of the usual accumulations of living—signed photographs, knickknacks, the small comforts of old age. It had a look of impersonality. The old man sat at a desk with his back to the window; light shone through his fluffy white hair. He wore no glasses; his hearing was perfect. The face was bony, strongly outlined, and this leanness extended to his body, giving a noticeable effect of youth. He spoke quietly, slowly; there was an austerity about him. I had the astonished feeling (I have not had it before or since) that I was talking to a saint —a saint moreover with a quick, remarkable intelligence that made itself manifest before he spoke.—Catherine Drinker Bowen, "The Magnificence of Age," *Harper's*

(2) Show character traits in action. In your paper, describe what people *do* in order to show what kinds of people they are. Describe what people do to show that they are kind, or generous, or stingy. In your own words, what kind of person is described in the following passage?

> "Thou shalt not be dirty" and "Thou shalt not be impudent" were the two commandments of Grandmother Henderson upon which hung our total salvation. Each night in the bitterest winter we were forced to wash faces, arms, necks, legs and feet before going to bed. She . . . was famous for pulling the quilts off after we had fallen asleep to examine our feet. . . . The impudent child was detested by God and a shame to its parents and could bring destruction to its house and line. All adults had to be addressed as Mister, Missus, Miss, Auntie, Cousin, Uncle . . . and a thousand other appellations indicating familial relationship and the lowliness of the addressor.—Maya Angelou, *I Know Why the Caged Bird Sings*

(3) Study the way a person talks for clues to his or her personality. Quote characteristic sayings: "You can't win them all"; "What is this world coming to!" The way we react to someone often has something to do with the way that person talks. Why did the boys in the following passage react to the "cub-engineer" the way they did?

Whenever his boat was laid up he would come home and swell around the town in his blackest and greasiest clothes, so that nobody could help remembering that he was a steamboatman. He used all sorts of steamboat technicalities in his talk, as if he were so used to them that he forgot common people could not understand them. He would speak of the "labboard" side of a horse in an easy, natural way that would make one wish he was dead. And he was always talking about "St Looy" like an old citizen; he would refer casually to occasions when he was "coming down Fourth Street," or when he was "passing by the Planter's House," or when there was a fire and he took a turn on the brakes of "the old Big Missouri." Then he would go on and lie about how many towns the size of ours were burned down there that day. Two or three of the boys had long been persons of consideration among us because they had been to St. Louis once and had a vague general knowledge of its wonders, but the day of their glory was over now. They lapsed into a humble silence, and learned to disappear when the ruthless "cub"-engineer approached.—Mark Twain, *Life on the Mississippi*

(4) Look for a person's major interest, desire, or ambition. Is there something that means more to the person than anything else? Does the person have some special talent he or she is trying to develop? What is the person's idea of how to be a success or of how to be happy? The subject of the following passage becomes identified in the reader's mind with a central interest or ambition:

There was a bugler in our camp who was the first expert, in any field, that I had known. He had no other talent but his music. He was a good-natured, chubby, curly-headed Italian boy, rather lazy, and when he was not back in the woods practicing his cornet he walked round with a dreamy look, as though our own handicrafts could not possibly be of interest to him. Paolo had a silver trumpet and he preferred it to the bugle. He wanted to be a great musician. He would take his horn and music back into a pine clearing a quarter of a mile from the camp and all day long we could hear him practicing the runs. He blew the trumpet with a clear, sweet tone. We had supreme confidence as we stood at attention on the parade grounds and the flag came down the creaking flagpole pulley in the late afternoon sunlight, and Paolo stood alone, with everyone watching, and bugled. We were proud of him when visitors came.—Thomas Sancton, "The Silver Horn," *Harper's*

A TRIP INTO AMERICA'S PAST

Pretend you are one of the people shown in these pictures. Tell your story.

What kind of person is described in the following passages? Point out details or examples that show the person's characteristic traits.

1. His shack was small, and it had grown smaller inside every year. Layers of things saved grew inward from the walls until Washington could barely move inside it. . . . If he found a board in a ditch as he walked home from the day's work, and if the board had a bent nail in it, he would hammer the nail out of the board with a rock and take it home. If the board would make kindling or if it was strong enough to build with, he would take it along too. He would straighten the nail with a hammer on the anvil at his leanto shop and put it in a box with other nails of the same dimensions. He might have to move a dozen other boxes to find the right one, but he would know where it was. It wasn't that he was a miser, because he cared nothing for the money he saved by collecting used nails. He saved the nails because it was a sin to allow good material to go to waste. Everyone knows the story about the box of pieces of string, found in an old attic, labeled "String too short to be saved."—Donald Hall, *String Too Short to Be Saved*

2. I realized how few things are needed to make a "home" when I took my seven-year-old daughter on her first sea voyage. The ship—the *Marine Jumper,* an unrenovated troopship with iron decks—was crowded with over a thousand students. They were bunked below where the troops had slept, while Cathy and I shared one cabin with six other members of the staff. Cathy climbed into her upper berth, opened the little packages that had been given to her as going-away presents, and arranged them in a circle around her. Then she leaned over the side of the berth and said, "Now I am ready to see the ship."—Margaret Mead, *Blackberry Winter*

3. My friend A_____ with whom I went once into the Canadian woods has genuine humor, and no one can be a more satisfactory comrade. I do not recall that he said many comic things, and at bottom he was serious as the best humorists are. But in him there was a kind of joy and exaltation that lasted throughout the day. If the duffle were piled too high and fell about his ears, if the dinner was burned or the tent blew down in a driving storm at night, he met these mishaps as though they were the very things he had come north to get, as though without them the trip would have lacked its spice. This is an easy philosophy in retrospect but hard when the wet canvas falls across you and the rain beats in. A_____ laughed at the very moment of disaster as another man will laugh later in an easy chair. I see him now swinging his axe for firewood to dry ourselves when we were spilled in a rapids; and again, while pitching our tent on a sandy beach when another storm had drowned us.—Charles S. Brooks, *Chimney Pot Papers*

Composition

EXERCISE 2

Write a *one-paragraph* theme to show a character trait of a person you have observed or know well. Start your paragraph with examples or with events that show the character trait in action. Then, at the end, state or sum up what the examples show.

EXERCISE 3

Write a *two-paragraph* theme about a person for whom you have mixed feelings. Write one paragraph each about the two sides of his or her personality.

PROSE MODEL 2

Read the following "elegy" written by a son on the occasion of his father's death. How real does the father sound to you?

BURT PRELUTSKY

A Remarkable Person

Two days ago I returned from a weekend in San Francisco to learn that my father had died.

Sam Prelutsky had been born in Russia, in 1901, or 1902. He never knew for certain. It didn't seem to bother him.

As a young man in America, he settled in a part of Illinois where the most popular organization going was the Ku Klux Klan. After the Cossacks, though, I guess farmers wearing sheets weren't such a big deal. Years later, he used to laugh about his former neighbors inviting him—*him* with his nose and his accent—on Klan outings. Maybe they had decided to overlook the obvious evidence in the belief that Jewish people didn't raise chickens or candle eggs.

Later, after he was married, he moved to Chicago. For a while he worked for a cigar company, rolling the stogies he couldn't stand to smoke. But for most of the time, he was a fruit and vegetable wholesaler. He'd drive his truck to the big central market at 3 A.M., pick up his load, and spend the next 12 hours delivering produce. In the dead of winter, he'd be out on that truck, *schlepping* sacks of potatoes. In the middle of summer, he'd be muscling crates of watermelons—just begging for the hernia he eventually got.

In '46, we moved to L. A. At that point he came to the conclusion that the people he'd been delivering to over the years had been living the life of Reilly, home in bed, snoozing, while he was up *schlepping*. He decided to tackle the retail end. A few months at a bad location ate up most of his savings, and sent him back to the truck. But L. A., massive sprawl that it was even then, was murder compared to Chicago.

His next venture was a cigar stand in the Harris-Newmark Building, at 9th and Los Angeles. Not counting the drive, it was still a 12-hour day, spent mostly on his feet. But at least the lifting and carrying was limited to soft drink cases and trash barrels. On the other hand, you had to learn to live with the *goniffs* who swiped candy bars during the noon rush, and the merchant princes of the garment industry who'd run up good-sized cigar bills and let you stew until they were ready to pay up. And my father would stew because he couldn't afford to offend the pot-bellied, cigar-chewing sweat shop aristocrats.

He was not an educated man. He couldn't correctly spell the names of those sodas and candy bars he sold six days a week. I don't know if he read two dozen books in his life. He loved America, Israel, pinochle, F. D. R., and the Democratic Party. . . .

He wanted me to get good grades, a college degree and have a profession—something safe, and preferably lucrative, like medicine or the law. He couldn't understand someone's wanting to write. Still, when I sold a poem at the age of 13 for fifty cents, he cashed the check for me—and later I found out he always carried that undeposited check around in his wallet. . . .

This afternoon, we buried my father. I didn't think I would, but I shed tears. I cried because he had worked too hard for too long for too little. For many years I had resented him because he had never told me he loved me. Now I wept because I'd never told him.

The rabbi's speech was short and simple. What is there, after all, to say at the funeral of such a man? Had the responsibility been mine, I would have said, *Sam Prelutsky, who was born in a small village 7,000 miles from here, 67 or 68 years ago, was a remarkable person. He was not a great man, but he was the very best man Sam Prelutsky could be. Now, let there be no more tears today—for we are laying to rest a man who's earned one.*

1. Why would a person with the author's ethnic background know words like *Cossack, schlep,* and *goniff?* What do they mean?
2. What is the difference between an "elegy" and a "eulogy"? How well does either of these labels fit the selection you have just read?
3. Suppose you were asked to do a one-paragraph portrait of the author's father. What would you include? Why?
4. Are there any facts of the father's life or any traits in his character that seemed familiar? Did any seem strange to you? Explain why.
5. Suppose you could write a few sentences about yourself, to be read as your eulogy at the end of a long career. What would you say? Write your own imaginary eulogy.

READING QUESTIONS

1. If you were asked to give a "short and simple" speech about the person closest to you in your family, what would you say? Write out what you would say.

2. Often we know people only through casual conversation, or through being with them in routine tasks. Sometimes, however, we have a chance to *know a person well*—through a heart-to-heart talk, or through being with the person in a crisis. Tell the story of how you came to understand someone that you used to know only superficially.

3. Sometimes, we have a chance to learn something about an *important human motive* or a common attitude. For instance, have you ever known someone who tried to talk and act "tougher" than he or she really was? Or, have you ever known someone who had to turn everything into a joke? Write a character study of this person. Concentrate on this one outstanding trait.

4. From newspapers, television, movies, and similar sources, we may form an idea of the typical schoolteacher or the typical private detective. Have you ever had a chance to compare such a notion of the *typical representative of a group* with firsthand knowledge of an actual person? Write a paper in which you compare and contrast the "typical" and an actual politician, police officer, private detective, teacher, labor-union official, cowhand, marine, physician, lawyer, nurse, convict, or the like.

5. Look back over your recent reading, or over recent movies, television programs, or plays. In any of these, have you encountered a character that seemed exceptionally *true to life?* Describe the character as fully as you can—setting, appearance, behavior, use of language, and the like. Concentrate on details that show your reader what kind of person the character was. Show why you consider him or her more lifelike than other characters.

C3c

**Writing About
an Incident**

Write vivid accounts of incidents, actions, and events.

A vivid account of an incident makes readers feel that they are actually present as witnesses. To achieve this eyewitness effect, observe the following advice:

(1) Use words that vividly describe actions, movements, sounds. Can you find all the action words and all the sound words in the following passage? What does each action or sound bring to mind:

> I pushed the door open, the hinges squeaking only a little. A bird or two stirred—I could hear them—but nothing flew and there was a faint starlight through the holes in the roof.

I padded across the floor, got the ladder up and the light ready, and slithered up the ladder till my head and arms were over the shelf. Everything was dark as pitch except for the starlight at the little place back of the shelf near the eaves. With the light to blind them, they'd never make it. I had them. I reached my arm carefully over in order to be ready to seize whatever was there and I put the flash on the edge of the shelf where it would stand by itself when I turned it on. That way I'd be able to use both hands. . . . I snapped on the flash and sure enough there was a great beating and feathers flying, but instead of my having them, they, or rather he, had me. He had my hand, that is, and for a small hawk not much bigger than my fist he was doing all right. I heard him give one short metallic cry when the light went on and my hand descended on the bird beside him; after that he was busy with his claws and his beak was sunk in my thumb. In the struggle I knocked the lamp over on the shelf, and his mate got her sight back and whisked neatly through the hole in the roof and off among the stars outside.
—Loren Eiseley, *The Immense Journey*

(2) Emphasize features that make an incident or event dramatic. See whether you can create the *tension* that comes from the conflict of opposing forces. See whether you can evoke *surprise* when things take an unexpected turn. What is there about the following passage that shows that it was written by someone who knew how to tell a story?

I sat impatiently with my family around me, waiting for the nurse to walk in with my thirteen-year-old sister, Loly. After two weeks of treatment for emotional disturbance, she was finally going to be returned to us. We watched the door, waiting and not knowing what to expect. She once saw us all as her enemies. She denied us as being her family. How would she react to us now? She walked into the room slowly, taking each step cautiously. Her hair was stringy and oily. Her once large, round, and gentle eyes were surrounded with a shadow of sleeplessness. There was a daze in them, almost as if she could see right through us, right through the walls and beyond. She stared blankly, then after a few seconds ran to my father and embraced him with a smile. We were a family again. There was a lump in my throat and my eyes burned as I held back the tears. She didn't see us as enemies any longer.

(3) Select details that reinforce the prevailing mood. You can steer the readers' emotions without having to announce: "This is sad" or "This is hilarious," "This is revolting" or "This is frightening." If you put in the right details, your readers cannot *help* having the right reaction.

How does the author of the following passage use vivid, dramatic details to contribute to the overall impression of terror and suffering?

> Time after time, when the great blaze suddenly *lashed out* at the fire fighters like an angry snake, the crews had to turn and *flee for their lives,* leaving their trucks and bulldozers and pumps and hose and axes and shovels to burn on the spot. Throughout the region deer in small herds and alone, *frantic and confused,* moved westward ahead of the flames, but many were caught and killed in their tracks. Cougars, the great cats of the woods, *ranged with fear and uncertainty* through the heavy smoke, *coughing like humans and paying no heed to humans or deer.* In a hundred streams, till then cool and clear, pools were soon white with the bellies of trout, dead from charcoal stomachs. One could only guess, by the *pitiful balls of naked flesh* found after the fire had passed over, how the myriads of grouse and pheasants had fared.— Steward H. Holbrook, *Burning an Empire*

(4) Quote what people say. Help readers imagine that they are watching actual people by making them hear the people's voices. Quote words and expressions that reveal character or that help give authentic local color to the setting. Quoted phrases can help make your characters more realistic and more believable.

Do you agree that the following account would be much less real to the reader without the quoted phrases?

> Cora was a good, easygoing woman who worked hard to keep her children in food and clothing, but . . . she was a soft touch for charming down-and-outers like Uncle Charlie and Larry Hickman, a three-hundred-pound sometime bandleader, whose belly flopped up and down when he walked. Hick, a balding man with round dancing eyes, swapped humor and long-winded tales for food, hypnotizing everyone into inactivity as he talked, ate, and refilled his plate. My sister, finally wise to his ways, offered up an amusing prayer at the supper table one night. Our heads were bowed and Hick was eyeing a chicken leg. *"Dear Lord,"* my sister began, *"make us thankful for what we are about to receive—and allow us to fill our plates before Hick fills our heart with lies. This we ask for our stomach's sake. Amen."* We fell into uproarious laughter. Maurice and I dropped to the floor, tears streaming from our eyes. It was Marcella who got us back to the table. *"You had better come and eat. Hick is already on his second plate."*—Gordon Parks, *A Choice of Weapons*

Point out all details and comparisons that make the following student-written paragraph exceptionally real and vivid for the reader.

EXERCISE 1

At noon, four glider pilots were to put on a short "Sky Ballet." We watched as their tow planes pulled them down the runway toward the take-off. The gliders looked like big, awkward birds being dragged steadily skyward. They reached altitude and suddenly were cut free of their bonds. The small tow planes gunned their engines in a defiant way and left the gliders as if they were hawks who, after carrying their prey aloft, dropped them and then circled, waiting for them to fall out of the sky. But the gliders caught the air currents and floated smoothly back and forth across the sky. The four tow planes zoomed away like angry bees as the gliders played games with the air currents. They soared wingtip to wingtip, peeling off to the left and right, then slowly creating figure eights in the sky. Then, as if there were a curving wire in the sky which was hooked to each glider's nose, they slowly spiraled down in unison and softly touched the ground to slide past like proud swans.

In the following paper, a student describes an incident that brought into focus a basic issue that many young people confront. What is that issue? Explain it in your own words.

EXERCISE 2

I am in a classroom. I am very young. I am practicing my handwriting. The teacher has a ruler in her hand. I've seen that ruler smash many a hand before. As I spell out the letter "a" on my paper, I am very conscious of the teacher peering over different kids' shoulders, checking their pencil grips to see if they are correct. Even then, holding a pencil a certain way because the teacher said it was right seemed a little absurd. I continued using my own grip. Only when the teacher approached me would I change to the standard grip. I can feel her watching me now. I feel clumsy. She passes by and I quickly regrip my pencil. Maybe this brief glimpse into my past reveals something that relates to me. Society sets these so-called standards. Must we live up to them? Must we adhere to them? Perhaps many people would be able to answer these questions with very little thought. I know in my own mind it would take a great deal of thought.

> Do one of the following:
>
> 1. Write a reply to the student writer; or,
> 2. Write about an incident that highlighted an important issue.

PROSE MODEL 3   The most disappointing story is the kind that goes on "and then" and "and then"—and finally arrives nowhere. A well-told story *has a point*. It leaves us with a better understanding of some human feeling or motive. It gives us a more vivid appreciation of some familiar fact. Study the following passage carefully and write down your answers to the questions that follow it.

ALICE MUNRO

Half a Grapefruit

I had to cross a bridge to get to high school. The bridge separated the town of Hanratty from West Hanratty, which was a straggling outgrowth where poor and sometimes lawless people lived. We lived there, being poor, though not lawless, and at that not as poor as some. My stepmother Flo had a store, a grocery-and-general store. My father had once done furniture repair, but was too sick to do it any more.

High school was dazzling after the school in West Hanratty. There were four large, clean windows along the wall. There were new fluorescent lights. One class was "Health and Guidance," a modern idea—boys and girls mixed until after Christmas, when we got on to "Family Life." The teacher was dashing in a red suit that flared over the hips. She went up and down, up and down the rows, making everybody say what they had for breakfast, to see if we were keeping Canada's Food Rules.

Differences soon became evident between town and country.
The country side answered first:
"Fried potatoes."
"Bread and corn syrup."
"Tea and porridge."
"Tea and bread."
"Tea and fried eggs and cottage roll."
"Raisin pie."
There was some laughing from the town side, with the teacher making ineffectual, scolding faces.

A rough sort of segregation was maintained voluntarily in the classroom, and now she was getting to the town side of the room. People claimed to have eaten toast and marmalade, bacon and eggs, corn flakes, even waffles and syrup. Orange juice, said a few.

I was the only one from West Hanratty, and I had stuck myself onto the back of a town row. I was wanting badly to align myself with towners, to attach myself to those waffle-eating, coffee-drinking, aloof and knowledgeable possessors of breakfast nooks.

"Half a grapefruit," I said boldly. Nobody else had thought of it.

As a matter of fact, my stepmother would have thought eating grapefruit for breakfast as bad as drinking champagne. I don't think we even sold grapefruit in the store. Flo didn't go in much for fresh fruit—a few spotty bananas, small, unpromising oranges. She believed, as many country people did, that anything not well cooked was bad for your stomach. For breakfast we too had tea and porridge; puffed rice in the summertime. The first morning that puffed rice, light as pollen, came spilling into the bowl was as festive, as encouraging a time as the first day walking on the hard road without rubbers, or the first day the door could be left open in the lovely, brief time between frost and flies.

I was pleased with myself for thinking of the grapefruit and with the way I had said it, in so bold yet natural a voice. My voice could go dry altogether in school; my heart could roll itself up into a thumping ball and lodge in my throat; sweat could plaster my blouse to my arms in spite of Mum.

I was walking home across the bridge a few days later and I heard someone calling—not my name, but I knew it was meant for me, so I softened my steps on the boards and listened. The voices were underneath me, it seemed, though I could look down through the cracks and see nothing but fast-running water. Somebody must be hidden down by the pilings. The voices were wistful, so delicately disguised that I could not tell if they were boys' or girls'.

"Half-a-grapefruit!"

I would hear that called now and again for years, called out from an alley or a dark window. I would never let on I heard, but would soon have to touch my face, wipe the moisture away from my upper lip. We sweat for our pretensions.

It could have been worse. Disgrace was the easiest thing to come by. High-school life was hazardous in that harsh, clean light, and nothing was ever forgotten. Every day when I got home I would tell Flo about what went on in school. Half-a-grapefruit she never got to hear about.—from *Redbook Magazine*

READING
QUESTIONS

1. Explain briefly each of the following words: *evident, ineffectual, align, aloof, festive, wistful.*
2. What would a part of town be like that is a "straggling outgrowth"?
3. Mention several details that helped make the high school "dazzling."
4. Later in the story, the author mentions several things that were very special "festive" and "encouraging" occasions in the yearly routine at the girl's home. What were they?
5. Toward the end, the author several times uses physical details that help us share in how a person feels. Find several of these.
6. Where is there a sentence that for you sums up the point of the story?

WRITING
TOPICS

1. Though they do not always admit it, people are often afraid of things that others brush off as *superstition.* Have you ever had an experience that was scary or spooky? Tell your story. Make an effort to have your reader share your feelings.

2. Did you ever undertake to do something that proved too much, or almost too much, for you? Describe an incident (or series of events) that required unusual *effort,* or put you under unusual *strain.* Try to make the reader feel that he or she is an eyewitness of the events you describe.

3. We often do not appreciate the strength of a feeling or *emotion* till we experience it for ourselves. Tell the story of an incident that taught you something about the true nature of one of the following: disappointment, resentment, jealousy, envy, anger, indignation, anxiety, grief.

C4
WRITING AND THINKING

Make your writing show that you have thought about your subject.

Writing a paper does not just mean stating our views. It means thinking about the subject. Careful writers collect evidence before they make up their minds. They are willing to look at the other side. They think about the needs and probable reactions of their readers.

C4a
Writing to Define

Define important terms to make their exact meaning clear to the reader.

When we define a term, we sketch out and limit the territory it is supposed to cover. We "draw the line." Definition becomes necessary whenever the reader is likely to ask, "What do you mean?" On the following pages are several kinds of terms that are likely to need definition:

SOME MEMORABLE DEFINITIONS

Look at the following capsule definitions. What makes each memorable? Which do you like best?

1. "Loneliness is the ability to hear your own footsteps when you are walking down the street."
2. "Willpower is trying hard *not* to do something that you really want to do."
3. "Prejudice is being down on somebody you're not up on."
4. "Prejudice is thinking ill of others without sufficient warrant."
5. "This is the final test of a gentleman: his respect for those who can be of no possible service to him." (William Lyon Phelps)
6. "A friend is a person with whom I may be sincere." (Emerson)

Do your own capsule definition of three or more of the following:

      friendship   pollution   honesty   good taste
      manners   dissent   popularity   loyalty
      prejudice   the American dream

TECHNICAL TERMS: Every occupation, hobby, or field of study has its own special terms that confuse the outsider:

Almost every island has developed species that are *endemic* —that is, they are peculiar to it alone and are duplicated nowhere else on earth. (Rachel Carson)

OVERLAPPING TERMS: Two terms may have closely related meanings that must be carefully distinguished. A single term may have several meanings that *differ* in important respects:

By studying I do not mean cramming. *Cramming* is learning the whole amount of material in the evening before the test. *Studying* requires the student to keep up with the material as it is presented.

KEY CONCEPTS: Writers need convenient or striking labels for key categories and key ideas. Sometimes these are terms they have made up or adapted themselves. Sometimes they share them with many other writers interested in the same subject:

About ten percent of the violence on children's television programs was labeled as *"tension producing."* By this was meant the presence of ominous background music; shadowy, dark lighting; stealthy movement; screaming, moaning, and similar sound effects; clear expressions of terror on the part of the characters.

FAMILIAR GENERAL TERMS: Many familiar terms are "umbrella terms" that cover much ground. Who could list all the political activities and institutions that come under the heading *democracy?* To use such terms meaningfully, we often have to tell the reader what we want to *include* under the term and where we want to draw the line:

> The word *democracy* refers to a system of government in which the people elect representatives in regularly scheduled free elections and in which citizens are urged to express freely their views on political issues.

Technical terms, and terms with fairly limited or specific meanings, can often be defined in a sentence or perhaps a short paragraph. More general terms often need **extended definition.** In working out an extended definition, go through the following steps:

(1) Collect examples of where and how the term is used. Start with actual situations where the term might be applied. Here are examples that came to mind when a student wanted to explain what kind of person we call a "wise guy":

- removes the chair while you are sitting down
- turns on the water from the drinking fountain full strength so that it will give your face a bath
- puts detergent in the salt shaker
- calls and uses "guess who" tactics on the telephone
- gives clever answers to serious questions

(2) Find the common denominator. What do the examples that you have collected have in common? Is there one basic common feature or perhaps *several* key qualities that are illustrated over and over again in different ways? When you look over the kind of things we associate with the "wise guy," what seems to be the common element or the common motive for the various different examples of the "wise guy's" behavior?

Here are some attempts to sum up the characteristic qualities of "democratic" societies or institutions:

> Democracy is the form of government that tries to give every citizen *a share*, however small, *in the management of the community*. Everyone has the right to be heard and to be a part of decisions that affect his or her own well-being and that of the community.

> Democracy is based upon the assumption that most people are people of *goodwill*, and if left alone to self-govern as much as possible, each will behave, on the whole, in a fair, just, and amicable fashion toward his or her fellow citizens.

Most societies have in the past forbidden *free criticism* of existing institutions and of the ideas on which they were based. Only in a democracy is free criticism and free expression of many different opinions encouraged as the highest virtue.

(3) *Adjust your definition to make sure it covers no more and no less than the intended territory.* Can you see why the following definitions need to be *narrowed down?*

TOO BROAD: Democracy is the form of government that carries out the wishes of the majority.

MORE LIMITED: Democracy is the form of government that carries out the wishes of the majority, *with due respect for the rights of minorities.*

TOO BROAD: To live in a free society means to be safe in your home from government supervision or intrusion by the police.

MORE LIMITED: To live in a free society means to be safe in your home from *unreasonable or unauthorized* instrusion by the police.

(4) *Try to sum up the main content of your definition in one sentence, observing conventional definition form.* The clearest way of stating a definition is to line it up in three parts: the term to be defined ("democracy"); the general class or heading under which the term belongs ("a form of government"); and finally the distinguishing features that set it apart from other members of the same class.

The following definitions are stated in accordance with conventional form:

TERM	CLASS	FEATURES
Democracy	is a form of government	that allows all citizens to participate in the political process.
Free enterprise	is an economic system	stressing individual initiative and the private ownership of industry.
Prejudice	is a generalization	formed without adequate evidence and held onto in spite of facts to the contrary.

(5) *As necessary, draw on familiar helps to definition:*

DICTIONARY DEFINITIONS: A dictionary definition sums up very briefly the meaning (or meanings) a word has in its most common use. The dictionary does *not* discuss the complications that arise when we try to fit a very general term to specific situations and events.

HISTORY OF A TERM: Democracy originated in ancient Greece; the word literally means "the rule of the people." Many democratic traditions, such as the tradition of political oratory, go back to Greek origins.

COMPARISON AND CONTRAST: You can show what you mean by democracy by contrasting it with other terms describing governmental systems, like *dictatorship* or *tyranny*.

NOTE: In a paper presenting your finished definition, you will usually tell your reader *early* in the paper what your definition is. You can then fill in the examples that show what your definition means in practice. If you are more ambitious, however, you may try a more difficult plan. For instance, in your paper you may prefer to examine several trial definitions until you *finally* reach the one that is adequate.

EXERCISE 1

Complete the following definition sentences. Give as exact information as you can. Write the missing part of each sentence after the number of the sentence. (Write on a separate sheet.)

EXAMPLE: A thermostat is a device that _____ .
(Answer) *regulates temperature*

1. A discount is an amount of money that _____ .
2. A probationary employee is a worker who _____ .
3. A disinfectant is a chemical that _____ .
4. Arthritis is a disease that _____ .
5. Metabolism is the process that _____ .
6. An absentee ballot is the arrangement by which _____ .
7. Immunity is the ability of an organism to _____ .
8. An anesthetic is a means of _____ .
9. A duplicate is a copy that _____ .
10. An affidavit is a statement made _____ .
11. Probation is a system that _____ .
12. A filibuster is a spate of speech-making that _____ .
13. Initiative is a personal quality that _____ .
14. Recycling is the procedure that _____ .
15. A naturalized citizen is someone who _____ .
16. A prejudice is an attitude that _____ .
17. The diameter is the measure that _____ .
18. Censorship is the practice of _____ .
19. An exposé is an article or program that _____ .
20. An amnesty is an action by which _____ .
21. Cloning is the procedure by which _____ .
22. Irrigation is a process whereby _____ .

23. Collaboration is a situation in which _____ .
24. Vertigo is a condition that _____ .
25. Enthusiasm is an attitude that _____ .

Study the following example of a definition paragraph. Restate in your own words the information it includes. Then write a similar one-paragraph definition of one of the following:

EXERCISE 2

1. a cooperative
2. a military academy
3. a business franchise
4. a labor union
5. a fraternity or sorority
6. the Olympics
7. a jury
8. a seminary
9. a musical
10. the FBI

EXAMPLE: Credit unions are nonprofit, cooperative institutions owned by their members. The basic intent is to encourage savings by offering a good return on the dollar and to help members get loans at favorable terms, even when the members have been turned down by other lenders. Credit unions are organized by people who have a common bond. They may work at the same place, belong to the same unions, go to the same church, share the same interests through a club, or live in the same geographical area. (Margaret Daly)

Words like *fairness* or *sportsmanship* are impossible to define without a careful look at examples. Study the following sample paragraph about fishing as a true sport. To judge from this example, what did the writer consider the most basic quality of a true sport? Then write a paragraph in which you give a detailed example of one of the following: fairness; considerateness; prejudice; a true sport; grassroots democracy.

EXERCISE 3

EXAMPLE: Fishing is a sport, a matter of concern only to fish and angler. It is not a competition between people. Respect for the fish is the real basis of the whole thing. It is not an enemy, merely an adversary. Whatever its type and species, it has certain qualities that make for sport, and it must be given a chance to show them to best advantage. It is entitled to the consideration of the lightest gear and the subtlest method the angler can use with a reasonable chance of success.

EXERCISE 4

Often related terms shade over into each other without a clear borderline. Discuss the difference between the two words in each of the following pairs. Use detailed examples.

1. When does an *amateur* become a *professional?*
2. When does a *firm* parent (or teacher) become *tyrannical?*
3. When does a *prank* become *vandalism?*
4. When does *horseplay* become *rowdyism?*
5. When does *opposition* become *obstructionism?*
6. When does an *individualist* become a *crank?*
7. When does a *crowd* become a *mob?*
8. When does *emphasis* on athletics become *overemphasis?*
9. When does something *colorful* become *gaudy?*
10. Is there a difference between a *fashion* and a *fad?*

(Your teacher may ask you to write a paper showing the difference between two of these terms.)

PROSE MODEL 4

Everyone has heard the term *privacy.* But the exact meaning and limits of the word often remain confused. The author of the following passage was a world-famous expert on the rules and customs people follow in living together as a group. In the following passage, she tries to explain what privacy is and why it is important. Study the passage carefully. Write down the answers to the questions that follow the passage. Be prepared to discuss your answers in class.

MARGARET MEAD

How Do We Define Privacy?

Privacy is important to every living being. Recognition of the right to privacy, however it is expressed, is the world's way—and the family's way too—of recognizing the fact that each individual is in some sense unique and must have some freedom to be herself for herself alone. Privacy protects the inner core of the individual's being.

But if one looks around the world, it is clear that respect for the privacy of another person can be expressed in very different —and, to us, quite unexpected—ways: by never touching another person without express permission; by leaving a space around a person; by assigning to each person a house, a room, or even a special place within a room that others may not enter without invitation; by never looking someone directly in the eye; even by never calling a person by her or his given name.

I know of no society without rules that protect personal privacy. But in most societies privacy is also a privilege that is unevenly accorded—more to adults than to children, more to women or to men, more to the well than to the sick, more to the rich than to the poor and, very often, more to those of high rank than of low rank. However, the rules also may be reversed, so that kings and all persons in important public positions may be almost totally deprived of real privacy.

Whatever the standards of privacy are, they must be observed. Otherwise, the person whose privacy has been invaded is almost certain to feel insulted, outraged, and denigrated. Invasions of privacy affect very different aspects of living. In our own society, for example, almost every one of us would feel violated if there were no privacy for sexual relations, if we had to bathe or excrete in public, if we were forced to reveal details of our income, if we were made to admit irregularities in our private life or if we found that someone—anyone—had opened and read a private letter.

Respect for the privacy of all those who live together in a home is one way in which each one of us learns and expresses a basic concern for the individuality of other people. As part of her learning, a child comes to value both what she keeps to herself as an individual and what, by her own choice, she shares with others. The rules for the protection of privacy may change radically over a lifetime, as they have in our own and most other societies. But having learned at home within the intimacy of one's own family how valuable privacy is, one can learn new rules and live by them. And one can learn in the same way to respect the rules, different from one's own, by which another person—one's grandmother or equally, a stranger in a strange land—protects her individuality.—*Redbook Magazine*

1. Explain or define briefly: *unique, reverse, deprive, denigrate, affect, intimacy, radically.*
2. Write a one-sentence definition of each, using conventional definition form: *privilege, insult, individuality.*
3. How many different examples of privacy are given by the author? Which of these seem most important to you? Which seem strange, and why?
4. Sum up in your own words this author's definition of privacy.
5. What does your dictionary tell you about the history of the following terms: *private, public, social, individual?*
6. Where would you draw the line between what should be private and what should be public? Select a test case or important example for discussion.

READING QUESTIONS

1. Write a definition paper in which you examine three or four test cases. Then present your definition *at the end*. Choose one of the following: fairness, a true sport, grassroots democracy, privacy, true leadership.

2. Among typical American expressions, *goodwill* is one of the most familiar. Define and illustrate goodwill as it exists in everyday American life today. What do people mean when they use this term? What do they expect?

3. Many familiar terms are used to express a negative judgment: *sensational, sentimental, conventional, cynical*. Choose one. Define the term and give several detailed examples.

4. Young people are often told to act grown-up or adult or mature. What does the term *mature* really mean? Write a paper in which you present your definition of maturity.

C4b

Pro and Con

Draw a balanced conclusion after weighing conflicting points of view.

Often when we look at an issue seriously, we find that there is no simple answer. We have to look at evidence that points in different directions. We have to weigh the pros and cons. This is the way to get a serious hearing from a reader who feels: "There is conflicting evidence here, and there are conflicting points of view. What do you make of it?"

The following advice will help you get a balanced view:

(1) Avoid hasty or sweeping generalizations. Look out for exceptions and contradictory evidence. A careful writer very seldom starts a sentence with "All high school students . . ." or "Every teenager. . . ." Can you see how the following statements should be changed in view of the exceptions?

GENERALIZATION: To be successful in American politics, a person must be an outgoing, sociable type—a good neighbor, and preferably something of a "joiner."

EXCEPTION: Abraham Lincoln is often described as a taciturn and even brooding man—something of a "loner."

GENERALIZATION: To be successful in American politics, a person must be a practical person, a doer. "Tinkering" is very American. Benjamin Franklin represents an ideal combination— someone who experiments with something new but on a level that the ordinary person can understand.

EXCEPTION: Woodrow Wilson had been a college professor; he was a student of ideas, a scholar, and an intellectual.

WHERE DO YOU STAND?

What would you say if you were asked to take sides on the issue raised in the following exchange? How would you defend your stand? Write a letter to the girl, or to the mother, or to Dear Abby.

Four-Letter Words Offend Mother

Abigail Van Buren

DEAR ABBY:

I have a 21-year-old daughter who will be a college freshman. She was raised in a moral and decent home. Lately she has begun to pepper her language with filthy four-letter words.

When I told her that I found her language offensive, she said everybody talks that way nowadays, and I should "get with it."

I am 50 years old and am not about to "get with" filthy language.

My daughter says, "They are only words and it's a person's right to use the words he wants to use."

I would like your opinion.

OFFENDED MOM

DEAR MOM:

The "right" to swing one's arms ends where the other fellow's nose begins. Tell your daughter to "get with it" and launder her language in your presence. No one has the right to pollute the atmosphere with audible garbage.

(2) Avoid stereotypes. A **stereotype** is a familiar generalization, usually about a group of people, that we have not tested against actual experience. Familiar stereotypes are the Frenchman who is a passionate lover and great talker; the beer-drinking, hardworking, methodical German; the happy-go-lucky black with "natural rhythm." Other stereotypes are the cynical businessman, the absentminded professor, the corrupt politician.

Everyone has a right to be judged by his or her character, not by nationality; by performance, not by prejudices we might have against a profession. Test familiar stereotypes against personal experience, as shown in the extract on the following page:

I like politicians. Ever since I started work as a city-hall reporter in New Mexico some thirty years ago, I have spent a lot of time in their company—*in smoke-filled rooms, jails, campaign trains, shabby courthouse offices, Senate cloakrooms, and the White House itself.* Mostly I've been reporting their doings, but on occasion I have served them *as speech writer, district leader, campaign choreboy, and civil servant.* On the whole, they have proved better company than any other professional group I've had a chance to know well. . . .—John Fischer, "Please Don't Bite the Politicians," *Harper's*

(3) Admit complications when looking for cause and effect. Many situations have more than *one* cause. People often have mixed feelings or conflicting motives. Recognize complications that are an important part of the total picture:

As Americans we worship bigness, yet we idealize the "little person." *On the one hand,* much of our business life is conducted by giant corporations, like General Motors. *On the other hand,* we believe that the important thing in business life is individual effort, that in politics every individual vote counts.

What is the attitude of Americans toward individuals who are truly outstanding or who are extremely successful? *On the one hand,* we tend to feel that we are just as good as the next person; and we make remarks about people who "put on airs." *On the other hand,* we believe that the American way of life gives everyone a chance to get ahead, to better himself or herself; and we admire the outstanding individual as living proof that our dream can come true. We do not really feel envious of successful people. They provide the model that we ourselves would like to imitate.

(4) Take into account other people's points of view. When someone disagrees with you on the minimum age for voting or the advantages of going to a parochial school, do not simply reject the view as foolish or wrongheaded. Try to find out what *makes* the person think the way he or she does.

What would you expect a teacher or a school administrator to say about school dropouts? How is the following statement different? How much is there to what the person is saying?

Many students drop out of school because they are treated as nothing; and out in the world, on a motorcycle, as a drifter, as a mechanic, waitress, or a dancer they can feel they are somebody. The school guarantees the dropout—the kid who cannot adjust to being on time and respectful—one big hassle. Attendance officers are excellent record keepers and spend 80 percent of their time with 5 percent of the school's students, busting kids for tardiness or truancy.

Here are some possible ways of organizing a paper based on a careful weighing of the pros and cons:

INITIAL THESIS: State your general conclusion at the *beginning* of the paper. Then devote the rest of the paper to presenting your supporting evidence. Include the *exceptions or objections* you took into account.

FINDING MIDDLE GROUND: Line up clearly the arguments on two sides of an issue. Organize your paper something like this: "arguments on one side—arguments on the other side—balanced conclusion emerging *at the end.*"

PROCESS OF ELIMINATION: Discuss three or four major possible solutions to a problem. Examine the *unsatisfactory* ones and show why you found them wanting. At the end, present the solution that is best. Show why it is free from the defects you have previously pointed out.

An important part of education is to study and think about ideas different from our own. What is your reaction to the point of view expressed in the following passage? Write a similar passage in which you present as fully and as fairly as you can an idea that was at first new or strange to you.

EXERCISE 1

Western marriage is supposedly based on love. The object of the marriage is above all the happiness of the couple involved. In India, by contrast, one of the primary objects of marriage is the continuation of the family line. A woman who does not give her husband many children, including a son, may be divorced. Our pride in our own ways naturally makes us assume that the love marriage is superior to the kind contracted primarily with the family in mind. If in all American marriages the goal of happiness were achieved, there would be little room for argument. But statistics show that a rising percentage of American marriages end in divorce. Polls show that only one out of every two marriages is considered successful by the couple involved. The partners apparently erred in choosing their partners. In India, divorce is uncommon. Perhaps putting love first and the family second is not the best basis for a stable and successful marriage.

EXERCISE 2

Television serials are sometimes accused of strengthening familiar stereotypes. Report on how programs you have recently watched *reinforce or counteract one of the following:*

- The typical American is a white Anglo-Saxon Protestant.
- The occupations that best suit a woman are those of nurse and secretary.
- Women with unusual intelligence or superior sophistication are likely to turn out bad.
- The most prestigious professions are those of doctor and lawyer.
- The working-class American tends to be a bigoted "hard hat."
- Orientals or South American types make good villains.
- A woman's best bet for success on the job is to humor and flatter the males.
- Being an artist is not normal for the red-blooded American.

PROSE MODEL 5

Can you see how the author of the following passage forces the reader to take a new look at something familiar? Study the passage carefully. Write down your answers to the questions that follow the passage, and be prepared to discuss your answers in class.

JOSEPH MARGOLIS

The Latter-Day Knights

The adult world thinks of these delinquents as outlaws, ir-responsibles; and it is baffled by its inability to contain them. But the juveniles themselves actually form a string of genuine and relatively stable neighborhoods, with a day-to-day code of conduct, a system of sanctions and rewards, a calendar of community life, an educational program, and facilities for communications and the provision and distribution of goods and services. It is a simple society in which everyone is known by name and face and accomplishment. . . . It is in fact *the* society to which these juveniles belong. The adult world, from their point of view, is vaguely defined and alien, usually threatening in its intermittent contact with their own; although, of course, the juvenile cannot ever be entirely free of a subordinate participation in that adult world.

The juvenile neighborhood has, I should say, two principal rituals to perform. It is, as a matter of fact, overwhelmingly concerned with ritual forms. But the two I have in mind bear most directly on the terror and violence that have so shocked the adult world. One is the initiation ritual, and the other is what I can only call the ritual sortie. They are indistinguishable as far as overt behavior is concerned; they are different only in their purpose. The initiation ritual has to do with recruitment, the selection of suitable members of an elite society. The ritual sortie has to do with status and prestige within that society, both a requirement of members in good standing and an opportunity for the advancement of the ambitious and the talented. The society is usually, at its most audacious, a society of warriors and "free" souls who accept only those limitations upon conduct that they themselves impose. But it is also a society of pranksters, gaming companions, exhibitionists, children, concerned as much with extremities of style in dress and speech as with murder and theft. It is always, however, a loyal brotherhood provided with a more or less clear schedule of honors. And it leads what is essentially a public life, protected as far as possible from the eyes of law-enforcement agencies. . . .

The routine of ordinary, unadventurous life is quite worthless, boring, idle to our juveniles. It is made supportable only by celebrating previous sorties and by preparation for others. In an odd sense, then, the juvenile does not wish to be idle—idleness is death to him. But, curiously, he considers the life of the adult world (and his submission to it) an idle life and, correspondingly, the adult world views his exploits also as a species of idling. The significance of his life lies exclusively in the perilous mountain peaks of the adventures he enters into so wholeheartedly. So he proves himself from episode to episode—whether by theft, fighting, vandalism, drinking—always in accord with the strict code of his own society.—from "Juvenile Delinquents: The Latter-Day Knights," *The American Scholar*

READING QUESTIONS

1. In a word or phrase, indicate the meaning of each of the following: *sanction, intermittent, ritual, initiation, sortie, overt, elite, audacious.*
2. Sum up in one short paragraph what you take to be the prevailing popular stereotype of the "juvenile delinquent."
3. What, to you, is the most striking or unexpected way in which the author *departs from* the popular stereotype?
4. Where, in your opinion, has the author been most successful in his effort to understand typical attitudes or motives of the young people he describes? Point out one observation or comment that you can confirm from your own observation, experience, or reading.
5. Can you state one important *objection* to this way of analyzing the behavior of the juvenile delinquent?
6. What, in your opinion, is the most serious problem that adults encounter in trying to regain the trust and cooperation of the juvenile delinquent?

1. When listening to people, how often do you feel that there is something to be said "for the other side"? Write a paper that would make people take a look at the other side on one of the following topics: dropouts; a type of unpopular teacher (or student); some other group around school that is often the subject of disapproval.

2. On which of the following topics do you feel that you could see both sides? Choose it as the subject for a paper in which you weigh the pros and cons.

   - Should smoking be made illegal everywhere as a threat to public health?
   - Should high school students be able to choose more of their own courses?
   - Should juvenile offenders be treated like adults when accused of serious crimes?
   - Should public officials have a right to keep their private lives or their own business affairs private?
   - Should a private club or other private organization have the right to limit membership on the basis of sex, race, or religion?
   - Should minority groups be encouraged to preserve their own cultural identity? Or should they be encouraged to merge in the mainstream of American life?
   - Should schools avoid all references to religion and all use of religious material?
   - Should young schoolchildren learn early of the darker pages in American history?

C4c

**Writing to
Persuade**

Know effective ways of persuading your reader.

Often writing serves an immediate purpose. We want readers to endorse a proposal or adopt a program for action. We want them to *change their minds*. We then ask: "What is the best strategy? What are the most effective means of persuasion?"

There are no surefire ways to persuade a reader. But some methods produce results if used in the right way at the right time:

EMPHATIC LANGUAGE: To make a strong impact, use strong language. Sometimes, we want to be sure we are *heard*. We come right out and forcefully express praise or blame. No one is likely to miss the point of the following passage:

> American civilization tends to stand in such awe of its teenage segment that it is in danger of becoming a *teenage society,* with *permanently teenage standards of thought,* culture and goals. As a result, American society is *growing down rather than growing up.* —Grace and Fred Hechinger, *Teenage Tyranny*

APPEALS TO FACT AND AUTHORITIES: To show that their own conclusions are solidly based on the facts, writers will "look at the record." They will quote statistics, official documents, authorities. The following excerpts, from the same book on "teenage tyranny," create the impression that the authors are drawing on authoritative factual evidence:

> *New York Times* reporter Gay Talese says it is impossible to determine accurately the number of hot-rodders in the country. But there are *sixteen hot rod magazines* on the stands today, with a *total monthly circulation of three million*. . . .

> How do teenagers themselves feel about the matter? *A Gallup survey* found them to be "tolerant." . . . Almost *half of the college students*. . . . *More than 20 percent of the high school seniors*. . . . *10 percent of the sophomores*. . . .

APPEALS TO EMOTION: In order to channel the readers' reactions in the right direction, the writer may try to bring strong emotions into play. Parents have strong feelings about the safety of their children. Business owners care strongly about free enterprise, teachers about freedom of speech, veterans about loyalty to country. Each such group is more likely to support a program or proposal if it can be shown to be related to their ideals.

Everyone can be influenced by fear of injury, or of inflation, or of trickery. Can you see the persuasive effect of the following?

> Once a driver knows that a head-on collision between two cars doing 30 miles an hour produces the same impact as a dive off a nine-story building he is apt to be a bit more careful.

> Whatever the reasons, teenage marriages do fail alarmingly often. Divorce and annulment rates are higher than for the population as a whole. Bureau of Census figures show that divorces are 12.6 percent for women married between the ages of 15 and 19, compared with 4.8 percent for those married between 21 and 25.

EFFECTIVE STRATEGY: Effective writers plan their line of attack. If their own view or program is not clearly desirable in itself, they can try to show that it is a lesser evil. Can you see the "lesser-evil" strategy at work in the following passage?

> Some people argue against spectator sports on the grounds that the spectator is only indulging in "passive" experience. They feel that he should do something active with his leisure hours. But the most popular leisure entertainment is watching television. Is it not better that the fan is at the field, instead of crouching in silence before the screen? In the middle of the desert, the thirsty man should not shun cactus milk because champagne would be more desirable.

Remember: In trying to persuade, it is easy to *try too hard*. Readers may feel that they are being shouted at and tune us out. Watch out for the following:

(1) Avoid overstatement or obvious exaggeration. Do without wild charges and exaggerated claims. Avoid words like "tremendous," "wonderful," "unique," "disastrous," "incredible," "colossal," "magnificent," "stupendous." How many customers really expect tremendous savings when they see a sign that says "Tremendous Savings"?

(2) Avoid name-calling and uncritical praise. Think twice before you use terms like "treason," "fraud," "betrayal," "trash." If we call a dissenter a traitor, what are we going to call a real traitor? If we call a second-rate novel trash, what are we going to call a third-rate novel? Be careful with expressions that insult or belittle people:

"*wormed* their way upward"
"have not *sloughed* off their old habits" (like snakes?)
"descended like *locusts*"
"*wallowed* in luxury" (like pigs?)

(3) Avoid irrelevant associations. When a prominent citizen opposes a bond issue, fair argument would center on the merits of the bond issue itself. If the person is a contractor or owner of much real estate, personal interest might become an issue. But many other matters are irrelevant: whether the person is short, or fat, or bald; married or divorced; born here or elsewhere.

EXERCISE 1

The italicized words in the following sentences are often used by people trying to make a strong impact on their audience. They carry a strong emotional charge. For each word, ask: What is the intended effect of each word on its audience? What gives each word its added charge? Do you react the way the writer or speaker wanted you to? Why, or why not? (Your teacher may ask you to check into the *history* of some of these words.)

1. We should not simply swallow the *propaganda* put out by the public health department in favor of fluoridation.
2. If play reading is not to *degenerate* into a spectator sport, readers must have a chance to express their reactions.
3. The chamber of commerce is starting a *crusade* to keep our city streets clean.
4. Prejudice and *bigotry* do not automatically disappear with parenthood.
5. In allowing the last large potential park site within the city limits to be subdivided by real-estate developers, the city council has reached the ultimate in political *cynicism*.

6. As the result of the tree-planting and clean-up program of the local merchants, the downtown area of the city is experiencing a veritable *renaissance.*

7. It is a sad spectacle to see Democratic legislators *connive* with the Republican minority to kill this much-needed legislation.

8. One member of the review board turned the investigation into a *witch hunt.*

9. No one should miss the chance to examine our *glamorous* new spring fabrics.

10. The building of the new shopping center marks a new chapter in our town's history of *progress.*

11. To substitute the "one citizen—one vote" principle for the present federal system of regional representation would be an open invitation to *mob rule.*

12. To call for public support of our police and then to deny the police officer higher wages is sheer *hypocrisy.*

13. Obviously the mayor has *brainwashed* the city council to the point where they will adopt her program without protest.

14. As a veteran of two wars, our senator speaks on military questions with *authority.*

15. To abandon these necessary regulations would be an open invitation to *anarchy.*

In a recent magazine, find a full-page ad that illustrates well several methods of persuasion used by advertisers. Explain the methods used and their effects. What kind of reader does the ad seem to aim at? How effective do you think it is, and why. (Bring a copy of the ad to class if you can.)

EXERCISE 2

How persuasive is the following newspaper article? What tactics does the author use to convince his audience? Arthur Ashe won the first United States Open tennis championship as an amateur in 1968. He won the traditional Wimbledon tournament in England in 1975. Study the article and answer the questions that follow it.

PROSE MODEL 6

ARTHUR ASHE

An Athlete Talks About Education

Since my sophomore year at UCLA, I have become convinced that we blacks spend too much time on the playing fields and too little time in the libraries. Consider these facts: for the major professional sports of hockey, football, basketball, baseball, golf, tennis and boxing, there are roughly only 3170 major league positions available (attributing 200 positions to golf, 200 to tennis and 100 to boxing). And the annual turnover is small.

There must be some way to assure that those who try but don't make it to pro sports don't wind up on street corners or in unemployment lines. Unfortunately, our most widely recognized role models are athletes and entertainers—"runnin'" and "jumpin'" and "singin'" and "dancin'."

Our greatest heroes of the century have been athletes—Jack Johnson, Joe Louis, and Muhammad Ali. Racial and economic discrimination forced us to channel our energies into athletics and entertainment. These were the ways out of the ghetto, the ways to get that Cadillac, those regular shoes, that cashmere sport coat.

Somehow, parents must instill a desire for learning alongside the desire to be Walt Frazier. Why not start by sending black professional athletes into high schools to explain the facts of life?

I have often addressed high school audiences and my message is always the same. For every hour you spend on the athletic field, spend two in the library. Even if you make it as a pro athlete, your career will be over by the time you are 35. You will need that diploma.

Have these pro athletes explain what happens if you break a leg, get a sore arm, have one bad year or don't make the cut for five or six tournaments. Explain to them the star system, wherein for every star earning millions there are six or seven others making $15,000 or $20,000 or $30,000. Invite a benchwarmer or a guy who didn't make it. Ask him if he sleeps every night. Ask him whether he was graduated. Ask him what he would do if he became disabled tomorrow. Ask him where his old high school athletic buddies are.

We have been on the same roads—sports and entertainment—too long. We need to pull over, fill up at the library and speed away to Congress and the Supreme Court, the unions and the business world.

I'll never forget how proud my grandmother was when I graduated from UCLA. Never mind the Davis Cup. Never mind the Wimbledon title. To this day, she still doesn't know what those names mean. What mattered to her was that of her more than thirty children and grandchildren, I was the first to be graduated from college, and a famous college at that. Somehow, that made up for all those floors she scrubbed all those years.—*New York Times*

1. How much use does the author make of facts and figures to help persuade his readers?
2. A persuasive writer often influences readers by making them fear undesirable consequences. How much use does this writer make of this strategy, and where?
3. How and where does the author appeal to positive emotions of pride?
4. A persuasive writer has to decide how to treat those who represent a different position or a different way. Are there any examples of understanding and respect? Are there any examples of belittling or ridicule?
5. Sum up the author's message in your own words. Find the passage where the author himself states it most effectively.

1. Write an "open letter" to Arthur Ashe in which you give *your* reaction to what he said.

2. Assume that you have been invited to be guest editor of a local newspaper. Write an *editorial* on a current issue that is close to your heart. Remember that your readers will represent different backgrounds and differents shades of opinion. Try to persuade them rather than merely make them angry.

3. Write an *open letter* to an imaginary official who has been critical of the "younger generation." Try to correct one major misunderstanding often held by adults concerning people your own age.

4. Try to enlist public support for a cause that you think has been neglected. Try to bring in convincing material from your own experience.

5. Have you ever found that something you considered objectionable was perfectly legal? Or, have you ever found that something you considered harmless or beneficial was against the law? Write a paper advocating the necessary *changes* in the law. Try to convince the reader that the change would be not merely for your own private benefit or convenience.

Draw effectively on the work of other writers.

Much writing makes use of the author's reading. Much of what we know about the world we know at second hand. We supplement our own experience by studying the record others have left of *their* observations. We draw on the results of *their* studies and investigations. Use the results of your own reading to good advantage:

(1) Learn to choose promising sources. Learn to recognize books and articles that are worth reading. Learn which authorities are

worth consulting. Ask: Does this author merely state an opinion, or is the opinion *supported* in detail? Does the author merely state *personal* views, or are the views of others taken seriously?

(2) Make it a habit to take notes.   Have you ever looked for an important quotation in a 400-page novel? Have you ever tried to remember in which of three books you found important information that you forgot to write down? Record key statistics and important examples. Copy short quotations that sum up an important point.

(3) Represent authors fairly.   Remember that a passage you quote or discuss is part of a larger whole. Ask yourself: How does this passage fit into the author's argument? Is it the author's own opinion? Or is the author merely examining it as a possibility? Am I overemphasizing something that is not very important?

C5a
The Book Review

Give your reader an informative description and a fair evaluation of a book.

A good book review tells the reader whether the book is *worth reading*. A good review gives a vivid account of the ground the book covers. It discusses the features that make the book new or interesting or important. It identifies major strengths and weaknesses.

A good review has **focus**. It covers a few major points in detail. It makes them add up to a coherent impression. What the review will focus on will vary with the type of book: a novel; a biography; a treatment of a scientific subject for the general reader. Look for the following as possible points to emphasize:

SETTING—Reviewing a book about missionary work in China, you may emphasize the author's treatment of the country and its people: their history, their daily tasks, their customs, their attitude toward foreigners. In a novel, the setting is often more than a mere backdrop for the action: The struggle for life on a farm in the mountains of Vermont may in many ways *shape the outlook* of the people who live there.

CHARACTER—In reading a biography or a novel, our major interest is often *psychological*. We learn *why* a central character acts the way he or she does. Some authors give us a very **flat** picture of character. Their heroes are all heroic, their villains all bad. They recognize only a few simple motives: money, sex, revenge. The more challenging author usually gives us a **rounded** picture of character. The author takes us beyond the surface, showing us some of the contradictions in people.

PLEASE BUY MY BOOK

Look at the following capsule reviews. For each book, what kind of person would be the ideal reader? What kind of person would be most likely to buy and enjoy the book? What kind of person would probably dislike the book?

HOUR OF GOLD, HOUR OF LEAD: Diaries and Letters 1929-1932. By Anne Morrow Lindbergh (Harcourt Brace Jovanovich, $7.95)—Continuing from *Bring Me a Unicorn,* this second volume of memoirs covers the early years of marriage to Charles Lindbergh, the kidnapping (and murder) of their first son, the enormous publicity that intruded on their lives, and recounts it all with quiet emotion, courage, and grace.

MY LIFE IN THE MAFIA. By Vincent Teresa with Thomas C. Renner (Doubleday, $8.95)—A lively and compellingly readable account of the Mafia by a top-ranking insider who turned informer—his testimony helped indict more than 50 gangland figures—and whose story a gifted reporter has assembled (and checked) from taped interviews conducted in the limbo of Teresa's hideaways.

NEWS FROM NOWHERE: Television and the News. By Edward J. Epstein (Random House, $7.95)—A careful and incisive report on network news: how it is gathered, processed, and financed, and how the prosaic needs of commercial TV often determine what is "news" and what is not.

OUR BODIES, OURSELVES. By the Boston Women's Health Book Collective (Simon and Schuster, $8.95; paperback, $2.95)—A complete medical guide for, about, and by women, and a breakthrough book of feminine consciousness.

PLOT—Your review should not be simply a summary of what happened in the book. But the typical review will have at least a solid paragraph devoted to the actions and events that take place. It is *what happens* that puts the characters to the test, or reveals their motives, or explains their background and its influence on their present motivations. Often the action is carried forward as a result of a conflict related to character. There may be a conflict between people with different goals or ideals. There may be a struggle between people and their environment. There may be a conflict between opposed motives *within* a major character.

THEME —Once we know what events take place in a book, we want to know what they *mean*. Why are they presented to us? What do they show about people, or about life? A serious book seldom has a simple moral, like "Crime does not pay." But it may well make us realize something important about the nature of crime —even if we cannot sum it up in a simple formula. Perhaps we learned something about the many different motives and circumstances that can lead a person to crime. When we discuss the theme of a book, we try to spell out its *larger significance*. Setting, character, and plot all contribute in their own way to the major theme of a book.

STYLE —The way a book affects us has much to do with *the way things are said*. Something that would be insulting if said in cold blood might make us smile if said in a spoofing manner. Statements that would sound cheerful when taken out of context may seem cruel in a novel whose general tone is bleak and foreboding. The style is often the most *personal* thing about a book —we remember it the way we remember a person's voice or face.

As you write a review, ask yourself whether the reader needs to be told any of the following additional information:

(1) Who is the author? We usually assume that the author is simply an ordinary person commenting honestly to the general reader. But when someone writes about Russia, we like to know whether the writer was there as a diplomat or as a tourist. When someone writes about the American high school, we like to know whether the writer writes from the point of view of the teacher, the administrator, the legislator, the parent, or the student.

(2) Who is the intended audience? A scientist will write one way for fellow specialists but a different way for the nonspecialist. The outsider needs to have many things explained that the specialist takes for granted. A story of a tourist's adventures in Southeast Asia may make entertaining reading. But it might be useless for someone seriously studying the region.

(3) What has been the reception of the book? If many writers and critics have hailed the book as a masterpiece, your review might point this out. If the book has been denounced as scandalous by some critics, you might want to give your reader fair warning. Remember, though, that books, like people, do not always live up to their reputations.

Remember: Each major point you make should be supported by *direct reference* to the book. Mention specific events to support your statements about the plot or about the theme. Choose revealing short quotations to support your statements about a character or about the author's style. Try to use short quotations that clearly illustrate *one major point at a time:*

> The Puritans described by William Bradford in his *History of the Plymouth Plantation* believed that everything that happened was a showing of God's wrath or God's favor. At one time during the long sea voyage, a "proud and very profane young man" became ill with a grievous disease and died. The other people on board the ship "noted it to be the just hand of God upon him."

> Hemingway's *The Old Man and the Sea* is the story of a grim struggle. But the tone of the book is nowhere hopeless or defeatist. Hemingway says about the central character, "Everything about him was old except his eyes and they were the same color as the sea and were cheerful and undefeated."

EXERCISE 1

The following book review was adapted from a student-written review rated highly by a group of English teachers. Answer the following questions about this review:

1. Which of the *major elements* —setting, character, plot, theme, style— does it treat, and where?
2. What *additional information* does it provide?
3. How well is each major point supported by specific reference and *well-chosen quotations?* Point out several examples.
4. How successful is the review in giving you a picture of the book *as a whole?* Sum up in a few sentences the overall impression the reviewer gives you of the book.

A BOOK REVIEW

THE OLD MAN AND THE SEA
by
Ernest Hemingway

Ernest Hemingway's book, *The Old Man and the Sea,* is a simple story of "an old man who fished alone in a skiff in the Gulf Stream" and who "had gone eighty-four days now without taking a fish." During the first forty days a boy had been with him. But because the old man was "definitely and finally *salao,* which is the worst form of unlucky," the boy's parents had ordered him to another more fortunate boat. The old man, nevertheless, daily sailed from the Cuban shore, looking for a catch. Not only did he have to show the boy that he was a good fisherman, but also he had a reputation to live up to. On the eighty-fifth day, he ventured far into the Stream, and by afternoon had hooked a giant marlin. He fought and struggled with this great fish for two days and two nights. Finally, though nearly finished himself, he was triumphant and headed for home with the enormous body lashed to the side of his skiff. But, ironically, before he could reach shore, sharks attacked his prize and left only a stripped skeleton.

Principally a story of character, *The Old Man and the Sea* presents a splendid portrayal of the old man's life—its victories and its defeats. The old man lived in a shack "made of the tough budshields of the royal palm . . . and in it there was a bed, a table, one chair, and a place on the dirt floor to cook with charcoal." Yet his life was not dull or sad. As a boy, he had sailed to Africa; and every night now he lived along the coast, and in his dreams he saw lions on the beach. Moreover, he was a great baseball fan, and the "great DiMaggio" was his hero because the two had something in common. The old man was handicapped by his age and by hand cramps. The famous ball player was handicapped by a bone spur; but in spite of his handicap DiMaggio kept fighting and achieved greatness. In him, the old man found a sort of encouragement to endure his travail. "I must have confidence," he thought while battling the marlin, "and I must be worthy of the great DiMaggio who does all things perfectly even with the pain of the bone spur in his heel." The old man had many admirable qualities—perseverance, patience, humility, understanding, love of life. "Fish, I'll stay with you until I am dead," he once said aloud, and under overwhelming odds he did. Although his left hand was cramped and the line had cut both palms, he held on until he wore out the marlin. The old man also had a love and admiration for nature. He respected his foe as an individual, and more than once he pitied the fish and spoke to him. Even after he had killed the marlin, the old man fought dauntlessly to ward off the hungry sharks. What had been his foe now became his treasure, and the old man gave what strength he had left to protect. When his harpoon sank with the first shark, he lashed his knife blade to one of the oars and fought with it. He lost this weapon too, but as more sharks appeared, he desperately beat them off with a broken oar. He knew the fight was useless, though; the sharks had won. Their victory might seem a defeat for the old man, "but man is not made for defeat," he said. "A man can be destroyed but not defeated."

Hemingway tells his story in such a way that the reader himself battles the fish with the old man, feels every tug and pull on the line, experiences every pain. *The Old Man and the Sea* gives every indication that Hemingway is indeed thoroughly familiar with his subject. He lived in Cuba for many years and often experienced the difficult techniques of deep-sea fishing.

Hemingway's style is simple but effective. Many of his sentences and even whole paragraphs have a freshness about them that is rarely found in modern literature. Throughout the story are numerous concrete details. "He was bright in the sun and his head and back were dark purple and in the sun the stripes on his sides showed wide and a light lavender. His sword was as long as a baseball bat and tapered like a rapier and he rose his full length from the water and then reentered it, smoothly, like a diver and the old man saw the great scythe-blade of his tail go under and the line commenced to race out." And fitting the simplicity of the story, Hemingway uses a common and unadorned language. To add local color, he uses a number of rich, pleasant-sounding Spanish words.

Hemingway's highly realistic novel is a story of struggle, of the indisputable courage of the aged fisherman against unconquerable natural laws. The reader will not soon forget the tragic story of the old man and his struggle with the giant marlin.

EXERCISE 2

Suppose you had asked a teacher or a librarian for a list of books you might enjoy reading. You were given the following selection of "capsule plots." Which of these books do you think you would most enjoy reading? Which least? Prepare a brief report on your personal reading tastes, referring to the books below as examples.

1. Virginia Hamilton's *The Planet of Junior Brown* will be a hit with any student who isn't embarrassed by its larger-than-necessary print. Two black boys, one homeless and the other lacking in significant adult models to pattern his life after, find school a "drag" and hide out daily in the custodian's workroom. While there, the two learn more about life from the custodian (a fired teacher at the school) than they are getting in their classes, until their truancy is eventually discovered. The resolution of the plot is mildly optimistic as Junior Brown shakes off the dream world he is beginning to encompass.

2. Louise Wilson's *This Stranger, My Son* is the heartrending, true story of a doctor and his wife who search desperately and hopelessly for the medical and/or psychological help to aid their schizophrenic, brilliant son. His grim institutionalization is hauntingly described here.

3. A diary by an anonymous fifteen-year-old girl is fast becoming a hit with teenagers interested in the drug scene. *Go Ask Alice* is particularly good for the noncollege-bound student as it traces the last six months of the girl's life, from her innocent first exposure

to acid through her increasing dependence on it as a means of coping with an unhappy, affluent home. Her tragic death is told in a postscript just when the diary reveals that she has found a measure of success and acceptance with peers at school.

4. One of the most unheralded, suspenseful novels published is Celia Fremlin's *Possession,* the chilling story of a young couple whose prospective marriage is constantly interfered with by dominating mothers. The ending, blurred purposely, will haunt its teenaged reader.

5. *Don't Play Dead Until You Have To,* by Maia Wojciechowska (pronounced Voy-chay-hof-ska), tells of a teenaged "regular guy" who babysits with a brilliant youngster and humorously tries to teach the latter how to be tough and cool. The younger boy has a nervous breakdown when his parents get divorced; subsequently the older boy, his obvious idol, tries to help him gain the confidence and sense of security necessary for coping with life. The characters are particularly believable here.

6. Lesser-known but nonetheless well-told is Wojciechowska's *A Single Light,* the story of a frightened, illiterate deaf-mute girl who possessively fondles a treasured marble image of Christ sought after by villagers and exploiters, greedy for the opportunity of making their poverty-stricken hamlet a famous shrine.

EXERCISE 3

The following books are often recommended to high school students. Your teacher may ask you to choose one or more of these for a book review.

Harriet Beecher Stowe, *Uncle Tom's Cabin*
Ellen Glasgow, *Vein of Iron*
Jesse Stuart, *The Thread That Runs So True*
Willa Cather, *My Ántonia*
Hamlin Garland, *Son of the Middle Border*
Gordon Parks, *A Choice of Weapons*
Sinclair Lewis, *Main Street*
O. E. Rölvaag, *Giants in the Earth*
John Steinbeck, *Grapes of Wrath*
William Faulkner, *The Bear*
William Saroyan, *My Name Is Aram*
Elia Kazan, *America, America*
Rachel Carson, *The Sea Around Us*
N. Scott Momaday, *The Way to Rainy Mountain*
Mari Sandoz, *Cheyenne Autumn*
Maya Angelou, *I Know Why the Caged Bird Sings*

Write a short research paper that brings together material from several sources.

C5b

In a research paper, we do not trust our own personal impressions. We find sources of reliable information. Where authorities disagree, we weigh the evidence and reach our own conclusions. In addition, we enable the reader to *check* our use of our sources. We show what material we have taken from other writers, and where we have found it. In a paper drawing on several printed sources, your teacher may ask you to provide complete **documentation:**

- **footnotes** that will guide the reader to the right passage in an article or a book;
- a **bibliography** that lists all sources used in alphabetical order.

Writing a research paper is a major project. Break it up into major steps:

(1) Limit your topic and locate the available resources. First, choose an area of *general interest.* You should be able to write

---

THREE IMPORTANT CONCEPTS

RESEARCH: Research is a process of *finding out.* Writers engaged in research make up their minds after careful study and after examining the best available evidence. They do not merely look for evidence that will support a conclusion they had reached in advance. They do not merely adopt someone else's *ready-made* collection and evaluation of the evidence.

DOCUMENTATION: Documentation provides an *honest accounting* of your sources. Responsible writers do not simply claim that "Science has proved . . ." or "History has shown. . . ." Instead, they direct the reader to *specific pages* in articles or books by scientists or historians. The reader can check how fairly they have selected and interpreted their evidence.

PLAGIARISM: Plagiarism is passing off *other people's* words and ideas as your own. Most authorities will welcome your decision to draw on their findings—as long as you give them *due credit.* But to lift important evidence without acknowledgment is dishonest. To copy a whole paper with a few minor changes from a printed source is theft. Avoid any suspicion of plagiarism by giving credit for what others have contributed to your work.

(and your reader to read) your paper without the training of a specialist. Second, narrow your area down to a topic you can treat *in detail*. In a short paper, you could give only a sketchy summary of the history of the American Indian. But Indian legends about the creation of the world you could discuss in some detail. Third, make sure you can find relevant material in *several different sources*. Do not condense a ready-made treatment from an encyclopedia or textbook. Research means finding out for yourself—by comparing different accounts, by filling in the gaps in one source with material from another.

In practice, you will have to depend on the resources of your school library, perhaps supplemented by those of a public library. (See the resource guide on "Using the Library" in Chapter 7.) Here are some areas of general interest, with the kind of sample project for which a typical library will have source material:

HISTORY AND BIOGRAPHY: When we read a history book or a biography, we must form our own conclusions where the evidence is sketchy and uncertain. One biographer may leave out details that another biographer considers important. Compare different sources on *one* limited point.

Suppose a student becomes interested in Benjamin Franklin as the typical American. For instance, how extensive was his interest in the *practical* side of life? Here is an alphabetical listing of sources that the student might find. The list includes books on Franklin, chapters on Franklin in books on more general subjects, magazine articles about Franklin, and writings by Franklin himself:

Cohen, I. Bernard. <u>Benjamin Franklin's Experiment</u>. Cambridge: Harvard Univ. Press, 1941.

Crane, Verner W. <u>Benjamin Franklin and a Rising People</u>. Boston: Little, Brown, 1954.

Davidson, Marshall B. "Penn's City: American Athens." <u>American Heritage</u>, 12 (Feb. 1961), 10-29, 103-107.

Franklin, Benjamin. <u>The Autobiography</u>. New York: Modern Library, 1944.

Levin, David. "The Autobiography of Benjamin Franklin: The Puritan Experimenter in Life and Art." <u>Yale Review</u>, 53 (1964), 258-275.

Sherman, Stuart. "Franklin." In <u>The Cambridge History of American Literature</u>. Toronto: Macmillan, 1944.

Van Doren, Carl. <u>Meet Dr. Franklin</u>. Philadelphia: The Franklin Institute, 1943.

SCIENCE AND TECHNOLOGY: Explaining scientific theories and difficult technical details is a job for the expert. But there are many topics in science and technology that the apprentice researcher can explore. What happened to the Zeppelins? What is it like to be a Russian astronaut? What is the history of supersonic planes?

Can you tell from the following list of sources how the student writer collected material on the end of the Zeppelin era? First, apparently, she found an article on the "Airship" in a standard *encyclopedia*. Second, she found several articles about the airship listed in an *index to magazine articles*. (She probably checked the volumes of the *Readers' Guide* for the years 1937 and 1938, when the last big airship disaster was very much in the news.) Third, she checked the *card catalogue* of the library for books under a subject heading like "Zeppelin" or "airship."

Adelt, Leonhard. "Last Trip of the Hindenburg."
  Reader's Digest, 31 (Nov. 1937), 69-72.

"Airships." Encyclopaedia Britannica. 1968 ed.

Allen, Hugh. The Story of the Airship. Akron:
  Goodyear Tire and Rubber Company, Inc., 1942.

Lehmann, Ernst A. Zeppelin: The Story of Lighter-
  than-Air Craft. New York: Longmans, Green
  and Company, 1937.

Rosendahl, C. E. What About the Airship? New
  York: Scribner's, 1938.

Settle, Betty Sue. "The Death of a Monster." The
  Expositor, Fall 1970, pp. 42-50.

Teale, Edwin. "Can the Zeppelin Come Back?" Popular Science, 132, No. 4 (Apr. 1938), 29-31.

LITERATURE: A *comparative* study on a literary topic provides good training for the use of material from different sources. Here are some possible topics:

- Three novels about American women
- "Growing Up American": biographies of members of minorities
- The railroad in nineteenth-century poetry
- Stephen Crane and Ernest Hemingway on war
- Lincoln through the eyes of two American poets

Your teacher may require you to limit your study to the **primary sources**—the actual literary works. Or, you might be asked to include **secondary sources**—articles and books *about* the works.

(2) Keep a record of your sources, for use during your project and in a final bibliography. Make sure you have a full description of every book, pamphlet, or magazine article you are using. For a book, note not only the full name of the author and the complete title, but also the specific edition: original version or revision, hardcover edition or paperback reprint. For an article, note the issue or year ("volume") of the magazine and the exact page numbers.

For a project using less than half a dozen sources, you may record all bibliographical information simply on a single sheet of notepaper. For a larger project, you will put the information for each item on a separate 3 x 5 note card. This way you can easily put your bibliography cards in alphabetical order for use in a final bibliography at the end of your paper. On your bibliography cards (but not in your final bibliography) include the **library call number** for each item that you have located in the card catalogue. Put the call number in the upper lefthand corner of your card:

> | SAMPLE BIBLIOGRAPHY CARD |
> |---|
>
> 509
> C4730
>
>
> Conant, James Bryant.
> <u>On Understanding Science: An</u>
> <u>Historical Approach.</u>
> New Haven: Yale Univ. Press,
> 1947.

Why is it important to include the library call number on your bibliography cards? Why is it *not* necessary to include it in your final bibliography?

Use the following system for full identification of your sources, both on your bibliography cards and in a final bibliography. *Use abbreviations and punctuation as shown* unless your teacher requires you to follow another system:

1. STANDARD ENTRY FOR A BOOK:

Bradbury, Ray. The Martian Chronicles. New York: Doubleday,
    1950.

2. BOOK WITH SUBTITLES:

De Las Casas, Bartolome. The Tears of the Indians: A
    Historical and True Account of the Massacres Committed
    by the Spaniards in the West Indies. New York: Oriole,
    1972.

3. BOOK WITH SEVERAL AUTHORS:

McQuade, Donald, and Robert Atwan. Popular Writing in America.
    New York: Oxford Univ. Press, 1974.

4. BOOK COMPILED BY EDITOR:

Bontemps, Arna, ed. American Negro Poetry. New York: Hill
    and Wang, 1963.

5. NEW EDITION OF OLDER BOOK:

Jinks, William. The Celluloid Literature: Film in the Human-
    ities. 2nd ed. Beverly Hills: Glencoe, 1974.

6. TRANSLATION:

Homer. The Iliad. Trans. E. V. Rieu. Harmondsworth, Middlesex:
    Penguin Books, 1950.

7. WORK WITH SEVERAL VOLUMES:

Marchand, Leslie A. Byron: A Biography. 3 vols. New York:
    Knopf, 1957.

8. BOOK NEWLY EDITED BY OTHER THAN AUTHOR:

Carson, Kit. Autobiography. Ed. Milo Milton Quaife. Lincoln:
    Univ. of Nebraska Press, 1966.

9. STANDARD ENTRY FOR ARTICLE:

Katz, Molly. "A Blueprint for Writing." Change, 8 (Nov. 1976),
    46-47.

10. ANONYMOUS NEWSPAPER OR MAGAZINE ARTICLE:

"Helping the Poor Find Justice." Time, 2 July 1979, p. 35.

11. ARTICLE IN A COLLECTION:

Sontag, Susan. "The Dummy." The Uncommon Reader. Ed. Alice
    S. Morris. New York: Avon, 1965.

12. ARTICLE IN ENCYCLOPEDIA:

"Universities." Encyclopaedia Britannica. 1962 ed.

(3) Take clearly identified notes, recording details and quotations that you will need to support your conclusions. Basically, your notes will record the concrete detail that you will need to back up your conclusions when you present them in the finished paper. Many teachers recommend 4 x 6 inch cards. Note at the top the tentative *subtopic* under which the material on the card would fit. Note at the bottom, in shortened form, author, title, and *exact page number.* Limit each card to material that clearly relates to one major point— material that is likely to appear in the *same paragraph* in the finished paper.

The material on your note cards will fall roughly into three categories:

Summary —or overview of essential information:

SAMPLE NOTE CARDS

Survivors of Vanished Tribes

Ishi, last known survivor of the Yahi tribe, was found starving on a ranch near Oroville, California, in 1911. Scientists from the University of California at Berkeley made friends with him and gave him a home for the remaining four years and seven months of his life. Ishi learned enough English to teach them something of the language and customs of his tribe. His people had fished and hunted in the hills and forests of Northern California.

Carmona, The Lost Trail, pp. 13-17

Concrete detail —facts, figures, data related to one limited point, typically recorded in *your own words:*

Blue-Collar Occupations--Income

Printers earned more than reporters.
Many milk-truck drivers and waiters
earned over $150 per week. Tugboat
dispatchers earned between $9,000
and $10,000. Sanitation workers
earned as much as many social workers. Bricklayers and carpenters
earned more than bookkeepers.

Fredrick, <u>Facts About Jobs,</u> p. 35

Key quotations —short excerpts with the exact wording of the original text, to be used for key points. Sometimes you will quote word for word only some selected phrases. Sometimes you will quote several sentences or an important paragraph.

Blue-Collar Occupations--Attitudes

     Favorable attitude toward the job held often
changes with age. Older people in business or management often consider themselves "ready to reap
life's greatest rewards." Blue-collar workers often
consider themselves handicapped by age, "using more
elbow grease" and yet seeing their working days get
rougher.

Fredrick, <u>Facts</u>**, pp. 78-79**

Remember: To take notes means to *gather ammunition* for use in your finished paper. Learn to select material that will help you prove a point. Learn to condense and summarize. Make sure your finished paper does not give your reader big chunks of quoted material, with only an occasional sentence of your own.

(4) Work out an overall plan. At first your reading and note-taking will be exploratory. You will follow up some possible questions and possible leads. The more you become familiar with the area you are investigating, the better you will be able to do two essential things:

• Focus on a limited *problem* you want to explore, a specific *question* you want to answer. After you have immersed yourself in your materials, you will be able to work toward a tentative **thesis** statement. Sum up in one sentence your major point.

• Work out a tentative *strategy* for supporting your thesis. Sketch out a skeleton **outline** tracing possible major steps, or possible major divisions. Adjust your outline as needed as you proceed.

Study the way the author of the following passage has worked information and quotations into a unified piece of writing. Summarize what she sets out to do, and how she accomplishes her purpose:

RACHEL CARSON

The Sunless Sea

(Central Question)

They used to say that *nothing could live in the deep sea*. It was a belief that must have been easy to accept, for without proof to the contrary, how could anyone conceive of life in such a place?

(Earlier View)

A century ago the British biologist Edward Forbes wrote: "As we descend deeper and deeper into this region, the inhabitants become more and more modified, and fewer and fewer, indicating our approach to an abyss where life is either extinguished, or exhibits but a few sparks to mark its lingering presence." Yet Forbes urged further exploration of "this vast deep-sea region" to settle forever the question of the existence of life at great depths.

(Reexamination)

Even then, the evidence was accumulating. Sir John Ross, during his exploration of the arctic seas in 1818, had brought up from a depth of

1000 fathoms mud in which there were worms, "thus proving there was animal life in the bed of the ocean notwithstanding the darkness, stillness, silence, and immense pressure produced by more than a mile of superincumbent water."

Then from the surveying ship *Bulldog,* examining a proposed northern route for a cable from Faroe to Labrador in 1860, came another report. The *Bulldog's* sounding line, which at one place had been allowed to lie for some time on the bottom at a depth of 1260 fathoms, came up with 13 starfish clinging to it. Through these starfish, the ship's naturalist wrote, "the deep has sent forth the long coveted message." But not all the zoologists of the day were prepared to

(Remaining Doubts)

accept the message. Some doubters asserted that the starfish had "convulsively embraced" the line somewhere on the way back to the surface.

(Clinching Evidence)

In the same year, 1860, a cable in the Mediterranean was raised for repairs from a depth of 1200 fathoms. It was found to be heavily encrusted with corals and other sessile animals that had attached themselves at an early stage of development and grown to maturity over a period of months or years. There was not the slightest chance that they had become entangled in the cable as it was being raised to the surface.

(Further Support)

Then the *Challenger,* the first ship ever equipped for oceanographic exploration, set out from England in the year 1872 and traced a course around the globe. From bottoms lying under miles of water, from silent deeps carpeted with red clay ooze, and from all the lightless intermediate depths, net-haul after

(Answer to Original Question)

net-haul of strange and fantastic creatures came up and were spilled out on the decks. Poring over the weird beings thus brought up for the first time into the light of day, beings no man had ever seen before, the *Challenger* scientists realized that *life existed even on the deepest floor of the abyss.*—from *The Sea Around Us*

Remember: Throughout your note-taking, and in both the first and final draft of your paper, clearly set off in quotation marks all material copied *word for word*. **Paraphrase** material you do not want to quote directly. Give the information, or restate the argument, *in your own words*.

See **M6** for punctuation of direct and indirect quotations.

(5) Identify your sources, using conventional footnote form. When you come to the end of the sentence (or paragraph) with information or a quote from one of your sources, insert a *raised* footnote number. Number all footnotes consecutively, from 1 to 15 or 28 as the case may be. Leave room at the bottom of the page for the footnote showing your reader where to find the material in the original source. (In a short paper, simply put the footnotes on a separate sheet of paper at the end.) Give full identification the *first time* you mention the source:

1. STANDARD FOOTNOTE FOR A BOOK:

   [5]Ray Bradbury, The Martian Chronicles (New York: Doubleday, 1950), p. 68.

2. BOOK WITH SUBTITLE:

   [7]Bartolome de Las Casas, The Tears of the Indians: A Historical and True Account of the Massacres Committed by the Spaniards in the West Indies (New York: Oriole, 1972), p. 43.

3. BOOK WITH SEVERAL AUTHORS:

   [7]Donald McQuade and Robert Atwan, Popular Writing in America (New York: Oxford Univ. Press, 1974), p. 6.

4. BOOK COMPILED BY EDITOR:

   [4]Arna Bontemps, ed., American Negro Poetry (New York: Hill and Wang, 1963), p. xiii.

5. NEW EDITION OF OLDER BOOK:

   [3]William Jinks, The Celluloid Literature: Film in the Humanities, 2nd ed. (Beverly Hills: Glencoe, 1974), p. 7.

6. TRANSLATION:

   [4]Homer, Iliad, trans. E. V. Rieu (Harmondsworth, Middlesex: Penguin, 1950), p. 30.

7. ONE OF SEVERAL VOLUMES:

[5]Leslie A. Marchand, Byron: A Biography (New York: Knopf, 1957) II, 84.

8. BOOK NEWLY EDITED BY OTHER THAN AUTHOR:

[9]Kit Carson, Autobiography, ed. Milo Milton Quaife (Lincoln: Univ. of Nebraska Press, 1966), p. 67.

9. STANDARD FOOTNOTE FOR ARTICLE:

[6]Molly Katz, "A Blueprint for Writing," Change, 8 (Nov. 1976), 46.

10. ANONYMOUS NEWSPAPER OR MAGAZINE ARTICLE:

[8]"Helping the Poor Find Justice," Time, 2 July 1979, p. 35.

11. ARTICLE IN COLLECTION:

[11]Susan Sontag, "The Dummy," in The Uncommon Reader, ed. Alice S. Morris (New York: Avon, 1965), p. 327.

12. ARTICLE IN ENCYCLOPEDIA:

[12]"Universities," Encyclopaedia Britannica, 1962 ed., XXII, 852.

NOTE: The typical footnote differs from the typical bibliography entry: It does *not* put the last name of the author first. It does *not* use periods to separate the major parts. It *does* provide an exact page number. (In references to a Shakespeare play, you may substitute act and scene. In reference to the Bible, use chapter and verse as well as book: *Hamlet* III.ii, or Judges 13:5.)

The *second time* and each later time you refer to a source, identify it by the author's last name. If you are using several sources by the same author, add a shortened version of the title:

1. ONE SOURCE BY AUTHOR:

[3]Baugh, p. 78.

2. SEVERAL SOURCES BY SAME AUTHOR:

[3]Baugh, History, p. 78.

3. SAME PAGE AS LAST FOOTNOTE:

[3]Ibid.

Ibid. stands for *ibidem,* "in exactly the same place." (When used with a page number, it means "in the same source, but on a different page.") It always points back to the *last* source cited.

Here are some other common **abbreviations** that you may encounter in your research:

© 1965	the copyright date, usually found on the *back* of the title page (unless the copyright on a book has been *renewed,* the copyright date is the official year of publication)
ca. or c.	Latin *circa,* "approximately"; used for approximate dates and figures (*ca.* 1952)
cf.	Latin *confer,* "compare"; often used loosely instead of *see* in the sense of "consult for further relevant material" (Cf. Ecclesiastes xii. 12)
et al.	Latin *et alii,* "and others"; used in reference to books by several authors (G. B. Harrison *et al.*)
f., ff.	"and the following page," "and the following pages" (See pp. 16f.)
loc. cit.	Latin *loco citato,* "in the place cited"; used without page reference
MS, MSS	manuscript, manuscripts
n.d.	"no date," date of publication unknown
op. cit.	Latin *opere citato,* "in the work already cited," usually preceded by the author's name (Baugh, *op. cit.,* p. 37).
passim	Latin for "throughout"; "in various places in the work under discussion" (See pp. 54–56 *et passim*)
q.v.	Latin *quod vide;* "which you should consult"

Should you footnote *every* piece of information you use in a documented paper? No, because some information is "common knowledge." For instance, many facts about Benjamin Franklin's life are so widely known that you could have obtained them from a dozen different sources. There is no need, for example, to footnote the information that Franklin was born in 1706, or that he worked in his brother's printing house as an apprentice. On the other hand, you *should* footnote little-known facts about Franklin's life that a researcher had to go to some trouble to collect. You *should* footnote as well recent discoveries that showed earlier information about Franklin to be mistaken.

How good a researcher are you? Find the answers to *five* or more of the following questions. Where do you turn?

1. What Indian languages are still spoken in the United States?
2. How much English is taught in Puerto Rico? How many of the people there know English?
3. How many Puerto Rican students attend school in New York City?
4. How much Japanese is spoken in Hawaii? By whom?
5. How do other countries—Mexico, Canada—deal with children whose home language is different from the school language?
6. Suppose you meet children whose native language is one of the following: Choctaw, Chamorro, Tagalog, Mandarin. Where do the children come from?
7. What is Creole? Does anyone still speak it?
8. How many Spanish-speaking children are there in the schools of Texas? Colorado? Arizona? New Mexico? California?
9. How many Americans speak English as a second language? How many of them are of school age?
10. Does your state have laws concerning the use of English as a compulsory school language for all children?

Find *five* different sources—articles and books—that throw light on one of the following topics that reflect American popular culture. List them in an alphabetized *bibliography*.

1. Disneyland
2. The movies of Charles Chaplin or Buster Keaton
3. Henry Ford
4. Broadway musicals
5. The books of Horatio Alger
6. Billy Graham
7. *Life* magazine or *Saturday Evening Post*
8. Early Hollywood movie queens
9. Dixieland jazz
10. Carry Nation and other temperance leaders

Prepare a set of five *note cards* recording material from *one* of the following books. Collect evidence or supporting material related to one limited question. For instance, what were predictions for space flight made around 1950? Make your cards illustrate different kinds of notes: summary, concrete detail, direct quotation.

1. Wolfgang Langewiesche, *A Flyer's World* (or another book on flying or aviation by the same author)

2. Arthur C. Clarke, *The Exploration of Space* (or another book on inter-planetary travel by the same author)
3. Alan Devoe, *Lives Around Us* (or another book on nature or natural history by the same author)
4. Rachel Carson, *The Sea Around Us* (or another book about the sea by the same author)
5. Bruce Catton, *A Stillness at Appomattox* (or another book about American history by the same author)

EXERCISE 4

Study the following sample *footnotes*. In your own words, re-state all information they give the reader about the sources to which they refer.

³Margaret Truman, Women of Courage (New York: William Morrow, 1976), p. 101.

⁴Robert C. Yeager, "Savagery on the Playing Fields," Reader's Digest, July 1977, p. 23.

¹¹Gina Pischel, A World History of Art, rev. ed. (New York: Simon & Schuster, 1975), p. 59.

⁷Shirley Hill Witt and Stan Steiner, eds., The Way: An Anthology of American Indian Literature (New York: Alfred A. Knopf, 1972), pp. 18-19.

⁴Robert Harrison, trans., The Song of Roland (New York: New American Library, 1970), p. 7.

⁹Theodora Kroeber, Ishi in Two Worlds: A Biography of the Last Wild Indian in North America (Berkeley: Univ. of California Press, 1976), p. 158.

³"U. S. Prestige at New Low," Oakland News, 24 May 1979, p. 34.

¹²Joan Baum, "The Politics of Back-to-Basics," Change, 8 (Nov. 1976), 32.

EXERCISE 5

Study the following model of a *short* research paper. Then do the follow-up assignments at the end.

Before the white settlers arrived in North America, all
the organisms lived in harmony with one another. There was
a balance of food chains and ecological systems that has
vanished since the arrival of the Europeans. As white people
conquered the New World, the balance was upset. Animals that
could not tolerate the onslaught became extinct. Others
became endangered, and still others were able to adapt to
their new world.

The endangered species list is composed of plants and
animals that are on the verge of extinction. Many of the
animals are predators and rely on other organisms for food.
When people destroy its natural habitat or contaminate its
food source, the survival of the animal is threatened. When
the farmer sprays fields to prevent crop damage from insects,
the birds or rodents that feed off the crops or insects
develop small concentrations of the pesticide within their
tissues. If these organisms are in turn eaten by an organism higher in the food web, the concentration increases its
level in the organism. This is the case of the birds of
prey, especially the larger eagles.

The bald eagle became the national symbol in 1782, and
there were nesting pairs in all the lower 48 states. The
current bald eagle population has been estimated at 5,000
in the lower 48 states. As of 1975, only 627 nests remained
active, and they produced approximately 500 young.[1] There
are two types, the Southern species, which is endangered,
and the Northern species. The Southern species main strong-
hold is the Everglades in Florida. Bald eagles are protected

under federal law, which was amended in the early sixties to include the golden eagle.

The increasing levels of pesticides in the diet of the eagles have been directly related to their decline. Poisons such as dieldrin affect hormone levels and are suspected of causing embryo deaths. DDT has long been suspected of affecting the calcium metabolism causing thinning of egg shells, and recent research has found related substances such as DDE to be the actual cause:

> Shells on eggs containing DDE are less porous, and they thus reduce oxygen supply to the embryo. Also, DDE is toxic to unhatched chicks and has been associated with abnormal behavior of chicks after hatching.[2]

Bald eagles apparently mate for life, returning to the same nest year after year. As with most long-lived birds, their reproductive potential is low. The high concentrations of pesticides can alter their reproductive cycle, resulting in the laying of infertile eggs. In some areas where pesticide concentrations are high, the breeding success is as low as 5%. This is characteristic of the New England area and around the Great Lakes.[3] Biologists are currently transplanting the fertile eggs to the non-fertile nests in an attempt to re-establish populations.

If pesticides are used in the agricultural areas, what is the reason for the decline of the eagle out West? The problem out there is different. Many of the stockmen fail to realize the role predators play in controlling rodents. They believe that all predators are harmful and should be exterminated. This attitude is most strongly held for the coyote, and government trappers working for the U.S. Fish and Wildlife

Service try to keep the predators' numbers down by using poison baits, traps, and bullets.

The government trapper would take a carcass, lace it with a prescribed amount of poison and leave it in the field at a marked location. But poisons do not discriminate; they will kill valuable fur-bearing animals or any other animal that eats some of the meat. At one time, the trappers were using a poison known commercially as 1080, which is so potent a single ounce used at maximum efficiency could kill over 200 adult humans or 20,000 coyotes.[4] Needless to say, it was very effective at controlling coyotes, but it also killed other organisms. Since 1080 decomposes only if burned or if immersed in large quantities of water, the other bodies became poisonous bait also. Fortunately, the Environmental Protection Agency has outlawed the use of 1080 because of its filtration into the food chain, much to the dismay of the rancher.

Occasionally, ranchers are not satisfied with the work of the government, and they take matters into their own hands. Their main concern is keeping their herds healthy and alive. For this concern, many ranchers consider all predators as being potentially dangerous, and they want to rid the country-side of them. As a writer said in the Audubon magazine, "The notion that eagles, like other hawks, are simply feathered vermin persists among certain people, especially in the far West."[5]

In the fall of 1971, a total of 25 eagles were found dead or dying in Jackson Canyon in Wyoming. The eagles were sent to the U.S. Wildlife Lab at Patuxent, MD., for an autopsy. The results showed the eagles had excessive quantities of thallium sulfate, a poison used in controlling predators. The poison bait carcasses had been set out by ranchers, not the U.S. Fish and Wildlife Service. This was evident in the amount of poison the ranchers used. Although a single ounce of the poison is enough to make 100 pounds of meat lethal, one rancher used 25 pounds of it to treat 30 sheep carcasses and two cow carcasses. The eagles had eaten the meat and awaited the days to die a convulsive death. The rancher, apparently a powerful figure in the Wyoming Wool Growers Association, had violated a total of twenty-nine Fish and Game Laws. But he and his attorney made a plea of nolo contendere to Prosecuting Attorney John Burk, who reduced the charges to fines totalling $675, plus $4 costs.[6]

People are becoming more aware of the abuse of the environment, and they are wondering what they can do to help preserve it and the organisms. A new eagle refuge, the first National Wildlife refuge for bald eagles, was purchased from the money people donated at 7/Eleven food chain stores.[7] The land is 825 acres in the southeastern corner of South Dakota, which has been a natural wintering ground for decades.

In more recent years there have been stricter controls on government poisons, and a greater enforcement of the Bald Eagle Protection Act. Some states have fines of up to $10,000 for shooting the eagles.[8] The National Wildlife Federation is also giving a reward of $500 for information leading to the conviction of persons shooting eagles. The same organization is also funding the research in developing a different design in powerline structures to prevent the electrocution of the eagle when its wings touch two lines.

All living things have a delicate role to play in the

balance of nature. As this role is disrupted, the organism must adapt to survive. The earth is a forgiving sphere. Given time, it will mend itself back to where it was in the beginning. We must understand this interrelationship of living organisms, for it is the key to our survival.

Notes

[1]Frank Graham Jr., "Will the Bald Eagle Survive to 2076?" Audubon, 78 (March 1976), 99.

[2]"Pesticides and Birds," Chemistry, 48 (Sept. 1975), 20.

[3]John E. Mathisen, "The American Bald Eagle," American Forests, 80 (Sept. 1974), 48.

[4]Jack Olsen, Slaughter the Animals, Poison the Earth (New York: Simon & Schuster, 1971), p. 112.

[5]Graham, p. 100.

[6]Ed Christopherson, "The Massacre of Jackson's Canyon," Outdoor Life, 149 (Feb. 1972), 39-41.

[7]George Laycock, "Bald Eagle at Bay," National Wildlife, 12 (Aurust-Sept. 1974), 35.

[8]Mathisen, p. 48.

Composition

FOLLOW-UP ACTIVITIES

1. How would you state the central idea of this paper? Write a *thesis statement* that the writer could add early in the paper.

2. Prepare a brief *written outline* that could have been handed in with this paper. (See C2e for form of outlines.) Be prepared to explain the writer's overall plan and strategy in your own words.

3. Point out different kinds of information that the writer has gathered from the various sources. (Can you find one or two examples of information where the source is not clear?)

4. Prepare an alphabetical *bibliography* that could have been handed in with this paper. Use the following complete page numbers for the magazine articles:

   - *Audubon:* 99–101.
   - *Chemistry:* 20.
   - *American Forests:* 48.
   - *Outdoor Life:* 39–41.
   - *National Wildlife:* 34–36.

RESEARCH PAPER TOPICS

A. Write a short documented paper based on your investigation of one important feature of a *newspaper*. Use documented references to several different issues of the newspaper to support your answer to one of the following questions. Use different kinds of direct quotation and paraphrase.

1. Is it true that "a surprising amount of space is being devoted to booster material for the paper itself or for local business groups"?
2. What kind of education news is the newspaper reader likely to encounter? What picture of the local public schools is the reader likely to get from it?
3. What kind of people and activities are treated on the typical society page? *How* are they treated?
4. Is crime news played up or played down?
5. What kind of guidance does the reader get from movie or television reviews?

B. Much has been written in recent years about the *endangered wildlife* of our planet. What is the current status of an endangered animal species or an endangered kind of plant? You may want to investigate, for instance, one of the following: whales, wolves, the California redwoods, the buffalo, pelicans. Bring together material from at least *three* printed sources. Make sure some of your sources help you bring the story up to date.

C. Write a documented paper about a *development in science or technology* that at one time attracted much popular attention. Draw on at least five different sources, including *contemporary* newspaper reports or magazine articles. Here are some possible areas for investigation: the passing of the airship; the discovery of radiation; the first jet planes; the first space satellite; the beginnings of color television. Give unity to your paper by concentrating on one major point: a major hurdle or a crucial achievement. Provide a bibliography.

D. Write a documented paper drawing on at *least five books and articles* about an outstanding figure in *American history*. Focus your paper on a major area or problem in the person's life or career. Provide a bibliography.

Here are some examples:

1. Benjamin Franklin's interest in science, technology, or civic improvements
2. Thomas Jefferson's reading
3. George Washington's religious beliefs
4. Andrew Jackson's political convictions
5. Abraham Lincoln's early education
6. Franklin Roosevelt's struggle with illness
7. Harriet Tubman's fight against slavery
8. Susan B. Anthony and the right to vote
9. Jefferson Davis and the Confederacy
10. Booker T. Washington and education

Know how to write an effective business letter.

When we write a business letter, we want to show that what we have to say matters to us. We want the people who receive it to give it their polite attention. We want the letter to make a good impression when it arrives.

C 6
WRITING
BUSINESS LETTERS

Use a conventional format and an effective style.

Whenever you can, type your letter. If your letter is written by hand, make sure your handwriting is easy to read. Use blue or black ink. For a typed letter, use standard typing paper. (Use onion-skin paper only for carbon copies.) Use unruled white paper for handwritten letters—not paper from a notebook. Avoid unusual abbreviations and other shortcuts. Do a letter over when smudges or erasures would cause it to make a poor first impression.

Remember the following when writing business letters:

C6a
Form and Style

(1) Follow a conventional format. Study the following elements of a conventional business letter. Study them at work in the two full-page model business letters that accompany this section:

HEADING AND OPENING PART

① **RETURN ADDRESS:** Write your return address at the top of the page, toward the right. On printed business stationery, the return address is usually part of the printed **letterhead.**

② **DATE:** Type the date directly under your address. With a printed letterhead, drop down several spaces and put the date on the right side.

③ **INSIDE ADDRESS:** Drop down four or five spaces and put the address of the person or firm you are writing to. Put it in the conventional three- or four-line block, flush left:

```
Mr. Winfred Simson
13591 Bosinger Drive
El Paso, Texas 79998
```

④ **GREETING:** **(Salutation)** Put the greeting flush left, followed by a colon: "Dear Mr. Simson:" Some people continue to use the traditional *Mrs.* or *Miss.* Others prefer the new *Ms.* for either. Sometimes you will write to an office or a firm without knowing the name of the person in charge. Here are some possible greetings:

```
Ladies and Gentlemen:        Dear Madam:
Gentlemen:                   Dear Sir:
Ladies:                      Dear Madam or Sir:
```

On the next page are two examples of the opening portion of two typical business letters. The first is from an individual who has typed the return address. The second is from an organization that uses a printed letterhead:

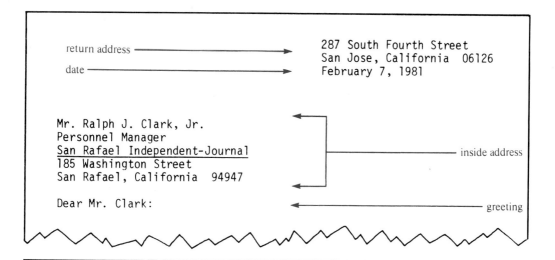

return address ⟶ 287 South Fourth Street
San Jose, California 06126
date ⟶ February 7, 1981

Mr. Ralph J. Clark, Jr.
Personnel Manager
<u>San Rafael Independent-Journal</u>   *inside address*
185 Washington Street
San Rafael, California 94947

Dear Mr. Clark: *greeting*

INSTITUTE FOR BUSINESS WRITING
2134 Glendale Boulevard
Los Angeles, California 90025

June 14, 1981

Ms. Joan P. Hansen
12 Wilshire Boulevard, N.E.
Atlanta, Georgia 30312

Dear Ms. Hansen:

BODY OF
LETTER

(5) **SPACING:**   Single-space each paragraph of a typed letter. Use double-spacing between para-
graphs.

(6) **INDENTATION:**   Many modern business letters now use a
block format. Each paragraph starts flush
left—it is not indented. But many people
still prefer indented paragraphs, as in other
kinds of writing.

(7) **MARGINS:**   Allow about a one-inch margin on each side.

```
┌─────────────┐
│ CONCLUDING  │────────────────────────────────────────────────
│   PART      │
└─────────────┘
```

⑧ **CLOSING:**   The concluding greeting is called the **complimentary closing.** In closing, use "Sincerely," or "Sincerely yours," or "Yours sincerely," (note the comma at the end of the greeting).

⑨ **SIGNATURE:**   Type or print your name below your signature. A representative of a firm or group will often include a title or a position below the name.

⑩ **NOTATIONS:**   Capital initials in the left bottom corner are usually those of the writer, followed by the typist's initials in lower-case letters. Other notations may follow: Sometimes a letter you receive carries a note like "cc: Gloria Miller." This means that a carbon copy has gone to someone else who should know what was in the letter. "Encl." means that something has been enclosed with the letter. A price list, or a poster, may have been sent along.

Here is an example of the concluding part of a letter. Note the use of the title below the signature.

```
                                    Sincerely yours,

                                    Sylvia Gomez
                                    Sylvia Gomez
                                    Treasurer


        SG:lbd
        cc: Frank Chute
        Encl.
```

ENVELOPE

(11) **RETURN ADDRESS:** Put your complete return address on the envelope in the left-hand corner.

(12) **RECEIVER:** Put the receiver's address on the right half of the envelope, about halfway down. Use the conventional block format. Check names and addresses here and in the letter itself carefully. Make sure there are no misspellings or mistakes.

Here is a sample envelope:

Sheila Keilson
158 Rand Boulevard
Azusa, California 91702

Mrs. Eloise Benoit
Head, Public Relations
Hobby Services, Inc.
4378 Greatfield Drive
Northfield, Minnesota 55507

NOTE: Check your business letters for conventional punctuation. Check the following especially:

• Put a comma between *city and state:* Tacoma, Washington

• Put a comma between *title and office* when they appear on the same line: Manager, Products Division

• Put periods after *Mr., Ms., Mrs.* (but not *Miss*), *M.D.*

• Put a comma between *day and year* if the day follows the month: April 17, 1983 (but 17 April 1983).

A MODERN BUSINESS LETTER—Indented Format

THOMPSON BUSINESS INSTITUTE ————— letterhead
893 South Loop
Atlanta, Georgia 30312

March 19, 1979 ◀— date

inside
address ——— Byrd, Cointreau, and Terry Inc.
2085 Mandell Parkway
Fort Worth, TX 76111

greeting ——▶ Ladies and Gentlemen:

message ———
    In this kind of semiblocked letter, the first line of each
paragraph is indented--usually five spaces. This style has been
in very general use. The semiblocked letter is still popular
because of its traditional appearance. The indented paragraphs
give this style a distinctive look.

    Worth noting also in this letter are the following: (1) po-
sitioning the date at the right margin; (2) using standard
punctuation, which calls for a colon after the salutation and
a comma after the complimentary closing; and (3) using the carbon
copy notation at the bottom to indicate to whom copies of the
letter are being sent.

    Though other, more recent styles are now coming into use,
many people are very comfortable with this traditional letter
format. Please feel free to consult us again when you have questions about the form and content of modern business correspondence.

closing ———————————————————————————▶ Cordially yours,

Jasper F. Broussard

signer's name ———————————————————
and title   Jasper F. Broussard
                                 Senior Account Executive

initials of ——▶ JFB:vrs
writer and
typist   cc: Ms. J. Laver
                    Dr. T. Mauser

carbon copies

NOVELTY SERVICES COMPANY
3301 Butterfield Road
Oak Brook, Illinois 60521

July 28, 1979

Ms. Claire Salerno
Thompson Business Institute
893 South Loop
Atlanta, Georgia 30312

SUBJECT: Communication and Careers ◄——————————— subject line

Dear Ms. Salerno:

I enclose a Xerox copy of an application I received from a
high school graduate applying for our apprenticeship program.
This application is really very unsatisfactory in the way it
uses language. The autobiographical statement is skimpy and
awkward. There must be many eighth-graders who can put words
on paper more effectively than this writer.

This young person will probably not find a place in our training program. We believe that the ability to communicate is
even more important than technical skills and other qualities.

I am writing this letter to you because this young person's
case is not a unique situation. The inability of young
people to communicate effectively has been a popular subject
in the news for some time. I can truthfully say that in our
company we have many young people who are not advancing in
their careers because of inadequate communications skills.

I hope you and colleagues will make an effort to impress upon
your students that the ability to communicate clearly and
effectively is more important for their future career than any
other single quality.

Sincerely yours,

Rita E. Cherworth

Rita E. Cherworth
Director

REC: bb

PS: If you use the attached letter for purposes of illustra-⌉ postscript
tion, please leave out the writer's name.   ⌋ (last-minute
                                                                 addition)

Folding and Inserting Letters

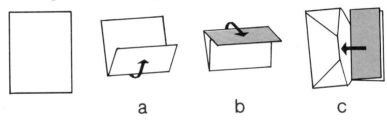

a. Bring the bottom third of the letter up and make a crease.
b. Fold the top of the letter down close to the crease you made in step *a*. Then make the second crease.
c. Put the creased edge you made in step *b* into the envelope first.

(2) *Aim at a businesslike but friendly and positive tone.* The main purpose of a business letter is to give clear and complete information. Tell the readers clearly what they need to know in order to understand the situation or to act on a request. To deal with business matters smoothly and effectively, however, you also have to use the right tone. The widely used guide *Business English and Communication*[1] gives the following advice on maintaining a friendly tone:

- It costs nothing in money or time to be courteous and friendly when answering someone else's letter.
- Expressing anger is a luxury that business people cannot afford because it interferes with good relations.
- Patience in answering questions can be one of your most valuable assets.
- Few people understand that what they write or say may *imply* criticism. Study the following illustrations and learn how to avoid hinting at carelessness, negligence, or dishonesty:

NEGATIVE: You are not entitled to the 2 percent discount because you did not pay within 10 days. *(What are you trying to do, cheat us?)*

POSITIVE: You probably did not notice that your check was dated July 1 and that by then the discount period had expired. *(You are such a busy person that this minor slip is understandable.)*

NEGATIVE: We expect immediate delivery of this order. *(You've been pretty slack in the past, but this time we're demanding immediate service.)*

POSITIVE: Help us make a big sale of your merchandise by shipping this order immediately. *(You're noted for superior service, and you'll be helping us to sell your own merchandise.)*

---

[1] Marie M. Stewart and others, *Business English and Communication*, 5th ed. (New York: McGraw-Hill, 1978).

NOTE: Often a postcard serves as well as a letter in making requests:

Dear Mr. Wykowski:

Please send me <u>Proper Telephone Techniques</u>, the booklet advertised in this month's <u>Management Methods</u> magazine. My address is 260 Carter Avenue, S.E., Atlanta, Georgia 30317.

I certainly appreciate your distributing this valuable publication.

Sincerely yours,

Sylvia Bialek

Sylvia Bialek

Study the following letters and answer the questions:

EXERCISE 1

1. What needed *information* is given to make clear the situation or the problem that the letter is about?
2. What *action* is requested or recommended?
3. What is done to maintain a *friendly relationship* or a positive tone?

LETTER 1

Dear Mrs. Wilcox:

Today I received a silver identification bracelet (your Invoice 753291) instead of the gold identification bracelet specified in my May 25 order.

I am returning the silver bracelet to you in a separate mailing. Please substitute a gold one with the name "Karen" engraved in script.

The quality of these identification bracelets is superb, and I am looking forward to receiving my gold bracelet as soon as possible.

Sincerely yours,

LETTER 2

Dear Mr. Paltz:

It is a pleasure to write you about the Stellar
stereo recordings (Mendelssohn's <u>Elijah</u> by the Hud-
dersfield Choral Society) that you returned recently.
I am sending you a replacement for the first record;
the other two have been checked by our inspectors and
are in excellent condition.

Upon examination of the records, our inspectors
found that Sides 1 and 2 of the first record were
apparently played with a blunt needle. May I suggest
that you examine the needle of your stereo before
playing any records? A record is only as good as the
needle playing it.

The enclosed booklet describes the various
needles recommended by Stellar--available at any au-
thorized Stellar record dealer.

Sincerely yours,

LETTER 3

Dear Ms. Beech:

As principal of Oakwood High School, you have a
great responsibility for the education of our youth.
Malor Industries thanks you for your efforts.

We hope the following invitation will help you
give students more insight into how products are
manufactured, packaged, and distributed to dealers.
You are invited to send your junior class to spend
the day with us. We will plan a full schedule of
activities for them and have them as guests for
lunch in our cafeteria. You may choose a date that
is most convenient for you.

Please call Sylvia Campbell, Public Relations
Director, at 555-3434 to make arrangements.

Sincerely yours,

Write one or more of the following business letters. On a separate sheet, draw a frame the size of a business envelope. Address it the way you would the real envelope.

1. Write to ask questions about a product or service you have seen offered in a *catalogue.* Choose something about which you would like to have more complete information. Identify the product or service clearly by referring to the catalogue and any number or description given there. Use the actual address of the firm or individual.

2. Write to a *government agency* to inform officials of some community problem with which you are concerned. Find the actual address of the agency in a phone book or other source.

3. Write to a *business firm* concerning some suggestion or complaint that you have. Write about their merchandise, service, advertising, or the like. If you can, address your letter to an actual person.

4. Write to a firm or agency that might be able to give you information about a kind of *job or career* that interests you. Explain your interest in that kind of work. Ask questions that are on your mind.

5. Write to a firm or agency to ask for *support* for some project in which you are interested. Explain the project and the support needed.

Know how to write an effective letter of application.

One of the most important kinds of letter people write is the letter of application for a job. Often such a letter helps an employer to select promising candidates for a closer look. When you ask someone for a job, try to include in your letter things that would show the following:

- you are familiar with the job or the area;
- you have had some previous experience;
- you have skills or training that would help;
- you would like the work;
- you would try to adjust to the employer's requirements concerning time, place, and the like;
- you would make every effort to appear for a personal interview.

Here is a summary of the instructions for writing the letter, as given in a guide to business English:

(1) A sloppy letter cannot be excused. It says "I didn't care enough to do it over." Employers are interested only in applicants who care enough to do the job properly.

(2) Address your letter to a specific person in the organization if it is possible to obtain his or her name.

*(3) A good beginning for an application letter is a summary state-
ment of your special qualifications.* This type of beginning gives the
prospective employer an immediate indication of your ability and
training. If these qualifications seem to be what is needed, the employer will read further.

*(4) In the body of the letter, offer support for the statements made
in the opening paragraph.* Emphasize the highlights of your educational background and experience that are related to the job. You
may also indicate why you would like to be employed by the firm to
which you are applying. To impress the company favorably, get some
of their literature and learn about their locations and activities.

(5) List references. Almost every employer likes to have information regarding the character, training, experience, and work
habits of job applicants. You may need to supply the names, titles,
and addresses of **references,** leaving to the interested employer the
task of obtaining the desired information. Before using a person's
name as a reference, request permission to do so. This permission may
be obtained in person, by telephone, or by a letter such as the following:

Dear Mrs. Wyman:

    I am applying for the position of assistant records
supervisor that is now open at the Wexler Corporation
in Bridgeton.

    Since I was a student in your office practice
class during the spring 1981 semester, I had excellent filing instruction. I would like permission to
use your name as a reference.

    I am enclosing a return postcard for reply.

                      Sincerely yours,

(You might use a return envelope instead of the postcard.)

(6) Prepare a written summary of your qualifications. This summary—called a **résumé,** a *data sheet,* or a *personal record* —is a description of your qualifications. It usually includes a statement of
your education, your employment record (experience), a list of references, and other data that will help you obtain the job you wish. A
résumé is highly useful. You may use it to accompany a letter of application, present it to an employer at the interview, or use it to assist
you in filling out an employment application form.

Study the following model letter. Then write an imaginary letter of application for a job that you think you may be interested in in the future. Include qualifications that by then you hope to have.

EXERCISE

SAMPLE LETTER
OF APPLICATION

4314 Sunset Road
Middletown, Illinois   62666
June 2, 1981

Box 176
The Herald
Middletown, Illinois   62666

Dear Ms. Foster:

Two years of high school accounting, followed by a year of accounting in the evening school program at Middletown Business School, have given me thorough preparation for accounting work. Therefore, I would appreciate your considering my application for an accounting position with your firm.

I am presently employed as an accounts receivable clerk. But I would like to find a position where I can make wider use of my accounting training and have an opportunity to get into a more advanced phase of accounting. I plan to continue my accounting training through an evening school program.

The enclosed resume provides the details of my education and experience and suggests a number of people from whom you may obtain information about my character and ability.

May I have a personal interview? I may be reached by telephone at 555-6967, Ext. 413, from 9 a.m. to 5 p.m. or at 555-8734 after 6 p.m.

Sincerely yours,

Pat Doyle

Pat Doyle

Pat M. Coakley
17 Fairview Avenue
Northville, Michigan 48167
Telephone: (313) 237-1710

POSITION SOUGHT: Administrative assistant in merchandising.

EXPERIENCE: Franklin Shops, Wayne, Michigan. August, 19--, to
                   present. Assistant to buyer of teen sportswear.
                   Supervisor: Mrs. Janice Davidson. Duties included
                   comparison shopping, producing bulletins for
                   members of staff, and helping in the preparation of
                   advertisements.

                   Hall's Department Store, Wayne, Michigan. August and
                   September, 19--. Member of College Fashion Board.
                   Supervisor: Mr. B. F. Thomas.

                   The Fashion Center, Northville, Michigan. Part time,
                   19-- and 19--. Salesclerk in the Junior Shop. Super-
                   visor: Miss Barbara Jameson.

EDUCATION: Merchandising Institute, Wayne, Michigan. Completed
                   one year of evening school courses in Textiles, Re-
                   tailing, and Fashion Trends in June, 19--.

                   Ellis College, Wayne, Michigan. Awarded certificate
                   upon completion of one-year business program in June
                   19--. Shorthand--120 w.p.m.; typing--65 w.p.m.

                   Memorial High School, Northville, Michigan. Graduated
                   with honors in June, 19--, upon completion of college
                   preparatory course.

REFERENCES: Dr. Marion J. Downes, Head, Department of Office
                   Education, Ellis College, Wayne, Michigan 48184

                   Mr. Francis Graves, 819 East Scott Road, Northville,
                   Michigan 48167

                   Ms. Estelle Lincoln, 63 Oakwood Terrace, Northville,
                   Michigan 48167

—Adapted from Henderson-Voiles, *Business English Essentials (5th ed.)*

BERKLEY WINSTON & STILLS, INC.

EMPLOYMENT APPLICATION

Date _July 10, 19--_

Personal Data

Applying for Position As _Clerk_   Salary Required _$150_   Date Available _July 17_

☐ Male ☑ Female

Name _Colborne,   Pat,   E._
    (Last),   (First),   (Middle)

Address _7 Maple Place,   Adelphi,   Maryland   20783_
    (Street)   (City)   (State)   (Zip Code)

Telephone Number _(301) 555-7040_   Social Security Number _734-89-2168_
    (Area Code)

Are you a U.S. citizen or an alien immigrant?   ☑ Yes   ☐ No

Birth Date _June   26,   1955_
    (Month)   (Day)   (Year)

Do you have or have you had any serious or prolonged illness?

Educational Data

SCHOOLS

GRADE SCHOOL

HIGH SCHOOL

COLLEGE

BUSINESS, TRADE, OR NIGHT SCHOOL

Approximate Scholastic

School and College

Skills

List any special skills you may have _Drive car_

List any hobbies or special interests outside of business _Tennis / Swimming / Reading_

Indicate the amount of time devoted to each. _3 hours a week / 2 hours a week / 1 hour a week_

What foreign languages do you speak, read, or write? _Spanish_   ☑ Speak   ☑ Read   ☑ Write   ☐ Speak   ☐ Read   ☐ Write

What business machines can you operate? _Calculator, Mimeograph, ditto, Monitor board_

Typing Speed _60_ words per minute   ☑ Electric   ☐ Manual   Steno Speed _120_ Words per minute   Method _Gregg_

EMPLOYMENT

Begin with most recent employer. List all emplo... no matter how short the term.

Company Name _Adel..._

Street Address

Ci...

From _6/71_ To _9/71_
   Mo.-Yr.   Mo.-Yr.

Tele. No. _555-1923_

Clerk-typist

Military Data

Have you ever served in the military service of the United States? _No_

Branch of Service

References

List three people who are not related to you and who are not former employers or supervisors.

NAME	ADDRESS	OCCUPATION
Mr. Richard Meyer	Adelphi Department Store, Adelphi, M.D.	Office Manager
Mrs. Rose Cellio	Adelphi High School, Adelphi, M.D.	Business Teacher

I certify that the above statements are true and complete to the best of my knowledge. I understand that employment is contingent upon the accuracy and acceptability of the statements herein.

Signature _Pat Colborne_

Date _July 10, 19--_

An employment application requests personal information, as well as a description of the applicant's job skills and experience.

FOR FURTHER STUDY

WRITING AND IMAGINATION

Make your writing come to life by using your imagination. Writing becomes gray and dull if it never appeals to our senses or stirs up our emotions. Good writers know how to make us take a fresh, imaginative look at a familiar subject. They know how to appeal to our feelings and our sense of humor. The following activities ask you to bring your imagination into play.

ACTIVITY 1

A writer with a strong or vivid imagination can make us see and feel something that before was just a word. Write a poem or prose passage that makes the reader see and feel what is involved in one of the following: *jealousy, envy, anger, pettiness, snobbery, generosity, gratitude, respect, callousness.*

ACTIVITY 2

What thing or object would you select as a *symbol* for life in twentieth-century America (or for a part of American life that you have had a good chance to observe)? Could you explain to your readers why the object you chose would make a good symbol? You and your class may want to discuss which of the following might be a good choice: the jet plane, the Statue of Liberty, a parking lot, a supermarket, an electric toothbrush, the bicycle, the computer, the commuter train, the subway, a roadside motel.

ACTIVITY 3

What goes into a paper or an article is determined by the writer's limited *point of view.* For instance, there is never just one version of an accident. There is the confused story of the dazed participant:

> Then I heard people screaming that there was a man trapped under the front tire of the other car. . . . I found Jack, who was completely stunned by the whole event. . . . I observed a girl sitting in the ambulance, and I realized that she also had been riding in the other car.

There is the fragmentary story of the innocent bystander, who more than likely was thinking of something else when the accident occurred:

> Suddenly I heard this screeching of tires and this tremendous crash. . . . I looked around and there was this smashed-up car facing the wrong way in traffic. . . .

There is the story of the newspaper reporter looking for sensational news:

> THREE PARTYGOERS KILLED IN FLAMING DOWNTOWN CRASH. . . .

There is the impersonal story of the police officer:

> This officer followed the yellow convertible proceeding north on Shattuck Avenue at speeds ranging from 50 to 60 miles. . . . When arriving at the scene of the accident I observed the car in the outer northbound lane. . . .

Tell the story of a recent news event as seen from three different points of view. Or give three different versions of a famous historical event, as reported by three different observers.

ACTIVITY 4

A writer can make us take a new look at familiar things by making us see them from the point of view of the *naive newcomer*. How would our everyday life look to people from a different civilization? Here is how Jonathan Swift had the little people of Lilliput react to Gulliver's watch:

> Out of the right fob hung a great silver chain, with a wonderful kind of engine at the bottom. We directed him to draw out whatever was fastened to that chain; which appeared to be a globe, half silver, and half of some transparent metal: for on the transparent side, we saw certain strange figures, circularly drawn, and thought we could touch them, till we found our fingers stopped by that lucid substance. He put his engine to our ears, which made an incessant noise, like that of a water-mill. And we conjecture it is either some unknown animal or the god that he worships; but we are more inclined to the latter opinion, because he assured us (if we understood him right, for he expressed himself very imperfectly), that he seldom did anything without consulting it. He called it his oracle, and said it pointed out the time for every action of his life.

Describe a familiar feature of everyday life as it would look to someone who saw it for the first time.

ACTIVITY 5

How would our society seem to a visitor from a different civilization? Write an imaginary report on a visit to contemporary America by a delegate from a *past civilization* that you have studied. For instance, suppose one of the following had come back to life to tour the United States: a Roman citizen, a Greek sculptor, a medieval knight, a British countess of the time of the American Revolution, or a British contemporary of William Shakespeare. What would strike the person as strange, interesting, or absurd?

ACTIVITY 6

Satire is the kind of writing that systematically uses humor for purposes of persuasion. The satirist uses humor to belittle and to ridicule. One of the favorite weapons of the satirist is *irony*. When we speak or write ironically, we achieve a humorous effect by saying the opposite of what we mean—in such a way that the audience *knows* we mean the opposite. At the time of the American Revolution, Benjamin Franklin wrote a piece in which he gave ironic advice to the British on "How a Great Empire May Be Reduced to a Small One." Write a paper in which you give ironic advice on a topic like the following:

- How a Great Football Team May Be Made Second-Rate
- How a Quiet Neighborhood May Be Made Unsafe
- How a Promising Student May Be Made an Enemy of Learning
- How a Beautiful Friendship May Be Turned into a Permanent Dislike

ACTIVITY 7

A *parody* is a close imitation that exaggerates ridiculous or objectionable features. How would you describe the kind of advertising that is being parodied in the following passage?

Recently I came into a room to find my eight-year-old son Catbird sprawled in a chair, idiot slackness on his face, with the doped eyes of an opium smoker. On the television screen stood a young woman with ice-cream hair listening to a man in thick glasses and a doctor's smock.

"What's happening?" I asked.

Catbird answered in the monotone of the sleeptalker which is known as television voice, "She is asking if she should dye her hair."

"What is the doctor's reaction?"

"If she uses Trutone it's all right," said Catbird. "But if she uses ordinary or adulterated products, her hair will split and lose its golden natural sheen. The big economy size is two dollars and ninety-eight cents if you act now," said Catbird.—John Steinbeck, "How to Tell Good Guys from Bad Buys," *The Reporter*

Write a parody of a type of movie, television program, or commercial that you find in some way ridiculous or objectionable.

How do you react to each of the following capsule plots from the world of science fiction? Select the plot you like best. Explain in detail how you react to it and why you prefer it to the others. Then follow up by writing your own capsule plot for a science-fiction story.

THE CROWDED GLOBE—The time is 2077. Birth control has finally become truly effective, but there are already ten billion people on earth. "Death control" is getting better all the time, so people live longer. The masses crowded together in huge cities find escape in "sniffer palaces" with exotic, nonaddictive drugs. Weird cults flourish, and strange fads abound. People have precious stones grafted in their skin and have strange surgical operations performed that give a bizarre appearance to their faces.

WINTER BOY—SUMMER GIRL—People of the future have learned to deal with the dwindling resources of the planet by learning to hibernate. By sleeping away the winter months, the large population can make do with the resources available. A small group of "winter watchers" takes care of things and watches over the cubicles in which the summer people sleep. In turn, some of the summer people watch over the winter watchers when they in turn "hibernate" during the summertime. Becoming acquainted through an accident, a winter boy and summer girl fall in love. Although they try to live in either part of the cycle, she cannot learn to live in his world nor he in hers.

PLANET OF THE APES—Because of complex genetic influences, reverse evolution has set in on our crowded planet. Fewer and fewer people are born with normal human intelligence. The majority of the population is reaching the level of intelligent apes. Because of their limited skills, the masses do little work but pursue incredibly crude amusements of all kinds. The members of the intelligent minority are incredibly overworked. One of them complains that in a single year he had to design a skyscraper, run a hospital, avert war with a neighboring country, and direct traffic at the airport. The masses love their automobiles, which they have been tricked into believing travel at fantastic speeds. But despite their sleek appearance and added sound effects, the cars drive at about twenty-five miles per hour, the highest speed their drivers can handle.

Guide to Manuscript Revision

ab . . . . . Spell out abbreviation (M7b)

adv . . . . . Use adverb form (U2c)

agr . . . . . Make verb agree with subject
(or pronoun with antecedent) (U3a, U3b)

ap . . . . . Use apostrophe (M2b)

cap . . . . . Capitalize (M2a)

coll . . . . . Use less colloquial word (U2a)

CS . . . . . Revise comma splice (M4a)

d . . . . . Improve diction (W4)

dev . . . . . Develop your point (C2a)

div . . . . . Revise word division (M7a)

DM . . . . . Revise dangling modifier (U3c)

frag . . . . . Revise sentence fragment (M3a)

FP . . . . . Revise faulty parallelism (U3f)

gr . . . . . Revise grammatical form or construction (U3d)

awk . . . . . Rewrite awkward sentence (U4)

lc . . . . . Use lower case (M2a)

MM . . . . . Shift misplaced modifier (U3c)

p . . . . . Improve punctuation (M3, M4, M5)

¶ . . . . . New paragraph (C1)

no ¶ . . . . . Take out paragraph break (M7a)

ref . . . . . Improve pronoun reference (U3b)

rep . . . . . Avoid repetition (U4)

shift . . . . . Avoid shift in perspective (U3e)

sl . . . . . Use less slangy word (U2a)

sp . . . . . Revise misspelled word (M1)

st . . . . . Improve sentence structure (U3)

t . . . . . Change tense of verb (U1a)

trans . . . . . Provide better transition (C2d)

w . . . . . Reduce wordiness (U4)

Chapter 4

Usage
Using Standard English

Chapter Preview 4

IN THIS CHAPTER:

- How to use standard forms of verbs, pronouns, adjectives, and adverbs.

- How to shift from spoken English to written English.

- How to handle agreement problems in written English.

- How to revise pronoun reference, position of modifiers, and mixed construction.

- How to improve sentence style through consistent point of view and parallel structure.

Use the right kind of language at the right time.

Everyone must learn to use the kind of language that is right for the time and place. The differences that set various kinds of English apart are called differences in **usage.** Differences in usage are of three major kinds:

- differences in the way we *pronounce* words;
- differences in the *words we choose* to describe the same thing;
- differences in the way we *combine words* in a phrase or sentence.

There are three important reasons for studying usage:

(1) The right kind of language counts on the job. Many jobs are open only to people who can use *standard* English.

(2) Writing is more formal than speech. Writers do not simply write the way they talk. The language we find in articles and books is less chatty than natural conversation. When we write, we *shift gears* to the more formal kind of English that we use in serious writing.

(3) An effective speaker and writer must have a good ear. Study the way different people use our common language. By studying the variety of English usage, you can learn to *vary* your speaking and writing to achieve different effects.

Often, two different ways of saying the same thing are both right. They are both used by people who know the language well and use it to good advantage. But often *how* we say something makes a difference. When we study usage, we concentrate on the choices that make a difference.

COMMON USAGE PROBLEMS

(M refers to Chapter 5, "Mechanics")

A CHECKLIST

DIAGNOSTIC TEST

In serious speech and writing, we should use formal standard English. Look at the blank in each sentence below. Which of the three choices would be right in serious written English? Put the letter for the right choice after the number of the sentence.

EXAMPLE: The relatives had sent tickets for his sister and _____.
         a. he   b. him   c. hisself
(Answer) *b*

1. The people who missed the bus had only _____ to blame.
    a. themself   b. themselves   c. theirselves

2. Changing all the familiar measurements _____ difficult.
   a. was   b. were   c. being

3. She reminded me to lock all windows and _____ off the light.
   a. turns   b. turn   c. turning

4. Almost everyone in our town _____ what had really happened.
   a. knowed   b. known   c. knew

5. _____ a miracle happens, the plant will close.
   a. Without   b. Unless   c. On account of

6. My uncle, my aunt, and _____ went everywhere together.
   a. I   b. me   c. mine

7. We lifted the heavy chest _____ .
   a. real careful   b. very careful   c. very carefully

8. Exercise is essential when people _____ at a desk all day.
   a. sit   b. set   c. sitting

9. As the plane lifted off, the engine _____ to sputter.
   a. begins   b. begun   c. began

10. You should _____ to us about the problem.
    a. of wrote   b. have wrote   c. have written

11. We did everything exactly _____ the instructions said.
    a. as   b. like   c. as if

12. Ron is the kind of person who takes good care of _____ .
    a. himself   b. hisself   c. themselves

13. _____ kind of suit went out of style years ago.
    a. Them   b. Those   c. That

14. There _____ a form and a self-addressed envelope on the desk.
    a. is   b. are   c. be

15. What I just told you is strictly between you and _____ .
    a. I   b. me   c. mine

16. The dog passed the spot where we _____ hidden.
    a. been   b. was   c. were

17. I studied languages, but he was not interested in _____ .
    a. it   b. them   c. this

18. Drivers should check the rearview mirror when _____ start the car.
    a. they   b. you   c. he

19. They loved leaving the trail and _____ a rare plant or bird.
    a. discover   b. to discover   c. discovering

20. The sheriff gave us advice on how to protect _____ own property.
    a. our   b. your   c. their

U1

STANDARD AND NONSTANDARD

Be able to speak and write standard English.

Standard English is the language of our institutions and of the mass media. We find it in almost everything that appears in print—newspapers, books, magazines, and circulars. It is the language of business correspondence, government paperwork, and legal documents. Anyone who works in an office must be able to speak and write standard English.

At home or on the job, many Americans speak a different kind of English. For want of a better word, we call their language **non-standard.** In many ways, the vocabulary and sentence structure of standard and nonstandard English are alike. The differences are in forms and expressions that are common in everyday speech:

He decided to do the work *hisself.*
The bus *don't* stop at this corner.
No one told us you *was* interested.
Has anyone seen *them* envelopes?

The forms of nonstandard English are not errors or mistakes. They are used by people the way they have learned them, according to the rules of their kind of English. But in many situations, nonstandard English is *out of place.* When someone is applying for a white-collar job, nonstandard English is a handicap. When dealing with anything that involves forms or regulations, the person who knows only nonstandard English is at a disadvantage. Do not let nonstandard English hold you back.

Use standard forms of verbs.

Verbs are words like *ask, bring, shorten,* and *accelerate.* Some verb forms of nonstandard English are different from those of standard English. Study and practice the standard forms:

(1) Use the final –s *for third person, singular.* Verbs change to show changes in *number.* When we talk about the present, verbs change to show the change from "one single third party" to "several." The change from one to several is the change from **singular** to **plural:**

The bus *stops.*	Several buses *stop.*
The mayor *agrees.*	My parents *agree.*

Use the –s form when talking about the present, and about one person or thing. In other words, use it when *he, she,* or *it* could take the place of the subject. These are the **third person** pronouns. They do not point to the person speaking (*I* or *we:* **first person**). They do not point to the "second party"—the one we are speaking to (*you:* **second person**). All of the following sentences talk about one third party, with "action now":

THIRD PERSON:	The owner *locks* the gate.	She *locks* it at night.
THIRD PERSON:	My brother *reads* the news.	He *reads* it every morning.
THIRD PERSON:	The bus *stops* here.	It *stops* here every time.

Be sure to use *doesn't* (or *does not*) for third person, singular:

NONSTANDARD:	The lock *don't* work.	She *don't* like me.
STANDARD:	The lock *doesn't* work.	She *doesn't* like me.

See **U3a** for agreement problems in the written sentence.

(2) Use standard forms for the past tense. Verbs change to show changes in *time*. Almost all English verbs change from present to past. Such changes are called changes in **tense.** Most English verbs, the **regular** verbs, form their past by adding *–d* or *–ed* to their present forms. Do not omit this ending:

NONSTANDARD:	Last year, she always *park* in the driveway.
STANDARD:	Last year, she always *parked* in the driveway.

Other English verbs, the **irregular** verbs, make up their past forms in their own ways: *know/knew, grow/grew, throw/threw, bring/brought. Knowed, growed, throwed,* and *brang* are nonstandard.

(3) Use standard forms for the perfect tenses. Many verbs have one form for the simple past. They have another form for use after *have (has, had)*. We call the forms that use *have* the **perfect** tenses. They often show that something has happened recently, or that it still mattered when something else took place:

PRESENT:	I *write* many letters.
PAST:	She *wrote* home every week.
PERFECT:	We *have written* to the mayor about it.
PAST PERFECT:	She *had written* careful instructions.

Study the past and perfect forms of familiar English verbs in the "Checklist of Standard Forms" on the next page. Take up one group of ten verbs at a time.

–S ENDING OF THE VERB FOR THIRD PERSON, SINGULAR:

VETERAN RETURNS MEDALS

Judge Sentences Bandit

Police Chief
Resigns

UNCLE SAM ADMITS WIRETAPS

TERRORIST HOLDS HOSTAGE

ENGLISH VERBS: A Checklist of Standard Forms

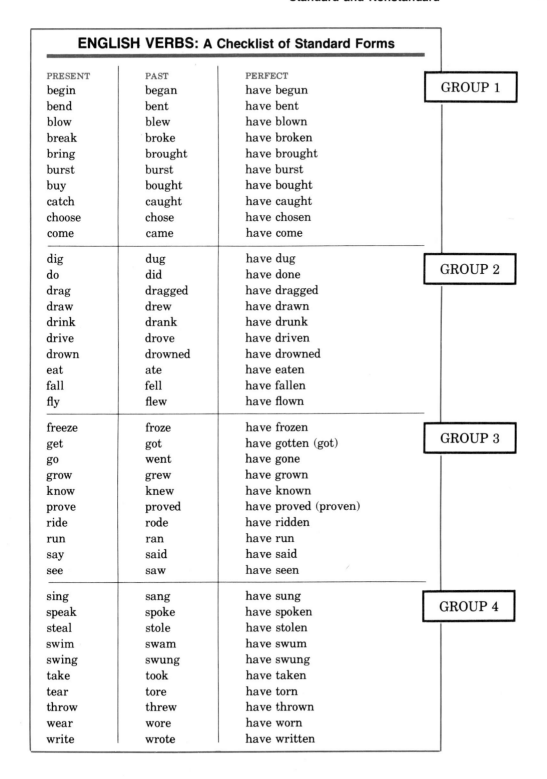

PRESENT	PAST	PERFECT	
begin	began	have begun	**GROUP 1**
bend	bent	have bent	
blow	blew	have blown	
break	broke	have broken	
bring	brought	have brought	
burst	burst	have burst	
buy	bought	have bought	
catch	caught	have caught	
choose	chose	have chosen	
come	came	have come	
dig	dug	have dug	**GROUP 2**
do	did	have done	
drag	dragged	have dragged	
draw	drew	have drawn	
drink	drank	have drunk	
drive	drove	have driven	
drown	drowned	have drowned	
eat	ate	have eaten	
fall	fell	have fallen	
fly	flew	have flown	
freeze	froze	have frozen	**GROUP 3**
get	got	have gotten (got)	
go	went	have gone	
grow	grew	have grown	
know	knew	have known	
prove	proved	have proved (proven)	
ride	rode	have ridden	
run	ran	have run	
say	said	have said	
see	saw	have seen	
sing	sang	have sung	**GROUP 4**
speak	spoke	have spoken	
steal	stole	have stolen	
swim	swam	have swum	
swing	swung	have swung	
take	took	have taken	
tear	tore	have torn	
throw	threw	have thrown	
wear	wore	have worn	
write	wrote	have written	

Remember especially:

• Do not use *wrote* and *went* after *have*. Forms like *had wrote* and *should have went* are nonstandard. Use *had written* and *should have gone* instead. (Never spell *could of* or *would of* instead of *could have* and *would have*.)

• In standard English, forms like *seen* and *done* cannot by themselves serve as complete verbs. Use auxiliaries as needed: Change "I *seen* him" to "I *have seen* him." Change "He *done* it" to "He *has done* it."

NOTE: The same form that follows *have* follows a form of *be (am, are, is, was, were)* when we use the passive:

PASSIVE: The letters *were written.*   The plans *had been stolen.*

(4) Use standard forms of be*. Be is different from all other verbs. It has three present forms: am, are, is. It has two past forms: was, were. Study the following chart:*

		SINGULAR	PLURAL
PRESENT	FIRST PERSON: SECOND PERSON: THIRD PERSON:	I *am* glad. You *are* right, Jim. Phil *is* absent. He *is* ill. Sue *is* here. She *is* well. The food *is* ready. It *is* hot.	We *are* glad. You *are* both right. The parcels *are* here. They *are* heavy.
PAST	FIRST PERSON: SECOND PERSON: THIRD PERSON:	I *was* glad. You *were* right, Jim. Phil *was* absent. He *was* ill. Sue *was* here. She *was* well. The food *was* ready. It *was* hot.	We *were* glad. You *were* both right. The parcels *were* here. They *were* heavy.

Remember: *We was, you was,* and *they was* are nonstandard. Use *we were, you were,* and *they were.*

EXERCISE 1

All of the following examples show the *right* verb forms for standard English. Read over the examples in each set several times.

1. I *work* late. He *works* nights. She *works* days. I *say* something. You *say* something back. She *says* little. The rules *say* nothing about it. This sentence *says* it all. We *ask* for support. Children always *ask* questions. He *asks* the right questions. She never *asks* anybody. My brother always *asks* me.

2. I *don't* believe it. They *don't* know. The instructions *don't* say. He *doesn't* believe you. She *doesn't* work here anymore. It *doesn't* matter. Flattery *doesn't* always work. Crime *doesn't* pay. Your friend *doesn't* know the difference. The pumps *don't* work. Many people *don't* care.

3. She *brought* it back yesterday. They *brought* good news. We *knew* the answer. I always *knew* the story. Her uncle *grew* flowers. Jean *grew* taller each year. Grandfather *grew* a beard. She shouted when she *threw* the ball. The court *threw* out the case. The pitcher *threw* a curve. The wind *blew* the roof off. Ray *blew* the trumpet.

4. He *wrote* it; I had *written* it. She *wrote* a letter; I have *written* a letter. He *went* home; she had *gone* home. Marion *went;* your friends have *gone.* They *came* in; they could have *come* in. He *broke* the seal; she had *broken* the seal; it had already been *broken.* He *wore* the new tie; he had *worn* it before. Somebody *stole* the car; the car had been *stolen.*

5. I *have done* nothing wrong; they *have done* everything they could; he *has done* something very unusual. We *have seen* your brother; she *has seen* the movie; I *have seen* nothing like it. He *has gone* home; she *has gone* downtown; I *have gone* there many times.

6. I *am* ready. He *is* late. She *is* missing. We *are* ready now. The stores *are* open. Rabbits *are* hard to catch. Nurses *are* underpaid. The store *is* closed. Their pancakes *are* the best. My cousin *is* hard to please. Some parents *are* hard to please. We*'re* happy to see you. You*'re* the only one.

7. The phone *was* ringing. I *was* awake. She *was* out of town. It *was* late. We *were* first. You *were* absent. They *were* rude. The stores *were* crowded. People *were* laughing. *Were* you working? What *were* they doing? Couples *were* dancing in the street. Flags *were* flapping. *Were* you invited? We *were* tired of it. They *were* trying. Some *were* trapped.

In each of the following sentences, you are given a choice of two forms. Write the *standard form* after the number of the sentence.

EXERCISE 2

(A) 1. The main characters in the story *is/are* a crippled girl named Betsy and a boy, Joe Anderson.
2. The story *is/are* about a home for the handicapped.
3. Betsy *meets/meet* Joe Anderson there.
4. Mostly teenagers and older people *lives/live* there.
5. All her friends *feels/feel* sorry for Betsy.
6. Betsy however *doesn't/don't* want pity.
7. Betsy and Joe *becomes/become* good friends.
8. They *shares/share* every minute of the day with each other.
9. At the end of the story, both *gets/get* well.
10. They *leaves/leave* the home where they met.

(B) 11. Your friends have already *went/gone* home.
12. She always *did/done* her work first.
13. She *was/were* sure it would rain.
14. Your sister should have *come/came* to the picnic.
15. The car had been *stole/stolen* from a parking garage.
16. The guard *saw/seen* them open the gate.
17. The owner *don't/doesn't* allow bare feet.
18. He had *wrote/written* the wrong address on the envelope.
19. Hundreds of people *was/were* ahead of us in the line.
20. They *threw/thrown* our baggage onto the back of the truck.

EXERCISE 3

In each of the following sentences, fill in the *standard form* of the verb listed at the end. After the number of the sentence, write down the form that fits into the blank space. (Do not add any *auxiliaries* not already supplied.) Write on a separate sheet of paper.

EXAMPLE: The wind had _____ the roof off. (blow)
(Answer) *blown*

1. They always look hurt when I _____ no. (say)
2. He never told us what he _____ last summer. (do)
3. If the letter _____ not come tomorrow, it will be too late. (do)
4. As we left, someone _____ rocks at us. (throw)
5. Where _____ you when the fire started? (be)
6. What have I _____ wrong? (do)
7. The band left, and the guests _____ home. (go)
8. When I saw her last, she _____ nothing about it. (know)
9. Fred had _____ an urgent letter to his parents. (write)
10. It was the biggest parade I had ever _____. (see)
11. Ralph had never _____ to anyone in his class. (speak)
12. Blizzards last winter _____ headaches for motorists. (bring)
13. Whenever I try to study, my brothers _____ making a racket. (be)
14. Most of the students had already _____ to the library. (go)
15. He has _____ the suit only a few times. (wear)
16. After she left, weeds _____ all over the yard. (grow)
17. I _____ last week that she would not agree. (know)
18. The neighbors _____ talking quietly when the police arrived. (be)
19. Remember that one swallow _____ not make a summer. (do)
20. The sky cleared, and a stiff wind _____. (blow)

U1b
Standard Pronoun Forms

Use the standard forms of pronouns.

Know the standard forms of several kinds of pronouns:

(1) Avoid nonstandard forms of **demonstrative** *pronouns.* These are the "pointing pronouns": *this* and *these; that* and *those.*

STANDARD FORMS OF PRONOUNS

A CHECKLIST

| Demonstrative: ("pointing" pronouns) | *this* book | *that* book |
| | *these* books | *those* books |

Possessive: (two sets)	*my* book	it's *mine*
	your book	it's *yours*
	his book	it's *his*
	her book	it's *hers*
	its book	it's *its*
	our book	it's *ours*
	their book	it's *theirs*

Reflexive: ("pointing back")	I did it *myself*
	you hurt *yourself* (singular)
	he did it *himself*
	she introduced *herself*
	it explained *itself*
	we covered *ourselves*
	you covered *yourselves* (plural)
	they did it *themselves*

Avoid expressions like *this here book* or *that there shelf.* Do not use expressions like *them books* or *them people.*

STANDARD: The apples are from *this* tree.
Put *that* package back on the shelf.
She found *those* nails in the shed.

(2) *Avoid nonstandard forms of* **reflexive** *pronouns.* These are the *–self* pronouns. The singular forms are *myself, yourself, himself, herself,* and *itself.* The plural forms are *ourselves, yourselves,* and *themselves.* Typically, the *–self* pronouns point back to something in the same sentence. Avoid the nonstandard forms *hisself, ourself, theirself* or *theirselves,* as well as *yourself* used as a plural.

STANDARD: He always checked the locks *himself.*
We introduced *ourselves* to the host.
You girls should be proud of *yourselves.*
They found the way by *themselves.*

(3) *Avoid nonstandard uses of* **possessive** *pronouns.* At one time, many people used nonstandard forms like *yourn, hisn, hern,*

or *ourn.* The standard forms for these are *yours, his, hers,* or *ours:*

STANDARD: Half of the money is *yours.*
The responsibility is *hers.*
Your car is parked next to *ours.*

NOTE: Standard English omits the added *he* or *she* in sentences like "My father, *he* asked them to leave" or "My aunt, *she* became a lawyer."

STANDARD: *My father asked* them to leave.   *My aunt became* a lawyer.

See **U2b** for subject forms and object forms of personal pronouns.

EXERCISE 1

In each of the following sentences, you are given a choice of two forms. Write the *standard form* after the number of the sentence. (Write on a separate sheet of paper.)

1. Take *them/those* boxes back to the basement.
2. You boys should make *yourself/yourselves* useful.
3. The singer had written all his songs *hisself/himself.*
4. As her only sister, you *yourself/yourselves* should have helped her.
5. No one tells *them/those* old tales the way my aunt does.
6. The Smiths yearned to see *theirself/themselves* in the social register.
7. The new boy very quickly made *hisself/himself* unpopular.
8. Take what is *yours/yourn* and leave the rest alone.
9. We excused *ourself/ourselves* as early as we could.
10. *This here/This* mansion was built in 1859.
11. We have to protect *ourself/ourselves.*
12. No one saw *that there/that* notice until today.
13. You should both prepare *yourself/yourselves* for bad news.
14. We only want what is *ours/ourn.*
15. The minister *himself/hisself* came to the door.
16. Her friends moved into one of *them/those* new apartment houses.
17. The newcomers introduced *themselves/theirselves* to us.
18. I refuse to believe *them/those* figures.
19. You were a guest and should have behaved *yourself/yourselves.*
20. *My friend he/My friend* was unable to help.

EXERCISE 2

In each of the following sentences, fill in the appropriate *standard form* of the missing pronoun. After the number of each sentence, write down the pronoun that would best fit into the blank space. (Write on a separate sheet of paper.)

EXAMPLE: I'll mind my business if you'll mind _____ .
(Answer) *yours*

1. Jim and I took off our coats, but Ted kept _____ on.
2. I enjoyed myself, but my guests enjoyed _____ more than I did.
3. They did their work and we did _____ .
4. We got our parcel in time, but the Smiths got _____ late.
5. The man carried his suitcase, and the woman carried _____ .
6. If a boy can introduce himself, girls can introduce _____ too.
7. If I can do the job by myself, why can't your brother do it by _____ ?
8. I will tell you my story after you tell me _____ .
9. When we went out, I paid my check and she paid _____ .
10. After we painted the kitchen ourselves, the Garcias decided to paint theirs _____ also.

Learn to avoid nonstandard expressions.

Some nonstandard expressions are common only in parts of the country, like the *reckon* in "I *reckon* I'll just have to be late." Others are in more general use. If you use any of the nonstandard expressions listed below, learn to shift to the standard ways of saying the same thing.

(1) Avoid the double negative. The **double negative** is an expression that says no twice. In "I *didn't* say *nothing*," the *didn't* already tells us no. Then the *nothing* tells us no again.

NONSTANDARD: I *didn't* say *nothing*.
STANDARD: I *didn't* say *anything*. I said *nothing*.

NONSTANDARD: She *couldn't* find *none*.
STANDARD: She *couldn't* find *any*. She found *none*.

Similar to double negatives are expressions like *couldn't hardly* or *can't barely:*

STANDARD: They *could barely* keep their eyes open.
Her uncle *could hardly* speak English.

NOTE: The word *irregardless* doubles the idea of "without." Use *regardless* instead.

(2) Avoid nonstandard plurals of nouns. We leave out the plural –s in hyphenated combinations that come before another noun: a *two-hour* interval, a *ten-year* stretch, a *two-inch* layer. But expressions like "five year" or "ten mile" are nonstandard when used by themselves in a sentence:

STANDARD: She worked there five *years*. We ran ten *miles*.

Do *not* add the plural –s to irregular plurals like *children, men, women, freshmen.* Know unusual plurals like *knives* and *calves.*

(3) Avoid double comparisons when using adjectives and adverbs. To show degree, use either the *–er* and *–est* endings, or the words *more* and *most*. Do not use both. Expressions like "more taller" and "most friendliest" are nonstandard:

STANDARD: She is *taller* than Ed. He is *friendliest.*

NOTE: *3ad, worse,* and *worst* are standard. Do not use forms like *worser* or *baddest.*

(4) Avoid nonstandard connectives. All of the following are nonstandard when they are used to mean *because: being as, being that, seeing as how,* and *on account of.*

NONSTANDARD: *Being as* he was a friend, I gave him the key.
STANDARD: *Because* he was a friend, I gave him the key.

NONSTANDARD: We failed *on account of* the rope broke.
STANDARD: We failed *because* the rope broke.

Without and *on account of* are standard as prepositions before a noun: *without* your help, *on account of* your friendship. They are nonstandard if they start a clause with its own subject and verb:

NONSTANDARD: They will sue *without* we pay the bill.
STANDARD: They will sue *unless* we pay the bill.

(5) Avoid using a *and* an *in nonstandard ways. An* is standard before words beginning with a vowel sound. *A* is standard only if the word does *not* start with a vowel sound:

An: *an* ear, *an* ace, *an* offer, *an* easy task, *an* hour, *an F*
A: *a* car, *a* tree, *a* station, *a* horse, *a C,* *a* useful tool

(6) Avoid other familiar nonstandard expressions. Watch out for the following:

learned me In standard English, a teacher *teaches* something to the student. The student *learns* something from the teacher:

STANDARD: *Teach* me what you have *learned.*
          I *learned* well in the classes he *taught.*

nowheres, some- The standard expressions are *nowhere, somewhere,* and
  wheres, nohow *not at all:*

STANDARD: She was *nowhere* to be found.
          We could *not* persuade him *at all.*

off of Use *off* or *from* instead of *off of:*

NONSTANDARD: He borrowed ten dollars *off of* his sister.
STANDARD: He borrowed ten dollars *from* his sister.

leave In standard English, *leave* means "to go away from," and *let* means "to permit or allow":

NONSTANDARD: Please *leave* me join the club.
STANDARD: Please *let* me join the club.

They is, Use *there is* or *there was* instead:
 They was

STANDARD: *There* is little time. *There's* not much left. *There* was trouble. *There* was more to it.

Read over the examples in the following sets to help you avoid double negatives and other nonstandard expressions. All examples show the forms that are right in standard English.

EXERCISE 1

1. We *don't* have *any* time. We have *no* time to lose.
   Jim *never* did *any* work for *any*body.
   We *weren't* afraid of *anyone*. We were afraid of *no one*.
   We *never* go *anywhere*. We *don't* ever go *anywhere*.

2. I *could hardly* keep from laughing.
   This room *would scarcely* hold all the people.
   The car *could barely* make it up the hill.
   I *can hardly* believe my eyes.

3. They were hiring people *regardless* of age.
   We should apply for the job *regardless*.
   Chris fixed the roof *without any* help.

4. She *taught* English to students *learning* it as a second language.
   We *learned* Spanish from someone *teaching* it by a new method.
   You should *let* us *leave* early.
   They *let* us eat what we wanted and *leave* the rest.

5. A young girl rode *a* horse down *a* street.
   An elderly man put *an* unsigned letter in *an* envelope.
   It's *a* pity it's such *an* old story.
   We wanted *a* total success or *an* absolute failure.

Each of the following sentences has one word or expression in it that is nonstandard English. After the number of the sentence, write the standard form that should replace it.

EXERCISE 2

EXAMPLE: My mother learned me to swim.
(Answer) *taught*

1. We couldn't do nothing to stop him.

283

2. The class hadn't hardly started.
3. We aren't going nowheres without you.
4. He went nowhere without we paid his way.
5. Seeing as how I was sorry, he let me go.
6. We moved out on account of the roof leaked.
7. My sister learned me to mow the lawn.
8. Being as it was late, we went home.
9. He hadn't never heard of the company.
10. Carol didn't tell nobody about her plans.
11. The noise continued irregardless of our complaints.
12. Being that I was ill, I ignored the request.
13. All I need is a excuse.
14. He borrowed money off of perfect strangers.
15. I realize I can't do nothing about it.
16. The hikers had gone about twenty mile.
17. She never told her family nothing about the accident.
18. There must be a more quicker way to notify them.
19. She was scheduled for a checkup by a ear specialist.
20. The injured player can't barely lift her right arm.

UNIT REVIEW EXERCISE

Revise examples of nonstandard English in the following sentences from Ring Lardner's short story "Haircut." After the number of each italicized word or expression, write down the appropriate standard form. If the expression *is* standard English, put *S* after the number instead.

A. You can see for yourself that this (1) *ain't no* New York City.
B. Most of the boys (2) *works* all day and (3) *don't have no leisure* to drop in here and get (4) *themselves* prettied up.
C. Jim and his wife (5) *wasn't* on very good terms.
D. (6) *She'd of divorced* him, only (7) *they wasn't no* chance to get alimony, and she (8) *didn't have no way* to take care of (9) *herself* and the kids.
E. Then (10) *they was* a story that Doc Stair's gal (11) *had throwed* him over, up in the Northern peninsula (12) *somewheres,* and the reason he (13) *come* here was to hide.
F. (14) *She'd came* on the same business I had.
G. Her mother (15) *had been* doctoring for years with Doc Gamble and Doc Foote (16) *without no results.*
H. Joe (17) *went* to Jim the next day and told him what would happen if he (18) *ever done* it again.
I. They (19) *was scared* to tell him, and he (20) *might of never knowed* only for Paul Dickson.
J. I (21) *ain't no* mind reader, but it (22) *was wrote* all over her face.
K. Paul (23) *hadn't never handled* a gun, and (24) *he was* nervous.
L. Jim was a sucker to (25) *leave* a new beginner have his gun.

Be able to shift from informal to formal standard English.

Standard English does not stay the same for all occasions. The basic difference is between informal and formal standard English:

(1) Informal English is typically spoken English. We speak informally when we are with friends, family, and other people we know. We write informally in most of our personal letters. We see informal English in print in pieces meant to be casual or entertaining. We see it when a writer has a character in a short story or novel tell the story the way the writer might tell it to friends.

In Walter Van Tilburg Clark's *The Ox-Bow Incident,* the whole story is told the way someone might tell it around a fire to a group of friends or neighbors. Do you recognize the features that make the following passage an example of informal English?

INFORMAL: Gil was *tight* enough so I could see him squinting, sometimes two or three times, to *make out* what he had in his hand, but he was having a big *run of luck.* I knew he *wasn't* cheating; Gil *didn't.* Even if *he'd* wanted to he *couldn't,* with hands like his, not even sober. But *with his gripe on* he *wasn't* taking his winning right. He *wasn't* showing any signs of being pleased, not boasting, or *bulling* the others along about *how thin they'd have to live,* the way you would in an ordinary game with a *bunch of friends.* He was just sitting there with a sullen dead-pan and *raking in the pots* slow and *contemptuous, like* he expected it. . . . You *couldn't* play long with a man acting like that *without getting your chin out,* especially when he was winning three hands out of four. I was *getting riled* myself.

(2) Formal English is typically written English. It is the language of reports, articles, editorials, and announcements. Formal written English is appropriate when you write a letter to the editor or to your congressional representative. It is appropriate when you write a paper on a serious topic or when you answer an examination question. We hear formal English *spoken* on serious public occasions: a lecture, a court hearing, or a board meeting.

In Van Tilburg Clark's novel, the judge and the minister use "platform speech" considerably more formal than that of the narrator. What features make their language formal, fit for public occasions?

FORMAL: You *cannot flinch* from what you believe to be your duty, of course, but certainly you *would not wish to* act *in the very spirit* which *begot the deed* you would punish. . . . If such an awful thing has actually *occurred,* it is *the more reason* that we should *retain our self-possession.* . . . *Let us not* act hastily; let us not do *that which we will regret.* We must act, certainly, but we must act in a *reasoned and legitimate manner,* not as a lawless mob.

U2a

Informal Words

Learn to recognize informal words and expressions.

Some words and expressions have a strong informal flavor. They seem out of place in a formal context. Such words are often labeled **colloquial**—conversational, fit for casual talk.

In the following sentences, the italicized words strongly suggest informal speech:

There was something about him which made people *cotton* to him.
Maybe if we do one job with our own hands, the law will *get a move on*.
He had his chin down on his chest, like he was both guilty and *licked*.

Remember:

(1) Replace words and expressions that are too informal for the occasion. Here are some colloquial words, with the formal words that might replace them in serious discussion and writing:

INFORMAL	FORMAL
act up	be unruly
boss	employer
bug	germ
flunk	fail
folks	people, family
gang up on	band together against
goof	make a mistake
gripe	complain
kid around	joke
mess	disorder
mope	brood, sulk
ornery	cantankerous
pal, buddy	friend
sloppy	untidy

Here are some *special colloquial* uses of words that are also used in other, more formal ways:

INFORMAL	FORMAL
a *lot* of money	*much* money
a *bunch* of people	a *group* of people
fire someone	*dismiss* someone
looked *funny*	looked *strange*
got *mad*	became *angry*

JOINING THE GREAT MAJORITY

What kind of language do we use when talking about the great milestones in human lives—birth, marriage, death? Often, there is a *formal* way of talking that makes the event seem solemn or dignified. At the same time, there is an *informal* way of talking that makes us look at the same event with wry humor or irreverence. In the following examples of expressions used about death, which is which? After the number of each expression, write *F* for "formal" or *Inf* for "informal." Explain what guided your choice in each case.

1. Your uncle has gone to his final reward.
2. Mr. Smith died in harness at the age of 62.
3. He is pushing up the daisies.
4. She has slipped into the great democracy of the dead.
5. She was taken by the Grim Reaper.
6. She finally popped off.
7. He has gone to his last sleep.
8. He's cashed in his chips.
9. He's been planted.
10. He came home feet first.
11. She was laid under the sod.
12. She had shuffled off this mortal coil.

Bonus Project: Euphemisms are "beautiful words" that we use to soften harsh realities. How many different euphemisms can you gather for the following: a dead person, a mortuary, a cemetery?

Here are some examples of *"shirt-sleeve"* English that would seem out of place in a serious study or report:

let's not kid ourselves	hassle over something
something's got to give	here's the pitch
throw in the sponge	have a crack at it
pull out all the stops	get down to brass tacks
pop the question	use some elbow grease

(2) Use abbreviations and contractions sparingly. Many of the shortcuts of everyday speech are *informal.* Informal English uses many shortened words like *tux, lab, math, bike,* and *phone.* It freely uses **contractions** like *don't, can't, won't, isn't,* and *aren't.*

(3) Use slang only for special purposes or special effects. When language becomes *extremely informal,* it becomes **slang.** Slang is

"language that is being slung about instead of being handled with stately consideration." It is often vigorous, colorful, and to the point. At the same time it is *limited* language. It is often the private language of a group and not shared by outsiders. It is often faddish, changing rapidly as new words are repeated over and over until they are in turn replaced. Much of it is disrespectful, exaggerated, or weird.

Can you see some of these features of slang illustrated in the following examples?

nonsense:	claptrap, bosh, flapdoodle, twaddle, baloney, bunk
money:	folding green, dough, bread, moolah
dullard:	chump, hayseed, rube, jerk, drip, sap, clod, dope, square
face:	kisser, mug
miser:	tightwad, cheapskate, skinflint
top person:	big shot, bigwig, big wheel, big cheese, VIP

NOTE: Formal words are not always "big words" that someone just found in the dictionary. Often they are short and simple, familiar to everyone. The main difference is that they sound more serious, more businesslike than "shirt-sleeve English."

EXERCISE 1

Study the italicized words or expressions in each of the following sentences. Which of the three is *more informal* than the rest of the sentence? Write it after the number of the sentence. (Write on a separate sheet.)

1. *A lot of* information is *available* on how to *find* a job.
2. The *important* thing is to *know* when you are *licked*.
3. There is *no point* in *having a crack at* a job if you are not *suited* to the work that will be required.
4. If you have *moist* hands, do not *knock yourself out* to become a *watchmaker.*
5. With their tiny parts *rusty* from the *moisture,* your watches would be *no good.*
6. If you are *extremely* short, *forget* any ambition to *become a trombonist.*
7. You have to have *fairly* long arms to *belt out* those *low notes.*
8. If you always *flub* your lines or have difficulty memorizing, you will not *succeed* in the *theater.*
9. If you are *sloppy,* you should not *train* to be a *manicurist.*
10. The armed services *refuse* to train *a bunch* of *incompetents.*
11. The other day I *ran across* a *brochure* from the *navy.*
12. The *services* would rather choose *alert* young people than *pooped* older people.
13. If you *sport* an *offensive* tattoo, you are *ineligible.*
14. Similarly, you *have had it* if you *happen* to be *extremely* ugly.
15. It seems *funny,* however, that an applicant *need not* know how to *swim.*

16. It is harder to *keep tabs on* what the army *expects of* its *recruits*.
17. It *does not* want *disturbed* people who *get into scrapes*.
18. It does not want *rebellious* people who *buck* superior *authority*.
19. *Goofing off* will *keep you out of* officer *training*.
20. The navy has *numerous* reasons for *telling* officer candidates to *beat it*.

EXERCISE 2

Study the words in each of the following sets. After the number of each set, write those words that you consider informal. (Be prepared to discuss your choices with your classmates.)

1. second-rate, so-so, mediocre
2. bush league, rookie, minor league
3. straphanger, road hog, commuter
4. wishy-washy, vice versa, hoity-toity
5. hogwash, eyewash, washed up
6. sit tight, stand firm, sit pretty
7. shindig, hoopla, party
8. slugfest, fight, fisticuffs
9. jalopy, Model T, hot rod
10. informer, snitch, stool pigeon

EXERCISE 3

Choose *five* of the following sets. For each expression in the set, write down a more formal expression with roughly the same meaning.

1. hit the books; hit the ceiling; hit pay dirt
2. monkeyshines; monkey business; grease monkey
3. looked beat; was a deadbeat; beat it!
4. a bum check; to bum a ride; machine went on the bum
5. souped-up model; got me into the soup; plane got lost in the soup
6. that figures; figure it out; I figured I was wrong
7. that bugs me; get the bugs out of the machine; flu bug
8. looked run down; run down the facts; gave me the runaround
9. show off; show up; show somebody up
10. sweat out a promotion; sweat blood; no sweat

EXERCISE 4

Find three examples of current *student slang* for which the outsider would need a translation. Explain and illustrate each expression in a short paragraph. (Your teacher may ask you to present your findings as an oral report or to hand them in as a short paper.)

EXAMPLE: "The beak" is a student term suggesting that one's nose gets pushed out of shape by some displeasing incident or remark. For example, "I got a low mark on the biology test—do I have the beak!"

U2b
Pronoun Case

Use the formal forms of pronouns.

Most personal pronouns have two forms. We use *I* or *me,* *she* or *her,* depending on how the pronoun fits into the sentence. *I, he, she, we,* and *they* are **subject forms.** We use the subject form when the pronoun is the *subject* of the sentence:

SUBJECT FORM		
I	asked them for advice.
She	went for an interview.
They	returned the merchandise.

Me, him, her, us, and *them* are **object forms.** We use the object form when the pronoun is the *object* of the verb. We also use it when the pronoun is the object of a preposition:

OBJECT FORM		
My friends supported	*me.*	
The company hired	*him.*	
The agency will send	*them* the forms.	
He left a package	for *me.*	
Carol received a letter	from *her.*	
We had been talking	about *them.*	

We will call the difference between subject form and object form a difference in pronoun **case.** In written English, and in formal speech, avoid familiar informal uses of pronoun forms:

(1) Choose the right pronoun when it is part of a **compound subject** *or* **compound object.** If there are several subjects for the same verb, use the pronoun form that would fit if there were only one subject. Do not use "Sue and *him* turned back." (We would not say "*him* turned back.")

SUBJECT: Sue *and I* had a quarrel.
She and her parents had gone.
They and their poodle went everywhere.
He and his brothers had left town.

If there are *several objects* for the same verb, use the form that would fit if there were only *one* object. Do not use "He asked Jim and *I.*" (You would not say "she asked *I.*")

OBJECT: We saw Tom *and her.*
They had invited the Smiths *and me.*

If there are *several objects* for the same preposition, use the form that would fit if there were only *one* object. Do not use "a letter for you and *I*." (You would not say "a letter for *I*.")

OBJECT: This is strictly between you *and me.*
They left a note for you *and her.*

(2) Choose the right form when a pronoun combines with a noun. Use the subject form when a combination like "we Texans" or "we scouts" is the subject. Use the object form ("us Texans," "us scouts") when the combination is the object of a verb or preposition:

FORMAL: *We scouts* trust each other. They trusted *us scouts.*
We Texans like open spaces. He liked *us Texans.*

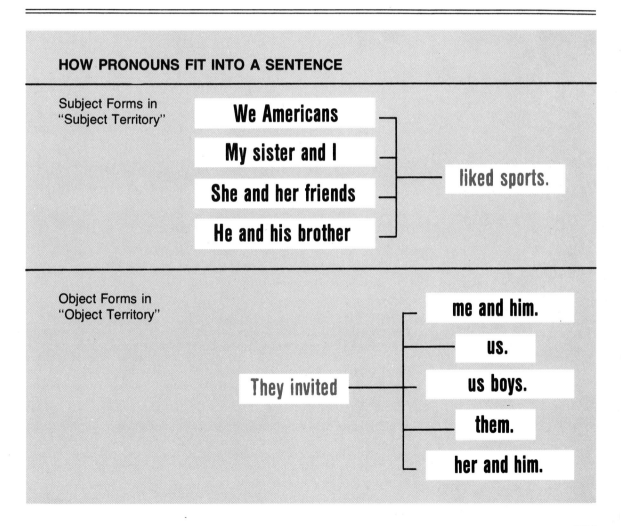

HOW PRONOUNS FIT INTO A SENTENCE

Subject Forms in "Subject Territory"

We Americans
My sister and I
She and her friends
He and his brother

liked sports.

Object Forms in "Object Territory"

They invited

me and him.
us.
us boys.
them.
her and him.

(3) Use the subject form after a form of be. *Be (is, was, has been, will be)* is a linking verb and does not take an object. After the linking verb, formal English requires the subject form. In formal usage, avoid *it's him, that's her, it's us, it's them.*

FORMAL: It is always *she* who does all the work.
The only people still there were *he* and his friend.

NOTE: Some informal uses of pronouns are so much a part of everyday speech that the formal choices have come to sound awkward. "It's me" is so generally accepted that "it is I" is almost never heard.

(4) Use the right form in shortened comparisons. Fill in the missing part of a comparison to decide whether the subject form or object form is right:

FORMAL: She knows more than *I* (do).
I know you better than (I know) *him*.
Few people dance as well as *he* (does).
They got up earlier than *we* (did).

(5) Use who *as a subject form and* whom *as an object form.* When used as a question word, *who* asks a question about the subject. Use it when *he* or *they* are possible answers. *Whom* asks a question about the object of a verb or preposition. Use it when *him* or *them* are possible answers:

FORMAL: *Who* told you? (*He* did.) *Whom* did you tell? (I told *him*.)
Who wrote that? (*He* did.) To *whom* did you write? (I wrote to *him*.)

Who as a relative pronoun is the *subject* of its clause. *Whom* is the *object* of a verb or preposition in its clause:

FORMAL: I remember the person/ *who* hired me. (*He* hired me.)
I remember the person/ *whom* I hired. (I hired *him*.)
I remember the person/ for *whom* I worked. (I worked for *her*.)

EXERCISE 1

The sentences in the following sets all show formal uses of pronouns. Read the sentences in each set over several times.

1. *He and* Marcia left. Sam *and I* knew. *We and* the neighbors never got along. *They and* their children love the snow. *She and* her cousin returned to Wyoming.

2. The officer questioned my brother *and me*. The agency had notified her husband *and her*. They asked only *us and them*. We saw Tom *and her*.

3. This is between you *and me*. The letter was for my brother *and me*. I have good news for you *and her*. I have nothing against you *and them*. There was no room for our guests *and us*. He stared at us *and them*.

4. *We* girls believed him. He trusted *us* girls. *We* Americans tend to be self-righteous. He admired *us* Americans. *We* foreigners never got to know the natives. The natives were watching *us* foreigners. The natives were suspicious of *us* foreigners. He felt sorry for *us* newcomers.

5. It was *they* who recommended this place. It was *she* who first asked me about it. The only people left were *she* and her friend. It was *we* who discovered the cave. It was *I* who was nominated. I knew it was *she*.

6. Her friend worked faster than *she* (did). I met you earlier than (I did) *her*. You speak Spanish better than *he* (does). You know me better than (you do) *him*. Few people sing as well as *he* (does). I know few people as well as (I do) *him*.

7. *Who* saw you? *Whom* did you see? With *whom* were you seen? *Who* called? *Whom* did you call? For *whom* was the call? *Who* is your friend? *Whom* did your friend invite? To *whom* did she address the invitation?

8. She is the woman *who* asked me. She is the woman *whom* I asked. She is the woman with *whom* I talked. People *who* know him well trust him. People *whom* he knows well enjoy his confidence. People with *whom* he works get to know him well.

Which of the two choices in each sentence is right in *formal usage*? Write the formal choice after the number of the sentence. (Write on a separate sheet of paper.)

EXERCISE 2

1. *She/her* and her friend walked down the street.
2. We had asked Jim and *she/her* to meet us at the corner.
3. It had been a bad year for *we/us* taxpayers.
4. To *who/whom* was the letter addressed?
5. What I say now will have to remain strictly between you and *I/me*.
6. His sister is much better at algebra than *he/him*.
7. I am sure it was *they/them* who called.
8. We talked to the woman *who/whom* was feeding the pigeons.
9. Your father gave me a message for you and *she/her*.
10. My friends and *I/me* loved to walk along the beach.
11. *He/him* and Hod Meyers used to keep this town in an uproar.
12. My uncle loved to send my brother and *I/me* on fool's errands.
13. The only people still waiting were *she/her* and her sister.
14. She was the kind of person for *who/whom* no task is too hard.
15. *We/us* Irish used to look at the English with suspicion.
16. No one sings the old songs as well as *she/her*.
17. It is always *he/him* who leaves first.
18. The man *who/whom* brought the flowers left no name.
19. *She/her* and Fred were sitting by the fire plucking their guitars.
20. *He/him* and his friends had left when we arrived.

EXERCISE 3

Check pronoun case in the following sample sentences. If all pronouns are right for formal use, put *S* for satisfactory after the number of the sentence. If a pronoun is used informally, put the form that would be right in formal usage.

EXAMPLE: She had long held a grudge against my family and I.
(Answer) *me*

1. Do not ask for whom the bell tolls.
2. Mother and me would sit at the window and watch the passersby.
3. The organ-grinder had a monkey who held out a tin cup to the crowd.
4. My sister had always been a better student than me.
5. There will be plenty of work for you and I.
6. The girl introduced my brother and me to her grandparents.
7. Whom would you recommend as a family doctor?
8. Us tourists were welcomed everywhere with open arms.
9. Who did you have in mind as a replacement?
10. She had arranged a crowded schedule for us visitors.
11. That is him over there in the blue shirt.
12. He divided the candy carefully between her sister and her.
13. It was she who taught me to enjoy good books.
14. It is always us boys who get blamed.
15. Jim had promised the boarders and us free tickets.
16. Few neighbors knew the woods as well as Anita and I.
17. Arvin and me had never been to the big city.
18. My brother married Hilda, whom he had met at the World's Fair.
19. We outdoor enthusiasts should help protect our parks and forests.
20. No one would do a better job than him.

U2c
Formal Adverbs

Know the adverb forms required in formal English.

Adjectives are words like *generous, real, smart,* and *lucky.* Adverbs are words like *generously, really, smartly,* and *luckily.* Adjectives modify nouns. They tell us "which one?" or "what kind?" Adverbs modify verbs. They tell how, when, or where something is done.

Notice the adverb forms in the following pairs:

ADJECTIVE: Many *poor* people lived in the neighborhood.
ADVERB: The whole team played *poorly.*

ADJECTIVE: The *quiet* boy on the right is my brother.
ADVERB: The girl was talking *quietly* with her friend.

Informal English often uses adverb forms that are *the same* as the adjective. Formal English uses the *separate* adverb form whenever there is a choice. Remember:

(1) Avoid unmarked informal adverbs in formal English. Remember that adjectives may follow a linking verb that pins a label on the subject. Adverbs modify action verbs, telling us *where, when,* or *how* an action takes place.

ADJECTIVE FOLLOWING A LINKING VERB:

Service was *slow.*
The music sounded *loud.*
Her reply seemed *quick.*

INFORMAL ADVERB WITH ACTION VERB:

We asked her to drive *slow.*
He always talks *loud.*
Come *quick!*

FORMAL ADVERB WITH ACTION VERB:

We asked her to drive *slowly.*
He always talks *loudly.*
Come *quickly!*

> **ADJECTIVE AND ADVERB**

Be sure to use the form with *–ly* to replace the unmarked informal adverbs in expressions like "She worked *steady*" and "It had changed *considerable*":

FORMAL: The women were working *steadily.*
My uncle had aged *considerably.*
We suffered *terribly.*

NOTE: A few adjectives and adverbs are the same in formal English: *fast, long, much, right.*

ADJECTIVE: The *long* march was over.
ADVERB: We did not want to wait *long.*

(2) Use well *and* badly *as formal adverbs to replace the adjectives* good *and* bad. Avoid using expressions like "clean it *good*" or "It was working *good.*" Use *well* to show approval of how something is done:

FORMAL: He is a *good* player. He plays *well.*
We bought a *good* toaster. It works *well.*
A *good* teacher taught her. She performs *well.*

FORMAL: It was a *bad* accident. They were hurt *badly.*
It was a *bad* start. It ended *badly.*

Remember that the adjective forms follow linking verbs: It sounds *good.* I feel *bad.* Everything tasted *bad.*

NOTE: The most common use of *well* is as the formal adverb to go with *good:* a *good* talk; he talked *well.* However, *well* is also used as an adjective in expressions like "He is not *well*" and "The sick child got *well* again."

(3) Avoid informal expressions like real smart *or* awful fast. In formal English, we use the form with *–ly* to modify other adjectives and other adverbs: *really smart, awfully fast, truly sorry, exceptionally well.* When *real* and *awful* are used as informal intensifiers in this way, the best replacement is often *very* or *extremely.* Use *fairly* to replace the *pretty* in *pretty good.*

FORMAL: The train was going *extremely fast.*
Attendance has been *fairly* good.

(4) Avoid the informal sure *used as a sentence modifier.*   Use *surely* or *certainly* as an adverb that applies to a statement as a whole.

FORMAL: They *certainly* work fast.
Surely there is some other way.

For more on adjective and adverb forms see **S1e.**

EXERCISE 1

The following sentences show the right uses of adjectives and adverbs in formal English. Read the sentences in each pair over several times.

1. She made a *good* choice. She chose *well.*
2. Business has been *good.* They knew their business *well.*
3. Spinach is *good* for you. Carlos cooks it *well.*
4. He is not *good* at arithmetic. He does not add very *well.*
5. We had made a *bad* choice. The car worked *badly.*
6. He had had *bad* teachers. He spoke English *badly.*
7. Juan felt *bad.* He had been treated *badly.*
8. The trick looked *easy.* I did it *easily.*
9. You should pay *careful* attention. Lift the lid *carefully.*
10. Look out for the *sharp* turn. The road turns *sharply.*
11. *Steady* work was hard to find. They were working *steadily.*
12. She gave a *solemn* speech. We listened *solemnly.*
13. They were *nice* to us. They treated us *nicely.*
14. Karen has been a *real* friend. She is *really* friendly.
15. We have had *extreme* cold. We are *extremely* sorry.
16. They were sent to *certain* death. You are *certainly* wrong.
17. We cannot be completely *sure.* He *surely* made a mistake.
18. A *fast* check confirmed the story. They answered *fast.*
19. There was a *long* wait. We had never waited so *long.*
20. Their sick child was getting *well.* I feel *well.*

Check all adverb forms in the following sentences. Put *S* (for satisfactory) after the number of the sentence if any adverbs in a sentence are right for formal English. If there is an unmarked informal adverb, write down the formal adverb that should replace it.

EXAMPLE: Her grandparents did not speak English very good.
(Answer) *well*

1. Robert did not understand mathematics very well.
2. It sure was a pleasure to see you again.
3. This material is extremely sensitive to changes in temperature.
4. Prices had gone up considerably since our last visit.
5. It had been raining steadily for three days.
6. Most of the downtown hotels were awful expensive.
7. None of us were really certain that we could win.
8. Several of the workers were hurt real bad.
9. Whatever he did he did well.
10. She will have to change her attitude considerable.
11. Until then the members of the crew had been getting along well.
12. Our plans will certainly have to be changed.
13. Claire knew the area extremely well.
14. Most of the children were terribly frightened.
15. I am dreadfully sorry that this had to happen.
16. Dogs generally do not see very well.
17. None of them seemed real eager to leave.
18. The man on the bed stirred uneasily in his sleep.
19. Jim didn't work very steady after he lost his position.
20. Billy shook hands solemnly, grinning under his mustache.

Avoid informal expressions that are often criticized.

Everyday talk is more informal than serious speech and writing. Learn to avoid the following familiar informal forms and expressions in formal English:

(1) Avoid these kind *and* those kind.   The *these kind* in "These kind of cars" mixes singular and plural. Use *this kind* or *that kind* (singular) or *these kinds* and *those kinds* (plural):

SINGULAR: We had never seen *this kind* of engine.
This kind of can is hard to open.
We tried to avoid *that kind* of argument.

PLURAL: We have to stock all *these* different *kinds*.
Those kinds of candy are all no longer made.

(2) Avoid the informal like *in "like I said" and "like we told you."*   Formal English uses *like* as a preposition: *like* my mother,

like a river. Do not use *like* as a connective to start a clause that has its own subject and verb. Use *as* or *as if* instead:

PREPOSITION: She looks *like* her older sister.
It looks *like* rain.
Like all newcomers, she was eager to learn.

CONNECTIVE: It looks *as if* it will rain.
The soup did not taste *as* it should.
The waiter acted *as if* we had insulted him.

(3) Avoid the informal was *in "If I was you."* After *if* and *as if,* use *were* instead to show that something is impossible or not now true. We call this special form to show the opposite of something real or factual the **subjunctive.** We use it also in expressions like "I wish it *were* true."

SUBJUNCTIVE: If I *were* you, I would complain.
If he *were* employed here, he could come in.
We would hire her if she *were* more experienced.
They talked about dancing as if it *were* a crime.
I wish the meeting *were* on a different day.

NOTE: Other special subjunctive forms appear after verbs like *request, command, order, suggest:*

We requested that the meeting *be* postponed.
She suggested that the work *continue* (or *should continue*).

(4) Avoid the informal use of lay *and* set. In formal English the verb for "being seated" is *sit,* or *sit down.* Its past form is *sat,* or *sat* down. The verb for "stretching out" is *lie,* or *lie down.* Its past form is *lay,* or *lay down.*

Remember: We just sit, or lie. But we set or lay *something:*

SIT/SET	Today I *sit* in the sun. Yesterday I *sat* in the sun. I *have sat* there before. I love *sitting* in the sun.	Today I *set something* up. Yesterday I *set something* down. I *have set up an appointment.* He hates *setting the tables.*
LIE/LAY	Today I *lie* in the sun. Yesterday I *lay* in the sun. I *have lain* in the sun too long. I should stop *lying* in the sun.	Today I *lay my cards* on the table. Yesterday I *laid tile.* I *have laid something* on the shelf. He was *laying bricks.*

(5) Avoid using plural pronouns to point back to words like everybody *and* nobody. *Everybody (everyone), anybody (anyone),*

somebody (someone), and *nobody (no one)* are **indefinite** pronouns. Though they refer to people in general, these words are treated as singulars in formal English. Avoid informal expressions like "Everybody took *theirs*" or "Nobody got *their* money back." Formal English requires singular pronouns like *he (him, his)* or *she (her)* to follow one of the indefinite pronouns:

FORMAL: *Everyone* brought *his* own lunch.

          No one complained about *her* assignment.

          When you train *somebody* new, you should give *her* complete instructions.

NOTE: To many readers, *he* or *him* seems misleading when *everybody* or *somebody* stands for both men and women. *He or she* (or *him or her*) is more accurate, but some readers consider it awkward. Sometimes the best solution is to make the whole sentence plural:

INFORMAL: *Everybody* parked *their* car behind the house.

FORMAL: *Everybody* parked *his or her* car behind the house.

FORMAL: *All the guests* parked *their* cars behind the house.

(6) Become aware of other informal expressions. Avoid the informal *most* in "*most* everybody." Use *almost* or *nearly* instead. Avoid as informal: *had ought to, used to could, didn't use to:*

FORMAL: *Almost* everyone had heard the story.

          They *ought to have* warned you.

          We *used to be able* to walk through the orchards.

          Wealthy people *did not usually* live here.

NOTE: Many expressions that used to be considered informal are today avoided only by very conservative writers. Conservative readers may object to *the reason is because* (instead of the more formal *the reason is that*). They may object to the split infinitive (to *speedily* correct; started to *slowly* change color).

Which of the following sentences contain an informal word or expression? Label such sentences *I* for "Informal." Which sentences are acceptable in serious discussion and writing? Label such sentences *F* for "Formal." (Write on a separate sheet.)

EXERCISE 1

EXAMPLE: They should have done as they were told.

          F

1. If I was you, I would write to the company.
2. Everybody gathered up their belongings and headed for the gate.
3. My sister treated me as if I were a burden to the family.
4. The problem with these kind of engines is the enormous heat.

5. Jim refused to sit next to the driver.
6. Tony quarreled with most everyone he ever met.
7. The nurse told her to lie down and rest.
8. Few Americans cook spaghetti as Italians do.
9. Someone on the fifth floor had left their lights on.
10. The dog was barking like the house was on fire.
11. No one can expect other people to agree with all of his ideas.
12. Father always lay down after dinner for a short nap.
13. No man should just sit all day after he retires.
14. I had heard about those kind of birds but never seen one before.
15. I had never seen anything like the Grand Canyon before.
16. On sunny days everyone usually took their lunch outside.
17. We always treated Herman like he was one of the family.
18. Nobody was admitted unless they could prove their identity.
19. If the room were a little larger, we could use it.
20. I was so excited I forgot to make the guests set down.

EXERCISE 2

Which of the two choices after each sentence is right for formal English? Write the formal choice after the number of the sentence.

EXAMPLE: He acted _____ he had known us for years. (like/as if)
(Answer) *as if*

1. The paper still _____ on the porch. (lay/laid)
2. Someone in the back of the room neighed _____ a horse. (like/as)
3. Everyone wishes my grandfather _____ still alive. (was/were)
4. He was _____ the strips of paper end to end. (lying/laying)
5. His dungarees always looked _____ they had just been washed. (like/as if)
6. She rejected an offer that _____ anyone else would have accepted. (most/almost)
7. You _____ the meeting. (hadn't ought to interrupt/ought not to have interrupted)
8. Many office workers _____ at a desk all day. (sit/set)
9. Everyone on the women's relay team was at _____ best. (her/their)
10. As the sun went down, we _____ around the fire singing songs. (set/sat)
11. She looked at me _____ she wanted to read my mind. (like/as if)
12. The form that had been _____ on the table had disappeared. (lying/laying)
13. We _____ see the mountains across the valley. (used to could/used to be able to)
14. _____ her mother, Sharon was very ambitious. (Like/As)
15. People out here _____ take their children to the doctor. (didn't use to/did not usually)

16. All candidates for the job were required to describe _____ past experience. (her/their)
17. All my friends were _____ in the back row. (sitting/setting)
18. _____ of microphone picks up the slightest sound. (This kind/These kind)
19. If he _____ taller, he would make a good basketball player. (was/were)
20. Everyone there has to wear _____ of uniform. (that kind/those kind)

In each of the following sentences, which of the two choices would be right in formal written English? Write the formal choice after the number of the sentence.

UNIT REVIEW EXERCISE

1. The new process for purifying the water worked *good/well*.
2. The council members got *angry/mad* at the mayor.
3. Archeologists sift dirt and debris very *cautious/cautiously*.
4. *We Catholics/Us Catholics* wore special uniforms to school.
5. A smudged or crumpled letter makes a *bad/badly* impression.
6. Their business was never *real/really* profitable.
7. My uncle sent round-trip tickets for my sister and *I/me*.
8. A *bunch/group* of well-wishers met the team at the airport.
9. They acted *like/as if* our quarrel had never happened.
10. We could hear perfectly even though we were *sitting/setting* in the back.
11. Alice wanted to be a doctor *like/as* her uncle.
12. Morale *sure/certainly* makes a difference.
13. *He/Him* and his friends used to help us with the harvest.
14. The list showed *who/whom* was working that weekend.
15. Everyone felt *bad/badly* when the decision was announced.
16. We received many reports of *that/those* kind of accidents.
17. He would have a better chance if he *was/were* younger.
18. My father hated to see money *lying/laying* around loose.
19. My aunt would not tell me *who/whom* she had hired.
20. My friend and *I/me* were scheduled for an appointment.

Revise your written sentences to make them clear and effective.

U3

REVISING WRITTEN SENTENCES

In conversation, we often leave something half said and then return to it later. We start a sentence one way and finish it another way. A good written sentence is more finished and more carefully put together. It clearly carries its message. It follows a clear pattern that the reader can follow. Learn how to revise sentences that seem hastily written or confused.

U3a

Check agreement between the subject and its verb.

Most English nouns have one form to show **singular**—*one* of a kind. They have a second form to show **plural**—*several* of a kind: *boy/boys, car/cars, building/buildings, child/children, crisis/crises.* When such a noun is the subject of a sentence, the sentence often shows this difference twice. The verb too may change from singular to plural. We say that the verb **agrees** with the subject.

In the following pairs, the subject and its verb change together:

SINGULAR: My cousin *works* at night.
PLURAL: My cousins *work* at night.

SINGULAR: Our neighbor *needs* a new car.
PLURAL: Our neighbors *need* a new car.

SINGULAR: The candidate *is* going to speak at the rally.
PLURAL: The candidates *are* going to have a debate.

SINGULAR: Anita *was* transferred to Kansas City.
PLURAL: Her friends *were* transferred to the new plant.

Check for agreement in the following situations:

(1) Check for agreement when something comes between the subject and its verb. The subject may be one thing among several. It may be a quality or an activity that applies to several things. Make the verb agree with its true subject:

The *ringleader* of the rebels *was* eighteen years old.
The *attitude* of the students *has* improved.

Changing familiar habits *is* difficult.
Filing the necessary forms and reports *takes* much time.

A similar wedge may separate a plural subject and its verb:

The *witnesses* who saw the accident *have* disappeared.
The *engines* for this new kind of car *use* less fuel.

(2) Check for agreement when the subject follows the verb. In formal English, we often start a sentence with *there is* or *there was* regardless of whether a singular or a plural subject follows. Make the verb that follows *there* agree with the postponed subject:

SINGULAR: There *is* only *one tree* in the whole neighborhood.
PLURAL: There *are* always *several stores* to let.
PLURAL: There *are* a *drugstore* and a *small grocery* at the corner.

(3) Check for agreement in sentences with more than one subject. We call two subjects joined by *and* or *or* a **compound subject.** *And* adds two singular subjects and makes them plural. *Or* makes us

choose one singular subject. *As well as* and *together with* are used as prepositions and leave a singular subject singular:

PLURAL: A teacher *and* an assistant *supervise* the lab.
SINGULAR: A teacher *or* an assistant *supervises* the lab.
SINGULAR: The warden *as well as* a helper *was* clawed by the lion.

NOTE: A compound subject may be singular when the whole combination is the name of a single thing:

SINGULAR: *Fish and chips is* a familiar English meal.
SINGULAR: *The Stars and Stripes was* flying from the flagpole.

   (4) Check for agreement when form and meaning do not clearly point in the same direction. Each and *either* point to more than one person or thing. But we are thinking of each individually:

SINGULAR: *Each* of the applicants *is* thoroughly examined.
SINGULAR: *Either* answer *was* acceptable.

   Collective nouns, such as *class, team, police, jury,* and *committee,* are singular when we think of the whole group together. They are plural when we think of the members of the group:

SINGULAR: The team *is* leaving tomorrow.
PLURAL: The team *were* changing their clothes.

   Expressions like *two-thirds* or *thirty dollars* are singular when they stand for the whole amount. *A number of* is plural when it means "several":

SINGULAR: *Five hours does* not give us enough time.
           Three-fourths of the oil *was* already gone.
PLURAL: *A number of* people *were* already waiting.

   (5) Check for agreement of other sentence elements. Sometimes sentence elements other than the verb need to be changed to bring them into logical agreement with the subject:

ILLOGICAL: *His grandparents* had spent most of their *life* in Guatemala.
LOGICAL: *His grandparents* had spent most of their *lives* in Guatemala.

   Know *unusual plurals* borrowed from Latin and Greek:

   (6) Check for agreement in relative clauses. The relative pronouns *who, which,* and *that* may point back to a singular or a plural.

SINGULAR: She was the only runner who *was* selected.
PLURAL: She was not one of the runners who *were* selected.

NOTE: Know unusual plurals borrowed from Latin and Greek.
   (crisis) The *crises* are over.
   (species) These *species* are extinct.

Usage

EXERCISE 1

Which of the two choices in each of the following would be right in a written sentence? Write the form that agrees with the subject after the number of the sentence. (Write on a separate sheet.)

1. The patience of the listeners *was/were* surprising.
2. Finding a parking space at school *is/was* not easy.
3. There *has/have* been many complaints about the noise.
4. Radioactivity from nuclear tests *has/have* made the island uninhabitable.
5. A guard or a store detective *is/are* always on duty.
6. The doctor on duty in the emergency room *take/takes* over.
7. Equipment for use in emergencies *is/are* stored upstairs.
8. Reading long-winded instructions always *confuse/confuses* me.
9. There *was/were* prehistoric paintings in some of the caves.
10. The excuses for their behavior *convince/convinces* nobody.
11. Her motive as well as her action *has/have* to be considered.
12. There *is/are* an old barn and an abandoned well on the property.
13. Each of the proposals *has/have* serious drawbacks.
14. There *is/are* many different ways of cooking fish.
15. The analyses of earlier researchers *was/were* proven wrong.
16. His interest in the creatures of the ocean floor *is/are* well known.
17. The new media *is/are* changing our ways of learning.
18. Ham and eggs *is/are* my favorite breakfast.
19. Sorting out conflicting facts *is/are* part of a scientist's job.
20. Television together with the other mass media *has/have* changed our way of life.

EXERCISE 2

Which of the sentences are acceptable in formal written English? Write *S* for satisfactory after the number of each sentence. Which of the sentences should be revised? Write down the form that should replace the italicized word.

EXAMPLE: The frequency of his visits *are* suspicious.
(Answer) *is*

1. The study of foreign languages *is* a challenge.
2. German as well as Spanish or French *is* offered in many schools.
3. Each of these languages *are* about equally difficult.
4. For someone learning a language, three years *is* only a short time.
5. The vocabulary and the grammar of the language *requires* careful attention.
6. Often the pronunciation of foreign words *causes* trouble.
7. Hearing the foreign sounds *are* difficult for the beginner.
8. However, there *are* many rewards for the patient learner.
9. There *is* truth in the saying that practice makes perfect.
10. Listening to foreign speakers *becomes* a real pleasure.
11. Understanding a visiting South American *is* a real thrill.

12. Often there *is* a foreign exchange club and a small foreign language library.
13. An exchange student or exchange teacher often *serves* as a model.
14. Films or filmstrips *are* furnished by foreign consulates.
15. In my own school, there *was* many opportunities to study a language.
16. Each of my language classes *was* different.
17. Students in one class *were* often busy writing letters to foreign friends.
18. With another teacher, singing French songs *were* our favorite pastime.
19. Talking to foreign students *has* taught me one important thing.
20. Each of us *is* proud of our own language and country.

EXERCISE 3

Each of the following sentences contains an example of unsatisfactory subject-verb agreement. Find the word that causes the problem. After the number of the sentence, write its corrected form.

1. The spaceship settles on the moon's surface, and all the hard work and the preparation pays off.
2. Many times teenagers are observing the adult's life and finds that the adult is not worthy to be a leader.
3. The sun's rays seldom penetrates the gloom.
4. A few shots was heard by the neighbors.
5. The distortion of facial muscles show his physical anguish.
6. A long row of towels were blown away by a forceful wind.
7. The surroundings of the village is a cheerful sight.
8. For a few seconds, everyone were yelling, and people were thrown around by the impact.
9. The historical sites in this part of the country is world-famous.
10. We admired the ivy and dogwoods that enhances the architecture of of the mansion.

U3b

Pronoun
Reference

Make the reference of your pronouns clear.

Pronouns are pointing words. *He* may point to *Charles* or to *Paul*. *She* may point to *Sue* or to *Jean*. We call the word that a pronoun points back to its **antecedent**—"what has gone before." A pronoun becomes confusing when it does not point clearly to its antecedent. A pronoun becomes ambiguous when we cannot tell which of two people or things is meant.

To make things clear, you may have to *drop* a confusing pronoun and spell out what it stands for:

CONFUSING: The nurse brought the child's pudding, but *it* ran away.
(The pudding?)
CLEAR: The *child* ran away when the nurse brought *its* pudding.

Make a pronoun clearer by *shifting* things in a sentence:

CONFUSING: *Bill* talked to *Mr. Greene* about *his* absence.
(Who was absent? Bill or Mr. Greene?)
CLEAR: *Bill* discussed *his* absence with *Mr. Greene.*

(1) Make the pronoun point to something clearly stated. Revise sentences if *it* or *they* points to an implied antecedent:

CONFUSING: My father was a teacher, and I too want to make *it* my career.
(The *it* points back to *teaching,* which is only implied.)
CLEAR: My father's profession was *teaching,* and I too want to make *it* my career.

CONFUSING: We had advertised free kittens, but *they* had stopped running.
CLEAR: We had advertised free kittens, but *the ads* had stopped running.

Avoid the informal *they* that points to "the people concerned":

INFORMAL: In New York, *they* have humid summers.
FORMAL: *The people who* live in New York have humid summers.

(2) Avoid vague this *and* which. These pronouns are often ambiguous when they point back to the whole idea expressed in what has gone before. Revise ambiguous "idea reference":

CONFUSING: The supervisor reprimanded Jim for leaving his job.
This is bad for the morale of the other workers. (The reprimand —or leaving the job?)
CLEAR: The supervisor reprimanded Jim for leaving his job.
These lectures are bad for the morale of the other workers.

CONFUSING: She always gets help on our weekly quiz, *which* annoys me.
(The quiz—or her getting help?)
CLEAR: She always does her weekly quiz with outside *help, which* annoys me.

(3) Avoid the informal you. *You* is informal when it points to people in general. Use it to mean "you, the reader."

INFORMAL: A hundred years ago, *you* had to be male to be able to vote.
FORMAL: A hundred years ago, *a person* had to be male to be able to vote.

EXERCISE 1

In each of the following pairs, one sentence includes a confusing or informal pronoun. After the number of the pair, put the letter for the sentence that would be *right* in written English.

EXAMPLE: (a) They are tearing down the old courthouse.
(b) The city is tearing down the old courthouse.
(Answer) *b*

1. (a) In *Reader's Digest*, they adapt articles from other magazines.
   (b) The editors of *Reader's Digest* adapt articles from other magazines.

2. (a) Ann is taking up ornithology. This field of study intrigues me.
   (b) Ann is taking up ornithology. This intrigues me.

3. (a) When a boy dates a girl only once, he knows nothing about her.
   (b) When you date a girl only once, you know nothing about her.

4. (a) Kate was arrested for rioting. This is undemocratic.
   (b) Kate was arrested for rioting. Such arrests are undemocratic.

5. (a) The barber could not cut the youngster's hair, though his father was holding him.
   (b) Though the youngster was held by his father, the barber could not cut his hair.

6. (a) At Union High, they thought of students as people.
   (b) At Union High, teachers thought of students as people.

7. (a) When he tried to put the saddle on the horse, it ran away.
   (b) When he tried to put on the horse's saddle, it ran away.

8. (a) He much less frequently flattered her, which she liked.
   (b) His flattering remarks, which she liked, were much less frequent.

9. (a) Beth argued with the driver, who finally threw her off the bus.
   (b) Beth and the driver argued, and she finally threw her off the bus.

10. (a) In Russia, they have cold winters and warm summers.
    (b) Russians have cold winters and warm summers.

In each of the following sentences, find the pronoun that needs to be revised. Write it after the number of the sentence. (Your teacher may ask you to rewrite five or more of these sentences to make them acceptable in written English.)

EXERCISE 2

EXAMPLE: The teachers were on strike, but they kept the school open.
(Answer) *they*

1. When there were fights, my mother would settle it with a few calm words.
2. In a new suburb, students may have a long bus ride because they have not yet built schools in the area.
3. During the blizzard, we sat around the house because it was too deep to go anywhere else.
4. Near the ski slopes, they had a place where we could go to get warm.
5. In the old days, you had to know Latin to be considered educated.
6. Our astronauts have to be in good health, because it requires alertness and stamina.

7. My relatives disliked our neighbors because they were conceited.
8. When a job became available, I told them I was interested in it.
9. Paris had kidnapped Helen, queen of Troy, which started the war.
10. To be paroled, you have to get a favorable decision from the parole board.
11. I quit work at the gas station, because they paid me the lowest wage.
12. My favorite winter was last year, because it was the biggest snowstorm I ever saw.
13. We went inside his friend's house for a while and helped his father.
14. I used to go to the firehouse next to our house and sled on their hill.
15. The king orders the rebel's destruction after the attempt to take over his position.
16. In Vermont, they pride themselves on a tradition of sturdy independence.
17. He said that his horoscope had predicted the accident, but it seemed unbelievable.
18. Our school stayed open in spite of the blizzard, which was rare in that part of Canada.
19. Lori talked to my aunt about moving, but she was still hesitating.
20. When a team cannot protect its quarterback, you have to be able to move quickly.

U3c

Position of Modifiers

Place modifiers carefully in a sentence.

A modifier changes or narrows down the meaning of some other part of a sentence. A **dangling modifier** appears in a sentence *without* what it is supposed to modify:

DANGLING: *Taking a rest,* the telephone suddenly rang.
            (The telephone was taking a rest?)
REVISED: Taking a rest, *I* suddenly heard the phone ring.

A **misplaced modifier** seems to go *with the wrong part* of a sentence:

MISPLACED: We contributed clothes for the victims *that were still usable.*
REVISED: We contributed *clothes* that were still usable for the victims.

A "squinting modifier" may seem to look in the wrong direction:

MISPLACED: Many people who teach here *at night* work at other jobs.
REVISED: Many people who teach here work at other jobs *at night.*

(1) Place adverbs where they point clearly to what they modify. Adverbs like *only, just,* and *almost* are confusing when they appear in the wrong place:

CONFUSING: We have dances on Wednesdays *only* for members.
CLEAR: We have dances on Wednesdays for members *only.*
CLEAR: We have dances for members on Wednesdays *only.*

CONFUSING: His car *almost* broke down on every trip.

CLEAR: His car broke down on *almost* every trip.

CLEAR: On every trip, his car *almost* broke down.

(2) Move prepositional phrases if necessary. They start with a preposition like *at, with, on, by, for, through,* or *without.* These prepositions bring a noun and other possible material into the sentence:

CONFUSING: I heard a lecture on rebellious children *by a specialist.* (The specialist had rebellious children?)

REVISED: I heard a specialist give a lecture on rebellious children. (Other people had rebellious children.)

CONFUSING: He brought chairs for his guests *with straight backs and spindly legs.*

REVISED: For his guests, he brought chairs with straight backs and spindly legs.

(3) Revise dangling and misplaced verbal phrases. Many dangling or misplaced modifiers start with a verbal like *cleaning, driving, opening;* or like *driven, written, opened.* To revise these verbal phrases, shift or add things in the sentence as needed:

DANGLING: *Walking around the corner,* the gym came into view.

REVISED: *As we walked* around the corner, the gym came into view.

REVISED: Walking around the corner, *we saw* the gym.

MISPLACED: *Opened by mistake,* I carefully resealed the envelope.

REVISED: I carefully resealed the enveloped *opened by mistake.*

(4) Make appositives point clearly to what they modify. An appositive is a second noun that tells us more about another noun (or sometimes, a pronoun): "Margaret Smith, *the senator.*" Make sure it relates clearly to the other noun:

AWKWARD: We have only one vacancy, *a typist.*

REVISED: We need only one person, *a typist.*

(5) Make relative clauses point clearly to what they modify. Make sure the *who, which,* or *that* at the beginning of the clause points in the right direction:

CONFUSING: He showed me the leader of the band *that was getting married.*

REVISED: He showed me the band leader that was getting married.

NOTE: Some verbals are technically danglers but are *acceptable* in formal English. They clarify the intention or attitude of the speaker or writer. They point to an implied "I" or "we":

Generally speaking, that is true.
Considering our costs, the price is low.

309

EXERCISE 1

In each of the following pairs, which sentence is the *clearer or more satisfactory* one? Put its letter after the number of the pair.

1. (a) Having eaten our lunch, the work continued.
   (b) Having eaten our lunch, we went back to work.

2. (a) He corrected the girl sitting in front of him with great glee.
   (b) With great glee, he corrected the girl sitting in front of him.

3. (a) She showed me her uncle's car, a battered wreck.
   (b) She showed me the car of her uncle, a battered wreck.

4. (a) At the age of ten, Grandfather came to live with us.
   (b) When I was ten, Grandfather came to live with us.

5. (a) He stared at the statue of Washington with his mouth open.
   (b) With his mouth open, he stared at the statue of Washington.

6. (a) Jim had met the girl he married by accident.
   (b) Jim and the girl he married had met by accident.

7. (a) Being a sickly child, I was often sent home.
   (b) Being a sickly child, my teacher often sent me home.

8. (a) We have night lights for children that glow in the dark.
   (b) For children, we have night lights that glow in the dark.

9. (a) Singing and dancing, the revels continued until dawn.
   (b) Singing and dancing, the guests continued their revels.

10. (a) Driving the jeep down the road, we came upon a herd of giraffes.
    (b) Driving the jeep down the road, a herd of giraffes came into view.

EXERCISE 2

Write *U* for "Unsatisfactory" after the number of each modifier that is *dangling, misplaced,* or *confusing.* Write *S* for "Satisfactory" after the number of each modifier that points clearly to what it modifies. (How would you revise the unsatisfactory modifiers?)

The first people (1) *that spoke English* came to England in the fifth century A.D. (2) *Rowing their shallow ships up the rivers,* these invaders ravaged the land. (3) *Having burned and plundered the cities,* the families were brought across the sea. Many of the newcomers were farmers (4) *looking for rich fields and pasture.* Others hunted the whales and seals that roamed the seas (5) *with primitive equipment.* (6) *Founded by the Romans,* ruin and decay overtook many English cities. (7) *Almost* none of the invaders moved into the abandoned houses and villas. Christianity (8) *only* survived in the part of England that remained unconquered. The newcomers lived in log cabins built (9) *with split trunks of forest timber.* The two major tribes were the Angles and the Saxons, (10) *often called by the common name of Anglo-Saxons.*

Which of the following sentences have modifiers that do not point clearly to what they modify? Rewrite each unsatisfactory sentence. If a sentence is satisfactory, write *S* after the number of the sentence.

EXERCISE 3

1. After showing interest in the job, the neighbor took me for an interview with the employer.
2. The engine was derailed en route to the storage yard blocking both main line tracks.
3. The agency listed only one vacancy, a position for a dispatcher.
4. Going for the milk, my roommate asked me to get him some too.
5. He bought a watch for my cousin, a cheap-looking thing.
6. The scouts carefully cleaned the fish that they had just caught with their new equipment.
7. Visiting the zoo, the elephants and the dromedaries had been moved to new locations.
8. The realtor specialized in apartments for families with children that are hard to find.
9. The dean carried a list of students looking for on-campus housing in his briefcase.
10. Changing our itinerary frequently, we saw many sights not usually seen by tourists.
11. The customs official only looked at my sister's suitcase.
12. With their winnings in the lottery, my aunt and uncle started their own business.
13. Each worker received a telegram, an emergency at the factory.
14. Having finished our salads, the waiter let us sit there for a long time before bringing the meat.
15. Being very angry, the painter spattered paint on passersby on purpose.
16. We drove to a drive-in restaurant singing our fight song.
17. Speaking English very poorly, people would sometimes take advantage of my grandparents.
18. The company refused to take back the items ordered by mistake.
19. Being still a small child, my family moved back to Canada.
20. Snails are a nuisance when planting a garden.

Avoid unnecessary repetition and other kinds of mixed construction.

Revise sentences that confuse two different ways of saying the same thing. When we speak, we often start a sentence one way. Then we change to what may seem a better way. Look for the following kinds of duplication and mixed construction:

(1) Remove unnecessary repetition of sentence parts. In hasty writing, parts of the sentence machinery may appear twice. Look

for unnecessary duplication of connectives like *that,* or of prepositions like *on, to,* and *with:*

WRONG: She said *that* if we invited her *that* she would come.
REVISED: She said *that* if we invited her she would come.

WRONG: I need a calculator *on* which I can depend *on.*
REVISED: I need a calculator *on* which I can depend.

NOTE: Sometimes, we go too far in leaving out elements that seem to duplicate some other part of a sentence. When a similar idea is expressed by two *different* prepositions, or by two *different* verb forms, both are needed.

WRONG: Everyone was enthusiastic and loyal to the project.
REVISED: Everyone was enthusiastic *about* and loyal *to* the project.

WRONG: A dog was lying in the sun and chickens scurrying about.
REVISED: A dog *was* lying in the sun, and chickens *were* scurrying about.

(2) Revise sentences that unintentionally repeat the same idea in different ways.   We call such sentences **redundant.** (Something is redundant when it "overflows.") "At three a.m. in the morning" is redundant because three a.m. has to be in the morning. Take out the second italicized part in sentences like the following:

> *As a rule,* the door is *usually* left open.
> We should *return* the package *back* to the sender.

In hasty writing, the verb may repeat all or part of the subject:

REDUNDANT: The *choice* of our new car *was selected* by my brother.
REVISED: Our new car *was selected* by my brother.

REDUNDANT: We are ready for any *eventualities* that *may happen.*
REVISED: We are ready for whatever *may happen.*

(3) Revise sentences if two ways of putting the sentence together have become mixed.   Make the sentence follow either one possible pattern or the other:

MIXED: The boy was bitten by the dog but did not cause rabies.
CLEAR: The boy *was bitten by the dog but did not* catch rabies.
CLEAR: The boy was bitten by the dog, but the bites *did not cause rabies.*

MIXED: Any small noise he became panicky.
CLEAR: *Any small noise* made him panic.
CLEAR: Whenever he heard a noise, *he became panicky.*

MIXED: We canceled the show because of our funds ran out.
CLEAR: We canceled the show *because of* insufficient funds.
CLEAR: We canceled the show *because* our funds ran out.

(4) *Avoid informal uses of adverbial clauses that replace a noun in a sentence.* *When* and *because* usually introduce *adverbial* clauses. They show the time or the reason for whatever happens in the main clause. Avoid a *when* clause after *is* in definitions. The *when* clause would then take the place of a noun:

INFORMAL: Democracy *is when* people run their own affairs.

FORMAL: Democracy is *a system* that enables people to run their own affairs.

Avoid a *because* clause that replaces the subject of the main clause:

INFORMAL: *Because you say so* doesn't make it right.

FORMAL: *Your saying so* does not make it right.

FORMAL: It is not right merely *because you say so.*

INFORMAL: *Because he was nominated* does not mean he will be elected.

FORMAL: *That he was nominated* does not mean he will be elected.

FORMAL: *Being nominated* does not mean being elected.

(5) *Straighten out illogical or incomplete comparisons.* Comparisons easily move off the track as they proceed from one thing being compared to another:

ILLOGICAL: The end was more valuable than any player on the team.

REVISED: The end was more valuable than any *other* player on the team.

AMBIGUOUS: The slides taught the students more than the teacher.

CLEAR: The slides taught the students more than the teacher *did.*

CLEAR: The slides taught the students more than *they did* the teacher.

Which of the sentences in each of the following pairs is the original unsatisfactory sentence? Which is the *revised version?* Put the letter for the revised version after the number of the pair.

EXERCISE 1

1. (a) A conflagration is when an ordinary fire gets out of hand.
   (b) A conflagration is an ordinary fire that has gotten out of hand.

2. (a) He wrote to us after he arrived but has not written since.
   (b) We received a letter after his arrival but has not written since.

3. (a) Our lot is not as hard as many other people in the world.
   (b) Our lot is not as hard as that of many other people in the world.

4. (a) Their goal is peace but seem unable to achieve it.
   (b) Their goal is peace, but they seem unable to achieve it.

5. (a) That you do well on tests does not mean you are a genius.
   (b) Because you do well on tests does not mean you are a genius.

6. (a) You should wash the car in the shade and be dried with a soft cloth.
   (b) You should wash the car in the shade and dry it with a soft cloth.

7. (a) We never had a chance to quarrel with or dissent from his view.
   (b) We never had a chance to quarrel or dissent from his view.

8. (a) Is the work of today's students equal to the schools of years ago?
   (b) Is the work of today's students equal to that done by students years ago?

9. (a) Exceptions cannot and have not been allowed.
   (b) Exceptions cannot be and have not been allowed.

10. (a) A camel's gait is quite different from a horse's.
    (b) A camel's gait is quite different from a horse.

EXERCISE 2

Check each of the following sentences for unnecessary repetition or mixed construction. After the number of the sentence, write *S* if the sentence is satisfactory. Write a revised version of the sentence if it is unsatisfactory.

1. She left an address to which we could forward her mail to.
2. My title is sales assistant, in which I stock shelves and arrange displays.
3. The constant stream of visitors endangers our ancient redwood groves.
4. I have several years' experience at a job which I like and could earn a living doing it.
5. Recall is a procedure by which officials can be stripped of their offices.
6. What matters is the employer's attitude toward me as a person, not a machine working for the company.
7. I want a job with a steady routine and also deals with the public.
8. The purpose of the valve was designed to relieve excess pressure.
9. A recount is when you challenge the count of the election officials.
10. The car used much less fuel than earlier experimental models.
11. The President should spend more time on domestic policy here at home.
12. My parents always encouraged me more than my brothers.
13. Because the bank had been robbed, additional guards were on duty.
14. They had always liked Emily Dickinson more than any other poet.
15. Because his father was a governor does not mean that he is entitled to special treatment.
16. The experts were afraid that when an earthquake struck that the dam might give way.
17. The division of the property was divided among several surviving nephews and nieces.
18. We have defeated them before and will defeat them again.
19. A teacher's job is becoming as dangerous as that of a taxi driver.
20. The police kept an eye on but did not interfere with his activities.

Avoid confusing shifts in point of view.

As you write, be aware of how you look at people and events. For instance, you may describe events as though they were happening now. Or you may describe them as having happened in the past. If you shift back and forth between present and past, you will confuse the reader. A sentence is **consistent** if it keeps the same perspective toward people and events.

Watch out for three kinds of shift:

(1) Avoid shifts in time. The **tense** forms of verbs show the relationship of events in time. Do not shift from the past *to the present* when some event becomes especially vivid in your mind:

SHIFT: As we *marched* along the shore road, I suddenly *remember* our picnic basket.

CONSISTENT: As we *marched* along the shore road, I suddenly *remembered* our picnic basket.

Use the **perfect** tense, formed with *have* or *has,* for something that has happened in the past but still matters. Use the **past perfect,** formed with *had,* to take us back to a time *before* other events in the past took place:

PERFECT: I profit (now) from what I *have learned.*
     During this decade, many new techniques *have developed* (and are now being used).

PAST PERFECT: I profited from what I *had learned.*
     By 1970, many new techniques *had been developed.*

Do not show events as having happened at the same time if one actually came before the other:

SHIFT: The lawyer *explained* to the grieving family what *happened* to the estate.

CONSISTENT: The lawyer *explained* to the grieving family what *had happened* to the estate.

(2) Avoid shifts in reference. Stay with one way of referring to yourself, to your reader, or to people in general. Do not start with an expression like *one* or *a person* and then shift to the more personal *you:*

SHIFT: If *a person* wants to study geography, *you* must learn to read maps.

CONSISTENT: If *you* took a map of the world and drew a line 30° north of the Equator and another 30° south of it, *you* would have outlined in general the waters where reef corals are found at the present time. (Rachel Carson)

EVENTS IN TIME	PRESENT (present or habitual action, or past events treated *as if* they were happening now): When I *see* him, I *laugh*.
	PAST (events past and done with): When I *saw* him, I *laughed*.
	PERFECT (past events with a bearing on the *present*): I profit now from what I *have learned*.
	PAST PERFECT (past events *prior to* other events in the past): I profited from what I *had already learned*.

Do not shift from a reference to yourself to a general reference:

SHIFT: *I* don't want to live in a small town where everyone knows all about *you*.

CONSISTENT: *A person* living in a small town must not be surprised if *his or her* actions are known to everyone.

(3) Avoid shifts to the passive.   The **passive** makes the target or the result of an action the subject of the sentence. It turns the usual "actor-action" pattern of the active sentence around:

ACTIVE: The guide *explained* the exhibits.

PASSIVE: The exhibits *had been loaned* by their owners.

Do not shift from the active to the passive when *the same person (or thing)* is still doing things in the sentence:

SHIFT: The partners *obtained* a loan, and a chicken farm *was started*.

CONSISTENT: The partners *obtained* a loan and *started* a chicken farm.

EXERCISE 1

In each of the following pairs, one sentence shows a shift in perspective. The other is more consistent. Write the letter of the more *satisfactory* sentence after the number of the pair.

1. (a) When we noticed that an employee was tired, she would be sent home to rest.
   (b) When we noticed that an employee was tired, we would send her home to rest.

2. (a) People cannot find lasting warmth in money, but they can find it in love.
   (b) One cannot find lasting warmth in money, but you can find it in love.

3. (a) I would rather not have a vacation if half of the time you have to stay home with your little sister.
   (b) I would rather not have a vacation if half of the time I have to stay home with my little sister.

4. (a) If people drink contaminated water, typhoid may be contracted.
   (b) If people drink contaminated water, they may contract typhoid.

5. (a) One should not trust rumors without checking for yourself.
   (b) People should not trust rumors without checking for themselves.

6. (a) A person can stop anywhere if you drive a car.
   (b) A traveler can stop anywhere if he or she drives a car.

7. (a) The mayor was criticized by the press and lost many supporters.
   (b) The principal called me in, and I was severely criticized.

8. (a) When I was halfway through the poem, Marion rushes in.
   (b) When a class is listening to a poem, it should not be interrupted.

9. (a) My aunt told us that she was a very sickly child.
   (b) My aunt told us that she had been a very sickly child.

10. (a) Before I started to write, my pencil was sharpened and the assignment reread with great care.
    (b) Before I started to write, I sharpened my pencil and reread the assignment with great care.

Which of the following sentences show a shift in perspective? Rewrite each unsatisfactory sentence. If a sentence is consistent, write *S* for satisfactory after the number of the sentence.

EXERCISE 2

1. When a person watches television regularly, many familiar types may be observed.
2. The cave contained pottery made by people who had lived there thousands of years ago.
3. My friends and I rushed out into the snow-covered yard, and a giant snow gorilla was built.
4. In the old movies, when people are surrounded, someone always comes to your rescue at the last minute.
5. They were sitting around the fire when suddenly a dry twig breaks and betrays the presence of an enemy.
6. Sometimes, a second crop was planted during the summer and harvested late in the fall.
7. The stereotyped television Puritan had his Bible in one hand and his musket was carried in the other.
8. The woods ranger wore a coonskin cap and carried a long rifle.
9. They have already worked long and hard by the time the play opens.

10. The relatives discovered that the deceased had not made a will.
11. People living in a big city cannot be too careful about whom you trust.
12. The government met in an emergency session, and war was declared the same afternoon.
13. Usually, when my family was on the brink of poverty, something happens to give us back hope.
14. I could not live with a person who constantly makes jokes at your expense.
15. We dismantled the scaffolding and then stored it in the old warehouse.
16. People are often in their best sleep when the alarm clock goes off.
17. Older people often wonder what will become of your savings in the days ahead.
18. Modern science has developed drugs that are saving thousands of lives.
19. When you work at night, considerateness on the part of your family is very much appreciated.
20. When the balloon touched down, a cheer goes up from the crowd.

U3f

Parallel Structure

Line up similar sentence parts in parallel form.

Sentence parts joined by *and, or,* or *but* should be the same kind of word. A noun should be linked to a noun. An adjective should be linked to an adjective. When a vehicle has four wheels, we align the wheels so that they will run parallel. When a sentence has several similar parts, we make them **parallel** to help keep the sentence on its track. In each of the following, the linked parts are the same kind of word:

The visitors *danced* and *sang.*
The winner was *weary* but *happy.*
The state is famous for its *mountains, forests,* and *rivers.*

Do the following to revise nonparallel sentences:

(1) If you can, change the parts that are not parallel *from one kind of word to another:*

OFF-BALANCE: Her new friend was *handsome* and *a giant.* (adjective and noun)

PARALLEL: Her new friend was *tall* and *handsome.*

OFF-BALANCE: Most of the townspeople *do* factory work or *running* a small shop. (verb and verbal)

PARALLEL: Most of the townspeople *do* factory work or *run* a small shop.

OFF-BALANCE: He asked me *where the exit was* and *for his money back.* (clause and phrase)

PARALLEL: He asked me *to show* him the exit and *to give* him his money back.

(2) If necessary, *add* something to the sentence to make it parallel. Or take out the *and* altogether:

OFF-BALANCE: They had a good life, good pay, and *liked their work.*

PARALLEL: They *had* a good life, *received* good pay, and *liked* their work. (three verbs)

OFF-BALANCE: The owner was *a retired police officer* and *who had seen much of the world.* (noun and relative clause)

PARALLEL: The owner was a retired *police officer* who had seen much of the world. (*and* removed)

(3) Make *three or more* parts parallel when they appear in a **series.** When three or more things are linked, the first two may be parallel. Then the third upsets the pattern. (Sometimes all three parts of a series are a different kind of word.)

OFF-BALANCE: Our neighbors do factory work, service work, and *a few small tradespeople.*

PARALLEL: Our neighbors are factory workers, service workers, and a few small tradespeople.

OFF-BALANCE: People are classified by birth, race, *where they live,* and occupation.

PARALLEL: People are classified by birth, race, residence, and occupation.

(4) *Use parallel elements with* **paired connectives.** Check for parallel structure when similar elements are joined by combinations like *not only . . . but also* or *either . . . or.* Make sure the *not only* or the *either* appears in the most logical position:

OFF-BALANCE: He not only *insulted* me but also *my family.*

PARALLEL: He insulted not only *me* but also *my family.*

OFF-BALANCE: We were forced either *to spend* the night there or *walking back* into town.

PARALLEL: We were forced either *to spend* the night there or *to walk* back into town.

After the number of each of the following pairs, put the letter for the sentence that shows parallel structure.

EXERCISE 1

1. (a) When I ride my bike, I like putting on the brakes and spin.
   (b) When I ride my bike, I like to put on the brakes and spin.

2. (a) The interviewer asked me whether I had any retail experience, my address, and telephone number.
   (b) The interviewer asked me for my address and telephone number and wanted to know whether I had any retail experience.

3. (a) We like to go to the mountains and ski, rent snowmobiles, or go sleigh riding.
   (b) We like to go to the mountains and ski, snowmobile, or sleigh riding.

4. (a) For their hobbies, they needed a house with not only a large garage but also a full basement.
   (b) For their hobbies, they needed a house with not only a large garage but also having a full basement.

5. (a) I like to work the register and also stocking shelves, because time then goes quickly.
   (b) I like working the register and also stocking shelves, because time then goes quickly.

6. (a) Joan told us about the accident and that no one had been badly hurt.
   (b) Joan told us that an accident had happened but that no one had been badly hurt.

7. (a) The critic called the program dull, predictable, and sentimental.
   (b) The critic called the program dull, predictable, and an example of sentimentality.

8. (a) We worried about the new school and would Phil be able to keep up with the other children.
   (b) We worried about the new school and Phil's ability to keep up with the other children.

9. (a) The huge repair bill was unexpected and a total disaster.
   (b) The huge repair bill was unexpected and meant disaster.

10. (a) The guard pointed out the sign to us and made us leave the field.
    (b) The guard pointed out the sign to us and making us leave the field.

EXERCISE 2

Which of the following sentences are *parallel* in structure? Put S for satisfactory after the number of each such sentence. Which sentences are off-balance? Revise the unsatisfactory sentences. Write on a separate sheet of paper.

1. Father told us of his trip to the South Pole and many other stories.
2. Boxing requires stamina, speed, and skill.
3. Pat is good at asking questions and a good listener.
4. Children should have the opportunity to listen and deciding for themselves what music they prefer.
5. He did not care how we got here, why we are here, or what happens when we die.
6. She is either planning to run for governor or for senator.
7. He bought and sold old automobiles, worn-out refrigerators, and other cast-off things.

8. The sheriff told the prisoner that it was late and to walk faster.
9. To my father, a good life meant to labor, to save, and to care for one's own.
10. Modern science has changed not only the cars we drive but also the bread we eat.
11. Jim liked picnics and to roam through the woods.
12. The treasurer was asked to resign the post and for the return of the missing funds.
13. We were shown how supplies are collected, sorted, shipped, and distributed.
14. Her new friend was quiet, studious, and a perfect gentleman.
15. He promised to change his ways and that he would write soon.
16. She made up for her mistake by admitting it and trying to correct it.
17. We went across the icy road to the garage and helping the mechanic put on chains.
18. He wanted his children to follow in his footsteps and succeed where he failed.
19. We not only repaired the floor but also any cracks in the wall or the ceiling.
20. You should either get a new transmission or sell the car.

UNIT REVIEW EXERCISE

Some of the following sentences are acceptable in written English. Write *S* for satisfactory after the number of each such sentence. Other sentences show familiar sentence problems: agreement, pronoun reference, position of modifiers, mixed construction, shifts, or lack of parallel structure. Find each sentence that needs revision. Revise it to make it acceptable in written English. Write on a separate sheet of paper.

1. I would like an exciting position with flexible hours and would include some travel.
2. The appearance of several police cars on the scene has made the crowd angry.
3. The players need a room where you can change your clothes.
4. In the winter, we help shovel out the neighbor's car and who else needs help.
5. The influence of her immigrant parents have kept her from mingling with other people her age.
6. When you see people take other people's property, you should notify the police.
7. This novel made me realize that one should go after what they really want in life.
8. In my hometown, they talk about football as if it were a religion.
9. When I arrived, the coach had already started to assign the positions to the various team members.

10. The tribal council claimed that the government had broken several solemn treaties.
11. The officials called an offside penalty, and precious yards were marked off against our team.
12. He and his friends used to brag about the fish they caught while drinking beer in our backyard.
13. The cathedral had been badly damaged during the war and was just now being rebuilt.
14. They had parked their car next to a hydrant with the lights on.
15. There had been several accidents for which the company claimed not to be responsible for.
16. Needing medical attention desperately, the doctor arrived on the scene just in time.
17. The villagers were famous for their skills as weavers, potters, and silversmiths.
18. There was only one small factory and a few stores in town.
19. A person should try different things before he or she chooses a definite career.
20. A nurse and one other attendant is always present during these operations.

U4
EFFECTIVE SENTENCE STYLE

Avoid features that make sentences awkward, roundabout, or dull.

Sometimes we look back over a sentence and say: "This sentence doesn't run the way I would like it to. It is too clumsy, too roundabout. The sentence machinery, instead of doing its job smoothly, gets in the way. How can I do better?"

Remember the following advice:

(1) Avoid the awkward, impersonal passive. The **passive** shifts attention from who *makes* something happen to *to whom* it happens: "The *attendants* brought in the patient" becomes "The *patient* was brought in."

EFFECTIVE: On a signal from the judge, *the prisoner was led out.*

The passive becomes annoying when the person who *makes things happen* is as important as ever but has been moved to some inconspicuous part of the sentence. The passive becomes impersonal or bureaucratic when the person who makes things happen has been omitted from the sentence altogether.

ROUNDABOUT: I doubt if *any of our actions were taken* completely disregarding how our fellow citizens will react.

DIRECT: I doubt if *we ever take any action* with complete disregard of how our fellow citizens react.

ROUNDABOUT: All *faculty vehicles will henceforth be parked* in the area designated for this use.

DIRECT: *Teachers should park* their cars in the lot reserved for them.

(2) Avoid roundabout, impersonal constructions with one, a person, *and* there is. Learn to remove the **deadwood** from sentences like the following:

AWKWARD: When *one* is a parent with several children, *he* looks at school taxes differently.

DIRECT: *Parents* with several children look at school taxes differently.

AWKWARD: *A person who travels frequently* cannot help learning many new things.

DIRECT: *A frequent traveler* cannot help learning many new things.

AWKWARD: While we stayed in the islands, *there was* tremendous damage *as the result of* an earthquake.

DIRECT: While we stayed in the islands, *an earthquake did* tremendous damage.

(3) Vary the length and the structure of your sentences. Use short sentences to sum up a point that your readers should remember. Use long sentences to give a rounded picture:

SHORT: *Our cities are aging.* Vast tracts of inner-city housing were built in the last century . . . .

LONG: The Sioux rode northward after annihilating Custer's five troops on the Little Big Horn, a whole nation on the move, driving the buffalo before them, and with soldiers from every army post in the West on their trail. (Wallace Stegner)

Try different kinds of sentence openers. Experiment with introductory modifiers or introductory dependent clauses to help give your sentences variety:

For nonconformity, the world whips you with its displeasure. (Emerson)

If we live truly, we shall see truly.

Racing with the clock, I hurried to complete my task.

Experiment with **inversion,** which pulls the object of the verb or a description of the subject to the beginning of the sentence for emphasis:

A better friend I never had.

Long indeed is the way home after a lost game.

(4) Line up related ideas in parallel form. Take ideas that are closely related *in meaning* and line them up in similar *form.* We call two or more parts of a sentence that fit into the same pattern

parallel in structure. Can you see how the parallel elements in the following sentences help us follow a consistent pattern?

> I have always felt sorry for people afraid
> *of feeling,*
> *of sentimentality,*
> *of emotion,*
> who *conceal* what they feel
> and *are unable* to weep with their whole heart. (Golda Meir)

EXERCISE 1

Which of the two sentences in each of the following pairs is more *vigorous and direct?* Put its letter after the number of the pair.

1. (a) The magazine that a person reads is usually one that appeals to his or her own personal interests.
   (b) Readers choose magazines that appeal to their personal interests.

2. (a) A member moved that the committee study the report further.
   (b) A motion was made by a member that the report receive further study.

3. (a) There was a riot caused by convicts dissatisfied with the prison food.
   (b) Convicts dissatisfied with the prison food started a riot.

4. (a) When one is a citizen, he or she should vote.
   (b) A citizen should vote.

5. (a) If a healthy outdoor sport is desired, people should buy horses if they have the money.
   (b) If people want a healthy outdoor sport and have the money, they should buy horses.

6. (a) The class asked the teacher to postpone the examination.
   (b) It was requested by the class that the examination be postponed.

7. (a) There was no explanation offered for my sister's late return.
   (b) My sister did not explain her late return.

8. (a) He was the only man who saw the strangers who visited the man who was slain.
   (b) Only he saw the strangers who visited the man before he was slain.

9. (a) The government negotiated a new treaty covering seal hunting.
   (b) A new treaty covering the hunting of seals has been negotiated by the government.

10. (a) If a person is determined to succeed as a student, he or she can usually make at least a passing grade.
    (b) A student determined to succeed can usually make at least a passing grade.

Rewrite the following sentences to make them more direct and vigorous.

1. When a person is a recruit in the marine corps, he or she is subjected to rigorous discipline.
2. In earlier societies, there was a tremendous amount of labor performed by the lower social classes for the glory of their masters.
3. A pyramid reminds us of the uncounted thousands who labored for the king who intended it as his tomb.
4. During his appointed rounds, all windows and doors are checked by the guard on duty.
5. If one is a guest at a party, he or she should refrain from circulating gossip about the host.

Often writers use a *short* sentence to make a point. Then they use one (or more) *longer* sentences to follow up. Look at this one-two effect in the following model pair of sentences by Mark Twain. Do one or more similar pairs of your own. Use the same overall pattern, but write on a subject of your own choice.

MODEL: *Noise proves nothing.* Often a hen who has merely laid an egg cackles as if she had laid an asteroid.

EXAMPLES: Laughter proves nothing. Often a grouch who has certainly caused misery smiles as if he had originated the joke.

            Laughter proves nothing. Often a hyena who is merely looking for a meal laughs as if he had already eaten the whole thing.

The following *model sentences* show the effective use of different sentence openers and of parallel structure. Choose three as models for sentences of your own. Write each sentence on a subject of your own choice, but keep it similar in structure to the original.

1. After years of wear, tear, dirt, grease, washing, patching, and more wear, jeans become molded to the owner's body.
2. Unlike gold, which will not corrode in the sea, silver turns black in the water.
3. If a robot can follow simple orders, do the housework, or run simple machines in a cut-and-dried repetitive way, most people are perfectly satisfied with its performance. (Isaac Asimov)
4. The past can only be remembered or forgotten, but the future can be molded, modeled, cast, created, shaped, and brought to life.
5. In my family, we all want the front seat, all want to answer the phone, and all want to get to the mailbox first.
6. No one wants to be taken advantage of, to be mistreated, to be misused.

VARIETIES OF AMERICAN ENGLISH

The colorful variety of American speech seldom shows on the printed page. Writing is usually *standardized*. Standard spelling does not allow for pronunciation differences. Formal usage makes little allowance for regional differences in word choice and grammar. Only when an author tries to reproduce in print the authentic speech of one of the characters do we get a glimpse of the different ways in which Americans talk.

The following assignments give you a chance to study some features that give color and variety to language that we hear around us everyday.

ACTIVITY 1

Look at the following examples of the dialect spoken by many people in Hawaii. Look at the word repeated in each set. Can you see that the word is used with a special twist? What would you have used instead? Could you use the word in a sentence or two of your own, speaking like a native?

1. I get one record. You get pencil? I get one cousin named Clifford. You folks get television? I get plenty marbles. I get more big kind.
2. You can make like this. I said no make! Hey, you, no can make like this.
3. I'm hungry—I like doughnuts, Auntie. Get off—I like ride your bicycle. He no like let me. Come on; I like play.
4. Andy stay catching bees. Stay here, the cow. When somebody stay, he no talk.
5. Roy, try look. Try stand up, Suzanne. Try come; we go make tent.
6. I brought home big kind dolly. This is marble kind agate. What kind she doing?
7. Plenty grasshopper here. Plenty guys come my house. I get plenty marbles.

Bonus Project: These sample sentences at the same time illustrate several other things that the local English of Hawaii does differently from mainland English. Point out the examples.

ACTIVITY 2

Eugene O'Neill's play *Desire Under the Elms* (1924) has as its setting a farm in New England around 1850. O'Neill makes the characters in the play speak a *rural New England* dialect. In the following excerpts, Eben and his two half-brothers, Peter and Simeon, talk about their harsh, domineering father,

Ephraim Cabot. What dialect features set the speech of these characters apart from standard English? Which of these features does their speech share with current nonstandard English?

1. Eben: I meant—I hain't his'n—I hain't like him—he hain't me!
   Peter: Wait till ye've growed his age!
   Eben: I'm Maw—every drop o' blood!

2. Simeon: What've ye got held agin us, Eben? Year arter year it's skulked in yer eye—somethin'.
   Peter: Ay-eh.
   Eben: Ay-eh. They's somethin'. Why didn't ye never stand between him 'n' my Maw when he was slavin' her to her grave—t' pay her back fur the kindness she done t' yew?

3. Simeon: We never had no time t' meddle.
   Peter: Yew was fifteen afore yer Maw died—an' big fur yer age. Why didn't ye never do nothin'?
   Eben: They was chores t' do, wa'nt they? It was on'y arter she died I come to think o' it.

4. Peter: Whar in tarnation d'ye s'pose he went, Sim.
   Simeon: Dunno. He druv off in the buggy, all spick an' span, with the mare all breshed an' shiny, druv off clackin' his tongue an' wavin' his whip. I remember it right well. . . . I yells "whar ye goin', Paw?" an' he hauls up by the stone wall a jiffy. His old snake's eyes was glitterin' in the sun.

5. Eben: It's nigh sunup. . . . He's gone an' married agen! . . .
   Peter: Who says?
   Simeon: They been stringin' ye!
   Eben: Think I'm a dunce, do ye? The hull village says. The preacher from New Dover, he brung the news.

6. Simeon: Waal—if it's done—
   Peter: It's done us. . . . They's gold in the fields o' Californi-a, Sim. No good a'stayin' here now.
   Simeon: Jest what I was a-thinkin'. . . . Let's light out and git this mornin'.—Act One, Scenes 2 and 3

John Steinbeck, in *The Grapes of Wrath,* tells the story of Southwestern farmers driven from their homes in Oklahoma by the drought and Depression of the early thirties. Describe as fully as you can the kind of *rural Southwestern* American that Steinbeck makes his characters speak.

ACTIVITY 3

"Look a the light comin'," said the preacher. "Silverylike. Didn' John never have no fambly?"

"Well, yes, he did, an' that'll show you the kind a fella he is—set in his ways. Pa tells about it. Uncle John, he had a young wife. Married four months. She was in a family way, too, an' one night she gets a pain in her stomick, an' she says, 'You better go for a doctor.' Well, John, he's settin' there, an' he says, 'You just got stomickache. You et too much. Take a dose a pain killer. You crowd up ya stomick an ya' get a stomickache,' he says. Nx' noon she's outa her head, an' she dies at about four in the afternoon."

"What was it?" Casey asked. "Poisoned from somepin she et?"

"No, somepin jus' bust in her. Ap—appendick or somepin. Well, Uncle John, he's always been a easy-goin' fella, an' he takes it hard. Takes it for a sin. For a long time he won't have nothin' to say to nobody. Just walks aroun' like he don't see nothin', an' he prays some. Took 'im two years to come out of it, an' then he ain't the same. Sort of wild. Made a nuisance of hisself. Ever' time one of us kids got worms or a gutache Uncle John brings a doctor out. Pa finally tol' him he got to stop. Kids all the time gettin' a gutache. He figures it's his fault his woman died. Funny fella. He's all the time makin' it up to somebody—givin' kids stuff, droppin' a sack a meal on somebody's porch. Give away about ever'thing he got, an' still he ain't very happy. Gets walkin' around alone at night sometimes. He's a good farmer, though. Keeps his lan' nice."

ACTIVITY 4

New York City speech has been much caricatured. Study the following dialogue, from Thomas Wolfe's short story, "Only the Dead Know Brooklyn." Point out all characteristic features that you can identify. If you live in or near a big city, your teacher may ask you to study any distinctive features of popular speech in your own city.

So like I say, I'm waitin' for my train t' come when I sees dis big guy standin' deh—dis is duh foist I eveh see of him. Well' he's lookin' wild, y'know, an' I can see dat he's had plenty, but still he's holdin' it; he talks good an' is walkin' straight enough. So den, dis big guy steps up to a little guy dat's standin' deh an' says, "How d'yuh get t' Eighteent' Avenoo an' Sixty-sevent' Street?" he says.

"Yuh got me, chief," duh little guy says to him. "I ain't ben heah long myself. Where is duh place?" he says. "Out in duh Flatbush sections somewhere?"

"Nah," duh big guy says. "It's out in Bensonhoist. But I was neveh deh befoeh. How d'yuh get deh?"

Duh little guy says, scratchin' his head, y'know—you could see duh little guy didn't know his way about—"yuh got me, chief. I neveh hoid of it. Do any of youse guys know where it is?" he says to me.

"Sure," I says. "It's out in Bensonhoist. Yuh take duh Fourt' Avenoo express, get off at Fifty-nint' Street, change to a Sea Beach local deh, get off at Eighteent' Avenoo an' Sixty-toid, an' den walk down foeh blocks. Dat's all yuh got to do," I says.

ACTIVITY 5

The following excerpts are from the story of a family that moved to New York City in search of a better life. Where are these people from? How many of the Spanish words they use do you recognize? Where have you heard them? Which of them are related to familiar English words? Do you hear Spanish spoken in your hometown?

1. Failed chicken farmers and bankrupt grocers—gallineros and bodegueros—my father and his younger brother gave up on their situation and beat it to Nueva York. World War II had just ended; flights on converted planes were cheap; jobs in hotel kitchens and factories were waiting for unskilled jibaros.

2. He meant that we were not going to follow in his stumbling footsteps, that we were not going to hang around with bandoleros, that when we came around to making good Catholic friends in school, we could bring *them* home; no public-school amigos for us.

3. We told Mami we wanted to go back to the Island, but she said, "Muy tarde," too late. We were americanos—not she, not Papi, but *we,* los hijos—and we'd just have to make the most of that situation.

4. Mami was always afraid we'd get found out; but she went along with Papi's maromas.

5. Third Avenue was an unbroken strip of ladrones, highwaymen posing as respectable merchants. We had a Spanglish word for what Papi brought home from la Avenida Tercera: "fakerias."

6. "Maybe her husband is the Latino. It's a fake name for her."

7. She waited for the "clientes" to disperse, to go cash their checks at Mr. Matamorros' bodega . . . or Mr. Cohn's farmacia, before she slipped the check out.

8. Illness was another diablo in his life.

9. Sometimes kids would stare at him from the stairwell window of the adjoining building. They called him "Mr. Telescopios." He'd just shrug and call them "mala leña," bad wood.

10. He wanted me to hear out his fabulous chicken-farm scheme and to reassure him that muy pronto he'd be walking again.
   —Edward Rivera, "La Situación," *New York*

Bonus: Do you know Americans who still regularly hear a language other than English? Do a report on some of the words and expressions that have come into their English from the other language.

Chapter 5

Mechanics
Words on the Page

Chapter Preview 5

IN THIS CHAPTER:

- How to improve your spelling through memory helps and spelling rules.

- How to use capital letters, apostrophes, and hyphens.

- How to avoid sentence fragments, comma splices, and other punctuation problems.

- How to punctuate restrictive and nonrestrictive sentence elements.

- How to punctuate equal parts, interrupters, and quotations.

Make your written work look right on the page.

When writers handle spelling and punctuation in a business-like way, we assume that they are serious about reaching us with their message.

Remember the following points:

(1) Some features of our writing system are truly functional. A mark we use has a definite purpose, a clear meaning. The exclamation mark, for instance, signals emphasis. The question mark turns a statement into a question. The colon typically means "as follows."

(2) Some features of our writing system have historical reasons. Much of our spelling made better sense five hundred years ago than it does today. The *k* and the *gh* in the word *knight* once stood for actual sounds.

(3) Some features of our writing system are merely conventional. We usually write *high school* as two words, *highway* as one. When we ask why, the answer often is: "This is the way it is conventionally done."

DIAGNOSTIC TEST

How well do you know basic requirements for satisfactory spelling and punctuation? Study the three possible choices for the blank space in each of the following passages. Put the letter of the best choice after the number of the passage.

EXAMPLE: She turned the dial to a differ_____ channel.
   a. ant   b. ent   c. int
(Answer) *b*

1. You may flood the _____ you pump the gas pedal.
   a. engine if   b. engine, if   c. engine. If

2. The head office is at 2987 _____ .
   a. main street   b. Main street   c. Main Street

3. The corner gas station hired several new _____ .
   a. attendance   b. attendants   c. attendents

4. She was going to school in _____ .
   a. Portland Oregon   b. Portland, oregon   c. Portland, Oregon

5. Her aunt had just re_____ved a jury summons.
   a. cei   b. cie   c. cea

6. The store sold _____ and other gift items.
   a. candles, sandals,   b. candles; sandals   c. candles; sandals;

7. He admired General _____ had been his commanding officer.
   a. Bradley. Who   b. Bradley, who   c. Bradley who

8. The fire _____ caused terrible destruction.
   a. could of   b. couldve   c. could have

9. Athletes always enjoyed special priv_____ .
   a. eleges   b. ileges   c. iledges

10. He helped us open the _____ a special key.
    a. door with   b. door. With   c. door; with

11. The deadline had _____ we were out of luck.
    a. passed therefore,   b. passed; therefore,   c. passed, therefore

12. Somehow they always seemed to win _____ .
    a. nevertheless   b. never the less   c. never-the-less

13. The other man kept re_____ to his stepdaughter.
    a. ffering   b. fering   c. ferring

14. There was a thick bandage around the _____ ankle.
    a. quarterbacks   b. quarterbacks'   c. quarterback's

15. She told us _____ applications had been approved.
    a. whose   b. who's   c. whos

16. The plan_____ for the outing had been very poor.
    a. ing   b. ning   c. nyng

17. The factory had a big lot for _____ cars.
    a. employees   b. employees'   c. employee's

18. The new law produced a noti_____ drop in the accident rate.
    a. ssable   b. cable   c. ceable

19. The President was finishing a three _____ tour of Europe.
    a. weeks   b. weeks'   c. week's

20. She voted for the _____ candidate for governor.
    a. write-in   b. writein   c. write in

M1

SPELLING

Treat poor spelling as a serious but avoidable handicap.

Poor spelling puts a barrier between your message and the reader. Rightly or wrongly, most readers feel that someone who cannot spell will not have much that is worthwhile to say. Wherever there is competition for a job, poor spellers put themselves at the end of the line.

If you have a spelling problem, overcoming it requires work. To make real progress, study and act on the following advice:

(1) Identify words that cause trouble for you, and work on them until they have ceased to be a problem. Some common words are misspelled over and over again: *believe, definite, athlete.* Keep a spelling log, and include all the common spelling demons that you have had difficulty with. Add other words that you misspell on quizzes, exams, or themes.

(2) Remember that spelling is a matter of habit building. A word ceases to be a spelling problem when the correct spelling has become *automatic.* Over and over again, run your eyes over the individual letters and the shape of the word as a whole. Give the word a chance to become firmly imprinted in your mind. Spell the letters out loud, so that your ears will remember the word, as well as your eyes. Trace the word repeatedly in exceptionally large letters. Go back over the same word at the next session and the next.

(3) Do not just copy a new or difficult word from the dictionary. You will have to go back to the dictionary the next time the word comes up. Take a minute or two then and there to fix the word in your mind. Copy it a few times. Add it to your list of new or difficult words.

VOWELS

a (as in *lane*)	also	*ai:*	vain, constrain, maid
		ei:	vein, sleigh, weigh
		ay:	bray, clay, stray
		ey:	they, whey
		ea:	break, steak
e (as in *me*)	also	*ee:*	deed, creed, keen
		ea:	beam, team, steam
		ei:	receive, ceiling, leisure
		ie:	believe, retrieve
i (as in *hit*)	also	*y:*	hymn, gymnasium
		ui:	build, guild
i (as in *hide*)	also	*ai:*	aisle
		ei:	height, stein
		ey:	eye
		uy:	buy, guy
		y:	sky, defy, rye
o (as in *tone*)	also	*oa:*	toad, shoal, foal
		ou:	soul, though
		ow:	low, crow, stow
u (as in *use*)	also	*eu:*	feud, queue
		ew:	few, curfew, dew
		iew:	view, review

CONSONANTS

f (as in *father*)	also	*ph:*	phone, phrase, emphatic
		gh:	laugh, cough, enough
g (as in *go*)	also	*gh:*	ghost, ghastly
		gu:	guess, guest, brogue
h (as in *hot*)	also	*wh:*	whole, who
j (as in *jam*)	also	*g:*	gypsy, oxygen, logic
		dg:	budget, knowledge, grudge
k (as in *kin*)	also	*c:*	castle, account, coat
		ch:	chemist, chlorinate, chrome
		qu:	clique
n (as in *noon*)	also	*gn:*	gnat, gnarled, gnash
		kn:	knife, knave, knight
		pn:	pneumonia
r (as in *run*)	also	*rh:*	rhythm, rhapsody, rhubarb
		wr:	wrong, wrangle, wry
s (as in *sit*)	also	*c:*	cent, decide, decimate
		sc:	scent, descent science
		ps:	psychology, psalm, pseudonym
sh (as in *shine*)	also	*ch:*	machine, chef
		ci:	special, vicious, delicious
		si:	impression, possession, tension
		ti:	notion, imagination
		sci:	conscious, conscience
z (as in *zero*)	also	*x:*	xylophone

M1a

Memory Aids

Make use of memory aids to help you with common spelling problems.

Many of the spelling errors in student writing are caused by a few dozen common words. Master them once and for all. Try to fix them in your mind by *association*—link them to some similiar or related word. Fit them into a jingle or saying. You are more likely to recall a whole phrase or a sentence than an isolated word.

Following are three groups of common words that you cannot afford to spell incorrectly:

GROUP ONE

accept	When you *accept* an invitation, or *accept* a ride, you take something *in*. (The word *except* takes things or people *out of* a group: "everyone *except* you and me.") REMEMBER: The boy with the **accent** *acc*epted the blame for the **acc**ident.
all right	Two separate words. REMEMBER: *All right* means **all** is **right.**
a lot	Two separate words: We can say "a *whole* lot." REMEMBER: a lump, a little, *a lot.*
beginning	*Begin* has a single *n; beginning* has a double *n.* REMEMBER: The **inning** is beg*inning.*
believe	One of the most frequently misspelled words in the language. Use *ie* in *believe* and *belief.* REMEMBER: **Eve** and St**eve** beli*eve.*
business	The *i* in *business* is not pronounced but must be written. REMEMBER: Put an *i* in bus*i*ness.
choose	We *now* choose something (with a double *o*). In the *past,* we chose something (with a single *o*). REMEMBER: Ch**oo**se rhymes with **oo**ze. Ch*ose* rhymes with **h***ose.*
coming	Never double the *m* in co*m*ing.
conscience	Someone who has been badly hurt may still be *conscious* when the doctor gets there. Someone who has stolen a wallet may be bothered by his or her *conscience.*
definite	The problem is the *i* in the *–ite* ending. Compare this word with related words like defin*i*tion and infin*i*te. REMEMBER: Spell **–ite** as in **kite** to get *definite* right.
disastrous	The *e* drops out of the word *disaster* when we change it to *disastrous.*

friend Make sure you have *ie*. REMEMBER: His best *friend* was a **fi**end.

government Preserve the *n* at the end when you change *govern* to *government*. REMEMBER: Citizens who **govern** make up a *government*.

grammar This word is spelled with *ar* at the end. REMEMBER: **Marg**aret loves *grammar*.

hoping When you have hope, you are *hoping* (with a single *p*). When you hop about on one foot, you are *hopping* (with a double *p*). REMEMBER: *Hoping* rhymes with m**oping;** *hopping* rhymes with st**opping.**

GROUP TWO

its *Its* is a pronoun and points back to a noun: "The *horse* bared *its* teeth." *It's,* with the apostrophe, shows that something has been *omitted*. The complete version is *it is*. Never use the apostrophe unless you can substitute *it is:* "*It's* (it is) a shame that you had to miss the party."

library Notice the *r* that follows the *b*. REMEMBER: The lib**r**arians **br**ought **br**icks for the **br**anch *library*.

lose When you have a losing streak, you lose all the time (single *o*). When a car door rattles, something has come l**oo**se (double *o*). REMEMBER: *Lose* rhymes with wh**ose;** *loose* rhymes with g**oose.**

necessary First a *c,* then double *s*. REMEMBER: The re**c**ess was ne**c**essary.

occasion Watch for the double *c* and the *s*. REMEMBER: **occ**ur, **occ**upy, *occ*asion; inva**s**ion, occa**s**ion.

occurred Single *r* in *occur* and *occurs;* double *r* in *occurred* and *occurring*. REMEMBER: Double *r* occu**rr**ed in occu**rr**ed.

perform It's *per* in *per*form and *per*formance. REMEMBER: **per**cent, **per**mit, *per*form.

prejudice People with prejudices have made *judgments* *pre*maturely. They *pre*judge people and ideas without giving them a fair hearing.

principle A basic idea or basic rule is a princi*ple* (with *ple* at the end). The person who runs a school is a princi*pal* (with *pal* at the end). REMEMBER: He paid us tri**ple** on prin**ciple.**

privilege   There is a second *i* in the middle and a simple *g* toward the end. REMEMBER: sac*ri*le*g*e, pri*vi*le*g*e.

probably   The *ab* in prob*ab*le is kept in prob*ab*ly. REMEMBER: **ably,** cap**ably,** prob*ab*ly.

quantity   Make sure to put in the first *t*. REMEMBER: We w**ant** the same qu*ant*ity.

quiet   The word with *ite* means "entirely" (your arguments are *quite* right). The word with *iet* means "silent" (keep *quiet* in the library). REMEMBER: *Quite* rhymes with **kite;** *quiet* rhymes with **diet.**

receive   One of the three or four most common spelling problems. It's *e* after *c*. REMEMBER: **ceiling, deceive, re**ce**ive**.

recommend   Double *m*. REMEMBER: Double *m* is reco**mm**ended in reco*mm*end.

GROUP THREE

referred   Single *r* in *refer* and *refers;* double *r* in *referred* and *referring*. REMEMBER: Refe*r* spells like h**er;** refe*rr*ing spells like h**erring.**

separate   This word is another all-time misspelling champion. It is spelled with *ate* at the end. REMEMBER: The customers in the restaurant **ate** at sep*ar*ate tables.

similar   Concentrate on the *–lar* ending. REMEMBER: circu**lar,** popu**lar,** simi*lar*.

studying   The *y* in *study* is kept in *studying*. REMEMBER: Stud**ying** is done in a **study.**

succeed   Double *c* in su*cc*eed and su*cc*ess. REMEMBER: A**cc**elerate if you want to su*cc*eed.

surprise   The first syllable is *sur–*. REMEMBER: When the **surf**er **surf**aced we were *sur*prised.

than   Use the *a* in comparisons (brighter *than*). Use the *e* in talking about time (now and *then*).

there   Use the *–eir* spelling only when you talk about what *they* do or what belongs to *them* (*their* car, *their* behavior). Use the *–ere* spelling when pointing to a place (over *there*) and in the *there is/there are* combination (*there* is time). Use *they're* only when you can substitute *they are*. REMEMBER: Th*eir* car was not th*ere*.

to	*To* shows direction (*to* church, *to* school). It is also used in the *to* form of the verb (He started *to* run). *Too* shows that there is *too* much of something, but it means "also," *too*. REMEMBER: *Too* late, he *too* came *to* school *to* learn.
together	When groups of people ga*the*r (with *a*), they are toge*the*r (with *e*).
tries	It's *y* in *try*, but *ie* in *tries* and *tried*. REMEMBER: cry, fly, try; cr*ie*s, fl*ie*s, tr*ie*s.
villain	The *a* is first, then the *i*. REMEMBER: The vill*ai*n went to Sp*ai*n.
whose	"Wh*ose* house?" means "belonging to whom?" Use *who's* only if you can substitute *who is*. REMEMBER: Wh*o's* the girl wh*ose* book you found?
women	It's one wom*a*n (with *a*), but several wom*e*n (with *e*).
writing	Single *t* in wri*t*e and wri*t*ing, double *t* in wri*tt*en. REMEMBER: Wri*t*ing rhymes with **biting;** wri*tt*en rhymes with **bitten.**

Read over the words in each set several times. Use this exercise to help fix the right spelling of familiar spelling problems in your mind.

EXERCISE 1

1. surfer, surplus, *surprise*
2. inning, winning, *beginning*
3. permanent, perfect, *performance*
4. regular, popular, *similar*
5. occur, occult, *occasion*
6. ceiling, receipt, *receive*
7. biting, igniting, *writing*
8. all here, all wrong, *all right*
9. relief, belief, *believe*
10. a little, *a lot, a lot* less
11. *their* car, *their* rights, *their* house
12. commence, commerce, *recommend*
13. probable, improbable, *probably*
14. diet, *quiet, quiet*ly
15. *succeed, success, success*ful
16. preferred, transferred, *referred*
17. rate, separation, *separate*
18. *privilege, privileged,* under*privileged*
19. finish, definition, *definite*
20. presence, absence, *conscience*

Mechanics

EXERCISE 2   Have someone dictate the following sentences to you. Then check your spelling of each word that is a familiar spelling problem. Give the words that you have misspelled your special attention.

1. They are *beginning* to *accept* my *friends.*
2. We are *studying together* in the *library.*
3. You will *receive* a large *quantity.*
4. They are *probably coming* in *separate* cars.
5. *Principles* are ideas we *definitely believe* in.
6. The *government* helped *women* in *business* to *succeed.*
7. To our *surprise,* the *villain* had a *conscience.*
8. She was *writing* about *unnecessary privileges.*
9. This *disastrous occasion* showed *their prejudices.*
10. They *recommend* that she *perform* a *similar* operation.
11. He *referred* to someone who *tries quite* hard.
12. *They're hoping* we will *choose to* stay *there.*
13. Keeping *quiet* is *all right too.*
14. I know at *whose* house it *occurred.*
15. The dollar may *lose a lot* of *its* value.

M1b
Spelling Rules

Use spelling rules to help you with words that follow a common pattern.

English spelling does not follow simple rules. However, some groups of words do follow a common pattern. The rule that applies to them will usually have its exceptions. But it will help you memorize many words that you would otherwise have to learn one by one.

(1) Spell i *before* e *except after* c.   In some words the *ee* sound is spelled *ie,* in others *ei.* When you sort out these words, you get the following pattern:

I BEFORE *E*		
ie:	believe, achieve, grief, niece, piece (of pie)
cei:	receive, ceiling, conceited, receipt, deceive

In the second line above, the *ei* always follows *c.* Exceptions to this rule:

EXCEPTIONS		
ei:	either, neither, leisure, seize, weird
cie:	financier, species

340

(2) Double a single final consonant before endings that start with a vowel. Double the final consonant before the verb endings *–ed* and *–ing* or the adjective endings *–er* and *–est.* Make sure the final letter is a single consonant, coming after a single vowel:

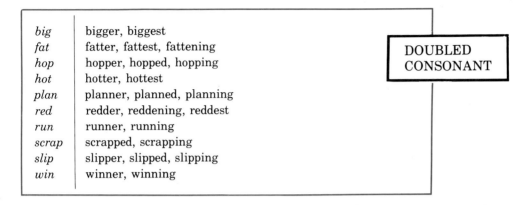

big	bigger, biggest
fat	fatter, fattest, fattening
hop	hopper, hopped, hopping
hot	hotter, hottest
plan	planner, planned, planning
red	redder, reddening, reddest
run	runner, running
scrap	scrapped, scrapping
slip	slipper, slipped, slipping
win	winner, winning

DOUBLED
CONSONANT

Do not double the consonant if the final syllable has a double vowel (*oo, oa, ea,* etc.) or a silent *e:*

DOUBLE VOWEL	SILENT E
heat—heated, heating	*hate*—hated, hating
read—reading, reader	*plane*—planed, planing
neat—neater, neatest	*love*—lover, loving
sleep—sleeper, sleeping	*hope*—hoped, hoping
doom—dooming, doomed	*dome*—domed, doming

NO DOUBLING

Double the consonant only if it is part of the syllable that is *stressed* as you pronounce the word. Do not double the letter if the stress shifts away from the syllable:

DOUBLING	NO DOUBLING
adMIT, adMITTed	BENefit, BENefited
overLAP, overLAPPing	deVELop, deVELoping
reGRET, reGRETTed	exHIBit, exHIBited
beGIN, beGINNing	WEAKen, WEAKening
forGET, forGETTing	ORBit, ORBiting
reFER, reFERRed	REFerence
preFER, preFERRing	PREFerable

(3) Drop a silent e *before an ending that starts with a vowel.*
Keep the silent *e* if the ending starts with a consonant:

	VOWEL	CONSONANT
love	loving	lovely
bore	boring	boredom
fate	fatal	fateful
like	likable	likely
state	stating	statement

SILENT *E*

Exceptions: *argue—argument, true—truly, due—duly, mile—mileage, whole—wholly.* Also, do not apply this rule to the *e* that accounts for the *dge* sound in change*a*ble, courag*e*ous, and outrag*e*ous; or the *ss* sound in notic*e*able.

(4) Change a final single y *to* i *or* ie *before endings other than*
ing. Change the *y* to *ie* when you add *–s*. Change it to *i* before most other endings. Keep the *y* before *–ing:*

FINAL Y

ie: try—tries, dry—dries, family—families,
quantity—quantities, carry—carries, hurry—hurries

i: easy—easily, beauty—beautiful, happy—happiness,
dry—drier, copy—copied

y: carrying, studying, copying, hurrying

When it follows another vowel, the *y* usually remains unchanged: *played, joys, delays, valleys, grayness.*

Exceptions to this rule: *day—daily, pay—paid, say—said,
gay—gaily, lay—laid.*

(5) Know the spellings of unusual plurals. A number of common words change their spelling when we go from one to several, from singular to plural:

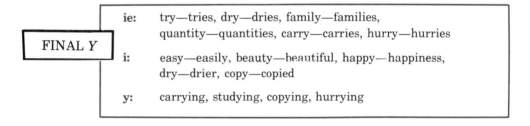

SINGULAR *o:*	hero	potato	tomato	veto
PLURAL *oes:*	heroes	potatoes	tomatoes	vetoes

SINGULAR *man:*	man	woman	freshman	chairwoman
PLURAL *men:*	men	women	freshmen	chairwomen

SINGULAR *f (fe):*	life	knife	calf	wife
PLURAL *ves:*	lives	knives	calves	wives

NOTE: Some of the less common words ending in *o* or *f* do not change their spelling in the plural: *solo—solos, soprano—sopranos, cello—cellos; hoof—hoofs* (or *hooves*), *scarf—scarfs* (or *scarves*). Check your dictionary when you are in doubt.

EXERCISE 1

On a separate sheet of paper, write down the words called for in the following instructions.

1. Fill in *ei* or *ie:* rec__ve, bel__f, c__ling, ach__ve, rec__pt, n__ce, s__ze, bel__ve, conc__ted, dec__t.
2. Write the *plural* of the following words: *quality, valley, mailman, half, subsidy, hero, study, family, woman, veto, fly, knife, quantity, potato, freshman.*
3. Write the *past* form of the following verbs: *plan, copy, orbit, prefer, play, pay, wipe, cheat, regret, permit, say, shun, stop, hope, overlap.*
4. Add *–ing* to the following words: *study, benefit, live, prefer, hate, edit, bat, float, run, hurry, drop, try, carry, dry, permit.*
5. Add *–er* to the following words: *mad, lonely, swim, grim, white, write, hot, busy, carry, flat.*
6. Add *–able* to the following words: *notice, like, change, envy, enjoy, forgive, break, exchange, pity, regret.*

EXERCISE 2

Of the two possible words in each sentence, write down the one that fits the context.

1. The noise of the machines was *dining/dinning* in his ears.
2. They *bared/barred* their heads as they entered the church.
3. The cantankerous old man never tired of *spiting/spitting* his family.
4. The teacher recommended a *griping/gripping* suspense drama.
5. We are *hoping/hopping* to visit Ireland next summer.
6. After the mate disappeared, the bird *pined/pinned* away.
7. The enemy spoiled our *well-planed/well-planned* strategy.
8. The hermit had a long beard and *mated/matted* hair.
9. Fall was the *caning/canning* season for fruits and vegetables.
10. The burglar had *robed/robbed* several neighborhood stores.

EXERCISE 3

Look up the plural forms of the following words in your dictionary:

1. buffalo
2. cargo
3. Eskimo
4. mosquito
5. motto
6. piano
7. solo
8. veto
9. wharf
10. roof

M1c
Confusing Pairs

Make a special effort to master confusing pairs.

Learn to distinguish the words in these confusing pairs:

(1) Know how to spell the same root word in different uses:

courte*ous*	but	courte*sy*
descri*be*	but	descri*ption*
four, *four*teen	but	*for*ty
gener*ous*	but	gener*osity*
ni*ne*, ni*ne*ty	but	ni*n*th
prono*u*nce	but	pron*u*nciation
spea*k*ing	but	spee*ch*
till	but	un*til*

Remember the following:

We advi*se* you to try.   (verb)
He gave us advi*ce*.   (noun)

We pa*ssed* the turnoff.   (verb)
Let us forget the pa*st*.   (noun)

We found little preju*dice*.   (noun)
He was extremely preju*diced*.   (adjective)

We us*e* cardboard and tape.   (present)
We us*ed* to meet in the hall.   (past)

(2) Know how to spell words that sound similar or alike:

accept	He *acc*epted my apology; his terms are not *acc*eptable; I cannot *acc*ept the money
except	everyone *exc*ept Judy; he made an *exc*eption for us; to *exc*ept (exempt, exclude) present company
capital	Paris is the capit*al* of France; a bank needs capit*al*; print in capit*al* letters
capitol	the capit*ol* is the building where the legislature meets
censor	in wartime letters are cen*sor*ed; object to cen*sor*ship
censure	he was cen*sur*ed (blamed, condemned) for his behavior; a vote of cen*sur*e
cite	he was *c*ited for bravery; he *c*ited several books by experts
site	the *s*ite of the new school (it's situated there)
counsel	the coun*sel*ing staff coun*sel*s or gives advice (its members are coun*sel*ors)
council	a coun*cil* is a governing board (its members are coun*cil*ors)

desert	we drove through the de*s*ert; he de*s*erted his friends; he got his just de*s*erts
dessert	we had pie for de*ss*ert

effect	she *effe*cted many changes (she brought them about, produced them); far-reaching *effe*cts; an *effe*ctive speech
affect	it *affe*cted my grade (had an influence on it); the bill won't *affe*ct (change) your status; he spoke with an *affe*cted (artificial) accent

personal	these are my own per*sonal* affairs; he got too per*sonal*
personnel	the manager hired additional perso*nnel;* the organization had a perso*nnel* problem

presents	he bought us presen*ts* (gifts)
presence	your presen*ce* is essential (opposite of absen*ce*)

principal	her princi*pal* (main) argument; a school princi*pal* (chief administrator)
principle	princi*ples* (rules, standards) of conduct; he acted on princi*ple*

quiet	be quie*t;* a quie*t* neighborhood
quite	the house was qu*ite* old; not qu*ite* ready

weather	stormy *wea*ther; to *wea*ther the storm
whether	*whe*ther or not

(3) Know how to spell words with parts that sound similar or alike:

–able:	accept*a*ble, avail*a*ble, indispens*a*ble (as in dispens*a*ry)
–ible:	poss*i*ble (also poss*i*bility), plaus*i*ble, irresist*i*ble

–ance:	attend*a*nce, perform*a*nce, acquaint*a*nce, guid*a*nce
–ence:	occurr*e*nce, experi*e*nce, exist*e*nce, excell*e*nce

–ant:	attend*a*nt, brilli*a*nt, abund*a*nt, predomin*a*nt
–ent:	excell*e*nt, promin*e*nt, independ*e*nt, differ*e*nt

–cede:	pre*cede*, se*cede*, con*cede*
–ceed:	suc*ceed*, pro*ceed* (but pro*cede*ure)

NOTE: Make sure to spell out the *have* that sounds like a shortened *of* in the following combinations:

could *have* come	(never *could of*)
should *have* stayed	(never *should of*)
would *have* written	(never *would of*)
might *have* worked	(never *might of*)

345

Mechanics

EXERCISE 1

After the number of the sentence, write down the word that fits the context. Write on a separate sheet of paper.

1. The lawyer refused to *accept/except* money for her work.
2. The class taught the basic *principles/principals* of modern business.
3. The bad weather is bound to *effect/affect* the gate receipts.
4. You should not have listened to your friend's *advise/advice*.
5. My brother is *prejudice/prejudiced* against lawyers.
6. During lunch the plane had *passed/past* over Kansas.
7. The bag contained most of my *personal/personnel* belongings.
8. The Gregors *use/used* to live in Canada.
9. We asked *weather/whether* dogs were allowed on board.
10. The hero of the novel was the strong *quiet/quite* type.
11. When she called her relatives greedy, she *accepted/excepted* her uncle.
12. The officer was going to *cite/site* my cousin for speeding.
13. They signed the documents in the *presence/presents* of witnesses.
14. I knew he would *counsel/council* us to wait.
15. The missing parts of the paper had been *censored/censured*.
16. The town called itself the artichoke *capital/capitol* of the world.
17. The new law goes into *affect/effect* on July 1.
18. It never crossed their minds to *desert/dessert* the sick and wounded.
19. Your friend should *of/have* left a forwarding address.
20. He always complained that the younger generation had no *principals/principles*.

EXERCISE 2

Write the following words, adding any missing letters. Write on a separate sheet of paper.

1. proc_____d
2. proc_____dure
3. pron_____nciation
4. pron_____nced
5. abund_____nt
6. independ_____nt
7. independ_____nce
8. until_____
9. occurr_____nce
10. curi_____sity
11. succ_____d
12. experi_____nce
13. experi_____nced
14. avail_____ble
15. indispen_____able
16. nin_____ty
17. fo_____rty
18. gener_____s
19. promin_____nt
20. descri_____tion

M1d
Spelling Lists

Study words frequently misspelled in order to avoid predictable errors.

The following boxes contain words frequently misspelled by student writers. If your spelling problem is serious, you will profit from studying these words, taking up a column at each sitting. If your spelling problem is more limited, you may have someone dictate a whole group of words to you. Then give special attention to the words that have given you trouble.

GROUP 1

absence	acknowledgment	afraid
accessible	acquaintance	against
accidentally	acquire	aggravate
accommodate	acquitted	aggressive
accompanied	across	allotted
accomplish	address	allowed
accumulate	adequate	all right
accurately	admit	already
accuses	adolescent	altar
accustom	advantageous	altogether
achievement	advertisement	always

GROUP 2

amateur	appearance	arrangement
among	applies	article
amount	applying	ascend
analysis	appreciate	assent
analyze	approach	athlete
annual	appropriate	attack
anticipate	approximately	attendance
anxiety	area	audience
apologize	arguing	authority
apology	argument	
apparent	arising	bargain

GROUP 3

basically	brilliant	cemetery
basis	Britain	challenge
beauty	burial	changeable
becoming	business	character
before	busy	chief
beginning		choose
belief	calendar	chose
believe	candidate	clothes
beneficial	career	coarse
benefited	careless	column
breath	carrying	comfortable

Mechanics

GROUP 4

comfortably	condemn	convenience
coming	confident	convenient
commercial	confidential	coolly
committed	conscience	courageous
committee	conscientious	course
companies	conscious	courteous
competition	considerably	criticism
competitor	consistent	criticize
completely	continually	
conceive	control	dealt
concentrate	controlled	deceive

GROUP 5

decision	develop	disastrous
definite	development	discipline
definitely	device	disease
definition	difference	disgusted
dependent	different	dissatisfaction
describe	difficult	dissatisfied
description	dilemma	doesn't
desirable	dining	due
despair	disagree	during
desperate	disappearance	
destruction	disappoint	efficiency

GROUP 6

efficient	equipped	extraordinary
eighth	especially	extremely
eliminate	etc.	
embarrass	exaggerate	familiar
embarrassment	excellent	families
eminent	exceptionally	fashion
emphasize	exercise	favorite
endeavor	exhaust	foreign
enough	existence	forward
entertain	experience	friend
environment	explanation	fulfill

GROUP 7

fundamentally	happily	hurriedly
further	happiness	hypocrisy
	height	hypocrite
generally	heroes	
genius	heroine	ignorant
government	hindrance	imaginary
governor	hopeful	imagination
group	huge	immediately
guaranteed	humorous	immensely
guidance	hundred	incidentally
	hungry	indefinite

GROUP 8

independent	irrelevant	likely
indispensable	irresistible	literature
inevitable	itself	livelihood
influence		loneliness
ingenious	jealous	losing
intellectual		
intelligence	knowledge	magnificent
interest		maintain
interpret	laboratory	maintenance
interrupt	laid	maneuver
involve	leisure	manufacturer

GROUP 9

marriage	muscle	occasionally
mathematics	mysterious	occurred
meant		occurrence
medicine	naïve	omit
medieval	necessarily	operate
method	necessary	opinion
mileage	ninety	opponent
miniature	noticeable	opportunity
minute		optimism
mischievous	obstacle	original
morale	occasion	

Mechanics

paid	persistent	practical
parallel	persuade	practice
paralysis	pertain	precede
paralyze	phase	prepare
particularly	philosophy	prevalent
peace	physical	primitive
peculiar	piece	professional
perceive	playwright	prominent
perform	political	propaganda
performance	possess	psychology
permanent	possession	pursue

quantity	resource	sense
	response	separate
really	reveal	several
recognize	rhythm	shining
recommend	ridiculous	significance
regard		similar
relief	sacrifice	simple
relieve	safety	sincerely
religion	satisfactorily	sophomore
repetition	schedule	sponsor
representative	seize	strength

stretch	together	writing
strictly	tragedy	
subtle	transferred	
sufficient	tremendous	
superintendent		
surprise	undoubtedly	
	unnecessary	
temperament	useful	
tendency	using	
therefore	various	
thorough	weird	

Test your mastery of common spelling problems by having someone dictate the following sentences to you. They contain 100 frequently misspelled words taken from the groups above that you have just finished studying.

1. The *principal* and the *superintendent disagree* on *discipline*.
2. My *friend* was *arguing* with an *adolescent* from *Britain*.
3. *Amateurs* face *competition* from *professional athletes*.
4. I *referred* him to his *counselor* for *guidance* and *advice*.
5. My *opponent* was of *tremendous height* and *strength*.
6. The city *council* chose a *convenient* and *accessible site*.
7. We were *studying* the *methods* of *medieval medicine*.
8. The *speech* was an *attack* on *political practices*.
9. The *performance* was *interrupted* by the *inevitable commercials*.
10. The *committee recommended* more *grammar* and *mathematics*.
11. The *playwright's characters* were neither *villains* nor *heroes*.
12. Because of their *privileges*, the *morale* of the *group* was *magnificent*.
13. The *beginner* should *seize* every *opportunity* for *writing*.
14. *Dining* with a *hungry acquaintance* can be *embarrassing*.
15. She is a *recognized authority* on *primitive religions*.
16. The *manufacturers* of *clothes* promote *weird fashions*.
17. His *conscientious* roll call *accidentally revealed* my *absence*.
18. Her *busy schedule* may *aggravate* the *disease*.
19. A *mysterious* event *occurred minutes* before the *burial*.
20. *Peace* is often *preceded* by *bargaining* and *maneuvers*.
21. *Several* workers were *dropped during* the *efficiency* drive.
22. He *accused* his *competitors* of his own *favorite devices*.
23. A *simple* but *sincere apology* will be *sufficient*.
24. *Exercise* is not *likely* to *affect* her *appearance*.
25. He *sacrificed* the *safety* and *quiet* of his former *existence*.

In your own words, explain briefly the difference between the two words in each of the following pairs. Be prepared to discuss the different definitions in class. (Your teacher may ask you to use each in a brief sample sentence.)

1. assent/ascent
2. conscious/conscientious
3. precede/proceed
4. mussel/muscle
5. moral/morale
6. eliminate/illuminate
7. course/coarse
8. a lot/allot
9. alter/altar
10. through/thorough

Mechanics

Choose the missing words or the missing letters for the blank in each of the following sentences. Put the letter for the right choice after the number of the sentence.

1. Everyone had rec_____ved an invitation.
   a. ei   b. ie   c. ea

2. The check was in a separ_____ letter.
   a. ete   b. ate   c. ite

3. Chipmunks _____ sun themselves on these rocks.
   a. use to   b. useto   c. used to

4. She _____ a position in a different state.
   a. excepted   b. acepted   c. accepted

5. We checked the pron_____nciation of the word.
   a. ou   b. uo   c. u

6. He had learned _____ during his trip.
   a. alot   b. a lot   c. allot

7. After the robbery, his _____ bothered him.
   a. conscience   b. conscious   c. conscientious

8. All books should be returned to the lib_____.
   a. rary   b. ary   c. erry

9. They were driving very simi_____ cars.
   a. ler   b. lar   c. liar

10. We had planned a _____prise party for her birthday.
    a. su   b. sur   c. sup

11. She was wri_____ her autobiography.
    a. tting   b. teing   c. ting

12. The class was stud_____ Spanish.
    a. ying   b. ding   c. ing

13. We bel_____ved none of these predictions.
    a. ei   b. ea   c. ie

14. The Italian club was pla_____ a picnic.
    a. nning   b. ning   c. nyng

15. They had experienced much unhapp_____.
    a. yness   b. ynes   c. iness

16. Teachers took attend_____ at the beginning of the hour.
    a. ence   b. ance   c. ants

17. The injury had _____ his hearing.
    a. affected   b. effected   c. afected

18. She was voted most likely to suc_____ .
    a. ede   b. cede   c. ceed

19. No one had suspected the exist_____ of these tribes.
    a. ence   b. ance   c. ents

20. That Christmas, there were very few pres_____ .
    a. ence   b. ents   c. ance

Learn how to use capital letters, apostrophes, and hyphens.

M2

CAPITALS AND SPECIAL MARKS

When we transfer spoken words to the written page, we use not only the ordinary alphabet but also capital letters and special marks. These marks often do not have an exact equivalent in speech. They are not pronounced in a way that would clearly signal when to put them in. We have to study and practice how each is used.

Use capital letters for proper names, for most of the words in a title, and for the first word of a sentence.

M2a

Using Capitals

The most basic function of a capital letter is to start a **proper name.** A proper name sets an individual or a group off from other examples of the same kind. In a group of children, only one may be called *Mary.* In a softball league, only one team is likely to be called the *Padres.* Look at the difference between general words and proper names in the following examples:

GENERAL WORD: freshman, sophomore, athlete, swimmer
PROPER NAME: Tom, Marcia, Cynthia, Dennis

GENERAL WORD: hunter, tribe, nation, people
PROPER NAME: Cherokees, Danes, Mexicans, Canadians

GENERAL WORD: car, vehicle, motorcycle, truck
PROPER NAME: Buick, Honda, Chevrolet, Volkswagen

In addition, capital letters serve some special purposes: We capitalize the pronoun *I.* We capitalize the first word of a new sentence.

Remember to use capital letters for the following purposes:

(1) Capitalize the first word of a sentence. Also capitalize the first word in a quotation that is a complete sentence:

The coach said, "Now I have heard everything."

(2) Capitalize all major words in titles. Capitalize the first word in titles of books, newspapers, articles, poems, movies, songs, television shows, and the like. Also capitalize all other words in such titles except articles *(a, an, the);* prepositions *(at, of, for, with,* and the like*);*

and connectives *(and, but, when, if,* and the like). Capitalize even the prepositions and connectives when they have five or more letters *(through, without, across, about):*

Women of Courage	The Little House on the Prairie
Singing in the Rain	Much Ado About Nothing
A Choice of Weapons	A Tale of Two Cities

NOTE: Capitalize words this way when you write the title of your *own* theme and when you mention a book or article *in* your theme.

See **M6b** for italicizing of titles.

(3) Capitalize the names and initials of persons. Also capitalize any titles or ranks used with the name. Study the contrast between a general and a specific use of a title or rank:

GENERAL WORD: The two judges had written the decision together.
PROPER NAME: Judge Cermak and Judge Rey wrote the decision.

GENERAL WORD: The sergeant had filed a report.
PROPER NAME: We sent Sergeant Blake to investigate.

We capitalize *Father* and *Mother* and similar family names when we use them as the name of the person. We do not capitalize them when they follow a pronoun like *my, his,* or *her:*

GENERAL WORD: Her father and his mother attended the ceremony.
PROPER NAME: As usual, Mother and Father were late.

NOTE: We sometimes use a title that is used alone. "A *president,*" "a *queen,*" or "a *pope*" means "one of several." "The *President,*" "the *Queen,*" or "the *Pope*" means "the only one."

(4) Capitalize the names of major groups: religions, denominations, nationalities, races, and political parties:

Protestant, Episcopalian, Canadian, Eskimo, Democratic

Remember that words like *democratic* and *republican* are also used to describe a type of institution or idea:

GENERAL WORD: Ancient Greece developed democratic institutions. (examples of a type)
PROPER NAME: She voted for the Democratic party. (name of one party)

(5) Capitalize the names of places and geographical features. Use a capital letter for the names of countries, cities, towns, streets, rivers, mountains, lakes, and the like:

Zambia, Oregon, Los Angeles, Outer Drive, Mount Hood, the Ohio River, Lake Tahoe, Purvis Tunnel

SOME CAPITALIZED NAMES

An Overview

PEOPLE:	Eleanor Roosevelt, Langston Hughes, Norma Lorre Goodrich, Edna St. Vincent Millay	PERSONAL NAMES
TITLES:	Dr. Brothers, Senator Kennedy, Queen Elizabeth, Pope John; the President	
IMAGINARY PEOPLE:	Apollo, Captain Nemo, Cleopatra, the Wizard of Oz, Maid Marian	
CONTINENTS:	Asia, America, Europe, Australia, the Antarctic	GEOGRAPHIC NAMES
COUNTRIES:	United States of America, Canada, Great Britain, Mexico, Denmark, Japan	
REGIONS:	the South, the East, the Near East, the Midwest	
STATES:	Kansas, North Dakota, Louisiana, Rhode Island	
CITIES:	Oklahoma City, Dallas, Baltimore, Los Angeles; Washington, D.C.	
SIGHTS:	Lake Erie, Mount Hood, Death Valley, Walden Pond	
ADDRESSES:	Park Lane, Fleet Avenue, Oak Street, Independence Square	
MONTHS:	January, March, July, October	CALENDAR NAMES
WEEKDAYS:	Monday, Wednesday, Saturday, Sunday	
HOLIDAYS:	Labor Day, Thanksgiving, Easter, the Sabbath, Mother's Day, the Fourth of July	
INSTITUTIONS:	the Supreme Court, the Department of Agriculture, the U.S. Senate	INSTITUTIONAL NAMES
BUSINESSES:	Ford Motor Company, General Electric, Sears	
SCHOOLS:	Oakdale High School, Las Vistas Junior College, University of Maine	
GROUPS:	the Democratic Party, the American Legion, the Garment Workers' Union	
PROPER NAMES:	the Virgin Mary, St. Thomas, Luther	RELIGIOUS NAMES
FAITHS:	Christian, Muslim, Jewish, Buddhist	
DENOMINATIONS:	Methodist, Mormon, Unitarian, Roman Catholic	

(6) Capitalize the names of buildings and institutions. Use a capital letter for the names of churches, schools, clubs, and other organizations. Study the difference between general and proper names in the following pair:

GENERAL WORD: A boy from my high school had to go to the hospital.

PROPER NAME: A boy from Independence High School was admitted to the Fairwoods Memorial Hospital.

(7) Capitalize the names of historical events, periods, and documents. Study the following pairs:

GENERAL WORD: They fought in two world wars.

PROPER NAME: They fought in World War I and World War II.

GENERAL WORD: The constitutions of several states should be amended.

PROPER NAME: The Constitution of the United States is a famous political document.

(8) Capitalize calendar names: days of the week, months, and holidays. Do *not* capitalize the names of the seasons:

Tuesday, February, Easter, the Fourth of July, Christmas
spring, summer, autumn, winter

(9) Capitalize compass points only when they name a region: the South, the Northwest, the East. Do not capitalize them when they show a general direction:

GENERAL WORD: We had to turn east to reach the lake.

PROPER NAME: She had spent all her life in the East.

GENERAL WORD: The wind was coming from the southwest.

PROPER NAME: The crew worked on irrigation projects throughout the Southwest.

(10) Capitalize the names of all languages. Do not capitalize the names of other school subjects, unless they are part of a course title:

Jim speaks English, French, and Spanish.
She is now taking a course in Russian.
I intend to take Algebra I and Art II.

I intend to take algebra and art.

(11) Capitalize the name of the Deity. Also capitalize all pronouns referring to Him. The names of sacred figures, the Bible, and parts of the Bible are also generally capitalized:

The Lord gives and He may take away; blessed be His name.
Virgin Mary, Holy Ghost, Genesis

(12) Capitalize adjectives made from proper nouns.   But do not capitalize the nouns following such adjectives unless they themselves are proper nouns:

Danish pastry (first made in Denmark)
French bread (first made in France)
Italian pizza (first made in Italy)
an African country (located in Africa)
a Roman emperor (who reigned in Rome)

(13) When something has been named after a person, capitalize the person's name:

Geiger counter, Ferris wheel, Morse code

Sometimes the person who gave something its name has been forgotten, and a lower case letter is used:

diesel engine, a maverick senator, pasteurized milk

(14) Capitalize trade names of all kinds.   Do not capitalize the word following the trade name unless it is part of it:

Coca-Cola, Alka-Seltzer, Bayer Aspirin, a Xerox copier

NOTE: Do not capitalize the following when they are part of a proper name: the articles *(the, a, an);* short prepositions and connectives— less than five letters *(of, by, with; and):*

Institute for the Blind
Fourth of July
Speech and Drama Department

Study the use of capital letters in the following exercise. Read it over several times. Pay special attention to pairs where the same word is used once with and once without a capital letter.

EXERCISE 1

1. A city in Kansas, Oklahoma City, Dearborn Township, a small town, Washtenaw County, El Paso, District of Columbia.
2. The Atlantic, Lake Huron, an island in the Pacific, Long Island, a rocky trail, the Rocky Mountains, the Erie Canal.
3. The Postmaster General, Professor Smith, an English teacher, the Reverend Brown, our new mayor, Mayor Santos.
4. A Ford truck, the Ford Motor Company, General Motors, General Electric appliances.
5. A side street, Main Street, the Ambassador Hotel, the Good Samaritan Hospital, a business college, O'Connor Hall.
6. The *Congressional Record, The New York Times,* the *Merryvale News; Gone with the Wind, The Bridge of San Luis Rey, Brave New World, A Midsummer Night's Dream, Much Ado About Nothing.*

7. The Greek gods, God Almighty, Christ and his disciples, the New Testament.
8. Mother's Day, Easter, last spring, Christmas Eve, the last Saturday in November, the Middle Ages, a middle-aged man.
9. The Civil War, a civil war, the Democratic ticket, democratic ideals.
10. The U.S. Army, the Senate, the Inaugural Ball, the Fourth of July, the Declaration of Independence, the Bill of Rights.

EXERCISE 2

After the number of each sentence, write down (and capitalize) each word that should have started with a capital letter. (You need not include the first word of the sentence.) Write on a separate sheet of paper.

(A) 1. Mark twain grew up in hannibal, missouri, on the banks of the mississippi.
    2. His parents were from virginia and kentucky, and he was for a short spell a confederate officer.
    3. In *life on the mississippi,* he paints the south he knew as a river pilot.
    4. In *the innocents abroad,* he describes a european tour on the steamship *quaker city,* which took him to the holy land.
    5. In *a connecticut yankee at king arthur's court,* a new englander finds himself in ancient britain.
    6. He tells the catholic english of the early middle ages that his first wife was a baptist.
    7. He plots to install republican institutions on the american model, bringing democracy not only to the british but to the germans and russians as well.
    8. Mark twain's humor is a blend of new england wryness and the tall tale of the west.
    9. He attacked christians tolerating slavery and exposed the corruption he saw after the civil war.
   10. His admirers have included people of every country from italy to new zealand.

(B) 11. Jean stafford was a well-known contemporary american writer of short stories.
   12. Her stories appeared in magazines like *the new yorker, harper's,* and the *saturday evening post.*
   13. Her father was a writer of westerns and had published a novel called *when cattle kingdom fell.*
   14. A cousin had written a book called *a stepdaughter of the prairie* about her childhood in kansas.
   15. In her first stories, jean stafford wrote about cattle drives from the texas panhandle to dodge city and about bloody incidents south of the border in mexico.

16. Though her roots were in colorado, she said parts of her belonged to the south, the midwest, new england, and new york.

17. Like many other american writers, she crossed the atlantic to study european ways.

18. One of her stories takes place on a cold december day in maine.

19. A lonely old woman puts up a christmas wreath for the holiday season but then blames her maid for the "monstrosity."

20. Another character has only one friend—a cat that looks like a halloween mask and hates most people.

After the number of each sentence, write down and capitalize all words that should have been capitalized. If there are no such words in the sentence, write *No* after the number of the sentence. Write on a separate sheet of paper.

EXERCISE 3

1. Walt disney is one of the names that hollywood has made famous around the world.

2. Millions in countries like germany, italy, and russia know and love mickey mouse and donald duck.

3. Later, disney made cartoon versions of european fairy tales like cinderella, snow white, and sleeping beauty.

4. In 1954, he filmed *20,000 leagues under the sea* by Jules verne, a french writer.

5. In 1868, a french scientist and his assistant are guests on an american warship searching the pacific for a legendary sea monster.

6. A famous german actor, peter lorre, plays the assistant.

7. An actor who plays a roman slave and a greek general in other-classic movies plays an american sailor who joins the expedition in san francisco.

8. He sings sailors' songs like those heard on sailing ships going around cape horn or on the whaling ships of new england.

9. The sea monster is really the submarine *nautilus,* commanded by captain nemo.

10. The captain and his crew have developed scientific secrets way ahead of their time.

11. Operating from the island base of volcania, the *nautilus* destroys ships used by nations like france and england in the service of oppression and war.

12. When the warship is sunk, the scientist, his assistant, and the sailor become prisoners on the undersea vessel.

13. They see treasures like those hunted by sir francis drake or looted by the spaniards in peru.

14. The sailor saves captain nemo's life in the climactic battle with a giant squid.

15. The three prisoners are the only survivors when the *nautilus* sinks after its last battle.

M2b
Using Apostrophes

Use the apostrophe to show contractions and the possessive of nouns.

Like a capital letter, the apostrophe is strictly a *written* symbol. We cannot hear it when we read a sentence aloud. Know the three major uses of the apostrophe:

(1) Use the apostrophe to show where letters have been left out. In speech we often shorten (contract) words by leaving out sounds. We say *I'd* for *I would, she'll* for *she will, don't* for *do not.* Look at the use of the apostrophe in the following **contractions:**

I am	*I'm* tired.
you are	*You're* right.
he is	*He's* gone.
we would	*We'd* call.
they will	*They'll* change.

Many contractions contain a shortened form of *not.* Take care not to misspell these, especially *doesn't* (*does* not) and *don't* (*do* not):

cannot	I *can't* tell.
have not	We *haven't* heard.
is not	It *isn't* true.
will not	He *won't* believe you.
do not	They *don't* like it here.
does not	It *doesn't* count.

Some contractions sound exactly like other forms that have quite different uses. Make sure you *spell* them differently:

It's means *it is:*	*It's* too late.
Its means *of it:*	The ship kept *its* course.
Who's means *who is:*	*Who's* your friend?
Whose means *of whom:*	*Whose* car did you borrow?
They're means *they are:*	*They're* my assistants.
Their means *of them:*	We found *their* hideout.

NOTE: Use contractions mainly when reporting a conversation. An occasional *don't* or *it's* may appear in a serious article. But many readers consider contractions too informal for formal reports, research papers, or letters of application.

(2) Use the apostrophe and –s to form the possessive of nouns. The **possessive** shows where or to whom something belongs. We

produce the possessive form when instead of putting an *of* between two nouns we put the *second noun* first. This noun is then usually followed by the apostrophe plus *–s:*

the leader of the *group* ⟶ the *group's* leader
the face of the *child* ⟶ the *child's* face
the speech of the *mayor* ⟶ the *mayor's* speech
the father of the *children* ⟶ the *children's* father

The same form is used in many common expressions dealing with time and price:

a *day's* work	a *week's* pay
a *night's* sleep	a *year's* leave
a *moment's* notice	a *dollar's* worth
tonight's paper	a *dime's* worth

Sometimes, the first noun already ends in *–s.* In that case, use *only* the apostrophe to form the possessive of the noun. Do *not* use an additional *–s:*

the girls ⟶ the *girls'* uniforms (several girls)
the parents ⟶ the *parents'* duty (both parents)

two *weeks* ⟶ two *weeks'* pay
five *dollars* ⟶ five *dollars'* worth

When a proper name ends in *–s, either* of the following is acceptable: *Charles'* letter, or *Charles's* letter.

NOTE: Use the apostrophe plus *–s* for the possessive of the **indefinite pronouns:** *one, everybody (everyone), somebody (someone), anybody (anyone), nobody (no one).* But never use the apostrophe for the possessive forms of **personal pronouns.** Never use an apostrophe in *his, hers, its, ours, yours, theirs.* Contrast the sentences in each of the following pairs:

The noise gets on *one's* nerves.
The noise got on *his* nerves.

The story aroused *everyone's* curiosity.
The bird shook *its* tailfeathers.

The car must be *somebody's.* (= somebody's car)
The car must be *hers.* (= her car)

(3) Use the apostrophe to separate the plural –s from the name of a letter or of a number or from a word discussed as a word:

His record showed many C's and a few B's.
There were three 7's in the number.
His speech contained many if's and but's.

EXERCISE 1

Rewrite each of the following. Substitute the possessive form or the contraction using the apostrophe.

1. the owner of the dog
2. the owners of the dogs
3. the schedule of the team
4. the relay team of the women
5. the obligations of the jurors
6. to the surprise of everybody
7. the day off of the lifeguard
8. a drive of two hours
9. the pay of one week
10. the work of several days
11. we cannot tell
12. we do not agree
13. who is there?
14. it is unlikely
15. they are out of town

EXERCISE 2

Write down the right choice after the number of the sentence. Write on a separate sheet.

1. The company owed him a *weeks/week's* pay.
2. When she will be back is *anybodys/anybody's* guess.
3. The first prize in the raffle was five *dollar's/dollars'* worth of merchandise from the book store.
4. Jean had repaired the *minister's/ministers'* bicycle.
5. The school needs a bigger lot for the *students/students'* cars.
6. Her sister-in-law was active in several *women's/womens'* business organizations.
7. The testimony of all *witnesses/witnesses'* was re-examined.
8. Some *childrens/children's* programs are very imaginative.
9. *Somebodys/Somebody's* dog was always tearing up the lawn and the flower beds.
10. The husbands saw their *wives/wives'* point of view.
11. No one knows *who's/whose* fault it was.
12. What do these *girl's/girls'* parents think?
13. The bird ruffled *it's/its* feathers and eyed me suspiciously.
14. While we were gone, two new *families/family's* had moved in.
15. Grandfather always worried about the *family's/families* good name.
16. I wonder *who's/whose* going to pay the bill.
17. The next day he had already forgotten the *girls/girls'* names.
18. The accident was *no one's/no ones* fault.
19. He was looking for *yesterdays/yesterday's* newspaper.
20. Jim had been trying to organize a *citizens/citizens'* patrol.

Use the hyphen in compound words that have not yet become a single word.

Use the hyphen in the following situations:

(1) Use the hyphen in compound numbers from twenty-one *to* ninety-nine:

Their ages ranged from nineteen to *forty-nine.*

(2) Use the hyphen for combinations that are at the halfway stage between one word and several. We call such combined words **compound words.** Some have already merged into a single word. Others are still separate. Still others are hyphenated:

ONE WORD: headache, darkroom, highway, newspaper, stepmother, grandfather, birthplace, bittersweet, freestyle, greenbelt

SEVERAL WORDS: high school, labor union, commander in chief, second cousin, bird dog, ground plan, pony express, side effect

HYPHEN: bull's-eye, cave-in, court-martial, great-grandfather, in-laws, brother-in-law, Mexican-American, left-handed, merry-go-round, hand-picked, able-bodied

Make sure to get the following right:

ONE WORD: today, tomorrow, nevertheless, nowadays
TWO WORDS: all right, a lot (of things, such as time), be able, no one

NOTE: Many words that used to be hyphenated are now written solidly. Others are used either way. When you are in doubt, use the word the way it is listed in your dictionary.

(3) Use the hyphen to separate some prefixes from the word that follows. A **prefix** is an exchangeable part that can appear in front of many different words. Most prefixes combine with the word that follows into a single unit. Put a hyphen after the prefix in the following situations:

- After *all–, ex–* (when it means "former"), and *self–:*

  all-knowing, all-powerful; ex-champion, ex-president; self-conscious, self-respect

- Before a *capital* letter:

  all-American, pro-British, anti-German, non-Catholic

- Between two *identical vowels:*

  anti-intellectual, semi-independent

(4) Use the hyphen with group modifiers. Several words that are normally kept separate may combine as a **group modifier**

that is put in front of a noun. Use hyphens whenever such a group of words takes the place of a single adjective: *first-class* mail, *four-wheel* drive, *high-grade* ore.

SEPARATE: We decided to *wait and see.*
HYPHENS: She adopted a *wait-and-see* attitude.

SEPARATE: The meal was *well balanced.*
HYPHENS: They served a *well-balanced* meal.

SEPARATE: The speech was followed by *questions and answers.*
HYPHENS: There was a *question-and-answer* period.

Do not use hyphens when one part of the group modifier is an adverb ending in *–ly:*

a *rapidly growing* city
a *carefully prepared* demonstration

For hyphen dividing words at end of line, see **M7a.**

EXERCISE 1

After the number of each group of words, write it the way it should appear. Use hyphens where they are required. Make changes only if they are necessary.

EXAMPLE: an ex champion
(Answer) *an ex-champion*

1. a play by play account
2. her new brother in law
3. wall to wall carpets
4. he was twenty one
5. a smoothly running operation
6. improved self confidence
7. a well chosen cast
8. a strictly personal question
9. a two lane high way
10. my person to person call
11. her non Catholic friends
12. our fast talking ex governor
13. a run of the mill performance
14. new heavy duty tires
15. anti American feeling
16. Spanish speaking voters
17. a heavily traveled road
18. a Polish American club
19. her hand picked successor
20. an old fashioned labor union

In each sentence, find the combination that needs one or more hyphens. Write the hyphenated expression after the number of the sentence. Write on a separate sheet of paper.

1. He suffered from a badly disguised lack of self confidence.
2. A station to station call made from one's home phone costs less than a call made from person to person.
3. The new pro American government stayed close to the middle of the road on domestic issues.
4. Grandfather thought that most people on welfare were able bodied paupers.
5. He went through a point by point comparison of the two plans.
6. As usual, the slowly deteriorating local movie palace offered a third rate movie.
7. The new process at the recycling plant made the use of low grade ore economically feasible.
8. We overcame his anti Catholic sentiments step by step.
9. The busboy was listening to a play by play account of the day's game instead of clearing the table.
10. The ex President had been sharply critical of labor unions.

Look at the three possible choices for the blank in each of the following sentences. After the number of the sentence, put the letter for the right choice.

1. Goats and sheep wandered around in the _____ zoo.
   a. childrens   b. children's   c. childrens'

2. Alex Haley wrote a book called _____ .
   a. *roots*   b. *Roots*   c. *Root's*

3. The next Sunday, he went to his _____ house.
   a. in-laws'   b. inlaws   c. inlaws'

4. The road followed the coastline of _____ .
   a. Lake Huron   b. lake Huron   c. lake huron

5. Her last employer owed her two _____ pay.
   a. months   b. month's   c. months'

6. No one could make _____ understand that children grow up.
   a. father   b. Father   c. father's

7. We visited the Massachusetts _____ Technology.
   a. Institute of   b. Institute Of   c. institute of

8. A driver may feel responsible for a _____ carelessness.
   a. passengers   b. passenger's   c. passengers'

9. Jane Austen wrote a novel called *Pride* _____ .
   a. *and Prejudice*   b. *And Prejudice*   c. *and prejudice*

10. Several members of her family were attending a _____ .
    a. Junior College   b. Junior college   c. junior college

11. She refused to give her _____ the day off.
    a. employees   b. employee's   c. employees'

12. All three networks carried the _____ message.
    a. Presidents   b. president's   c. President's

13. There were two _____ players on the team.
    a. all American   b. all-American   c. all-american

14. The title of the book was *Goalie* _____ *Mask*.
    a. *without a*   b. *Without a*   c. *Without A*

15. The city had been chosen as the site of the _____ .
    a. olympic games   b. Olympic games   c. Olympic Games

16. The Australian player won the _____ singles match.
    a. women's   b. womens   c. womans

17. We had to cancel our _____ .
    a. spanish lesson   b. Spanish Lesson   c. Spanish lesson

18. The proposal had to be approved by a _____ majority.
    a. two-thirds   b. two thirds   c. two-third's

19. It was rare for the coach to ask an _____ opinion.
    a. athlete's   b. athletes   c. athletes'

20. Houston was the fastest-growing city in the _____ .
    a. southwest   b. Southwest   c. south-west

M3

END PUNCTUATION

Mark the end of a sentence by a period, a question mark, or an exclamation mark.

In speech, the end of something we say is signaled by definite breaks, accompanied by a rising or falling tone of voice. The written symbols of these breaks are the period, the question mark, and the exclamation mark.

M3a

Sentences and Fragments

Use the period at the end of a complete sentence.

The **period** separates one complete sentence from another. A complete sentence has its own subject and its own verb. (In request sentences, the subject has often been left out, but *you* is understood as the subject.)

PUNCTUATION MARKS
A Reference Chart

COMMA
before coordinating connectives	M4a
with adverbial clauses	M4b
with relative clauses	M4c
with nonrestrictive modifiers	M5a
after introductory modifiers	M5a
with adverbial connectives	M4a
with *especially, namely, for example*	M3a
with *of course* and other sentence modifiers	M5a
between items in a series	M5b
in a series of parallel clauses	M4a
between coordinate adjectives	M5b
with dates, addresses, etc.	M5b
with direct address and other light interrupters	M5c
between contrasted elements	M5c
with quotations	M6a

SEMICOLON
between independent clauses	M4a
before adverbial connectives	M4a
before coordinating connectives	M4a
between items in a series	M5b

COLON
to introduce a list or explanation	M3a
to introduce a quotation	M6a

PERIOD
at end of sentence	M3a
ellipsis	M6a
with abbreviations	M7b

DASH
break in thought	M3a
with heavy interrupters	M5c

QUOTATION MARKS
with direct quotation	M6a
quotation within quotation	M6a
with slang or technical terms	M6b
to set off titles	M6b

EXCLAMATION MARK	M3b
QUESTION MARK	M3b
PARENTHESES	M5c

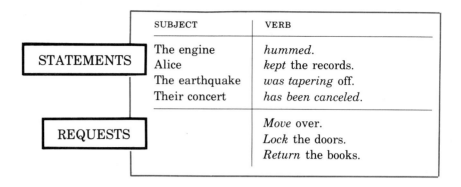

	SUBJECT	VERB
STATEMENTS	The engine	*hummed.*
	Alice	*kept* the records.
	The earthquake	*was tapering* off.
	Their concert	*has been canceled.*
REQUESTS		*Move* over.
		Lock the doors.
		Return the books.

Do *not* use a period to set off a group of words that is not a complete sentence. If you do, the result will be a **sentence fragment.** Usually, what is missing from a fragment is *all or part of the verb.* Often, both part of the verb and a possible subject are missing:

FRAGMENT: We had an additional passenger. *My brother.*

COMPLETE: We had an additional passenger. My brother *joined* us.

FRAGMENT: We watched the raccoon. *Stealing the cat food.*

COMPLETE: We watched the raccoon. *It was* stealing the cat food.

Avoid especially four kinds of sentence fragments:

(1) Do not separate prepositional phrases from the rest of the sentence. Prepositional phrases start with a preposition like *in, at, with, for, on,* or *without.* Do not separate them from the sentence to which they belong:

FRAGMENT: Sue had painted the shed. *With leftover paint.*

COMPLETE: Sue had painted the shed *with leftover paint.*

FRAGMENT: He had crossed the Rocky Mountains. *On a bicycle.*

COMPLETE: He had crossed the Rocky Mountains *on a bicycle.*

(2) Do not separate appositives from the rest of the sentence. An appositive is a second noun that is put after the first noun and gives us further information about it. Often the second noun carries with it other material to make up an appositive phrase. There is no verb to make a second complete sentence:

FRAGMENT: We protected our key player. *The goalkeeper.*

COMPLETE: We protected our key player, *the goalkeeper.*

FRAGMENT: He pawned his last treasure. *A silver flute.*

COMPLETE: He pawned his last treasure, *a silver flute.*

(3) Do not separate verbals from the rest of the sentence. Many verbal phrases start with an *–ing* form (participle) or a *to* form

(infinitive). To become part of a complete verb, such forms have to follow an auxiliary like *am, was, has, had, will, can, may,* or *should.* Do not separate verbals from the sentence if there is no auxiliary:

FRAGMENT: She had twisted her ankle. *Playing volleyball.*
COMPLETE: She had twisted her ankle *playing volleyball.*

FRAGMENT: They had gone downtown. *To find a job.*
COMPLETE: They had gone downtown *to find a job.*

(4) *Do not separate dependent clauses from their main clauses.* A clause that starts with a subordinator—*if, because, although, whereas*—cannot stand by itself. It turns into a fragment when separated from the main clause by a period. A clause that starts with a relative pronoun—*who, which, that*—also turns into a fragment when set off:

FRAGMENT: We returned to the pier. *Because the boat was overloaded.*
COMPLETE: We returned to the pier *because the boat was overloaded.*

FRAGMENT: We went to see my uncle. *Who had promised to help.*
COMPLETE: We went to see my uncle, *who had promised to help.*

Remember the major ways a fragment may be punctuated as part of a complete sentence:

• Many fragments can become part of the sentence without any break in speech and *without any punctuation* in writing. Use no comma or other mark before most adverbs and prepositional phrases, and many verbals:

Tell them to return the car *right away.*
We will meet you at five *at the corner of Main Street.*
She went to the county building *to register.*

• Most appositives and many verbals and dependent clauses are separated from a sentence by a slight break in speech. Use a comma in writing:

We admired the heirloom, *a grandfather clock.*
They were up on the roof, *nailing down loose shingles.*

Use the comma also before *such as, especially, for example, for instance,* or *namely* when it adds examples to a more general statement: (A *second* comma is used in much formal writing after the last three of these.)

Many students had come from distant places, *such as Guam.*
You should slow down in the rain, *especially at night.*
Be prepared for the unexpected, *for instance, a stalled car ahead of you.*

See **M4** and **M5** for detailed instructions on using the comma.

• Use the **colon** to tie a detailed *list, description, or explanation* to the more general statement that comes before:

The sled carried our two most basic supplies: *flour and matches.*
Training was always the same: *running, exercising, and sparring.*
We lacked only one important thing: *a good coach.*

• Use the **dash** to *keep an afterthought apart* as something you add after a definite break. (Like other marks that call special attention to something we say, the dash easily loses its effect when overused.)

We had reached the moment of truth—*opening night.*
The driver pleaded and argued—*in vain.*
He slammed the door and left—*forever.*

• Sometimes it is difficult to work a fragment into a sentence in one of these ways. Turn such a fragment into a *complete separate sentence:*

FRAGMENT: The coupling had come loose. *Thus causing a slow leak.*
COMPLETE: The coupling had come loose. *A slow leak was the result.*

NOTE: **Permissible fragments** appear in writing when the writer imitates the natural flow of speech or thought.

You are likely to find such permissible fragments in the following kinds of material:

(1) Written records of *conversation,* the *dialogue* of a play, or *answers* to questions:

The family moved to Grass Valley last summer. *Beautiful country. Very dry, however.*
What have we got to lose? *Nothing.*
How do I feel? *Terrible!*

(2) *Descriptive passages* that put down impressions the way they would pass through the mind of the observer:

The sunrise was spectacular. *Spears of flame in the sky. Bird voices everywhere.*

(3) *Narrative passages* that record random, naturally moving thoughts:

Cleaner by far than that child right there, she thought. *Poor nasty little thing.* (Flannery O'Connor)

You may use such permissible fragments when reporting a conversation or writing a story. However, avoid these fragments when writing a more formal paper devoted to serious discussion, argument, or research.

Which of the following passages have the right punctuation?
Put *S* after the number of each satisfactory passage. Put *F* after
the number of each passage that contains a sentence fragment.

1. The couple walked from door to door. To sell Bibles.
2. Mrs. Hopewell was talking to her daughter. Joy ignored her completely.
3. Nothing is perfect. This was one of my aunt's favorite sayings.
4. They discussed all important matters in the kitchen. At breakfast or
   over dinner, but not during lunch.
5. The dog had lost an ear. In a hunting accident.
6. Joy saw a young man. Carrying a heavy valise.
7. Charles always arrived during a meal. He would watch us eat.
8. He kept looking at me. Like a child watching a bird at the zoo.
9. Mrs. Hopewell hated her daughter's new name. She would not use it.
10. The girl had achieved her goal. Without even trying.
11. Paul hated the sight of the bathroom: the grimy tub, the cracked mirror,
    the dripping faucets, the greasy tiles.
12. He heard something else. The high whining yelp of a dog.
13. Old-fashioned tires did not just go flat. They went with a bang like a
    cannon cracker on the Fourth of July.
14. Most driving tests are the same. Driving through the town, stopping
    and starting at signals, and parking.
15. Under the back seat, we had a complete workshop. Wrenches, tire
    patches, tire pumps, screwdrivers.
16. The lug bolts stood out. There were no hubcaps in those days.
17. The patch had to be cut on the bias. Tapering off toward the edges.
18. They lived close to the soil—being able to hunt, fish, and raise a garden.
19. We needed some special equipment, such as a black grease pencil and
    a ruler marked in millimeters.
20. A flat tire would cause the car to swerve. Careening wildly all over the
    road.

Which of the following are really two sentences, each with its
own subject and verb? After the number of each such pair, write
down the last word of the first sentence, followed by a period. Then
add and *capitalize* the first word of the second sentence. Put *F* for
fragment if the period would cause a sentence fragment.

EXAMPLE: We checked the fuel _____ the tank was empty.
(Answer) *fuel. The*

1. Language makes possible our sense of numbers _____ words enable us
   to count.
2. Numbers confuse animals _____ for instance, birds.
3. A bird will not return to its nest _____ if two of its four eggs have been
   taken.

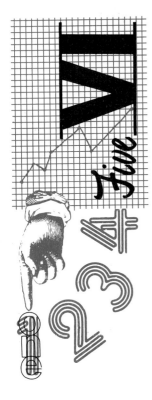

4. It will return to a nest with three eggs left _____ because it cannot count.
5. Some languages have only three number words _____ they are *one,* *two,* and *many.*
6. Words for *three* are often related to similar words _____ meaning "many."
7. *Thrice* is an old word for three times _____ a similar word may mean "frequently."
8. Many words take us back _____ to earlier methods of counting.
9. People counted by keeping a tally _____ they cut notches into a stick.
10. The word *calculate* reminds us of people _____ who counted with pebbles.
11. You can guess the word often used for *five* _____ the word for the hand.
12. Two hands often stand for *ten* _____ as you might expect.
13. Our ten fingers help us count by tens _____ we use a decimal system.
14. Some nations have counted by twenties _____ with ten fingers and ten toes.
15. Americans did some counting by twenties _____ fourscore and ten meant ninety.
16. Some people do not have a separate word for *eighty* _____ the French say "four times twenty."
17. The day of the Aztecs had twenty hours _____ compared with our twenty-four.
18. We still do some counting by twelves _____ in other words by dozens.
19. The Roman year had ten months _____ our own year has twelve.
20. We still use Roman names like December _____ which means the tenth month.

M3b

Questions and Exclamations

Remember to use question marks and exclamation marks where necessary.

Use marks to show that something is not a simple ordinary statement: -

(1) Use the question mark to end sentences that ask for a reply. Many questions are signaled by question words like *who, whom, whose, which, when, where, what, why,* and *how:*

> *Who* is it?
> *What* is the difference?
> *Which* is the shortest way?
> *Why* should we have to pay?

Many questions are signaled by a reversal of the subject and its verb (or auxiliary):

> *Was* the package ready?
> *Did* you tell her the truth?
> *Should* we ask them to return the money?
> *Has* the company been notified?

Remember to put a question mark at the end of a *long* question:

In this book, where does truth end and fiction begin?
How could they have done that when they know how I feel?

(2) Use the exclamation mark for special emphasis. It shows that something is urgent, or that it is unusual, or that it is a surprise. It marks orders, shouts, or urgent requests. Use the exclamation mark as needed with single words, groups of words, or complete sentences:

Stop!	They lost the game!
Put that back!	The supplies are gone!
What a story!	What faces they are going to make!

NOTE: Use either the question mark or a period after requests that are worded as questions for the sake of *politeness:*

Will you please return to the office at three o'clock?
Will you please return to the office at three o'clock.

Which of the following sentences illustrate *acceptable* end punctuation? Put *S* for satisfactory after the number of each such sentence. Which of the following sentences illustrate *unacceptable* end punctuation? Put *U* for unsatisfactory after the numbers of these sentences. Write on a separate sheet of paper.

EXERCISE

1. Are we going to vote for a program or for a handsome face?
2. Will you please tell your friends about our plans.
3. How are we going to find jobs for people poorly trained.
4. What a relief it was to see the rescue party arrive!
5. How important is it to know the right people!
6. Why do you always blame others when something goes wrong.
7. Would you be willing to help us with our project?
8. What is the point of trying hard when the cards are stacked?
9. This man was elected by a margin of three or four votes!
10. What can an individual do against a whole community.
11. Did you notice how his hands shook?
12. We have to evacuate the building!
13. Would you turn off the light on the way out.
14. This is the reward of faithful service?
15. How can anyone know what goes on in another person's mind.
16. Have all members been notified?
17. Do not enter the section if the warning signal shows red!
18. How will she be able to convince the jury.
19. Have you really read the instructions?
20. Have faith!

**UNIT REVIEW
EXERCISE**

Put *S* for satisfactory after the number of each passage with the right punctuation. Put *U* if a passage is unsatisfactory because of a sentence fragment or other punctuation problem.

1. We finally started our vacation. Once just a dream, now a reality.
2. My brother and I got up early. We were the first people skating. on the
3. Can we still afford to hunt just for the excitement of the game.
4. The eagle is a large bird of prey. With a hooked beak and powerful claws.
5. Gradually the leather begins to crack. The fresh leather smell disappears.
6. The eagle perches on a high cliff. Where it sees all.
7. Money for us children meant coins, such as pennies and dimes.
8. Do you have any idea how huge a large hall looks to a small child.
9. We would spend the whole day doing the same job, for instance, unloading shingles from railroad cars.
10. What changes a few years can make in the appearance of a neighborhood!
11. Deadlines scare me. Appointments bother me.
12. We need a happy medium between the serious learning of private schools. And the easy-going learning in public schools.
13. Who cares whether a gift is practical if it comes from the heart.
14. Long slopes led down to rocky creeks. There were no people around.
15. He wanted a credit card. Which would buy things for free.
16. We were lucky to find a specialist. A doctor with an excellent reputation.
17. No one said a word. We had all heard the bad news.
18. We moved to Los Angeles. Offering many cultural attractions new to us.
19. I enjoy the outdoors. Because it is a relaxing environment.
20. My aunt told us about her trip to Canada. What a story!

M4

LINKING
PUNCTUATION

Know when to put the semicolon or the comma between two clauses.

Often, two statements combine. Each becomes a subsentence in the larger combined sentence. We call such subsentences **clauses.** Each of the following sentences combines two clauses. Each clause has its own subject and verb:

The house was empty; *vandals had littered* the floor.
The team was losing, and *the crowd had quieted* down.
The manager turned her down, although *she had been promised* the job.

Remember that a request is still a complete sentence even though the subject is omitted (or "understood"). A clause may also be in the request form. It then *lacks a subject:*

The *lights are* still on; *turn* them off.
You may go now, but *be* careful.

How we punctuate such combined clauses depends on how they are joined. Study the way we join and punctuate two or more clauses.

Know when to use a comma or a semicolon between independent clauses.

We call clauses **independent** when they could easily separate and go their different ways. Know the major ways independent clauses can come together:

(1) Use a comma when two independent clauses are joined by a coordinating connective. Often two statements are joined by a *coordinator.* There are only seven words in this group: *and, but, for, so, yet, or,* and *nor.* The **comma** is the right punctuation when one of these words joins two complete clauses:

The thunder rolled, *and* thick drops began to fall.
The phone kept ringing, *but* nobody answered.
He was worried, *for* his application had gone in late.
It rained hard, *so* the parade was called off.
The food was average, *yet* we all asked for more.
You should confirm your reservation, *or* the airline will cancel it.
Norbert did not attend the rally, *nor* did his friends.

More than two independent clauses may be linked by coordinating connectives in the same sentence:

Marcia was humming, *but* Vince kept quiet, *for* he was still afraid.

NOTE: All the connectives in this group also have *other* uses. These often require no punctuation. Often, a coordinator joins two words or phrases:

The city needed more parks *and* playgrounds.

(2) Use a semicolon when two independent clauses are joined by an adverbial connective. Adverbial connectives are words like *however, therefore, consequently, nevertheless, besides, moreover, furthermore, accordingly, indeed,* and *in fact.* Put a **semicolon** between the two clauses joined by one of these words:

The crowd booed; *however,* the players kept calm.
Conditions were ideal for the wild horses; *therefore,* their numbers kept growing.
The officer kept waving on the other cars; *nevertheless,* everybody slowed down to look.
She has worked here regularly; *in fact,* she has not missed a day.

This kind of connective may *shift its place* in the second clause. The semicolon stays at the point where the two clauses join:

Many people had camped here; *therefore,* the grass was almost gone.
Many people had camped here; the grass, *therefore,* was almost gone.
Many people had camped here; the grass was almost gone, *therefore.*

NOTE: In formal writing, as in all of these examples, a **comma** usually keeps the adverbial connective apart from the rest of the second clause. If the connective appears in the middle of the second clause, *two* commas are needed. The commas used for this purpose are *optional* in informal writing.

(3) Use a semicolon when there is no connective between independent clauses that are closely related.   Often two statements go together even though there is no connective to join them. A **semicolon** may then replace the period.

In this case, the first word of the second statement is *not* capitalized as it would be following a period:

> The corral was empty; the horses were gone.
> A child is like clay; he or she needs a molding hand.
> The following Sunday was fine; the sodden November chill was broken. (Willa Cather)
> The hunted man saw all this over his shoulder; he was now swimming vigorously with the current. (Ambrose Bierce)

(4) Do not use a comma or eliminate punctuation entirely where a semicolon is required.   When you leave out the semicolon, the result is a **fused sentence.** When you use a comma instead, the result is a **comma splice:**

COMMA SPLICE:	There had been an accident, traffic was stalled for miles.
REVISED:	There had been an accident; traffic was stalled for miles.
COMMA SPLICE:	He answered the ad, however the job had been filled.
REVISED:	He answered the ad; however, the job had been filled.
FUSED:	Erin loved boats her mother had owned a marina.
REVISED:	Erin loved boats; her mother had owned a marina.
FUSED:	Rachel Carson wrote *Silent Spring* it warned against the use of pesticides.
REVISED:	Rachel Carson wrote *Silent Spring;* it warned against the use of pesticides.

Some writers use the comma between two independent clauses when they are very similar in structure or in meaning. In your own writing, use the semicolon to be safe.

NOTE: Here are some possible *variations* from the most common practice:

• A **period** is possible with adverbial connectives, and also at times with coordinators, for a stronger break. Both kinds of connectives leave the clauses they join independent. The period does not cause a sentence fragment:

The building has been declared unsafe. *Therefore,* all events scheduled for the fall had to be canceled.

There were no letters on the back, and nobody could tell the title of the book. *But* it was well known to be a book of magic. (Hawthorne)

• A **semicolon** is possible with all coordinating connectives, especially if the two clauses are *long or complicated:*

The situation seemed hopeless; but my cousin Albert, always ready with a new idea, knew a way out.

• A **colon** may join two clauses when the second is the *explanation or result* of the first:

Pepé turned in his saddle and looked back. He was in the open now: he could be seen from a distance. (John Steinbeck)

• *And, but,* and *or* sometimes appear *without punctuation* between clauses that are very short:

He talked *and* we listened.
They shouted *but* nothing moved.

See **S4a** for fuller treatment of independent clauses.

Most of the following sentences show the right punctuation between two independent clauses. Put *S* for satisfactory after the number of each such sentence. Some sentences are examples of the comma splice or the fused sentence. For each such sentence, write the last word of the first clause and the first word of the second. Put a comma or semicolon between them as required. (Use no other punctuation.)

EXERCISE 1

EXAMPLE: The office was cold and impersonal everybody concentrated on the work.
(Answer) *impersonal; everybody*

1. Sally is not very friendly, but she is not really mean.
2. Our guest left early, he was very tired.
3. I had my paycheck; the bank was closed, however.
4. The publicity did not help, in fact, it boomeranged.
5. Camp life taught me independence this is extremely important to learn at an early age.
6. Competition was keen, for the school had many top athletes.
7. After dinner we sat outside the dining room, or we walked along the beach.
8. My sister was cross; she had expected an apology.
9. The meeting was announced late; the crowd, accordingly, was smaller than we had hoped.

10. The car was expensive to buy, but it was economical to operate.
11. The sun was bright, and small boats dotted the lake.
12. We had trouble with the truck, the rear axle broke.
13. My brother and I are much alike we both enjoy music.
14. We went fishing upstream, or sometimes we just loafed.
15. Ink had been spilled, paper was scattered on the floor.
16. I had trouble in history, for my study habits were poor.
17. The band never won a prize, nor did it promote school spirit.
18. Love cannot be faked, it must come from the heart.
19. The plane shook violently, yet the pilot seemed calm.
20. I approve of early marriages my friends disagree, however.

EXERCISE 2

Connectives do not always join two complete clauses. Besides, words like *for* do double duty as prepositions or the like. Study the following sentences from John Steinbeck's short story "Flight." Find each break where a coordinator actually joins two complete clauses, each with its own subject and verb. Put *C* for "Comma" after the number of each such break. Put *No* for "no punctuation" after the number of all others. (Write on a separate sheet of paper.)

A. Fifty yards away he stopped (1) _____ and went back (2) _____ for he had forgotten his rifle.
B. He looked down (3) _____ for a moment (4) _____ and then pulled himself straight again.
C. For a moment her face had softened (5) _____ but now (6) _____ it grew stern again.
D. His voice was tired (7) _____ and patient (8) _____ but very firm.
E. His tongue tried to make words (9) _____ but only a thick hissing (10) _____ came from between his lips.
F. He threw back his head (11) _____ and looked up (12) _____ into the pale sky.
G. A big black bird (13) _____ circled nearly out of sight (14) _____ and far to the left another was sailing near.
H. He lifted his head to listen (15) _____ for a familiar sound had come to him (16) _____ from the valley.
I. He walked heavily down (17) _____ and poked about in the brush (18) _____ but he could not find his gun.
J. At first he tried to run (19) _____ but immediately he fell (20) _____ and rolled.

M4b
Adverbial Clauses

Use the comma to set off nonrestrictive adverbial clauses.

Some connectives do not merely join a second clause loosely to the first. They turn it into a *dependent clause,* which normally cannot stand by itself. For instance, subordinating connectives typically introduce **adverbial clauses.** Such clauses tell us when, where, why, or how. They may come *before* as well as after the main clause:

AFTER: They gave up the search *when the tide turned.*
BEFORE: *When the tide turned,* they gave up the search.

AFTER: The boat will leave at nine *if all goes well.*
BEFORE: *If all goes well,* the boat will leave at nine.

Remember:

(1) Use no punctuation when you add a restrictive clause to the main clause. Many subordinators deal with time, place, or conditions: *when, while, before, after, since, as, if, unless, as long as.* The clause that follows often makes *all the difference.* "You can have a car" means one thing. "You can have a car *when you earn the money*" means another. "When you earn the money" *restricts,* or narrows, the meaning of the main clause in an important way. It is called a **restrictive** clause.

The added clause in each of the following pairs *restricts* the original meaning:

VERY BROAD: Jean will accompany us.
RESTRICTIVE: Jean will accompany us *if her parents let her.*

VERY BROAD: All work will stop.
RESTRICTIVE: All work will stop *unless the supplies arrive.*

(2) Set off nonrestrictive clauses. Some subordinators set up a contrast: *though, although,* and *whereas;* also the combinations *no matter what* and *no matter how.* The clause that follows is **nonrestrictive.** It does not change the meaning of the main clause. It merely shows that something else is also true.

Use a **comma** when you add a nonrestrictive clause to the main clause:

Jim knows no Spanish, *although* he was born in Spain.
Cubans speak Spanish, *whereas* Brazilians speak Portuguese.
He never placed first, *no matter how* hard he tried.

(3) Use a comma when the dependent clause comes first. You then need not decide whether it is restrictive or nonrestrictive. Use a **comma** to show where the main clause starts:

When Eleanor Roosevelt entered the White House, she proved to be a different kind of First Lady.
As our plane droned on, I studied the passenger next to me.
After we first took off, she had been reading some reports.

NOTE: A few subordinators work two different ways. Connectives like *because* and *so that* start *either a restrictive or a nonrestrictive* clause, depending on the meaning of the whole sentence. Use no punctuation if the major point of the sentence follows the connective. Use the **comma** if the major point is in the main clause—with the adverbial clause giving additional information or explanation.

Study the difference in meaning, and listen to the break signaled by the comma, in the following pairs:

Why are you leaving? I am leaving *because I have to work.*
What are you doing? *I am leaving,* because I have to work.

Why did you leave? I left *so that she could work.*
What did you do? *I left,* so that she could work.

EXERCISE 1

What should be the punctuation at the break shown in each of the following sentences? Put *C* after the number of the sentence if there should be a comma. Put *No* if no punctuation is required.

1. My brother would come to my aid _____ if other boys made fun of me.
2. As the boat bumped over the waves _____ spray came over the side.
3. If an engine skips or hesitates _____ it may not be in tune.
4. My friends used to go to the movies _____ whereas I worked at the gas station.
5. There was no way to open the can _____ no matter what the instructions said.
6. We spent more time together _____ after we became friends.
7. We will have to close the store _____ unless business improves.
8. Each spring the river would rise over its banks _____ so that the fields were flooded every year.
9. As long as you keep up the payments _____ you can keep the set.
10. The team did its best _____ although the turnout was poor.
11. If you do not know manual transmissions _____ ask someone for help.
12. Some gymnasts reach their peak _____ before they are twenty.
13. The village has become a backwater _____ since the bypass was built.
14. She promised to help us _____ as much as she could.
15. The car stalled _____ as we reached the top of the hill.
16. When I dropped the ball _____ the crowd groaned.
17. Whales are warm-blooded and air-breathing mammals _____ though they live in the sea.
18. The whale's baleen works _____ as if it were a giant sieve straining food from the water.
19. Some species of whales may become extinct _____ no matter what measures are taken by concerned nations.
20. If a blue whale survives to maturity _____ it may reach a length of one hundred feet.

What would be the right punctuation at the break in each of the following sentences? Put *C* after the number of the sentence if the instructions you have studied require a comma. Put *No* after the number of the sentence if no comma is required. (Write on a separate sheet of paper.)

1. Language seems limited _____ when it is used by someone with a poor vocabulary.
2. When foreign students learn English _____ they soon become aware of our rich vocabulary resources.
3. No matter how many words they know _____ there are always more words to learn.
4. People often encounter new words _____ although they have known their language all their lives.
5. If there is a need for a word to describe a new technological process _____ our language provides the word.
6. Many words are in the language _____ because at one time there was a need for them.
7. Many such words were more widely used _____ when farming and hunting were common occupations.
8. Farmers might drive a team of horses _____ whereas they might also drive a yoke of oxen.
9. Where we see only two dead birds _____ a hunter might see a brace of quail.
10. Birds are a covey _____ when the older birds are accompanied by their young.
11. City dwellers do not know such terms _____ unless they have read them in a book.
12. Most of us have been away from farm life for a long time _____ so that we do not know a bushel from a peck.
13. What words do you use _____ when you name a group of domesticated animals?
14. We speak of a flock of sheep _____ though we refer to a herd of cattle.
15. What animals do you think of _____ after someone mentions a bevy or a gaggle?
16. While we are on this subject _____ what animals are commonly found in a shoal?
17. If you have relatives or friends who live on a farm _____ ask them about farmers' words.
18. Look for such words _____ as you read about life in nineteenth-century America.
19. Words no longer in common use will survive _____ as long as they appear in novels and plays.
20. Here we find the language of our ancestors _____ no matter how modern we have become.

LANGUAGE IN ACTION

FROM THE OLD NEWSPAPER FILE

Study the following sentences, adapted from a newspaper article published over a hundred years ago. (How would you reword these sentences in a more streamlined, modern newspaper style?)

Explain how each sentence illustrates linking punctuation in the larger combined sentence.

1. Things are quiet today after the town celebrated a glorious Fourth of July.
2. The citizens of our town awoke when booming big guns announced the holiday.
3. Edibles were for sale in numerous booths, yet few people partook to excess.
4. We saw very few intoxicated persons, and only one altercation occurred during the day.
5. It produced a bitten finger; moreover, it left two citizens badly demoralized.
6. In the morning the national insignia was raised on a staff which had been set up on the hill in front of town.
7. After the choir sang the anthem, the Declaration of Independence was read.
8. Singing followed, and then came the oration by the orator of the day.
9. We cannot publish the entire address, as we had no reporter on the ground.
10. Before noon had been reached, our streets were alive with patriotic citizens.
11. The hotels were full; eating houses and barber shops were busy.
12. The saloons were full; a number of citizens were also full.

M4c

Relative and Noun Clauses

Use the comma to set off nonrestrictive relative clauses.

Learn how to punctuate two special kinds of dependent clauses. The relative pronouns (*who, whom, whose, which, that*) start a **relative clause.** Relative clauses fill in information about one of the nouns in the main clause:

Joyce owned a plane, *which took mail to the islands.*
I looked for the boy *who had borrowed my bicycle.*
The boy *who had borrowed my bicycle* had disappeared.
The team *that had won the game* celebrated its victory.
The driver *whose car crashed* was not hurt in the accident.

That and question words like *why, how, where,* and *when* serve as special connectives starting a **noun clause.** A noun clause takes the place of one of the nouns in the main part of the sentence:

The manager admitted *that the price had been changed.*
Susan knew *where the family lived.*
My uncle told us *what he knew.*

See **S4c** and **S4d** for a review of relative and noun clauses.

Remember:

(1) Use no commas for relative clauses that are essential to the meaning of a sentence. Use no comma with *who (whom, whose)* and *which* when the relative clause is **restrictive.** A restrictive clause is essential *to identify* something. It tells us who, or which one, or what kind. The restrictive clause then becomes an essential part of the sentence:

RESTRICTIVE: The boy *who ate the mushrooms* became violently ill. (The other boys were fine.)

Often, something or somebody has already been identified. For instance, we know the name. The relative clause then merely adds information. It is **nonrestrictive**—not an essential part of the main statement. The nonrestrictive clause is set off by a **comma:**

RESTRICTIVE: I gave the key to the lifeguard *who took my place.*
(Tells us which one)
NONRESTRICTIVE: I gave the key to Sue Keller, *who took my place.*
(Tells us more about Sue)

NOTE: When *that* is used as a relative pronoun, the clause that follows is usually restrictive. Use no comma:

RESTRICTIVE: The Coast Guard looked for the shark *that had frightened the swimmers.*
Cars *that block the entrance* will be towed away.

The *that* is often left out in such sentences. Punctuation remains the same:

RESTRICTIVE: The shark *they had sighted* had disappeared.
The car *he had parked in the driveway* was towed away.

(2) Use two commas when a nonrestrictive clause interrupts the main clause. Make sure to use both of these:

Black Elk, *who had then been a young warrior,* told the story of Custer's defeat.
The Aztecs, *whose culture was destroyed by the Spaniards,* had beautiful poems about love and war.

(3) Use no commas to separate a noun clause from the rest of the sentence. Use no punctuation when *that* or question words like *why, how, where,* and *when* start a noun clause:

I suddenly remembered *that the meeting would start at eight.*
She would not tell us *why she had changed her mind.*
The article explained *how the whales could be saved.*
Tell me *who you are.*

EXERCISE 1

After the number of each sentence, put *S* if punctuation is satisfactory. Put *U* if punctuation is unsatisfactory.

1. Jesse Owens, whose name was known around the world, ran in the 1936 Olympic Games in Berlin.
2. She always shook hands with a player, who had defeated her.
3. People who live in glass houses should not throw stones.
4. We soon found out who was in charge.
5. I discovered that, few people were eager to help me with the work.
6. We won the opening game, which everyone had expected us to lose.
7. The family who moved in across the street from us owned numerous dogs and cats.
8. My brother disliked people, who always act tough.
9. The coach would not tell us, why the practice had been called off.
10. He could not decide which player he should let go.
11. The map we had brought did not show the new streets.
12. The number of fish they had caught, was well over the limit.
13. The last bus, which leaves around eleven, was just pulling out.
14. A Russian gymnast who had been unknown in the West became famous overnight.
15. Someone who does not make the team, should try again.
16. She lost to Billie Jean King who was making a comeback.
17. The school had a tutoring service for students who needed special help.
18. Robbers were unable to discover where the burial chamber was located.
19. I admire my oldest sister, who always speaks her mind.
20. He moved back to Boston, which was his favorite city.

EXERCISE 2

What would be the right punctuation at the breaks in each of the following sentences? Put *C* after the number of the sentence if the instructions you have studied require a comma (or two commas where a clause *interrupts* another). Put *No* after the number of the sentence if no comma is required. (Write on a separate sheet of paper.)

1. We all know the word *taboo* _____ which means "forbidden."
2. In the South Pacific, it refers to things _____ that are set aside as sacred or unclean.

3. Taboos are observed by people _____ who will not visit certain places or eat certain foods.

4. Our language _____ which now seems an everyday tool _____ was long governed by taboos.

5. People would not use a word _____ that might bring bad luck.

6. They thought _____ that names had magical properties.

7. Have you ever wondered _____ why Rumpelstiltskin wanted no one to know his name?

8. The Irish _____ whose ancient tales are full of magic _____ told many stories about taboos.

9. A hero _____ whose name meant dog _____ could not touch his namesake.

10. The ancient story tells us _____ how his breaking of the taboo brought disaster.

11. Religious awe surrounds the name of the Lord _____ which must not be taken in vain.

12. People _____ who swear _____ often substitute more harmless words.

13. We see this tendency in American English _____ which has many expressions like "my gosh."

14. The expressions "for Pete's sake" and "land's sakes" are other substitutes _____ we have all heard.

15. We all recognize the taboo _____ that bans four-letter words.

16. The courts long banned authors _____ who used such words in their books.

17. Some people criticize publishers _____ who include these words in dictionaries.

18. But not only sailors _____ whose language has always been salty _____ like colorful talk.

19. Many readers like critics _____ who on occasion call people insulting names.

20. Many voters admired President Truman _____ who often used strong language.

Most of the following sentences show the right punctuation for a sentence combining two clauses. Put *S* for satisfactory after the number of each such sentence. The remaining sentences illustrate unsatisfactory punctuation. Look for the following: (1) fused sentences, with no punctuation where there should be at least a comma, or even a semicolon; (2) comma splices, where there should be a semicolon *instead* of a comma; (3) unnecessary commas—a comma used with a restrictive clause or a noun clause. Put *U* after the number of each unsatisfactory sentence.

UNIT REVIEW EXERCISE

1. Return the money, or I will notify the police.
2. We were tired of studying, for it was May.
3. We abandoned the car, the rear axle broke.
4. We should notify the police unless she returns the money.

5. Hunters should not shoot from the car the law forbids this practice.
6. The band is fun; besides, it promotes school spirit.
7. He asked for my brother Jeremy, who had promised him a ride.
8. People in India believe, that certain animals are sacred.
9. I approve of long engagements; my mother disagrees, however.
10. When an important game came up, we staged a rally.
11. Jim was not the type who shouts himself hoarse at ball games.
12. Your friend is not a physician, therefore you should not listen to his advice on how much medicine to take.
13. My friends and I all share common interests we all enjoy swimming and boating.
14. People must learn self-control; life is impossible without it.
15. Books lined the shelves, there was a typewriter on a cluttered desk.
16. We had all hoped that she would reconsider her decision.
17. People in the nation's capital did not have a United States senator, though they voted in Presidential elections.
18. The city will build a new theater if the voters approve the funds.
19. My father admired President Kennedy who succeeded President Eisenhower in 1961.
20. I could never understand why children are fascinated with guns.

M5

INSIDE PUNCTUATION

Know when to use commas or other inside punctuation.

No punctuation is required *within* a single clause that contains only the most basic elements. We do not put a comma between a subject and its verb, or between a verb and its object. Nor do we use a comma when we go on from these basic elements and add phrases that state circumstances, reasons, or conditions:

Frank Pope passed through town yesterday.
Fort Morgan was an army outpost.
Mrs. Sutherland brought to town the first cabbages of the season.

Inside punctuation becomes necessary when we add things that make such a simple sentence more complicated:

Frank Pope, *the large cattle dealer,* passed through town.
Fort Morgan was an army outpost, *the largest on the Overland Trail.*
Mrs. Sutherland, *driving in from the Fontaine-qui-Bouille,* brought to town the first cabbages of the season.

M5a

Punctuating Modifiers

Use commas to set off nonrestrictive modifiers.

The basic elements in a sentence often carry along modifiers that clarify or in some way limit their meaning. Know the situations where a modifier requires a comma:

COMMAS FOR INSIDE PUNCTUATION
A Summary

The *comma* used for inside punctuation appears with the following sentence elements:

(1) *nonrestrictive modifiers*—modifiers *not used* to single out one or one of a kind:

The Lincoln Memorial, *a magnificent structure,* was next.

(2) *sentence modifiers*—modifiers that seem to apply to the sentence as a whole rather than to any one part:

To keep out the deer, we built a wooden fence.

(3) *series* of three or more elements of the same kind:

We talked about *art, music, and poetry.*

(4) *dates, addresses, and measurements* with two or more parts:

The family had moved to *Lincoln, Nebraska.*

(5) *interchangeable adjectives* modifying the same noun:

The settlers discovered a *cool, moist* valley.

(6) *names, questions, and comments* added to a sentence:

Your application, *John,* has been approved.

(7) *alternatives* inserted for contrast after *not* or *never:*

I wanted the hoe, *not the spade.*

---

(1) Use no commas with essential modifiers. Often, a modifier helps us single out one thing among several, or one kind of thing among several kinds. A modifier narrows down the possibilities; it helps us identify something. Such a modifier is **restrictive** and needs *no punctuation:*

The books *on the top shelf* belong to Marty.
(Which ones? The ones on the top shelf)

I returned the package *sent here by mistake.*
(Which one? The one sent by mistake)

The girl *sitting next to me* explained the chart.
(Which girl? The one sitting next to me)

(2) Use the comma with nonessential modifiers. When something has already been clearly identified, the modifier merely adds information. In this case, the modifier does not single something out. It just tells us more about it. Such a modifier is **nonrestrictive** and is set off by a **comma.** If the sentence continues after the modifier, two commas are needed:

> I talked to Muriel Browne, *the new director.*
> (After a proper name, the modifier gives further information.)

> Ed, *dressed in a bright green jacket,* opened the door.
> (The modifier tells us about Ed's appearance.)

> His new Buick, *parked illegally,* had been towed away.
> (We know *which* Buick—the modifier tells us more *about* it.)

(3) Set off modifiers that apply to the sentence as a whole. Such sentence modifiers are set off by one or more **commas** when they are stressed enough to stand out in speech, separated by a slight break. Always use this comma when a verbal or verbal phrase comes *at the beginning of a sentence.* Also, set off any verbal or verbal phrase that comes later in the sentence but seems to apply to the sentence as a whole:

> *To beat the rush-hour traffic,* we left early.
> *Smiling,* she opened the letter.

> The price is not bad, *considering the location.*
> Billie Jean King, *to name only one,* is a first-rate athlete.

(4) Use the comma with any introductory modifier of more than three words:

> *After a long introduction,* she came to the point.
> *To the ordinary person,* Sargent and Whistler are merely names.
> *Throughout the school year,* I get up at 6:00 A.M.

(5) Use commas with familiar expressions that comment on the whole sentence. Some of these link one sentence to the other. Set off expressions like *after all, of course, unfortunately, on the whole, as a rule, certainly,* and *on the other hand.* Remember that any modifier set off in the middle of a sentence requires *two commas:*

> You will submit the usual report, *of course.*
> No one, *unfortunately,* had a copy of the book.
> *On the whole,* his performance was satisfactory.

NOTE: The last two uses of the comma listed here are *optional.* In formal writing, however, it is strongly recommended that you use commas in these situations.

FROM THE OLD NEWSPAPER FILE

Which of the following sentences should have one or more commas? Put *C* after the number of each such sentence. Which sentence would be all right without inside punctuation? Put *No* after the number of each such sentence.

1. Colorado was created a territory _____ in 1861.
2. For the first few years _____ its capital shifted all over the place.
3. H. P. Farnum _____ arrested for robbing the mails _____ was freed on bail.
4. Colorado was admitted to the Union in 1876 _____ the 100th anniversary of American independence.
5. Digging down about ten inches _____ the deputies discovered a tin can wrapped in a woolen blanket.
6. People _____ living in Colorado _____ like to call their state the "Mother of the Rivers."
7. The accused had stolen a mail sack _____ containing about a thousand dollars in gold dust.
8. People associate Colorado with skiing _____ the Rockies _____ and the mile-high city of Denver.
9. The Ute reservation _____ occupied one-third of the arable land _____ of Colorado.
10. Black Kettle _____ chief of the Cheyennes _____ took part in the battle of Sand Creek.

Most of the following sentences show the right punctuation with modifiers. Put *S* after the number of each such sentence. Put *U* if punctuation is unsatisfactory.

1. In most modern societies, ancient ways and customs have disappeared.
2. A few isolated groups on the other hand, have kept a very old way of life.
3. Margaret Mead, born in Philadelphia, became America's best-known writer about older cultures.
4. *Growing Up in New Guinea,* her most famous book, was published in 1930.
5. Originally located in New England, her family had spread out through Ohio and Illinois.
6. Emily Togg Mead, her mother had been a sociologist.
7. Margaret's father, Edward Mead, had been an economist.
8. During her childhood years, Margaret Mead was strongly influenced by her grandmother.

9. The grandmother was a teacher with ideas considered very modern in her time.
10. The Mead family strongly believed in education to say the least.
11. To study old tribal ways, young Margaret Mead lived with faraway people.
12. She learned expressions, showing politeness or respect.
13. Considering her different upbringing, she communicated with the people very well.
14. People as a rule, consider these older cultures backward.
15. Someone describing the beautiful ancient ways can make us change our minds.

EXERCISE 2

What would be the right punctuation at the breaks in the following sentences? Put *C* after the number of the sentence if the instructions you have studied require a comma (or *two* commas where a modifier appears in the middle of a sentence). *Include all optional commas.* Put *No* after the number of the sentence if no comma is required. (Write on a separate sheet of paper.)

1. The American people _____ suspicious of authority _____ have worshiped few great leaders.
2. One exception is George Washington _____ the father of our country.
3. Americans _____ living in the nineteenth century _____ had his picture in their homes.
4. His Farewell Address _____ translated into many languages _____ was known to all.
5. The book _____ responsible for the popular view of Washington _____ was a biography by Parson Weems.
6. Published shortly after Washington's death _____ it called the general a saint.
7. Weems _____ the son of a Scottish immigrant _____ praised the great man in sermons and speeches.
8. He first told the story of the prayer at Valley Forge _____ considered an invention by American historians.
9. The cherry tree legend is also among the stories _____ first told by Weems.
10. Modern historians _____ as a rule _____ distinguish carefully between fact and legend.
11. Jared Sparks _____ a president of Harvard _____ collected Washington's letters and documents.
12. Together with an assistant _____ he made many changes in the manuscripts.
13. Words _____ showing the great man's temper _____ were left out.
14. The picture of Washington _____ seen on stamps and dollar bills _____ was done by Gilbert Stuart.

15. Like other pictures of famous men _____ it looks solemn.
16. The sculpture _____ standing in Virginia's state Capitol _____ was done by a French artist.
17. Looking timeless _____ Washington stands with a column under his left hand.
18. Modern historians _____ on the whole _____ do not believe in hero worship.
19. Some books _____ published in modern times _____ have been critical of Washington's personality.
20. Some writers _____ on the other hand _____ have stressed his warm human qualities.

Use commas where several elements of the same kind appear in a sentence.

Several items of the same kind often take the place of a single sentence part. When we have several parts of the same kind, there is often a connective like *and* or *or* to **coordinate** them—to tie them together. Often there are punctuation marks in addition to or in place of a connective:

(1) Use commas between elements in a series. Three or more elements of the same kind are called a **series.** In the most common kind of series, **commas** appear between the elements of a series, with the last comma followed by a connective that ties the whole group together. Study this "*A, B,* and *C*" pattern in each of the following examples:

> Washington's face looks at us from *monuments, coins,* and *stamps.*
> She *organized* an office, *secured* funds, and *hired* a staff.
> He painted his mailbox *red, white,* and *blue.*

The slots in the series may be filled not just by single words, but by groups of words or whole clauses:

> At midnight *the storm stopped, the clouds parted,* and *the stars glittered* above the camp.

A series can be expanded to *more than three* items:

> He *tried* one of the basement windows, *found* it open, *raised* it cautiously, and *scrambled* down to the floor.

NOTE: The last comma in a series is *optional.* Use it in your own writing, because it is never wrong.

(2) Use semicolons in a series where commas would be confusing. Sometimes the separate parts of a series already contain com-

---

M5b
Punctuating Equal Parts

mas. Use **semicolons** instead of additional commas to show the major breaks:

> Only three people came to the meeting: *Lucy, the president; Michael, the treasurer;* and *Gregory, a new member.*

(3) Use commas with information that comes in several parts. Dates, addresses, page references, and similar information often come in two or more parts. Use **commas** between the different elements. Use another comma *after the whole group,* unless the last word is at the same time the last word of the sentence:

> The fiesta lasted from *Monday, October 2,* to *Thursday, October 5, 1978.*
> *El Paso, Texas,* is across the river from *Juarez, Mexico.*
> We forwarded all their mail to *1134 Oak Street, Livermore, California.*
> You will find the quotation in *Chapter 5, page 243.*

Commas also separate the different parts of *measurements* that use more than one unit of measurement. Here no additional comma is used after the last item:

> The fullback was *six feet, two inches* tall.
> *Nine pounds, three ounces* is heavy for this kind of fish.

(4) Use commas between interchangeable adjectives. Two or more adjectives may modify the same noun. Sometimes these come in different layers. For instance, we first call someone a *public servant* and then say what kind: a *loyal public servant. Loyal* and *public* are not interchangeable (a *public loyal servant* would not make sense). When two adjectives *are* interchangeable, they may be coordinated by *and,* or instead by a **comma:**

> a rainy *and* blustery day
> a *rainy, blustery* day

> lonely *and* unhappy people
> *lonely, unhappy* people

EXERCISE 1

Most of the following sentences show the right punctuation of equal sentence parts. Put *S* for satisfactory after the number of each such sentence. Put *U* if punctuation is unsatisfactory.

1. Many of our Olympic athletes were training at Squaw Valley, California.
2. Women were moving into jobs in law enforcement equipment maintenance communications and radar technology.
3. The army needed people for the infantry, armor, and field artillery.
4. Her family had always been strong-minded, ambitious people.
5. The drought dried up water holes, ruined crops, and kindled brush fires.
6. The inmates were taught basketry, carpentry and other manual skills.

7. Olympics held in the Western Hemisphere include those at Montreal, Canada, and Mexico City, Mexico.

8. They ran a small restaurant featuring continental cuisine on Holmes Avenue Chicago, Illinois.

9. We found the quotation in Volume 2, chapter 3, page 48.

10. An angry, violent crowd disrupted a soccer game in Lima, Peru.

11. The weight was short by four pounds, three ounces.

12. Sunday, March 17 was announced as the new date.

13. The tour took them to London, England; Paris, France, and Frankfurt, Germany.

14. Folk, rock, pop, and jazz are the four best-known kinds of American music today.

15. She felt that there had been too little recognition for such a dedicated, public servant.

16. Six feet, three inches is not considered tall for a player in this game.

17. Their new address was 2398 Broadway, New York, New York.

18. People were getting tired of the stale, tasteless food.

19. Her birthday is Saturday November 22.

20. I wrote to Eileen, my sister; Alfredo, my cousin; and Charlie, my best friend.

At which of the numbered breaks in the following sentences should there be a comma? After the number of each break, put *C* for comma, *S* for semicolon, *No* if no punctuation is required. *Include all optional commas.* (Write on a separate sheet of paper.)

EXERCISE 2

A. Eggshells (1) _____ beer cans (2) _____ and scraps of paper (3) _____ litter the countryside next to our scenic highways.

B. I remember a trip from Reno (4) _____ Nevada (5) _____ to Sacramento (6) _____ California.

C. There were three of us in the car: John (7) _____ a sailor on leave (8) _____ Paolo (9) _____ an exchange student (10) _____ and I.

D. Paolo is a lively (11) _____ foreign (12) _____ student from Leghorn (13) _____ Italy. His birth date is the same as my brother's: March 16 (14) _____ 1965.

E. A sleek (15) _____ shiny sedan drove ahead of us on the narrow (16) _____ dangerous road.

F. The occupants were throwing gum wrappers (17) _____ Coke bottles (18) _____ and other refuse out of the car windows.

G. Later we stopped at a public (19) _____ picnic ground among the rolling hills (20) _____ majestic trees (21) _____ and peacefully grazing horses.

H. Paper was everywhere (22) _____ cans were rusting in the sun (23) _____ and smashed bottles littered the ground.

I. Paolo is only five feet (24) _____ three inches (25) _____ tall, but he looked tall when he denounced tourists for their behavior.

M5c

**Punctuating
Interrupters**

Use commas or other marks to set off interrupters.

Especially in conversation, we often *interrupt* a sentence. We interrupt what we are saying in order to call the listener by name. We stop to add some information that we forgot to mention. There are three major ways of setting off such interrupters from the rest of the sentence:

(1) Use commas to set off light interrupters. Light interrupters blend into the sentence with only a slight break. They need two **commas** when they appear in the middle of a sentence. They need only one comma when they are at the beginning or the end. Use the commas that go with light interrupters when you

- *address the listener or reader:*

  John, come over here.
  Here are the books, *Mrs. Brown.*

- *show how true something is, or who thought so:*

  The price, *you will agree,* is outrageous.
  That remark, *she felt,* was unnecessary.

- *start a sentence with* yes, no, well, why, *or a similar expression:*

  Yes, I know where it is.
  Well, all came out all right in the end.
  Why, I have never even heard the name.

- *tack on a short question addressed to the listener:*

  You are new here, *aren't you?*
  So he backed out, *did he?*

- *add something for contrast after* not *or* never:

  The passengers, *not the driver,* were to blame.
  The club meets Mondays, *never on Tuesdays.*

- *shift something to an unusual position in a sentence:*

  The walls, *with one exception,* had fallen in.
  The reason, *dear reader,* should be clear.

(2) Use dashes to set off heavy interrupters. Heavy interrupters cause a definite break in speech and are set off in writing by **dashes.** Overuse of the dash makes for jerky, disconnected writing. Use the dashes that go with heavy interrupters when you

- *stop in order to insert a complete sentence:*

  In Tulsa—*we moved there in June*—I found many friends.
  Pluto—*this was the cat's name*—was my favorite pet.

SOME MASTERS OF FICTION

Read the following sample sentences. Explain why and how each author used inside punctuation.

1. The hurt captain, lying against the water-jar in the bow, spoke always in a low voice. (Stephen Crane)
2. Mr. Oakhurst did not drink. It interfered with a profession which required coolness, impassiveness, and presence of mind. (Bret Harte)
3. It was a pity, she reflected, that she was so sensitive to public opinion. (Mary McCarthy)
4. In that advanced season, the party soon passed out of the moist, temperate regions of the foothills into the dry, cold, bracing air of the Sierras. (Bret Harte)
5. The hour's drive had sobered him somewhat—his arrival was merely hilarious—and Paula hoped that the evening was not spoiled. (F. Scott Fitzgerald)
6. His father, on principle, did not like to hear requests for money. (Willa Cather)
7. On the northern horizon a new light appeared, a small bluish gleam on the edge of the waters. (Stephen Crane)
8. He then handed him his money back, pushed him gently from the room, and so made a devoted slave of Tom Simson. (Bret Harte)
9. She springs to her feet, as if this were all planned (which it wasn't). (Joyce Carol Oates)
10. "My, their mother had a good imagination, didn't she!" (Jean McCord)

• *add a modifier that is exceptionally long or contains commas:*

The fur traders—*French, British, and Russian*—pushed in for beaver and other pelts.

• *make something stand out for an especially strong effect:*

He walked through the gates—*a free man.*
The lakes, the trees, the birds, the sun—without these she could not live in tranquility.

(3) Use parentheses to enclose less important information. Less important information is often given in a lower tone of voice and appears in writing in **parentheses.** Use parentheses instead of dashes when you

● *insert a complete sentence as an aside:*

> In Tulsa *(we moved there in June)* I found many new friends.
> Bixby tapped the big bell three times *(this was the signal to come in).*

● *insert page references, dates, and the like as supplementary information:*

> The author's summary *(p. 45)* was badly needed.
> Her birthday *(June 2)* is still several months off.
> MacDonald *(sometimes spelled Macdonald)* is a common family name.

NOTE: When a whole sentence appears *separately* in parentheses, it carries its own end punctuation with it:

> We gave him our telephone number. *(He never called.)*

EXERCISE 1

What should be the punctuation at the blank spaces in each of the following sentences? After the number of each space, write one of the following:

C   for comma;
D   for dash;
P   for parenthesis;
No for no punctuation.

(Use no other marks. Write on a separate sheet.)

A. People used to eat at home _____(1) not in restaurants.
B. The wild burros (at first only a few hundred _____(2) had taken over the range.
C. A town in Nevada—I have forgotten the name _____(3) has been kept exactly _____(4) as it once was.
D. The flight _____(5) ladies and gentlemen _____(6) has been canceled because of bad weather.
E. Our money order _____(7) the manager claimed, had never reached her.
F. Why _____(8) you are the Pallards' daughter _____(9) aren't you?
G. You will never guess _____(10) what we found _____(11) an old family Bible.
H. The media—their gossip columns, fan magazines _____(12) talk shows _____(13) help keep celebrities in the public eye.
I. The debt _____(14) everyone agreed, had to be paid off.
J. No _____(15) we have not noticed anything unusual _____(16) Officer Brown.
K. The earthquake (I believe it was in 1906 _____(17) destroyed most of the town _____(18) didn't it?
L. Your teammates, I am sure _____(19) will be glad to help you _____(20) John.

Most of the following sentences show the right punctuation of interrupters. Put *S* for satisfactory after the number of each such sentence. Put *U* for unsatisfactory after the number of each sentence that needs revision. Be prepared to explain what went wrong.

1. Most people, I am sure, take our system of writing for granted.
2. Some of us, it is true, grumble about English spelling.
3. We would like to write *rime,* not *rhyme.*
4. Simplified spellings—*thru, alright, dialog*—always find supporters.
5. But most people you will agree obey habit.
6. Well, the customary way is not the only way.
7. Do you realize, dear reader, that our sentences might look quite different?
8. Many languages—Hebrew and Arabic are examples—are written from right to left.
9. On the spines of some books, we read the title from the bottom up (British publishers seem to prefer this).
10. Pictographic writing (writing based on pictures) does not use letters for separate sounds.
11. A single symbol—resembling a bird, perhaps—would stand for a whole word or a syllable.
12. You have seen Chinese characters haven't you?
13. These symbols (more complicated than our letters stand for words not sounds.
14. A whole message—like "Happy New Year"—might require only two or three symbols.
15. Our own writing system, you realize, also has signs that do not stand for separate sounds.
16. Our numerals (1, 2, 3, and so on) make one single sign stand for the whole word.
17. Other symbols—asterisks, apostrophes, and the like—do not stand for sounds at all.
18. You know what *etc.* means, don't you?
19. Many people use Latin abbreviations *(i.e., etc.)* without knowing what the original words were.
20. Yes our writing system has many complications.

Test your command of different kinds of inside punctuation. In which of the following sentences should there be a comma at the space indicated? Put *C* after the number of each such sentence. Put *No* after the number of the sentence if no comma is required.

1. Scientists interested in language ＿＿＿ are building translation machines.
2. Building the machine is a long ＿＿＿ difficult job.
3. The machine must know words ＿＿＿ grammar, and idioms.

4. Idioms, you probably know _____ are individual expressions.
5. An idiom is a group of words _____ not just a single word.
6. "Give me a hand" is a familiar _____ American idiom.
7. Translating word by word _____ a German would get a wrong meaning.
8. The words translated separately _____ would mean "shake hands."
9. You can see the problem here _____ can't you?
10. The machine must recognize _____ and translate the whole group.
11. Single words _____ a simpler problem, also cause headaches.
12. We use the word *club* for a heavy stick _____ a suit of cards, and a group of people.
13. A machine translating the word _____ must know the difference.
14. The problem is like telling Abraham Lincoln from Lincoln _____ Nebraska.
15. To pick the right meaning for a word _____ we look at the words before and after it.
16. A translating machine _____ you can see, must store much information.
17. It must remember thousands of words _____ and meanings.
18. Perhaps machine translation _____ long considered impossible, will soon be a reality.
19. A good _____ public library might have translating machines for key languages.
20. Scientists _____ doctors, and diplomats would use them all the time.

M6
QUOTATION

Know how to work quoted material into your text.

Often we must make it clear that we are repeating words and ideas not our own. We must make it clear by punctuation and other means that we are recording what somebody else said, or copying what somebody else wrote.

M6a
Direct Quotation

Use quotation marks to set off someone's exact words.

When you repeat someone's exact words, you are using **direct quotation**. Though you may repeat only a part of what someone said or wrote, that part must be word for word the way it was first said. Material quoted word for word is enclosed in **quotation marks.**

Punctuate direct quotations as follows:

(1) Use a comma to separate a short quotation from its credit tag. Usually, a **comma** separates the quotation from the introductory statement—the credit tag that shows its source:

He said, "It's a beautiful day."
The guard replied, "I still have to see your I.D."
"We have checked your credit rating," the letter began.

Use the comma regardless of whether the credit tag appears at the beginning or at the end. If the credit tag *splits a complete sentence,* you need two commas:

> "Your father," my aunt would say, "would not have approved."
> "Few things," Mark Twain said, "are harder to put up with than the annoyance of a good example."

NOTE: If the credit tag separates two complete sentences, you need a comma before it and a *period* after it:

> "Adam was only human," Mark Twain said. "This explains it all."

(2) Use the colon to introduce long or formal quotations: Long quotations are often introduced by a **colon** rather than by a comma:

> She remembered a line by Elinor Wylie: "I love those skies, thin blue or snowy gray."

Long quotations running to more than half a dozen lines of prose or more than one full line of poetry are usually treated as **block quotations.** They are *not* enclosed in quotation marks but instead indented and, in a typed paper, single-spaced.

See the sample research paper in **C5b** for an example of a block quotation.

NOTE: When a single quoted word or phrase appears in a sentence, you do not need a comma or a colon to set it off:

> He always said "Good morning."
> Saying "I told you so" only makes matters worse.

(3) Know how to place the final quotation mark.   When a quotation ends or is interrupted, commas and periods stay *inside* the quotation. They come *before* the final quotation mark. Semicolons go outside the quotation. They follow the final quotation mark:

> She said, "There, that will do"; nevertheless, she kept making adjustments.

Question marks go inside the quotation if the quoted part asks a question. They go outside if you are asking a question *about the quotation.* Exclamation marks go inside if the quoted part was shouted or had strong stress on it. They go outside if you are making a strong point *about the quotation:*

> The stranger asked, "Which way do I turn?"
> Was it Mark Twain who said, "Training is everything"?
>
> Jones kept shouting: "We are half an hour late!"
> Don't you dare tell me, "We know your kind"!

NOTE: If a question mark or an exclamation mark appears at the end of a quotation, do *not* use an additional comma to separate the quotation from any remaining part of the sentence:

"What happened?" my brother asked.

(4) Show quotations within a quotation. Use **single quotation marks** to show that the person you are quoting is in turn quoting somebody else:

"You know what Gene Debs said, 'I want to rise with the ranks, not from the ranks,' " said Mac. (John Dos Passos)

(5) Show where something has been left out. Omissions from a quotation are shown by three spaced periods, called an **ellipsis.** Use four periods if the omission includes the period at the end of a complete sentence:

The report said, "Farming . . . has always been an uncertain business."

(6) Show where something has been added. Comments or corrections added to a quotation are put between **square brackets:**

The report said: "On Monday, October 3 [actually October 4], we set out across the ice for the mainland."

NOTE: In all the examples in this section, the first word of a quotation is *capitalized.* This is done whenever it would have been capitalized anyway if the quotation were written down separately, without being quoted in your text.

EXERCISE 1

Most of the following passages show the right punctuation of quotations. Put *S* for satisfactory after the number of each such passage. Put *U* after the number of each passage that is unsatisfactory. Be prepared to explain in class what went wrong. (Write on a separate sheet of paper.)

1. "Hurry up," Charles said, "and let's go over to the Meaders."
2. In a subsequent issue, the *Yale Review* said: "When you can drop just one atomic bomb and wipe out Paris or Berlin, war will have become monstrous and impossible."
3. She said in a firm voice, "May I come in"?
4. Reading the reference to the atomic bomb, the editor wrote "fanciful" in the margin.
5. "Most people," Dr. Gaudet says, "choose their life's work through a series of accidents."
6. She said, "We are always fighting in a losing cause!"
7. According to the brochure, "Today's youth seeks the satisfactions of leadership."

8. When the Texas rangers sent only one tall officer to help with a range war, the sheriff gasped, "What! Only *one* ranger?"

9. Calmly the ranger replied, "There's only one war, ain't there?"

10. According to one author of 125 Western novels, "The Western . . . stubbornly holds its popularity."

11. "You'll never catch them now," Jack grinned "they left three days ago."

12. Who said, "Power corrupts"?

13. "I'm very busy just now," she said halfheartedly. "I have things to do."

14. The announcer kept saying, "Time is up;" people were scrambling for the door.

15. Juan said, "That reminds me of his favorite saying: 'The watched pot never boils.' "

16. What a fool she was to say: "I'm the one"!

17. "General Smith and 110 horses have been captured by the rebels," Secretary of War Stanton announced one day.

18. "Well," said Lincoln, "I'm sure sorry about those horses."

19. "I could not, at any age," Eleanor Roosevelt said, "be content to take my place in a corner and simply look on."

20. "We have fished in these waters for many generations," the elders said, "no court will stop us."

After the number of each sentence, write down the mark or marks missing at the blank space in the sentence.

EXAMPLE: "We are leaving now _____ she casually said to her brother. (Answer) ,"

1. "The horses are gone _____ she shouted at the top of her voice.

2. Which President said: "We have nothing to fear but fear itself _____

3. "Life _____ Eleanor Roosevelt said, "is meant to be lived."

4. He quickly said _____ Thank you" and was gone.

5. "The bus has broken down," he announced _____ I am going for help."

6. I remembered a song that asked: "Where have all the flowers gone _____

7. The coach kept shouting, "Pass the ball! Pass the ball _____

8. The entry read: "Cascaro returned to the tent a few minutes later and very quietly said, 'We cannot go on _____

9. He usually told us _____ I am busy right now."

10. "All trains will run ten minutes late _____ the announcement read.

Use no punctuation with indirect quotations, but set off phrases quoted word for word.

We do not always reproduce the exact wording of what someone said. Instead we repeat it in our own words. This way of quoting someone is called **indirect** quotation. Indirect quotations often start with the special connective *that* or question words like *how, why, what,* and *where.* Such indirect quotations fit into the sentence *without punctuation*—no comma, no quotation marks:

INDIRECT: She claimed *that the manager owed her a week's wage.*
INDIRECT: We asked him *how we should proceed.*
INDIRECT: The President said *that unemployment was going down.*

A direct quotation looks at things from the point of view of the *speaker,* at the time the speaker was talking. An indirect quotation looks at things from the point of view of the person who *quotes,* at the time of quoting. Note how references to persons and to time change:

DIRECT: Sue asked him, "*Were you* there?"
INDIRECT: Sue asked him whether *he had been* there.

DIRECT: The manager told him, "*Your* hours *will* be changed."
INDIRECT: The manager told him that *his* hours *would* be changed.

Even when you are not using direct quotation, set the following off from your own text:

(1) Set off quoted words and phrases. Even in indirect quotations, show when you have kept some of the original words—because they are striking, or typical of the speaker, or especially important. Enclose such words and phrases (but not the rest of the quotation) in **quotation marks:**

The mayor said the criticism came from "well-meaning but uninformed" citizens.
Our teacher called Mark Twain "the Lincoln of our literature."

(2) Set off difficult or new or unusual terms. **Quotation marks** show that they are new or deserve special attention:

The engine has an "afterburner" especially designed for this plane.

(3) Set off words discussed as words, as in a discussion of word meanings. Use **italics** (or underlining in typed and handwritten papers) for this purpose:

The word *imply* means to hint or give to understand.

(4) Set off words borrowed from foreign languages and still considered foreign. For instance, many scientific and legal terms are borrowed from Latin. Use **italics:**

Poison sumac *(Rhus vernix)* has spoiled many a vacation trip.
The junta claimed to be the *de jure* government.

(5) Set off titles of publications. For complete publications, such as books and magazines, use **italics.** For *separate parts* of a publica-

tion—such as a chapter of a book, an article in a magazine, a poem in a collection—use **quotation marks**:

> A portion of Tillie Olsen's *Yonnondio,* called "The Iron Throat," was published in *Partisan Review.*

NOTE: Students often use quotation marks to set off words (often slang terms) for humorous effect. This practice is much overdone.

EXERCISE 1

Which of the following sentences include a direct quotation? Which include an indirect quotation? Copy each sentence, punctuating it correctly.

1. The speaker said I need the support of everyone in this hall
2. The candidate said that she had been encouraged by the many letters and phone calls she had received
3. The teacher asked us how many of us knew another language
4. The voice through the megaphone boomed all ashore that is going ashore
5. The guide asked us to stay on the designated paths
6. The sign said we are not responsible for personal belongings
7. I love my country the author said but at the same time I cannot forget that I was born Irish
8. He asked if you love the person you marry does that mean you no longer love your parents
9. She wanted to know if any of us had had trouble finding a ride.
10. My aunt told us what had made her parents leave everything behind and come to the United States

EXERCISE 2

The following sentences show the right way of setting off individual words and phrases. Explain why each word or phrase was set off the way it was.

1. *Junta* is a Spanish word meaning group or council.
2. Poe's "The Raven" was included in *Great American Poems.*
3. The word *gargoyle* is related to *gargle* and refers to a spout designed to throw rainwater clear of a building.
4. The rattlesnake weed *(Daucus pusillus)* is a weedy herb related to the carrot.
5. As Thoreau has pointed out, the partridge loves peas, but "not those that go with her into the pot."
6. To protect our divers from the "bends," a special decompression chamber had to be constructed.
7. Mr. Green was reading "Why Teachers Fail" in the current issue of *Harper's.*
8. In "The Minister's Black Veil," Hawthorne never quite says whether the veil really symbolizes "the consciousness of secret sin."

9. The new governor announced that offenders would be prosecuted "without fear or favor."

10. The defendant's lawyer entered a plea of *nolo contendere.*

<table>
<tr><td>

**UNIT REVIEW
EXERCISE**

</td><td>

Book reviews and literary criticism require of the author competent handling of titles, quotations, and the like. Find all examples in the following passage. Explain what each illustrates.

</td></tr>
</table>

"This country knows not yet, or in the least part, how great a son it has lost. . . . His soul was made for the noblest society; . . . wherever there is knowledge, wherever there is virtue, wherever there is beauty, he will find a home."

The people who were gathered 100 years ago in the parish church at Concord heard these words from Ralph Waldo Emerson as he spoke of his neighbor Henry David Thoreau, who had died three days before, on May 6, 1862. A friend recited a poem "To Henry." Bronson Alcott read a poem in which Thoreau had written of himself as "a bundle of vain strivings tied by a chance bond together."

Eight years earlier, Thoreau had published a book which most reviewers agreed was "more curious than useful." It told of his life alone by Walden Pond, a life he considered better than the "mean and sneaking lives" many other people lived. Five years before that, he had allowed publication of an essay on "Resistance to Civil Government," which told of his own arrest for failure to obey an ordinance of which he did not approve.

Since then, Thoreau had published little: articles about a visit to Cape Cod in *Putnam's Magazine* and about a walking trip to Maine in the *Atlantic Monthly;* a piece about "Slavery in Massachusetts"; and a study on "The Succession of Forest Trees."

M7

MANUSCRIPT FORM

Hand in clean and legible copy observing standard form.

The outward appearance of your paper shows what you think of your reader. Show that you care about your reader's convenience, eyesight, and standards of neatness.

M7a

Preparing Copy

Write or type your papers neatly, legibly, and in standard form.

Observe the following guidelines:

(1) Keep your handwriting clear and legible. Keep the loops open in letters like *e*. Keep the dots right over each *i* and cross your *t*'s. Do not run together combinations like *mm, mn, ing, tion.* Avoid excessive slanting and excessive crowding. Remember that

flourishes and squiggles easily annoy the reader. If your teacher does not require any special type of theme paper, use paper of *standard size,* ruled in *wide* lines.

(2) Type your papers whenever you can. Type the original copy on *nontransparent* paper—unlined, of standard size. Semitransparent sheets (onionskin) are for carbon copies. *Double-space* all material except block quotations and footnotes. Leave two spaces after a period or other end punctuation. Use two hyphens—with no space on either side—to make a dash.

(3) Leave adequate margins. Leave about an inch and a half on the left and at the top. Leave about an inch on the right and at the bottom. *Indent* the first line of a paragraph—about an inch in longhand, or five spaces in typed copy.

(4) Capitalize words in the title of your paper as you would in a title you mention (see also **M2a**). Observe the three *don'ts* for the title you give to your own theme: Do *not* underline or italicize it. Do *not* enclose it in quotation marks (unless it is indeed a quotation). Do *not* put a period at the end (but use a question mark or exclamation point where needed).

```
        Growing Up the Hard Way
        Are You in a Hurry?
        Save the Whales!
```

(5) Proofread a first draft carefully for misspellings or typing errors. The following last-minute **corrections** are permissible on the final copy if they are neat and few in number:

• Draw a line through words or phrases you want to omit. Do *not* use parentheses or square brackets for this purpose:

```
    clothes which had been bought for her sister
```

• To correct a word, draw a line through it and write the corrected word in the space immediately above. Do *not* cross out or insert individual letters:

```
            implied
        He inferred we were cheating.
```

• To add a missing word, insert a caret (∧) and write the word immediately above:

```
                is
        A new census ∧ being planned.
```

- To change the paragraphing of a paper, insert the symbol ¶ to indicate an additional paragraph break. Insert *no*¶ in the margin to indicate that an existing paragraph break should be ignored.

```
. . . was finished. ¶The second part of the program. . . .
```

(6) Divide words as recommended by your dictionary. Most dictionaries use centered dots to show the possible breaks (com•pli•ment). Divide words only if otherwise you would have an uneven right margin. Use the hyphen to divide words. Remember:

- Do not set off *single letters,* as for instance in *about, alone, many, via.* Do not set off the *–ed* ending in words like *asked* and *complained.*

- When a word is clearly a *combination* of other meaningful parts, divide at the point where the original parts are joined: *blue•bird, harm•ful.*

- Divide *hyphenated words* only at the point where the hyphen occurs, for instance in *un-American* or *sister-in-law.*

- Do not divide the *last word* on a page.

(7) Underline, or italicize, for emphasis. Use this device only rarely, when clearly appropriate:

```
"I know exactly what you mean," he replied.
```

M7b
Abbreviations and Numbers

Use abbreviations and figures only where they are appropriate.

Abbreviations and figures can help save much time and space in informal writing. In ordinary writing, however, you should try to avoid excessive shortcuts:

(1) Use abbreviations only if they are acceptable in ordinary writing:

- Before or after *names,* the titles *Mr., Mrs., Ms., Dr., St.* (Saint); the abbreviations *Jr.* and *Sr.;* degrees like *M.D.* and *Ph.D.:*

> We were introduced to Mr. and Mrs. Jones.
> The sign identified her as Jean E. Gielgud, M.D.

- Before or after *numerals,* the abbreviations *No., A.D.* and *B.C., A.M.* and *P.M.* (or *a.m.* and *p.m.*); and the symbol *$:*

> The battle of Marathon was fought in 490 B.C.
> The plane leaves at 9:25 A.M.

- *Initials* standing for the name of agencies, business firms, technical processes, and the like, providing these initials are in common use:

> Ranson had been an agent for the CIA.
> We studied an article about the NAACP.
> One of our major TV stations is ABC.

- *Latin abbreviations* such as *e.g.* (for example), *etc.* (and so on), *i.e.* (that is). (The modern tendency is to use the corresponding English expressions instead.)

> The writer discussed important new resources, e.g., solar energy.
> Know how to use various tools: saws, hammers, wrenches, etc.

(2) Know abbreviations that we use only for special purposes. Some abbreviations are acceptable in addresses, business records, and the like, but are *spelled out* in ordinary writing:

- Names of *countries, states, streets,* and the like (with a few exceptions: *U.S.S.R.;* Washington, *D.C.*):

> Our first stop in the United States was Buffalo, New York.
> Her office was on Union Street in Pittsburgh, Pennsylvania.

- *Units of measurement* like *lb.* (pound), *oz.* (ounce), *ft.* (foot), with the exception of *mph* and *rpm:*

> The fish she caught weighed three pounds, two ounces.
> The wall measured eight feet, six inches.

(3) Use exact figures where needed. Figures are generally acceptable in references to dates and years, street numbers, and page numbers. Use them also for exact sums and technical measurements, especially those referring to percentages or including decimal points:

> She was born on June 12, 1951.
> They lived at 1078 Washington Avenue.
> The town had 23,456 inhabitants.
> You will find that information on page 131.

(4) Know which figures to spell out. The following are usually spelled out: numbers from one to ten; round numbers requiring no more than two words; a number at the beginning of a sentence. (When they are spelled out, compound numbers from 21 to 99 are hyphenated.)

> The first issue of our paper sold about three hundred copies.
> Twenty-five years ago he was not even born.
> The nursery school was for children from two to six years old.

Most of the sentences in the following exercise use abbreviations and numbers in a way that would be satisfactory in ordinary writing. Put *S* after the number of each such sentence. The remaining sentences need to be revised. Put *R* after the number of each such sentence. Be prepared to explain why and how each of these should be revised. (Your teacher may ask you to write down the revised versions.)

1. Exactly $27.85 remained in the treasury.
2. In a fascist country, the FBI would infiltrate the PTA and the government would run the AFL-CIO.
3. We decided to call the Dr. the following a.m.
4. Each day, the cafeteria serves about 1000 people.
5. The population had reached a peak of 22,347 people.
6. The card identified them as Mr. and Mrs. Joseph Sparks, Jr.
7. UNESCO is the educational and cultural branch of the United Nations.
8. They first visited Oakland, Calif., in 1978.
9. 13 copies were sold, 8 were given away, and the rest were remaindered.
10. The coach was pleased to learn that Hank measured six feet, two inches.
11. The company moved from Poughkeepsie, New York, to Terre Haute, Indiana.
12. When he came back from his trip, he weighed a mere one hundred and thirteen lbs.
13. The vase had been made in China around 400 B.C.
14. To remodel the house would have cost the club ten thousand dollars.
15. We all know a few Irish words, e.g. *leprechaun* and *whiskey*.

THE PRINTER'S PRACTICE

Handbook instructions necessarily give a *simplified* account of the mechanics of written English. They can tell you what is typical and generally accepted. They cannot take stock of all the variations of current practice. The following assignments give you a chance to explore some of these variations on your own.

Much *modern journalism* employs "open punctuation," using fewer commas and semicolons than the more formal style taught in most English classes. Study punctuation in a recent issue of *Time* or *Newsweek*. Prepare a report on how the conventions employed differ from those of a more formal style. Provide sample sentences.

What conventions of punctuation do you encounter in your reading of *American fiction?* The following is a passage from a short story by Bret Harte. How does it follow or adapt the conventions outlined in this chapter?

The assemblage numbered about a hundred men. One or two of these were actual fugitives from justice, some were criminal, and all were reckless. Physically, they exhibited no indication of their past lives and character. The greatest scamp had a Raphael face, with a profusion of blond hair; Oakhurst, a gambler, had the melancholy air and intellectual abstraction of a Hamlet; the coolest and most courageous man was scarcely over five feet in height, with a soft voice and an embarrassed, timid manner. The term "roughs" applied to them was a distinction rather than a definition. Perhaps in the minor details of fingers, toes, ears, etc., the camp may have been deficient, but these slight omissions did not detract from their aggregate force. The strongest man had but three fingers on his right hand; the best shot had but one eye.

Chapter 6

Oral Language
You and the Audience

Chapter
Preview 6

Speak with confidence and a sense of purpose.

The applicant who is interviewed for a job, the sales representative who comes to the door, the citizen who speaks up at a public hearing—all these depend for success on the personal impression they make on their audience. And that personal impression depends to a large extent on how well they handle the spoken language.

When you watch successful speakers, look for three major qualities that contribute to their success:

(1) An effective speaker inspires confidence. The speaker may be worried before the speech starts, but no stage fright shows once it is time to speak. Looking the audience in the eye, the speaker starts in a firm but relaxed tone, reassuring the audience that he or she is in command of the material. A confident speaker puts the audience at ease and in an attentive mood.

(2) An effective speaker knows what he or she is doing. To hold our attention, a speaker must give us the feeling that the speech is moving ahead with a purpose. There is essential information to be conveyed or some important points to be made. Whether or not they agree with the speaker, an audience wants to know: "What is this all about? What are you trying to prove? What do you want us to do?"

(3) An effective speaker stays in control of the audience. He or she sizes up the listeners' moods and reactions and reacts to them in turn. Are the people in the back row nodding appreciatively? Or are they responding with a blank stare? An effective speaker does not stay tied to a set speech but instead makes adjustments that regain the attention of the audience.

Draw on the full range of the speaker's resources.

Speakers do not become effective unless they improvise and experiment. The following *limbering-up exercises* will give you much-needed practice in addressing an audience. They will give you a chance to explore the full range of the speaker's resources.

SOUND—*Make the sound fit the sense.* Try to read the following student-written poems in such a way that your audience will say: "I can hear it now! I can see it now!"

POEM 1   **Murder**

HONK! HOOOONK!
   went the horn.
SCREEEEEEEECH!
   went the tires on the pavement.
CRASH!
   went the cars into each other.
OUT!
   went three more lights of life.

The siren sounds pain:
   whimpers of a beaten dog.
Traffic
goes slow.
The curious take a moment
and wait.
Hungry
eyes watch:
to glimpse the dying,
   to lap the blood.

POEM 2   **Slurp! Went the Fizzling Surf**

watch the water slurp
   among the rocks
and listen to the foam
   pop and fizzle
notice how she slaps
   and slashes at the air
and watch her curl
   and crash upon the sand
do not move if she
   sprays your face—
her eagerness will last
   only a while

DIALOGUE—*Suggest the give-and-take of conversation.* Good speakers do not just announce everything from "on high." They know how to echo the give-and-take of question and answer. They know how to create suspense and how to bring in the punch line at the right moment. Find a brief dialogue that ends with a punch line or a clever answer—like the sample below. Use one that you have heard or read, or use one that you have made up yourself. First, act it out with a classmate. Then do the whole dialogue by yourself in such a way that your audience can hear the two different voices. Sample:

> In the old days, the only way to travel across some of the snowed-in mountain passes of Colorado was by horse-drawn sleigh. Here is a conversation that one passenger claimed he had with the driver:
> "How high is the mountain?"
> "It is 13,000 feet."
> "Can you fall all the way down?"
> "Well, not very easy. You hit a crag down about a thousand feet."
> "Do people fall very often?"
> "Only once."

IMPROVISATION—*Learn to think on your feet.* Effective speakers do not seem to be reading everything from cue cards. They know how to respond to an unexpected question or to an unforeseen situation. They know how to bring in the improvised remarks that make the talk sound like a live performance.

How good are you at thinking on your feet? What would you say if you unexpectedly found yourself in one of the following situations?

1. A friend complains to you about a job he or she has applied for but did not get. Though your friend had all the necessary qualifications, only people from ethnic or racial minorities were being hired because of minimum quotas for minority employees. What do you say to your friend?

2. A girl tells you that her mother wanted to become a dentist. When she entered dental school, she was the only woman. When she left dental school, the only way she could get started in her own career was to work in her father's dental office. The girl asks you what you think of this pattern of discrimination.

3. You work in a place where women are asking for equal pay for equal work. But some of the men complain that there are rules prohibiting women from lifting weights of over 45 pounds and that, when in a tight spot, women call on men for help.

ACTING OUT—*Use gestures to help your audience get into the spirit of the thing.* A good storyteller does not just use words. The whole person tells the story. With an effective speaker, what the face says and what the hands say are very much part of the message.

Look at the following student-written poems. Read them out loud —*act them out* with appropriate gestures. Make the full meanings of the words in these poems come to life. (You may want to team up with a classmate—have the speaker read the poem; have the other person "pantomime" the meaning of the poem.)

POEM 3

A Circle

A circle is divine
It has no beginning
and it never ends.
Someday I may find
someone to make
a circle with.

POEM 4

A bud, new and green, opens its dew filled shutters to
reveal a flower;
        the beginning of a season.
A leaf, dried and brown, shrivels its crinkly dryness and
drops;
        the end of a season.
A spring salmon, floating swiftly downstream to experience
growth and the big blue green world;
        the beginning of a season.
A salmon, scared and battered, depleted of its strength,
arrives at the place of its birth, drops its eggs then turns
over and floats into a fertilizer mound;
        the end of a season . . . .
   A Spring into Life -
           A Fall into Silence -
  The Seasons of the World.

POEM 5   The Flame

```
I am frightened that
the flame of hate
will burn me,
will scorch my pride,
scar my heart.
It will burn and I
cannot put it out.
I cannot call the fire department,
and they cannot put out the fire
within my soul.
I am frightened that the flame
of hurt will burn me.
If it does,
I will die.
```

HUMOR—*Show that you have a sense of humor*. Even a serious talk need not be grim. Experienced speakers know how to *disarm* an audience by humor at their own expense. How good are you at telling stories that are *humorous at your own expense?* Prepare to tell a collection of anecdotes at the expense of a group to which you yourself belong: Catholics, Baptists, Jews; Americans of Polish, German, Italian, Japanese descent; football players, campus politicians, musicians, model students.

EXERCISE 1

Choose one or more of the following:

1. Tell a story with different *animal characters* in it. Give to each a voice that fits its appearance and its role in the story. Try to give your performance some of the life and color that mark effective storytelling.

2. Memorize and recite a *poem with different speakers* in it. Make each voice distinct and appropriate. Or, recite stanzas from two or three poems *by the same author* but requiring a different speaking voice.

3. Select a number of passages by *different American authors,* all concerned with a major common theme: friendship, loss, separation, young love, or the like. Choose authors that differ widely in tone, style, personality. Prepare a recital in which you present these passages.

4. With your classmates, select passages in which different people talk about the *same experience:* life in a labor camp or camp for prisoners of war; life in prison; a wartime experience; a natural disaster. Assign each passage to a different reader. In a staged reading, have each reader try to assume the personality of the author of the assigned passage.

Prepare a talk in which you make a fresh attempt to tackle a *familiar prejudice*. Try to adopt some fresh and lively new approach that will make the prejudiced person take a new look at the subject. *Dramatize*—act out little scenes. Impersonate both the prejudiced person and the victim of prejudice, and the like.

EXERCISE 2

Prepare a short talk with a definite purpose.

Of the various purposes that a short planned talk may serve, three are the most basic. First, the major purpose of a speaker may be to *inform*. The speaker's task may be to explain a situation, or to bring the audience up-to-date on recent developments. The audience expects to hear someone who knows—who has facts, examples, statistics at his or her fingertips.

Or, the major purpose of the speaker may be to *persuade*. The audience expects a "talking to": Someone wants them to change their minds, or their habits, or their present course of action. They expect to hear someone who cares.

Or, the major purpose of the speaker may be to *inspire*. When troubled or discouraged, people look for guidance. They look for someone who can say the encouraging word. As you experiment with these three major purposes, remember some general guidelines:

(1) Become familiar with your subject. Make your audience feel that you know what you are talking about. Competent speakers know *more* about the subject than they are likely to use in the talk.

(2) Speak freely from notes. Few people can read a prepared speech, or recite it from memory, and still sound *natural*. Everyone has been to meetings where the steady drone of a read speech puts the audience to sleep. Color and movement return to a speech when speakers have their material in front of them. They put it into words freshly as they go along.

(3) Make sure your audience can follow the major outline of your talk. Your audience must have a sense of direction. It loses interest unless it knows where it is headed. Experienced speakers often use a very simple outline, stressing three or four major points. They make sure the audience knows early what will be the major steps in their argument or the major aspects of a problem.

Learn to present information in a businesslike and authoritative fashion.

A speaker presents to a group of people information they need to help them carry out their work. Often, a speaker presents to a group

O2
SPEAKING WITH A PURPOSE

O2a
The Background Talk

of nonspecialists information that will help them understand developments in a specialized field. The speaker provides essential background that helps people understand what is going on, how it came about, and what might be needed in the future.

If you check a current program of speeches and lectures offered in your community, you may find topics fitting under some of the following typical headings:

- Problems in newly emerging nations
- New discoveries in medicine
- Plans for urban renewal
- Current movements in modern art
- New educational methods

The first step in preparing a background talk is to become thoroughly familiar with available information. Draw on a *variety of sources*. If you want your material to be factual, try to check facts given in one source against those given in another. Compare different sources. Which seem superficial and secondhand? Which are more thorough—drawing on firsthand observation or detailed study? If you cannot get material from clearly *neutral* sources, make sure that not all the people you draw on had the same ax to grind.

As you work up your material into usable form, remember:

(1) Keep your outline clear and simple. Generally, use a simpler scheme than you would in writing. Readers can always backtrack, or stop and think. Listeners must be able to follow you the first time, or you have lost them for good. Make sure that in your listeners' minds your presentation falls into some clear general pattern, such as the following:

Outline 1: A theory and its application
    I. The basic theory
    II. First major practical application
    III. Second major practical application
    IV. Third major practical application

Outline 2: A program for action
    I. A program for action by a major interest group
    II. An alternative program by a rival group
    III. A third alternative of your own

(2) Emphasize key terms and key ideas. Obviously, you should not give too difficult technical terms, like *median terminal velocity* or *intermittent modular construct*. But give your listeners key terms that they can remember, like "functional form," or "guaranteed annual income." Such terms can serve as pegs to hang an argument on. They can help you give clear focus to your discussion.

(3) Use a few striking statistics to drive home major points. Make an honest attempt to sort out available figures. Statistics can help you dramatize a situation that might otherwise go unnoticed by your audience:

> The sciences have always received the lion's share of federal funds. A few years ago, government support of study and research was divided as follows: physical sciences, 69 percent; life sciences, 28 percent; social sciences, 2 percent; arts and humanities, less than ½ of 1 percent. Government support for studies of art and literature amounted to less than $\frac{1}{250}$ of 1 percent of the national budget.

(4) Make strategic use of references to authority. The audience wants to be reassured that you are not simply making things up. A quote from a well-known expert does not prove that you are right—experts disagree. But it shows that you have kept up. Learn to weave short, informal references into your talk:

> As *Marshall McLuhan suggests,* today's television children are attuned to up-to-the-minute "adult" news—rioting, war, taxes, crime. They are lost when they enter the different environment of the school, where they are asked for extended attention to distant causes, long-range effects, and minor details.

(5) Build up gradually to what is difficult or debatable. Prepare the ground for what is difficult to take. To explain a new medical or scientific concept, relate it first to more simple things that the audience already knows. When moving into controversial territory, try to take your audience along with you by gradual steps:

> First, we *all agree* that one result of the current trend is as follows . . . .
> Second, and this is a *more subtle effect* . . . .
> Third, and perhaps the most important result, *hardly ever noticed* by many people, is . . . .

Prepare a background talk on some *current topic or current development* of interest to a general audience. The following topics indicate some possible choices:

EXERCISE 1

- The two-year college
- Myths and facts about weight
- Yoga
- Astrology and the ancients
- A modern Bible
- How safe is your car?
- The future of space travel
- Growing your own food

EXERCISE 2

Attend a *public speech or lecture* on a subject of current general interest. Study the speaker's technique: How does he or she proceed? What is the tone or manner? What kind of material is used? How is it organized? Your teacher may ask you to present your findings as an oral report or as a short paper. Concentrate on a few major points that helped determine the speaker's effectiveness.

O2b
The Call to Action

Learn how to influence an audience faced with important decisions.

Effective speakers know how to help people make up their minds on important issues. They do not try to do the impossible. They do not expect to convert their listeners to a completely different point of view. But they know how to guide audiences when they are undecided. Effective speakers know how to appeal to their listeners' consciences when apathy or self-interest are keeping them from doing what is right.

The following examples are all taken from one famous persuasive speech: Patrick Henry's speech to the Virginia Convention in 1775. He is asking his fellow delegates to take steps leading to a definite break between the colonies and England. Can you see how his speech lives up to the following suggestions for an effective call to action?

(1) Treat with respect people who disagree with you. Resist the temptation to call listeners holding other views ignorant or dishonest. It is easier to insult people (and to make lifelong enemies) than it is to persuade them. Notice how respectfully Henry treats people that he wants to *bring over to his side:*

> No one thinks more highly than I do of the patriotism, as well as abilities, of the very worthy gentlemen who have just addressed the house. . . . I hope it will not be thought disrespectful to those gentlemen, if, entertaining as I do, opinions of a character very opposite to theirs, I shall speak forth my sentiments freely, and without reserve. . . .

(2) Appeal to your listeners' experience. Use evidence that your listeners can verify. Appeal to what they themselves have seen and heard and felt:

> I have but one lamp by which my feet are guided and that is the lamp of experience. I know of no way of judging of the future but by the past. And judging by the past, I wish to know what there has been in the conduct of the British ministry for the last ten years, to justify those hopes with which gentlemen have been pleased to solace themselves and the house. . . .

(3) Show weaknesses and contradictions in the opposing point of view. Here is how Henry answers those who saw hope in the relatively friendly reception of recent communications from the colonists:

> Ask yourselves how this gracious reception of our petition comports with those warlike preparations which cover our waters and darken our land. Are fleets and armies necessary to a work of love and reconciliation? Have we shown ourselves so unwilling to be reconciled, that force must be called in to win back our love? . . . These are the implements of war and subjugation, the last arguments to which kings resort. . . .

(4) Show that as a person of goodwill you have considered possible alternatives. Even in adopting a drastic course of action, people want to think of themselves as patient, reasonable, doing only what is right:

> We have done everything that could be done, to avert the storm which is now coming on. We have petitioned, . . . we have supplicated, we have prostrated ourselves before the throne, and have implored its interposition to arrest the tyrannical hands of the ministry and parliament. Our petitions have been slighted; our supplications have been disregarded; and we have been spurned, with contempt, from the foot of the throne. . . .

(5) Show that your own solution is logical and inevitable. It is a lonely and bitter task to go against the tide. People like to feel part of the mainstream. The audience is reassured when it supports a cause that is part of a powerful popular movement or of a strong current trend. Here is how Henry makes his own program for action seem inescapable:

> It is in vain, sir, to extenuate the matter. Gentlemen may cry, peace, peace—but there is no peace. The war is actually begun! The next gale that sweeps from the north will bring to our ears the clash of resounding arms! Our brethren are already in the field! Why stand we here idle?

NOTE: If you address an audience on a grave topic, remember an important principle: *Start in a low key and build up to a climax.* A speaker who starts at a high pitch may seem merely hysterical to the listeners. One of Henry's listeners reported:

> He commenced somewhat calmly, but the smothered excitement began more and more to play upon his features and thrill in the tones of his voice. . . . His voice rose louder and louder, until the walls of the building, and all within them, seemed to shake. . . . His last exclamation, "Give me liberty or give me death!", was like the shout of the leader which turns back the rout of battle.

EXERCISE 1

How effective a speaker are you? Prepare a *persuasive speech* in which you ask your audience to

- join an organization;
- support a candidate;
- endorse a park proposal, bond issue for schools, or similar community project;
- take effective action to upgrade a neighborhood or to preserve scenic beauty;
- endorse a new educational method or project.

EXERCISE 2

Prepare a talk calling for action in an area likely to cause *controversy:* censorship, zero population growth, family education, divorce laws, civil disobedience, or the like. Try to deal with an explosive issue in such a way that your point of view will get a fair hearing. What can you do to "defuse" the issue? What can you do to persuade people on a subject on which many have closed minds? How can you best get across new material that may influence your listeners?

EXERCISE 3

Prepare to *reenact a famous speech* designed to sway American popular opinion. Prepare an abridged version of the speech, preserving its high points and some of its general outline or development. If you can, find out about the appearance and mannerisms of the speaker. Here are some possible choices:

- Patrick Henry's speech to the Virginia Convention, 1775
- W. J. Bryan's "Cross of Gold" speech, 1896
- Woodrow Wilson's speech on the Fourteen Points (January 1918) or in support of the League of Nations (July 1919)
- a speech by Susan B. Anthony in favor of women's suffrage

O2c
The Inspirational Message

Study the ways an inspiring speaker builds morale.

Some people prefer to leave inspiration to commencement speakers and to the minister in the pulpit. But even the practical work of the world depends on people who by their words as well as their actions can inspire confidence, give a sense of direction. People have to feel that what they are doing is worthwhile. Many achievements that seem practical on the surface depend on loyalty, dedication, satisfaction in work well done.

Here are some of the morale-building qualities of an inaugural address delivered by President John F. Kennedy on January 20, 1961:

(1) Appeal to what unites people rather than what divides. Many people respond to a reminder of the common purposes often obscured by petty bickering and prejudice:

> We observe today not a victory of party but a celebration of freedom, symbolizing an end as well as a beginning, signifying renewal as well as change. . . .

(2) Emphasize human potential and the promise of the future rather than the shortcomings of the present. People cannot live in a fool's paradise, shutting their eyes to their present dilemmas. But the effective leader does not harp on present evils without offering a formula for what *can be done:*

> . . . United, there is little we cannot do in a host of cooperative ventures. . . . To those people in the huts and villages of half the globe struggling to break the bonds of mass misery, we pledge our best efforts to help them help themselves, for whatever period is required, not because the Communists may be doing it, not because we seek their votes, but because it is right. . . .

(3) Give fresh meaning to familiar values. Speakers appealing to our love of freedom must be able to talk about the problems of freedom here and now. They must be able to give new meaning to familiar terms. They have to offer a new perspective on old problems. Notice how the word *enemies* has a fresh contemporary meaning in the following quotation from President Kennedy's speech:

> Now the trumpet summons us again—not as a call to bear arms, though arms we need; not as a call to battle, though embattled we are; but a call to bear the burden of a long twilight struggle, year in and year out, "rejoicing in hope, patient in tribulation," a struggle against the common enemies: tyranny, poverty, disease and war itself.

EXERCISE 1

Prepare a short talk about *someone you admire.* For instance, talk about a diplomat, artist, explorer, or physician whose biography you have recently read. Avoid perfunctory, stereotyped praise—the kind of thing "everybody says." Convince your audience that the person you talk about means something to you personally.

EXERCISE 2

Have you recently been interested in an *unpopular or unsuccessful cause?* Prepare a short talk designed to restore the morale of its supporters. What can you say that is not merely cheap consolation? (Prepare a short preface filling in your classmates on the background of the cause and the kind of audience they will play.)

EXERCISE 3

Compare and contrast *inaugural addresses* by American Presidents. Prepare a short report on major differences in style. Which seems to you the most eloquent or inspiring? Some of the more famous addresses are those by Jefferson (1801), Lincoln (1861), Roosevelt (1933), and Kennedy (1961).

O3

DISCUSSION AND DEBATE

Participate actively in discussion and debate.

In much of the public speaking we do, we cannot follow a prepared manuscript. At a committee meeting or public hearing, we have to be able to think on our feet. Effective speakers must be able to speak vigorously and coherently on a subject that has just come up. Opportunities for improvised public speech vary a great deal:

• **Informal discussion** is an excellent way of exploring an issue. Discussion teaches us to *listen* as well as to talk. It allows us to air tentative ideas, to see how others will react. It makes us aware of possible doubts and objections. It helps us adopt a *balanced view.*

• A **panel discussion** makes it possible to give definite *direction* to an exchange of views. Three or four speakers present different *parts of a topic* or different but related *points of view.* Each speaker is expected to be somewhat of an expert on his or her part of the topic. The give-and-take that follows the initial presentation by each speaker can then be anchored to the material already presented. A **moderator** can help keep the discussion in focus by trying to sum up whatever consensus has emerged.

• A **public hearing** may merely allow the public to let off steam. But it may also sway officials who reckon with public opinion.

• The **formal debate** presents an opportunity for the full, systematic presentation of opposing views. Each side in a debate is allotted time to present the major arguments in support of its position. Then each side is given additional time for **rebuttal,** so that objections raised by the other side do not go unanswered. If the two sides are about equally matched, intellectual fireworks result.

The format of the debate is that of a contest. A debater is pushed toward taking a *definite stand.* Typically he or she speaks for or against a central **proposition:** "Capital punishment should be abolished." "The United States should recognize the new XYZ government." As a result, a debate tends to polarize opinion. Two opposed, and often somewhat extreme, views are presented.

No matter what the format of a discussion, remember:

(1) Let the audience know what you are driving at. Sum up your major point clearly and forcefully so that it can be recognized

and remembered. Evidence and argument are wasted when the audience is not sure what they are supposed to prove.

(2) *Let the other side have its turn.*   Audiences resent speakers who try to dominate a discussion, or who try to bully their opposition. Do not try to correct every error. Do not answer every charge. Concentrate on essentials; don't scatter your fire.

(3) *Work toward a meeting of minds.*   Even in a formal debate, the opposing sides can *agree* on a basic theory and yet *disagree* on important applications. Learn to look for common ground. When no agreement is possible, make sure that at least the disagreement is on *substantial* points, not over something minor.

EXERCISE 1

Stage a *panel discussion* on some current public health hazard: air pollution, smoking, contamination of the water supply, or the like. Make sure the members of the panel have authoritative information and represent different views. During the last third of the session, have the moderator accept questions from the audience.

EXERCISE 2

Stage a *public hearing* in which you assume that the education committee of a state legislature is exploring expert opinion and public sentiment on an important issue in education. Some possible topics are individualized instruction, course credit by examination, proficiency tests, busing. After the hearing, discuss whose contribution is likely to have made the strongest impression.

EXERCISE 3

Stage a *formal debate* on a political issue of current interest. For instance, should the U.S. Senate ratify an important new treaty? Should the House or Senate censure one of its members? Make sure the issue is clearly spelled out in the proposition to be debated. Have each side represented by a team of two or three members, with each speaker for the affirmative side followed by one for the negative. The class may vote on which side presented the *most persuasive* case, or it may appoint a panel of judges.

EXERCISE 4

Reenact, in a shortened version, one of the *famous debates of American politics.* For instance, study and reenact the Lincoln-Douglas debates of 1858 or the Kennedy-Nixon television debates of 1960. Have different classmates take the roles of the two major figures in different parts of the debate. The class may want to vote on who impersonated each major figure most convincingly.

FOR FURTHER STUDY

BEYOND THE CLICHÉ

Triteness is the bane of public speech. When a speaker repeats what we have heard a hundred times before, the audience finds it hard to stay awake. In listening to a speech, can you identify the phrases that have become clichés? Can you learn to avoid them in your own practice as a speaker? The following assignments give you a chance to explore some of the factors that make public speaking either tired and routine or fresh and worth listening to.

ACTIVITY 1

The following is an excerpt from John P. Marquand's novel *Point of No Return.* It describes a speech made in the twenties to the graduating class of a New England grammar school. How familiar are the phrases used by the speaker and the sentiments he expresses? How do they compare with phrases typical of graduation exercises and commencement speeches today? What would be your reaction to the speech if you were a member of the audience?

"Don't let anyone tell you, my young friends, that there is any such thing as luck. Do you think that you are here today, on the threshold of higher education, because of luck? No! . . ."

"No, no," Mr. Gifford was saying. "You are here because of the sacrifices of your parents and the work of every citizen and the very fine achievements of the wonderful ladies and gentlemen on your school committee, your teachers, and of your great mayor, my dear old friend, Francis X. Flynn."

He did not intone the name of Clyde's great mayor but ended it in a shout, and then he waited for the fluttering of applause.

"And what made it possible for them to give you these advantages and to make their sacrifices and their dreams for you come true?" Mr. Gifford was asking. "Was it accident? Was it luck? No! I'll tell you what made it possible." And he walked to the edge of the platform before he told them. "It was possible because you live in the greatest country in the world, in the United States of America, where all men, I thank God, are free and equal, living in the frame of freedom, life, liberty and the pursuit of happiness, where each of us can look the other in the eye and say, 'I am as free as you are; no matter how rich you may be, I have the same chance as you, because this great land of ours is the land of freedom.'"

Mr. Gifford mopped his forehead before he went on with the credo of Clyde.

"Oh, no—there is no such thing as luck, my dear young friends, not for American boys and girls. As you sit here, not so far from entering the contest for life's prizes, you are all starting even because this is America, no matter what may be your religion or race or bank account. There is no grease for palms in America. The only grease is elbow grease. Look at our greatest men, born on small farms in small houses, boys without a cent to their names. Did they get there by luck? Oh, no. They got there by making the most of opportunities which are open, thank God, to every American boy and girl."

Study Babbitt's Annual Address to the Zenith Real Estate Board in Sinclair Lewis' novel *Babbitt* (chapter 14). How familiar are the sentiments and phrases that Lewis is satirizing? (Identify them in detail.) *Babbitt* was published in 1922. Has Babbitt's kind of oratory become dated?

ACTIVITY 2

Study a recent speech by a United States senator with some reputation for skill as an orator. Does the senator's style as a whole seem conventional, stereotyped? Or does it seem fresh, individual? Support your answer by specific examples.

ACTIVITY 3

Read several reactions by columnists and editorial writers to an important recent speech. Apart from their stand on the issues, what *standards* do these writers seem to apply in judging the effectiveness of the speaker? Is there any substantial agreement among the different critics? How fair do the standards applied seem to *you?*

ACTIVITY 4

Chapter 7

Resources
Special Helps for Writers

R1

USING THE LIBRARY

Know your library.

An effective user of the library knows how to look for information and how to use the information to advantage.

R1a

Examining a Book

Learn how to examine a book for its possible usefulness.

In order to judge which books will best serve their purpose, students should know how to look briefly at a book and draw conclusions about its contents, purpose, and possible usefulness. Learn to use the following parts of a book:

(1) The *title page* gives information which is important to someone doing research. It may include

- the full *title* of the book;
- the full name of the *author* and often title and place of employment;
- the name of the *editor* if the book is a collection of material written by many people, or if it is adapted from earlier published works, or if one person has prepared the work of another for publication;
- the *translator* if this work was first printed in another language;
- the *edition* if the book is in any but its original printed form;
- the *publishing house* and the city or cities in which the publisher and any branches or affiliates are located.

On the reverse side of the title page, look for the copyright date and the name of the copyright owner. Since each edition is separately copyrighted, a list of copyright dates shows that the book has been through several revisions. *Printing dates do not indicate revision.* A popular book may be reprinted many times without revision. Recent books give their Library of Congress catalogue card number.

(2) A book may have both a *preface* and an *introduction*. In a preface the author explains the reasons for writing the book. When an author personally writes an introduction, it is often a message to the reader on how to benefit from the book. An introduction by someone other than the author may present background material on the author and the book. Both preface and introduction are well worth the short time it takes to read them. Often, reading them tells students whether the book contains information suitable for their research.

(3) The *table of contents* gives an idea of what the book contains by listing the chapters by page numbers. Sometimes it gives enough detail to serve as an outline of the book. You can often tell from the table of contents what parts of the book will prove useful for a project.

(4) The *bibliography* is the list of books and articles that the writer has read in preparation for writing the book. Sometimes authors will also provide lists of books that they recommend to the reader for further study of the subject. Both types of bibliography furnish valuable hints about other books (and articles) that might prove useful for your project.

(5) The *index* is a listing of all subjects covered in the text in alphabetical order, telling on what page or pages references to the subject are to be found. In the index, find one or two topics relevant to your project. Read the pages of the book mentioned for these topics to determine how extended and difficult the treatment is.

Several other possible features of a book are worth noting. Is the book heavily *footnoted?* If so, it may turn out to be a scholarly study paying much attention to technical detail. It might be a good book in which to find exact information on a difficult point, but it might not be a good book for making you see the broad outlines of a subject. Is there a *glossary of terms?* A glossary serves as a miniature dictionary of specialized terms and is a great help to the non-specialist reader.

Learn where to look for material for a research project.

R1b

Finding Material

Become familiar with the usefulness of the following sources:

(1) **Encyclopedias**—*Consult a general encyclopedia for an overview of the topic.* A quick reading will give you a familiarity with the terms associated with your topic, the people that may have been involved in a particular event, the beginning and ending dates (if it is a historical subject), etc. It will also give you some idea of the scope of the topic you have chosen. Let us assume you have been assigned a one-thousand word paper on the Mormons to fit in with a social studies unit about settlement of the western United States. Turning to "Mormons" in the *Encyclopaedia Britannica,* for example, you would find a cross-reference to "Latter-Day Saints," another name for the sect, and under that name you would discover five full pages of summary.

(2) **Special encyclopedias**—*Consult a specialized encyclopedia for a more technical survey of the subject.* A good special encyclo-

MORMONS AND MORMONISM-FICTION

SAMPLE SUBJECT
CARDS

Fisher, Vardis 1895-

Children of God; an American epic

769 p.   Vanguard 1939

Maps on lining papers

A story of the building of the Mormon empire,
told mainly in terms of two central and
dramatic figures — Joseph Smith and Brigham
Young

MORMONS AND MORMONISM

289.3

Mullen, Robert Rodolf 1908-

The Latter-Day Saints; the Mormons yesterday and today by Robert Mullen. 1st ed; Garden
City, New York, Doubleday, 1966

xvi, 316 p. illus. map (on lining paper)

"Bibliography and notes": p. 289-303

978   MORMONS AND MORMONISM-HISTORY

Stegner, Wallace Earle, 1909-

The gathering of Zion; the story of the
Mormons, by Wallace Stegner. 1st ed. New
York, McGraw-Hill, 1964

331 p. illus. maps 23 cm (American Trails
series)

Bibliography: p. 315-319

pedia for a paper about the Mormons would be the *Concise Dictionary of American History,* edited by Wayne Andrews. Although
called a dictionary, this is more exactly a historical encyclopedia
in two volumes. Under "Mormons," you would find several subtopics: "Mormon Battalion," "Mormon Expedition," "Mormon Trail,"
and "Mormon War" besides a full-page treatment of "Mormons."
These headings suggest ways to *limit* the larger general subject.

(3) **The card catalogue**—*Use the card catalogue to determine what relevant books a library might contain.* The card catalogue contains a card for every book in a library. Each book is listed
on at least three cards: one alphabetized by the author, one by
title, and one by subject. If you were interested in books on the subject "Mormons," you would look for the *subject cards.* Let us say there
are three cards in the catalogue on "Mormons and Mormonism":
The book *Children of God* has no call number because it is fiction.
The Latter-Day Saints is written from a religious viewpoint (its
Dewey decimal number is in the two hundreds). *The Gathering of
Zion* has been classified as history (with a nine-hundred number).

The **call numbers** help you or the librarian find books on the
shelves. Nonfiction or *factual books* are arranged numerically rather
than alphabetically. Two numbering systems are used:

• The **Dewey decimal system** is one classification system.
Dewey classified nonfiction into ten major categories and assigned
a numerical designation to each:

000–099 General reference works: dictionaries, encyclopedias, etc.
These are almost always kept apart from the other nonfiction books.
100–199 Philosophy, psychology, ethics
200–299 Religion (including mythology)
300–399 Social sciences: immigration, economics, government, education, folklore

Within these hundreds, groups of ten form subdivisions of the
large area. For instance, 970–979 is North American history; 980–
989 is South American history. Each digit within these groups of
ten further subdivides the classification system: For instance, 972
covers the history of Mexico; 973 the history of the United States. A
decimal added after these three numbers helps divide American
history into periods: Colonial history is 973.2. Even further subdivisions may be necessary, each with a reason of its own. A book dealing
with the French and Indian wars during colonial times may be
classified as 973.26.

• The **Library of Congress system** divides books into categories identified by letters of the alphabet. It then uses additional

letters and numerals to subdivide each main category. For instance, the call number of a book on religion starts with a capital *B;* the call number of a book on education starts with a capital *L.* Here are the letters used by the Library of Congress system:

A	General Works	M	Music
B	Philosophy, Religion	N	Fine Arts
C	History	P	Language and Literature
D	History and Topography (except America)	Q	Science
		R	Medicine
E	American (general)— U.S. (general)	S	Agriculture (plant and animal industry)
F	United States (local) and America (except U.S.)	T	Technology
		U	Military Science
G	Geography—Anthropology	V	Naval Science
H	Social Sciences	Z	Bibliography and Library Science
J	Political Science		
L	Education		

(4) **The vertical file**—*Use the vertical file to locate miscellaneous printed material.* The vertical file is an informal collection of pamphlets, newspaper clippings, and other forms of printed material that cannot be conveniently arranged on a shelf. It is stored in manila envelopes or folders and alphabetized in the manner of letter files in a business office. If you were looking for some material on Mormons, you might find some religious tracts and some clippings from local newspapers in the folder labeled MORMONS.

(5) **The Readers' Guide**—*Use the* Readers' Guide *to find magazine articles on a subject.* The *Readers' Guide* indexes articles appearing in over one hundred periodicals. The most recent issues of the *Readers' Guide* appear in booklet form. Back issues are hardbound in volumes covering two years. If you were searching for articles on Mormons, you would locate that entry in the alphabetical listing of subjects in the *Readers' Guide.* There you would find the titles and authors of all articles dealing with the Mormons that appeared in the periodicals indexed by the *Readers' Guide to Periodical Literature* during the years covered by that volume.

Entries give the following information: article title (without quotation marks); magazine (often abbreviated—key is found in the front of *Guide*); volume; pages; date of issue.

Sample subject entry:

> **POSTAGE stamps**
> Natural world of the post office; natural history theme on stamps. A. Ross. ii Natur
> Hist 77:28-31 Ja '68

Sample author entry:

> **ROSS, Arnold**
> Natural world of the post office. Natur Hist
> 77:28-31 Ja '68

Learn how to locate materials on topics of current interest.

Here are sources of material for discussion of current issues:

(1) **Newspapers**—*The most logical source of up-to-date information is the daily or weekly newspaper.* Most high schools subscribe to the local papers, the Sunday edition of *The New York Times,* and the *Christian Science Monitor.* Today's or this week's copy can usually be found hanging on a rack in the library. There is an index for *The New York Times,* but it is too expensive for most school libraries. The *Christian Science Monitor* is indexed and therefore the copies are apt to be stored for a few years at least.

A very useful paper is *Facts on File,* a weekly summary of world news indexed by topic and person for the year. One index covers January to September. A supplement is issued for the remaining three months. (This is a valuable instrument for a student of public speaking since it can be used quickly.)

(2) **Magazines**—Depending upon the time coverage of one's topic, the *Readers' Guide* may or may not be of help. If a subject is very recent, it is best to go to the open racks of magazines and look in the current issues. Periodicals such as *Time, Newsweek,* and *U.S. News and World Report* tell about events almost as they happen. Others such as *The Nation, Harper's,* and *The Atlantic Monthly* offer commentary upon current events but also treat topics of more long-range concern. You might also look into specialized magazines such as *Science News* or the *Bulletin of the United Nations.*

(3) **Microfilm**—Newspapers, magazines, and books are now often stored in miniature form. You can read them by using a special viewer. Find out what material your library has on microfilm.

(4) **Interlibrary loan**—*Some high school libraries belong to an association that works to exchange books and other material from one library to another.* If you know of a book, magazine, paper, or filmstrip that would help you in your research but that is not in your library, your librarian may be able to borrow it from another institution. In this way, high school students can use the resources of colleges and technical libraries without having to go to those places.

NOTE: *One of the biggest publishers in the United States is the federal government.* The United States government produces pamphlets and books on every subject from home repairs to outer space. A student may write to the Government Printing Office to inquire if there is literature on a subject or to secure a catalogue of all available titles. Many of the more substantial books put out by the government are found in high school libraries. These can be of great help in both historical and contemporary research, especially contemporary, because they are apt to be more up to date than the information found in encyclopedias. For example, each year a roster of government officials, foreign diplomats, and Washington newspaper correspondents is put out under the title *Congressional Directory for the Use of United States Congress*. The Bureau of the Census puts out an annual *Statistical Abstract of the United States* with the most recent figures on American population and business.

EXERCISE 1

Select a book that you have read recently or choose one from your school library. Answer the following questions about it.

1. Does the title page tell anything about the author other than his or her name? What?
2. Where was the book published?
3. When and in whose name was the book copyrighted? Is more than one copyright year indicated?
4. Does the book have an appendix? a glossary? an index?
5. Examine the table of contents and determine how many chapters the book has. Are the chapters named, numbered, or both?
6. Does the book have a preface? an introduction? Is the introduction written by someone other than the book's author?
7. What, in brief, does the book seem to be about?

EXERCISE 2

Consult an encyclopedia and make a preliminary judgment concerning *five* of the following subjects as a research topic. Should it be limited? If so, what would two or three possibilities be? Is there likely to be a reasonable amount of material in the high school library? not enough? too much?

1. Black literature
2. Lincoln's first term as President
3. History of the Chicano
4. History of jazz
5. Reservation life
6. Creole language and traditions
7. The story of the zeppelins
8. The life and work of Willa Cather
9. Printing types (pica, English, etc.)
10. The making of a dictionary

Assume that you are working on the following topic: military leaders of the Revolutionary War. Use the card catalogue in your library and select three books that sound as if they would be appropriate sources for material on the topic. Locate each book and examine it for appropriateness.

EXERCISE 3

Choose a topic that is currently of interest. Using various sources, prepare a list of books and articles that discuss the topic. Limit yourself to books and articles published within the last two years.

EXERCISE 4

Learn to distinguish between various dictionaries.

R2
THE DICTIONARY

Ideally, a dictionary is a file of all the words used in the language. The unabridged *Webster's Third New International Dictionary* (1961) cost the G. & C. Merriam Company, which published it, $3,500,000 and represents the effort of more than three hundred scholars working over a period of twenty-seven years. In order to produce *Webster's Third New International Dictionary,* dictionary editors read newspapers, magazines, and books—the printed English word wherever it was found. On 3 x 5 cards, or "citation slips," they recorded every new word or new use of an old word, as well as common words with unusual meanings. A good desk dictionary adapts and abridges the results of such scholarly work for practical everyday use.

Make full use of the information provided in a good desk dictionary.

R2a
Desk Dictionaries

Several of the best-known desk dictionaries are abridged versions of more comprehensive dictionaries. Authoritative collegiate dictionaries include:

Webster's New Collegiate Dictionary (Merriam-Webster)
The American Heritage Dictionary
Webster's New World Dictionary of the American Language
The Random House Dictionary, College Edition
Funk and Wagnalls Standard College Dictionary

Dictionaries intended especially for high school students are:

Webster's New Students Dictionary
Thorndike Barnhart Advanced Dictionary
Macmillan Dictionary

KINDS OF DICTIONARY INFORMATION

pil·grim (pil′grim, -grəm), *n.* **1.** a person who journeys, esp. a long distance, to some sacred place as an act of devotion. **2.** a traveler or wanderer. **3.** (*cap.*) one of the Pilgrim Fathers. [early ME *pilegrim*, *pelegrim*; c. OFris *pilegrim*, MLG *pelegrīm*, OHG *piligrīm*, Icel *pīlagrīmr*, all < ML *pelegrīnus*, dissimilated var. of L *peregrīnus* alien < *peregrē* abroad = *per-* PER- + *-egr-* (comb. form of *ager* field; see ACRE) + *-e* adv. suffix] —**Syn. 2.** wayfarer, sojourner. — Alternate pronunciation / Capitalization style / Synonym list

Pil·sen (pil′zən), *n.* a city in Bohemia, in W Czechoslovakia. 141,736 (1963). Czech, **Plzeň.** — Geographical entry (location, population and date, foreign name)

pin (pin), *n.*, *v.*, **pinned, pin·ning.** —*n.* **1.** a short, slender piece of metal with a point at one end and a head at the other, for fastening things together. **2.** a small, slender, often pointed piece of wood, metal, etc., used to fasten, support, or attach things. **3.** any of various forms of fasteners, ornaments, or badges consisting essentially or partly of a pointed or penetrating wire or shaft (often used in combination): *a fraternity pin; a tiepin.* **4.** a short metal rod, as a linchpin, driven through the holes of adjacent parts, as a hub and an axle, to keep them together. **5.** a short cylindrical rod or tube, as a wristpin or crankpin, joining two parts so as to permit them to move in one plane relative to each other. **6.** the part of a cylindrical key stem that enters a lock. **7.** a clothespin. **8.** a hairpin. **9.** See **rolling pin.** **10.** a peg, nail, or stud marking the center of a target. **11.** *Bowling.* one of the rounded wooden clubs set up as the target in tenpins, duckpins, etc. **12.** *Golf.* the flagstaff that identifies a hole. **13.** Usually, **pins.** *Informal.* the legs. **14.** *Music.* peg (def. 2). **15.** *Wrestling.* a fall. **16.** *Naut.* See **belaying pin. 17.** a very small amount; a trifle. —*v.t.* **18.** to fasten or attach with or as with a pin or pins. **19.** to hold fast in a spot or position. **20.** to give one's fraternity pin to (a girl) as a pledge of one's fondness or attachment. **21.** *Wrestling.* to obtain a fall over one's opponent. **22. pin down, a.** to bind or hold to a course of action, a promise, etc. **b.** to define with clarity and precision: *to pin down a vague intuition.* **23. pin something on someone,** *Slang.* to blame someone for something on the basis of real or manufactured evidence. [ME *pinne* OE *pinn* peg; c. D *pin*, G *Pinne*, Icel *pinni*; ? akin to MIr *benn* (for *bend), now *beann* peak, steeple, gable, etc.] — Verb forms (past tense and past participle; present participle) / Cross reference to multiple-word entry / Usage label / Cross reference to one word entry / Idiomatic phrase

pin·y (pī′nē), *adj.*, **pin·i·er, pin·i·est.** **1.** abounding in, covered with, or consisting of pine trees. **2.** pertaining to or suggestive of pine trees: *a piny fragrance.* Also, **piney.** — Adjective forms (comparative, superlative) / Example phrase

Pi·rith·o·üs (pī rith′ō əs), *n.* *Class. Myth.* a prince of the Lapithae and friend of Theseus, in whose company he attempted to abduct Persephone from Hades. — Mythological entry

pk, *pl.* **pks.** (in dry measure) peck. — Abbreviation

plan (plan), *n.*, *v.*, **planned, plan·ning.** —*n.* **1.** a method of action or procedure. **2.** a design or scheme of arrangement: *an elaborate plan for seating guests.* **3.** a project or definite purpose: *plans for the future.* **4.** a drawing made to scale to represent the top view or a horizontal section of a structure or a machine. **5.** a map or diagram: *a plan of the dock area.* **6.** (in perspective drawing) one of several planes in front of a represented object, and perpendicular to the line between the object and the eye. —*v.t.* **7.** to arrange or project a plan or scheme for (any work, enterprise, or proceeding): *to plan a new recreation center; to plan one's vacation.* **8.** to draw or make a plan of, as a building. —*v.i.* **9.** to make a plan; *to plan for one's retirement.* [< F: plane, plan, groundwork, scheme < L *plan(us)* level *planum* level ground. See PLANE[1], PLAIN[1]] —**Syn. 1.** plot, formula, system. PLAN, PROJECT, DESIGN, SCHEME imply a formulated method of doing something. PLAN refers to any method of thinking out acts and purposes beforehand: *What are your plans for today?* A PROJECT is a proposed or tentative plan, often elaborate or extensive: *an irrigation project.* DESIGN suggests art, dexterity, or craft (sometimes evil and selfish) in the elaboration or execution of a plan, and often tends to emphasize the purpose in view: *a disturbance brought about by design.* A SCHEME is apt to be either a speculative, possibly impractical, plan, or a selfish or dishonest one: *a scheme to swindle someone.* — Parts of speech / Consecutive definition numbers / Word History / Synonym study / Example in synonym study

—from *The Random House Dictionary, College Edition*

A dictionary offers the following information about every entry:

(1) SPELLING: Some words have *more than one* correct spelling. Example: *caddie* or *caddy*. The plural of *ski* is given as "*skis* or *ski* also *skiis*," meaning that *ski* or *skis* is equally common but that *skiis* is less often used. Different spellings may be listed as separate entries. In *The American College Dictionary* we find:

> **ee·rie** (ĭr′ĭ), *adj.*, **-rier, -riest. 1.** inspiring fear; weird, strange, or uncanny. **2.** affected with superstitious fear. [ME *eri*, d. var. of obs. *argh*, OE *earg* cowardly, c. G *arg* bad] —**ee′ri·ly**, *adv.* —**ee′ri·ness**, *n.* —**Syn. 1.** See **weird.**
> **ee·ry** (ĭr′ĭ), *adj.*, **-rier, -riest.** eerie.

(2) PRONUNCIATION: There is *no one standard system* for representing sounds. Each major dictionary uses its own way of indicating English pronunciation. The symbols used are explained, with examples, at the beginning of the book, and usually at the bottom of every page. Pronunciation is often indicated in parentheses:

> (ˌlek-sə-ˈkäg-rə-fē) or (lĕk′sə kŏg′rə fĭ).

NOTE: In some dictionaries, the stress marks (accents) come *after* the stressed syllable: **gra·vy** (grā′vē). In others, they come *before* the stressed syllable: **gra·vy** \ˈgrā-vē\.

(3) PART OF SPEECH: The grammatical status of a word usually appears in abbreviated form after its pronunciation: n. (noun); v. or vb. (verb); v.t. (transitive verb); v.i. (intransitive verb); adj. (adjective); adv. (adverb); conj. (conjunction, or connective); prep. (preposition); pron. (pronoun); interj. (interjection—words like *Ah* and *Oh*). Often a word is used in more than one way.

(4) CHANGING FORMS:

• *Plurals:* If the plural of a word is unusual it will be listed after the letters *pl.* Example: "*moose* (mōōs) n. pl. moose."

• *Past tense and participles:* If a verb is regular, that is, if it adds –*ed* for its past tense and past participle *(walk, walked, had walked, walking),* these forms are usually not listed. If it is irregular, the dictionary gives the variations; for example, "*take* (tāk), v., *took, taken, taking.*" Sometimes there is more than one past tense; for example, "*hang* (hang) v. *hung* or (esp. for capital punishment and suicide) *hanged; hanging.*"

• *Comparative or superlative:* No forms are given for adjectives and adverbs that are regularly compared *(small, smaller, smallest,* or *hostile, more hostile, most hostile).* However, if the adjective or adverb is irregular, the comparative and superlative are given in the dictionary; for example, "*little, less, least.*"

• *Other forms:* Adjectives and adverbs that follow logically from nouns in spelling and meaning may be put at the end of the noun entry. For example, if you look for the word *sarcastically,* you may find *sarcasm* as an entry. At the end of that entry may be *sarcastic* and *sarcastically.* Nouns directly formed from an adjective may be put at the end of the adjective entry. For example, under the entry *inseparable,* we find *inseparability* and *inseparableness,* as well as the adverb *inseparably.* Some words beginning with *in–* or *un–* and having a negative meaning are alphabetically included in the entries. Others whose meanings are directly opposite to their root words are listed in columns either under *in–* or *un–* or at the bottom of several pages of *in–* or *un–* words.

(5) DEFINITION: Most words have several meanings and, when used with other words, become expressions with still other meanings. The word *take* used as a transitive verb may have nineteen numbered definitions; as an intransitive verb, eight more. Then there will be expressions using *take* as a part of a verb phrase, such as *take account of, take heart, take place,* etc. A definition with several meanings may give the oldest one first—the original sense of the word—and then others chronologically. Or it may give the most common meaning first.

(6) STATUS LABELS: Be alert for italicized words or abbreviations before definitions. Some of the common ones are:

Obs.	Obsolete. Has not been standard usage for at least 200 years.
Archaic	Old-fashioned. Sometimes used now but not current modern usage.
Slang	Extremely informal. Not acceptable for serious speech or writing.
Substand. or Nonstand.	Not acceptable in standard use.
Dial.	Dialect. Regional (sometimes with part of country given).
Poetic or Literary	Not used in ordinary conversation or writing.
Colloq.	Informal, everyday speech and writing.

(7) ETYMOLOGY: Dictionaries give the derivation of words—they tell us where words came from and how they grew. The entry for *eerie* in *Webster's New Collegiate* adds in square brackets: [ME *eri,* fr OE *earg* cowardly, wretched]. ME stands for *Middle English,* fr

means *from,* and OE is *Old English.* An Old English word *earg* evolved into a Middle English word *eri* and then into our modern word *eerie.* Along with spelling change came meaning change, since the word no longer has the meaning of *cowardly.*

(8) SYNONYMS AND ANTONYMS: At the end of an entry you may find the abbreviation *Syn.* For example, after the word *center* we find *"Syn. 1. See middle."* This means that *middle* is like *center* in some, but not necessarily all, of its meanings. After *Syn.* there may be the abbreviation *Ant.* An antonym is a word that means the opposite or almost the opposite of the entry. For example, in the entry *large* we find *"Ant. 1. small."*

(9) ADDITIONAL INFORMATION: Trademarks, biography, mythical characters, historical events, geographical names, medical terms, and scientific names of plants and animals are often found in the main part of the collegiate-sized dictionary. Most collegiate dictionaries have, in addition, information at the front or back of the book. First and most important, there is always information on that particular dictionary and how to use it. There may be as well:

- a guide to punctuation
- abbreviations (sometimes included in main part)
- signs and symbols (mathematics, music, etc.)
- proofreaders' marks
- biographical names
- geographical names
- given names (with meanings)
- colleges and universities with locations
- weights and measures

Look up the following words. Check spelling, pronunciation, word class (how used in a sentence), other forms (like the plural of nouns), meaning, and history. Note especially if there is more than one way to spell, pronounce, or use the word.

EXERCISE 1

1. illustrate
2. dialog
3. stimulus
4. neologism
5. antibiotic
6. buffoon
7. animate
8. alkali
9. husband
10. finagle

EXERCISE 2

Check the following questions in *one* of the major desk dictionaries:

1. *Pronunciation:* What do you find on the pronunciation of *apricot, greasy, melee, oleomargarine, pall-mall, pshaw?* Are *gaol* and *jail* pronounced the same? What about the last syllable in *collage, garage, mirage?*

2. *Grammatical Information:* What do you learn about the uses of *annoy, set, like?* What about the past tense of *dive, hang, light?* What are the plurals of *datum, formula, alumna, antenna, prospectus?*

3. *Word History:* Why are *gypsies* so called? What kind of clothing did a *candidate* originally wear? What can you find out about the history of *cauliflower, champion, catharsis?* What is the common element in *pulse, propulsion, repulsive?*

4. *Encyclopedic Information:* What were the real names of Mark Twain, George Eliot, George Orwell, Voltaire? Who or what is *Anubis, Atreus, Ilium, Valhalla?* What associations or events do the following names bring to mind: Roland, Dreyfus, Nat Turner?

5. *New Words:* Does the dictionary include *disco, hippie, minibike, air bag, solid state, scuba?* Can you find three words that are currently in the news but not listed in the dictionary? (Your teacher may ask you to write a brief dictionary entry for each for use in a future edition.)

R2b
Special Dictionaries

Use specialized dictionaries as supplements to the general dictionary.

Among the supplements that every student should learn to use are thesauruses, dictionaries of synonyms, and dictionaries of usage.

(1) **Thesaurus**—*A thesaurus* is a "treasure-house" of words. *Roget's International Thesaurus* is a book of synonyms. Its purpose is to supply different ways of expressing an idea. Unlike a dictionary, the thesaurus is arranged by subjects rather than alphabetically. The student must work through an alphabetical index that refers to numbered subjects rather than to pages.

Suppose you turn to the index to find the word *good.* The noun uses are listed first. Among the noun contexts, you find "good persons, 983.6." The 983 refers to the section, and the .6 refers to a subsection within 983. Turning backward, you find guide numbers at the top of each page. You turn to 983, the sixth subsection, and read: "saint, angel, cherub, seraph; the good, the righteous." In the adjective references, you find *good* in the sense of "kind, 936.4." Under 936.4, you find "gracious," "kindhearted," "warmhearted," "softhearted," "tender," "sympathetic," "humane."

Here are parts of the entries for "zero" and "few":

> 101.Zero. N. ZERO, nothing; naught,
> nought; cipher, none, nobody; *nichts*
> [*Ger.*], goose egg [*U. S.*], duck [*slang*],
> nixie [*slang*]. nix [*slang*]; not a soul

> 103. FEWNESS.
> Adj. FEW; scant, scanty; thin, rare,
> scarce, sparse, thinly scattered, few and
> far between

(2) **Dictionaries of synonyms**—*There are several good dictionaries of synonyms that you may consult. Webster's Dictionary of Synonyms* is the best-known. Both synonyms and antonyms are covered. While some words have just lists of synonyms after them, others are followed by thorough discussion. For example, *good* is broken down and discussed in the following ways: *good* as opposed to *bad, good* as opposed to *poor,* and *good* as *right.*

(3) **Dictionaries of usage**—*Dictionaries of usage are intended as books of guidance.* They often do not tell us what *is* used but what *should* be used. They are also entertaining and fun for browsing. Here are three widely used dictionaries of usage:

- H. W. Fowler's *A Dictionary of Modern English Usage* is the classic in this field. It has been revised and brought up to date. Its form is more formal than the other books, and Fowler is even more decisive in his opinions than are the others. Much of the discussion in this book is based on British usage.
- Wilson Follett's *Modern American Usage, a Guide* presents lengthy discussions on both words and constructions. For example, eleven pages are devoted to the use of *a, an,* and *the.*
- *A Dictionary of Contemporary American Usage* by Bergen and Cornelia Evans answers questions about grammar, word preference, effective style, punctuation, idiomatic phrases, spelling, and so forth. This book too takes a highly *personal* attitude.

EXERCISE 1

Report on the words a thesaurus lists for *one* of the following ideas: *freedom, two, deceiver, ignorance, youth, age, loafing, success, failure, authority.*

EXERCISE 2

In browsing through *Webster's Dictionary of Synonyms,* find a set of words that you consider especially interesting and present it to your classmates.

EXERCISE 3

From a dictionary of usage, find out the difference in use between the words in *three* of the following pairs:

1. *amount* and *number*
2. *center* and *middle*
3. *tragedy* and *disaster*
4. *populace* and *population*
5. *kill* and *murder*
6. *nauseous* and *nauseated*
7. *human* and *humane*
8. *imply* and *infer*
9. *fortunate* and *fortuitous*
10. *like* and *as*

EXERCISE 4

Here is a list of nine words. Look them up first in your desk dictionary, then in Webster's unabridged, and finally in the Random House unabridged. Note on the chart below whether the word is included in the dictionaries and whether it bears a status label.

WORD	DESK DICTIONARY		WEBSTER'S UNABRIDGED		RANDOM HOUSE UNABRIDGED	
	Inc.	Label	Inc.	Label	Inc.	Label
hi						
mom						
dad						
hippie						
hijack						
newfangled						
bebop						
gal						
wingding						

R3
TAKING TESTS

Make sure tests show what you know and what you can do.

Tests are an ever-present feature of modern life. The more you know about them, the better you will be able to handle them in a businesslike way. Remember the following general advice:

(1) Always read instructions or directions carefully. What exactly are you asked to do? Take time to read and understand the key words in the directions you are given.

(2) Keep moving. Do not allow any part of any item on a test to use up too much time. Do not allow yourself to become flustered by something difficult or confusing. Move on; return to the difficult part later if you have the time.

(3) Use common sense about guessing. Some tests encourage guessing. If only *right* answers are counted for test results, even wild guessing cannot hurt. If a test states, "Wrong answers will be penalized," wild guessing is not advisable.

(4) Make some notes before answering essay questions. Even though you may be under some time pressure, pause to think before you begin to answer an essay question. While you are thinking, jot down a few key ideas. Take a moment to put those ideas in some logical or chronological order.

(5) Allow time to proofread essay tests. A comma where a period should be, a misspelled word, a "their" for a "there"—these may seem to be small things. But little errors like these make the writer appear careless or badly prepared. Take a minute or so before you hand in a test, and correct any errors you may find.

Know the different ways tests measure your knowledge of vocabulary.

Tests of vocabulary occur in batteries of tests from kindergarten through the graduate schools of universities. They are used in tests that are given to applicants for many kinds of jobs. In almost all intelligence tests, the verbal part of the test measures vocabulary. The most common tests used by colleges and universities for admission purposes include measures of the applicants' vocabulary. In general, students with the best vocabularies get the best grades in college. (Of course, some students with good vocabularies get poor college grades.)

The *Scholastic Aptitude Test,* published by the College Entrance Examination Board, is widely used by colleges and universities in selecting the freshman class from those who apply for admission. This test is commonly called the "S-A-T" and is frequently written as SAT. The SAT in recent years has used three kinds of test items to measure vocabulary. These sections are called: Antonyms Analogies, and Sentence Completion. The verbal part of the SAT also measures reading comprehension. It gives from five to seven reading passages, with five questions for each.

(1) SYNONYMS

The most common vocabulary tests ask you to find **synonyms.** For a test word, you select the word that is closest to it in meaning. In each of the following examples, the correct answer has been circled.

1. *melancholy*	a. fruitful	(b. gloomy)	c. suave	d. tuneful
2. *obsequious*	a. obscene	b. obscure	(c. servile)	d. tyrannical
3. *nurture*	a. dupe	(b. feed)	c. skitter	d. squat

(2) ANTONYMS

The Antonyms section of the SAT has directions similar to the following:

> *DIRECTIONS: In each test item, there is a word in capital letters followed by five answer choices. From these five choices select the one whose meaning is **opposite** to the meaning of the word in capital letters.*

Try to work these four sample items before reading the discussion that follows them:

A	PAUPER	B	CONTAMINATION
	(1) beggar		(1) conservation
	(2) follower		(2) continuation
	(3) isolationist		(3) pollution
	(4) millionaire		(4) prohibition
	(5) traveler		(5) purification
C	VIRTUOSO	D	JEOPARDY
	(1) artist		(1) danger
	(2) sinner		(2) frenzy
	(3) nonexpert		(3) hazard
	(4) villain		(4) modesty
	(5) wretch		(5) security

An **antonym** test makes us look for a word with the *opposite* meaning. Very often the author of antonym items will include synonyms among the wrong answer choices. In item B, *pollution* is a synonym for *contamination*. In item D both *danger* and *hazard* are synonyms for the word in capital letters. All of these are *wrong* answers on an antonym test.

- In item A, the word *pauper* means a person with very little money. The antonym must be a word that means a person with a lot of money. Although some travelers may have a lot of money, the only word that represents a person with money is *millionaire*. Therefore, the answer to item A is *millionaire*.

- In item B, a person who knows that *con–* and *pro–* are prefixes with opposite meanings may erroneously choose *prohibition* as the answer. The author also included two words that begin with the same prefix, *con–,* to confuse the examinee. The answer is *purification*.

- In item C, some students may confuse *virtuoso* with *virtuous*. They may choose either *sinner* or *villain* for the answer, and they would be wrong. A virtuoso is an expert musician; and, therefore, the answer is the opposite, *nonexpert*.

- In item D, as mentioned above, *jeopardy* means *danger* or *hazard*. The answer, therefore, is a word that is opposite to these words: *security*.

③ ANALOGIES

The Analogies section of the SAT has directions which are similar to the following:

> *DIRECTIONS: Each test item contains a pair of words in capital letters. Try to establish a relationship between these two words. Then from the five answer choices select the pair of words whose relationship to each other is the same as that between the two words in capital letters.*

This test involves more than a knowledge of word meanings. You will have to think about the relationship between the two words in each pair. Try to solve these four samples before reading the discussion that follows them:

E RENOUNCE : DISAVOW : :
  (1) abandon : discuss
  (2) announce : avowal
  (3) denounce : disprove
  (4) regain : recoup
  (5) resist : desist

F PYRE : PYROTECHNICS : :
  (1) Bible : bibliography
  (2) doctor : technicians
  (3) fire : meteors
  (4) heat : thermometer
  (5) pile : heap

G CAR : GARAGE : :
  (1) aerie : eagle
  (2) city : residents
  (3) ship : harbor
  (4) singer : choir
  (5) teacher : classroom

H CENT : MONEY : :
  (1) day : year
  (2) dollar : inflation
  (3) nickel : quarter
  (4) salmon : fish
  (5) wages : salary

- In sample E, you have to find the pair of words that are related to each other in the same way that *renounce* and *disavow* are related. Since renounce and disavow are synonyms, the correct answer must be a pair of synonyms. The only pair that are synonyms are *regain* and *recoup*.
- In sample F, the two words in capital letters are both based on the same Greek prefix, *pyr–,* which means fire. The answer to this item should be a pair of words based on the same prefix, probably Greek. *Bible* and *bibliography* are based on *bibl–,* a Greek prefix meaning book, and therefore they are the correct answer.
- In sample G, the relationship between *car* and *garage* is not difficult to determine. The answer should be a pair in which the first word represents something that rests in the second word when not in use. The answer then is *ship* and *harbor.* (An *eagle* rests, or nests, in an *aerie,* but this pair could not be the answer, because these words are not in the proper order.)
- In sample H, a *cent* is a kind of *money.* The only pair with a similar relationship is *salmon* and *fish.*

(4) SENTENCE COMPLETION

The directions for the Sentence Completion section of the SAT are similar to the following:

DIRECTIONS: *In each of the following sentences on the next page, one or two words are missing. Select the answer choice that fits the sentence best.*

Try to solve these four sample items before reading the discussion that follows them:

J   The President found it _____ not to mention it in public because, according to the polls, the _____ of people were against it.
- (1)   better . . . . demands
- (2)   convenient . . . . crowds
- (3)   dishonest . . . . feelings
- (4)   expedient . . . . majority
- (5)   impossible . . . . scruples

K   To _____ thieves, who had repeatedly removed all of the clothes from his sales racks, the _____ shop owner alternated the directions of the hangers.
- (1)   catch . . . . clumsy
- (2)   irritate . . . . tired
- (3)   prevent . . . . poor
- (4)   stop . . . . little
- (5)   thwart . . . . ingenious

L   She had hoped to give him an elegant gift, but the shop had nothing but _____ items on its shelves.
- (1)   antique
- (2)   expensive
- (3)   fragile
- (4)   souvenir
- (5)   tawdry

M His teammates considered his _____ objectionable, because he acted _____ to them.
- (1)   aloofness . . . . superior
- (2)   beard . . . . arrogant
- (3)   clothes . . . . attracted
- (4)   perfume . . . . inferior
- (5)   ranting . . . . unfriendly

In order to solve all of these items, you need to know accurate definitions of the answer words and to understand the way these words fit into the contexts of the sentences. To answer such items, read the sentence with each of the answer choices filled in. Some choices can be immediately eliminated because they make no sense or sound silly. However, many wrong choices are written so that they *sound* good, but when you know the meanings of the words, the wrong choices will not make sense.

• Item J tests your knowledge of the meaning of *expedient*. This word means "advantageous" or "advisable." If the *majority* was against something, it might be advisable for the President not to mention it. (*Demands* and *crowds* do not fit well in the second clause. *Dishonest* does not fit in the first clause. The fifth choice makes no sense.)

• In item K, the shop owner was *ingenious:* It was clever of him to think of alternating the hangers, because then the thieves had to remove the clothes one by one. This would certainly slow down the thieves, thereby *thwarting* them. (There is no reason to believe the shop owner was *clumsy* or *little*. *Irritate* and *prevent* are not appropriate words for the first blank.)

• In item L, the sentence suggests that nothing in the shop is elegant. Any one of the first four answer choices could possibly define something elegant. The answer, then, is *tawdry*, which means cheap and gaudy, or showy without good taste or elegance.

• In item M, the blanks need to be filled with two words that must go together. Persons who feel *superior* to others are often *aloof* and stay away from the others. (A *beard* does not necessarily go with *arrogance*, nor does *perfume* go with *inferiority*. *Attracted* is not appropriate for the second blank. The words *ranting* and *unfriendly* might go together, but they do not make good sense when used to complete this particular sentence.)

SAMPLE TEST A

I. **SYNONYMS**

In each test item, there is a word in capital letters followed by five answer choices. From these five choices select the one whose meaning is most nearly *like* the meaning of the word in capital letters. Write the letter of your choice in the space next to the number of the item.

_____ 1. REPUDIATE
  A blame
  B disclaim
  C prolong
  D recuperate
  E extinguish

_____ 2. MUTUAL
  A dependent
  B evident
  C loquacious
  D reciprocal
  E rural

_____ 3. INDULGENT
  A brilliant
  B intelligent
  C intolerant
  D lenient
  E obscure

_____ 4. FLAW
  A blemish
  B brandish
  C conceit
  D flee
  E patch

_____ 5. COMPENSATE
    A contend
    B incomplete
    C lengthen
    D remunerate
    E retrieve

_____ 6. CONCUR
    A agree
    B automate
    C expose
    D request
    E separate

_____ 7. RETRIBUTION
    A abandonment
    B aloofness
    C contribution
    D demand
    E retaliation

_____ 8. CULPABLE
    A blameworthy
    B dormant
    C edible
    D lucrative
    E reluctant

_____ 9. TURMOIL
    A harmony
    B melody
    C olive oil
    D conflict
    E detour

_____ 10. CELESTIAL
    A demonic
    B famous
    C heavenly
    D speedy
    E urban

II. ANTONYMS

In each test item, there is a word in capital letters followed by five answer choices. From these five choices select the one whose meaning is most nearly *opposite* in meaning to the word in capital letters. Write the letter of your choice in the space next to the number of the item.

_____ 1. BENEVOLENT
    A beneficent
    B emotional
    C malevolent
    D sneaky
    E sublime

_____ 2. VOLATILE
    A airy
    B apathetic
    C apparent
    D irrational
    E permanent

_____ 3. CHAOS
    A order
    B crescendo
    C falsetto
    D chorus
    E finale

_____ 4. DISCREET
    A careless
    B circumspect
    C colossal
    D determined
    E shoddy

_____ 5. INANIMATE
   A commercial
   B senseless
   C intimate
   D living
   E spirited

_____ 6. SYNTHETIC
   A cotton
   B irregular
   C natural
   D opposite
   E unreal

_____ 7. INDIGENT
   A affluent
   B digestible
   C dignified
   D expedient
   E healthy

_____ 8. COMPULSORY
   A absent
   B elementary
   C required
   D simple
   E voluntary

_____ 9. RESILIENCE
   A activity
   B elasticity
   C melee
   D quiet
   E rigidity

_____ 10. PRIMITIVE
   A civilized
   B fatalistic
   C final
   D inferior
   E urban

III. ANALOGIES

Try to establish a relationship between the two words in capital letters. Then select from the five answer choices the pair of words whose relationship to each other is the same as that of the two words in capital letters. Write the letter of your choice in the space next to the number of the item.

_____ 1. CONCORD : DISCORD : :
   A conceal : disguise
   B condole : grieve
   C dependent : independent
   D grapes : music
   E uncover : discover

_____ 2. STATUTE : STATE : :
   A gentile : gentle
   B law : lawyer
   C ordinance : city
   D Portland : Oregon
   E stature : tallness

_____ 3. ARIA : SOPRANO : :
   A hymn : choir
   B composer : opera
   C crescendo : finale
   D duet : solo
   E orchestra : conductor

_____ 4. PIZZA : ITALY : :
    A kimono : judo
    B pie : country
    C rice : France
    D sauerkraut : Germany
    E sierra : Spain

_____ 5. BIBLIOGRAPHY : BOOKS : :
    A demons : angels
    B Bible : Scriptures
    C crocodile : crocks
    D dictionary : words
    E library : catalog

_____ 6. SHYSTER : LAWYER : :
    A amateur : professional
    B bailiff : attorney
    C imposter : artist
    D Philadelphia : Washington
    E quack : doctor

_____ 7. SPIGOT : FAUCET : :
    A hose : pipe
    B muzzle : nozzle
    C shoal : shallows
    D spout : steam
    E water : milk

_____ 8. PLOW : PLOUGH : :
    A catalog : catalogue
    B row : rough
    C slow : slough
    D throw : through
    E tow : tough

_____ 9. SORROW : REJECTION : :
    A elation : popularity
    B grief : dejection
    C love : injection
    D sadness : sympathy
    E surprise : disillusionment

_____ 10. WIPEOUT : SURFING : :
    A erasure : writing
    B hit : baseball
    C knockdown : boxing
    D love : tennis
    E slalom : skiing

IV. SENTENCE COMPLETION

In each of the following sentences one or two words are missing. Five answer choices lettered A through E follow each sentence. From the five answer choices select the one that fits the sentence best. Write the letter of your choice in the space next to the number of the item.

_____ 1. I only wanted to _____ for a few minutes, but the boss accused me of _____.
  A chop . . . . . hacking
  B jog . . . . . dawdling
  C relax . . . . . loafing
  D sleep . . . . . daydreaming
  E watch . . . . . prying

_____ 2. The enterprise was so _____ that the owner became wealthier by the minute.
  A exciting
  B lucrative
  C novel
  D ominous
  E popular

_____ 3. After weeks of investigation, they found the _____ who had set all six fires.
  A criminal
  B felon
  C pyromaniac
  D thief
  E villain

_____ 4. His _____ for these people was reflected in his _____ manners.
  A adoration . . . . . revolting
  B contempt . . . . . abominable
  C disgust . . . . . revealing
  D hopes . . . . . scholarly
  E love . . . . . haughty

_____ 5. The town council voted sufficient funds to _____ the _____ of the town hall.
  A designate . . . . . painter
  B dissipate . . . . . elevator
  C facilitate . . . . . renovation
  D increase . . . . . remnants
  E revitalize . . . . . stairs

_____ 6. After _____ into the large hall, he _____ his way through the crowd.
- A hurrying . . . . . found
- B lumbering . . . . . elbowed
- C sneaking . . . . . retraced
- D stamping . . . . stumbled
- E walking . . . . . ran

_____ 7. She _____ the needless loss of lives, but she did nothing to prevent _____ occurrences of such tragedies.
- A abhorred . . . . . inevitable
- B applauded . . . . . similar
- C deplored . . . . . further
- D ignored . . . . . future
- E watched . . . . . more

_____ 8. The paper's limited _____ did not prevent its having a strong _____ on the thinking of the townspeople.
- A appeal . . . . . reminder
- B circulation . . . . . influence
- C editorials . . . . . intensity
- D news . . . . . sagacity
- E views . . . . . perspective

_____ 9. The candidate _____ a bitter attack on the reporter who asked _____ questions about the candidate's personal affairs.
- A beamed . . . . . intense
- B screamed . . . . . financial
- C stormed . . . . . original
- D suggested . . . . . sensitive
- E unleashed . . . . . prying

_____ 10. Sportswriters and news reporters write not only to give us _____ but also to provide _____.
- A facts . . . . . records
- B gossip . . . . . repetition
- C information . . . . . entertainment
- D news . . . . . intelligence
- E stories . . . . . endings

Know how tests measure your command of English.

Many different tests measure the student's ability to write standard English. These tests have names such as _Test of English Usage_, _Test of English Grammar_, _Test of Language Expression_, _Test_

R3b

**Tests of
Written English**

of Mechanics of English, and the like. The right or correct answer on such tests is the choice that is right for formal written English. Things to be marked wrong or incorrect will include problems of usage and mechanics, such as the following:

- informal or slang words;
- lack of agreement between subject and verb;
- nonstandard forms of verbs;
- nonstandard comparative or superlative forms;
- vague use of pronoun;
- wrong form of pronoun;
- double negatives;
- sentence fragments;
- wrong use of comma;
- problems with capitalization;
- wrong use of the apostrophe.

In senior high schools, these tests are usually included in a battery of achievement tests, which also measure reading and mathematics. Among the most widely used achievement batteries at this level are the *California Achievement Tests* (now called "CAT" by many users), the *Comprehensive Tests of Basic Skills* (CTBS), *Metropolitan Achievement Tests* (often called "Metro"), and the *Stanford Test of Academic Skills* (TASK). In colleges and universities, tests of English usage and the mechanics of written composition are often administered to entering students to aid in placing them in appropriate English classes.

The best way to find out if students have writing ability is to ask them to write an essay. Such tests are called essay tests. Standardized tests use multiple-choice test items to measure some of the knowledge and skills that are part of writing ability. The following is a sampling of test questions that you may be asked to answer:

① PARAGRAPH REVISION

This kind of test asks students to check a paragraph for usage problems or errors in mechanics. Portions of sentences in these paragraphs are underlined and numbered. The student is asked to mark each numbered phrase as follows:

- *U* for usage problem
- *P* for punctuation error
- *C* for capitalization
- *NE* for no error

Read the example on the following page:

A resident of Seattle <u>don't need</u> to leave town to find a
₁
woodsy waterfall. <u>They will</u> find one near shops, <u>restaurants and the</u>
₂   ₃
Kingdome in the middle of historic Pioneer Square. <u>Tiny</u>
<u>Waterfall Garden park</u>, as it is called, merges city and country
₄
shapes: <u>conifers,</u> <u>japanese maples,</u> azaleas, and rhododendrons
₅   ₆
harmonize behind concrete <u>borders, splashing</u> water cascades down
₇
basalt boulders.

In answering test items of this type, remember that all sentences should be written in formal standard English. Check each word or phrase for nonstandard English or slang. Look for verbs that do not agree with the subject. Check on the proper use of relative pronouns. If you find an informal or nonstandard use, mark the item *U*.

Then see if the underlined phrase contains any punctuation. If there is punctuation, ask yourself if it is the correct mark. If it is not, mark the item *P*. If there is no punctuation, ask yourself if it needs a comma, an apostrophe, quotation marks, or another mark of punctuation. If it does, mark the item *P*.

If there is no error in punctuation, look for an error in capitalization. Is there a capital in the underlined section? Is it correctly used? If not, mark the item with a *C*. If there is no capitalized word in the phrase, check each word to determine if one of the words should have been capitalized. If a capital letter is needed, mark the item *C*.

Mark *NE* to show there is no error. In tests of this kind, the authors always include several items without any error in them.

Here are the answers for the sample paragraph:

• In item 1, the apostrophe is correctly placed for the word *don't,* and no other punctuation is needed. Neither word needs capitalization. However, the subject of the sentence is singular: a *resident.* The verb should be *does not need* instead of *don't need.* The lack of agreement between subject and verb is a problem of usage. The answer is *U*.

• In item 2, no punctuation is needed. As the first word of a sentence, the word *They* is correctly capitalized. However, the pronoun *they* should point back to a plural word as its "antecedent." But it here points to a singular word, *resident.* This is a problem in pronoun reference. The answer is *U*.

• In item 3, a comma is expected after *restaurants,* because this is the second in a series of three things. The answer is *P*.

- In item 4, no other punctuation is needed. However, the name of the park should have capital letters for each word. Since *park* needs a capital letter, the answer is *C*.
- In item 5, the colon after *shapes* introduces the list of objects and the explanation that follows. There is no need for capitalization and no usage error. The answer is *NE*.
- In item 6, there is no need for punctuation, but the word *japanese* needs a capital letter. All words derived from proper names are capitalized. The answer is *C*.
- In item 7, following the colon after the word *shapes* are two clauses. The first clause ends with the word *borders*. *Splashing* starts a second clause that could be a separate sentence. The comma here causes a "comma splice." There should be a semicolon where the second clause begins. The answer is *P*.

② BEST-SENTENCE TESTS

Another item used to measure writing ability lists three or four sentences, each saying roughly the same thing. The student selects the one sentence that best expresses that idea. Often the best choice is the most direct statement: brief and clear, with an active verb, with the modifiers close to what they modify. Look at the following items and try to choose the *best* sentence for each:

8	A	Nylon makes a better parachute than cotton does.
	B	Nylon makes a parachute better than using cotton.
	C	Nylon makes a better parachute than to use cotton.
9	F	With a green head Jane painted a horse.
	G	With a green head, the horse was painted by Jane.
	H	Jane painted a horse with a green head.
10	K	Whoever stole the jewelry knew the house.
	L	They knew the house who stole the jewelry.
	M	The house was known by whom the jewelry was stolen.
11	A	He walked downtown in order to be able to see the parade.
	B	He walked downtown to see the parade.
	C	He walked downtown for the purpose of being able to see the parade.

Answers:
- In item 8, choices B and C lack parallel structure. In A, *Nylon makes* and *cotton does* have the same Noun–Verb structure; they are parallel. The answer is A.

• In item 9, the phrase *with a green head* belongs near *horse*, which it modifies. In F, it seems that Jane has the green head. In G, the phrase immediately precedes *horse,* but the use of the passive verb is awkward. The answer is H.

• In item 10, L is bad because the restrictive clause is misplaced. It was not the house that stole the jewelry. M is faulty. Does the word *by* belong with *known* or *stolen?* The answer is K.

• In item 11, answers A and C include words that are not needed. In A there is no need for *in order to be able.* Similarly in C, *for the purpose of being able* is unnecessary and awkward. The answer is B.

③ **SENTENCE REVISION**

Some tests ask the student to look for a problem—punctuation, capitalization, or usage—in two or three parts of a single sentence. Parts of the sentence are underlined and numbered. The student is asked to label the problem, if any, in each numbered section. The student marks:

P for a punctuation error   *C* for a capitalization error
U for a usage problem   *NE* for no error

Try to find the problem in each underlined phrase of the following sentences. If there is no error, mark *NE* on your worksheet.

The old woman tapped on the <u>door entered</u> the room and

<small>12</small>

asks, ''Can I help you <u>unpack</u>''?
<small>13</small>   <small>14</small>

<u>Setting on</u> the <u>sofa he</u> sang <u>soft while</u> playing the guitar.
<small>15</small>   <small>16</small>   <small>17</small>

Answers:

• In item 12, a comma is needed after *door* because there is a series of three verbs: *tapped, entered,* and *asked.* The answer is *P.*

• In item 13, the comma and quotation marks are correct. The capitalization is correct. There is a usage problem. The first two verbs are in the past tense. The third verb shifts to the present. It should be *asked.* The answer is *U.*

• Item 14 has a punctuation error. Because the quotation is a question, the question mark should come before the quotation mark. The answer is *P.*

• Item 15 uses the wrong verb for formal writing. Persons only *set* on sofas in informal English. The correct word for formal writing is *sitting.* The answer is *U.*

- In item 16, a comma is needed after *sofa*. When a verbal or verbal phrase introduces a sentence, it is set off by a comma. The answer is *P*.
- In item 17, an adverb is needed to modify the verb *sang*. *Soft* is an adjective. *Softly* would be the formal adverb form. The answer is *U*.

(4) **COMPLETION TESTS**

One widely used test of language expression provides paragraphs with several blanks. For each numbered blank, the student is given four choices. The student picks the choice that fits best. Sometimes the four choices are different forms of the same word. For other blanks the student must select the appropriate relative pronoun, or the proper comparative or superlative form of an adjective or adverb, or the right word to fit the context of the rest of the sentence.

The following paragraph is an example of this kind of completion test. Read the entire paragraph first and then go back to answer the sample items.

By defining the problems that have to be ____18____, we have set up a rough framework of influences on automotive design for the years to come. ____19____, it is not possible even for the ____20____ to call all the shots, even for the car of the near future. Automotive engineers and designers have prejudices and ____21____ of their own, as do government officials and auto buffs, and the outcome of these various ____22____ is difficult to predict.

18	A	created	19	F	Consequently
	B	defined		G	However
	C	named		H	Moreover
	D	solved		J	Furthermore
20	K	driver	21	A	cars
	L	journalist		B	families
	M	mechanic		C	hopes
	N	expert		D	jobs
22	F	influences			
	G	men			
	H	persons			
	J	problems			

Answers:

- For item 18, the best choice is *solved*. Problems need solutions. The answer is D.
- For item 19, the best transition word is *however,* because the sentence that follows limits or contradicts the sentence before it. None of the other words is appropriate. The answer is G.
- For item 20, we need a word for someone who knows more than others: *expert.* It is the best choice for this blank. The answer is *N.*
- For item 21, it is necessary to choose a word that represents something that is held by four groups: automotive engineers, designers, government officials, and auto buffs. All of these have *hopes* for the cars of the future. The answer is C.
- For item 22, there is a clue in the opening sentence of the paragraph: the word *influences.* The answer is F.

⑤ MISSING TRANSITIONS

Some tests include a paragraph with numbered blanks to be filled in with the right transitional expression. The missing link may be a coordinating connective or an adverbial connective. For each blank the student selects the best word from the four choices. Read the following paragraph and select the best transition word for each numbered blank from the lists of four choices below the paragraph.

Anita was scheduled for the high jump; ____23____, she was a member of our relay team. ____24____, she was feeling ill, and, ____25____, she did poorly in both events.

23	A	although	24	F	Because	25	K	besides
	B	but		G	For instance		L	consequently
	C	furthermore		H	However		M	in fact
	D	unless		J	Indeed		N	moreover

Answers:

- For item 23, the word needed should show that more information of the same kind will follow. *Furthermore* means *in addition to.* It brings in something similar. The answer is C.
- For item 24, an adverbial connective is needed that shows a contrast with the previous statement. *However* serves that purpose. The answer is H.

● For item 25, a word is needed that shows what follows is the result of the previous statement. *Consequently* is appropriate. The answer is L.

⑥ PARAGRAPH ORGANIZATION

Below are examples of test items that test your ability to develop a paragraph. Each item has a list of four sentences, numbered from one through four. You are asked to find the order of these sentences that would make the best paragraph.

---

26 1 My wealthy aunt, knowing I liked the outdoors, gave me a UFM for my birthday.
    2 I can stay home and watch TV while the UFM catches fish, cleans them, cooks them, and eats them.
    3 When the UFM comes home and I ask it what luck it had, it tells lies.
    4 A UFM is the Ultimate Fishing Machine.
       A 1–4–2–3
       B 2–3–4–1
       C 4–1–3–2
       D 4–3–2–1

27 1 The state may suspend or revoke the privilege.
    2 Permission to drive a car is legally considered a privilege.
    3 This action is taken if the court finds the privilege is abused.
    4 It is not considered a right, even if the person's livelihood depends on it.
       F 1–3–2–4
       G 1–4–2–3
       H 2–1–3–4
       J 2–4–1–3

Answers:
● In item 26, the four sentences apparently tell about an imaginary machine. The passage is meant to be humorous. In the usual order of events, sentence 3 would follow sentence 2. This eliminates answer choices C and D. In sentence 2, the words *the UFM* seem to require some previous explanation of what a UFM is. This eliminates answer B. Only answer A remains. Checking the order given in answer A, you can see that it makes a good paragraph. The answer is A.

• To answer item 27, similar reasoning is helpful. It deals with the privilege of permission to drive a car. Sentences 1, 3, and 4 all include words that point back to something that must have been mentioned earlier. In sentence 1, it is the words *the privilege*. In sentence 3, it is the first word *This*. In sentence 4, it is also the first word *It*. The opening sentence of the paragraph, therefore, must be sentence 2. The word *It* in sentence 4 points back to *permission to drive a car*. The only answer choice starting with 2—4 is J. In checking J, you will see that its order of the sentences makes a good paragraph. The answer is J.

I. ANSWER TO AN AD

The letter that follows on the next page was written in response to this ad:

SALES MANAGEMENT TRAINEE. Complete program. $15,300 salary + incentive plan. Generous benefits, national company. Send resume to Mr. Marsen, 3056 Sims Way, Suite 525, San Jose CA 95128.

Read the letter completely. Then go back and reread it carefully. When you come to a numbered, underlined section, look at the four answer choices whose number corresponds to that of the underlined section. Decide which of the four responses is the best choice. If you think that the underlined material is satisfactory as it is, mark the letter of the "No Change" response. If you think that one of the three alternative responses is the best choice, mark the letter of that choice. Write your choice in the space next to the number of the item.

4941 Monterey Road
San Jose, CA 95108
March 15, 1979

Mr. Marsen
3056 Sims Way, Suite 525
San Jose, California 95128

Dear Mr. Marsen:

I am writing in response to your ad of March 14 in the *Mercury* offering the position of sales management <u>trainee. I</u> feel that I am qualified for this training.
₁

In 1976 I graduated from <u>Buena Vista high school</u> in <u>Arizona where I</u> studied a commercial course. <u>After graduating,</u> Belton department store hired me as a salesclerk. Then, a year later my family moved to Modesto, where I was hired by Lucas Plymouth as a sales trainee. <u>I have work</u> for them to the present, being promoted to salesperson late in 1977.

I have for some time wanted to move to the San Jose area. I believe there would be opportunities for advancement for <u>my husband and I</u> if <u>we both</u> could find employment there. The sales manager at Lucas Plymouth is Walter Badgley. I know he would give me a good recommendation if you requested one.

<u>Me and my husband is</u> planning to move to your area in the near <u>future, therefore</u> I am looking for a challenging career position there. I would appreciate an opportunity to discuss your sales management trainee program in person with you in the <u>near future</u>.

Yours truly,

Juanita Nelson

Juanita Nelson

___ 1. A trainee, I
     B trainee—I
     C trainee I
     D No Change

___ 2. A Buena Vista High School
     B Buena vista high school
     C buena vista High School
     D No change

___ 3. A Arizona; where
     B Arizona, where
     C Arizona: where
     D No Change

___ 4. A After being graduated,
     B After graduating
     C After I graduated,
     D No Change

___ 5. A I work
     B I had worked
     C I have worked
     D No Change

___ 6. A me and my husband
     B my husband and me
     C me husband and I
     D No Change

___ 7. A he and me both
     B us both
     C him and me both
     D No Change

___ 8. A My husband and I is
     B My husband and I are
     C My husband and me are
     D No Change

___ 9. A future; so,
     B future—therefore
     C future; therefore,
     D No Change

___ 10. A coming future soon
     B future coming soon
     C near future soon
     D No Change

II. EDITORIAL

The editorial that follows this paragraph was written for a
school newspaper. Read it completely. Then go back and reread
it carefully. When you come to a numbered, underlined section,
look at the four answer choices for that section. Choose the best
answer. If you think that the underlined material is satisfactory as it is, mark the letter of the "No Change" response. If
you think that one of the three alternatives is the best choice,
mark the letter of that choice. Write your choice in the space
next to the number of the item.

CHILDREN OF THE WORLD NEED YOUR HELP

Hundreds of millions of children in the poor countries of

the world need help from you the students in American schools.
                                    1
These children suffer the effects of extreme poverty—hunger,
                                                  2

get <u>sick</u>, lack of education, and limited hope for the future.
₃
<u>A child</u> cannot select the place of their birth nor the religion,
₄
government, or culture of their communities. The <u>United</u>

<u>Nations Children's Fund</u> is helping over 100 countries—in
₅
Asia, Africa, Latin America, and the <u>middle east</u>—provide the
₆
basic health, <u>nutrition, and education</u> services that every child
₇
needs. <u>If you was</u> to skip a 35¢ package of <u>french fries</u> and give
₈ ₉
that money to <u>U.N.I.C.E.F.</u>, you could protect three children
₁₀
from blindness, buy ninety vitamin capsules, and buy seeds

for six hundred tomato plants. Please help.

___ 1. A you
    B you the Students
    C you, the students
    D No Change

___ 2. A poverty; hunger
    B poverty, hunger
    C poverty: hunger
    D No Change

___ 3. A disease
    B have poor health
    C need to get well
    D No Change

___ 4. A Children
    B No children
    C No child
    D No Change

___ 5. A United Nations
       childrens fund
    B United Nations
       Childrens Fund
    C united nations
       Children's Fund
    D No Change

___ 6. A middle East
    B Middle East
    C Middle-east
    D No Change

___ 7. A nutrition and education
    B nutrition and learning
    C food, and learning
    D No Change

___ 8. A If you were to
    B If you want to
    C If you will
    D No Change

___ 9. A French fries
    B french-fries
    C French-Fries
    D No Change

___ 10. A UNICEF
    B United Nation's C.F.
    C United Nations' C.F.
    D No Change

III. PARAGRAPH ORGANIZATION

Each of the following test items has a list of four sentences, numbered from one through four. Read all four sentences and decide in which order these sentences would make the best paragraph. If you can find that order among the four answer choices, mark the letter of that choice in the space provided.

_____ 1. 1 Most train wrecks happen because of faulty equipment.
        2 Of course, human misjudgments also often play a role.
        3 The most common examples are derailments because of defective tracks.
        4 Other examples are collisions caused by defective signaling systems.
          A 1–2–3–4
          B 1–3–2–4
          C 1–3–4–2
          D 3–2–4–1

_____ 2. 1 North America has its own version of the Loch Ness monster.
        2 Descriptions of it greatly resemble those of its Scottish counterpart.
        3 "Ogopogo" has been encountered by many persons in Okanogan Lake in Canada.
        4 Added to this coincidence is the similarity of their habitats; the lakes are very much alike.
          F 1–3–2–4
          G 1–4–3–2
          H 3–1–2–4
          J 3–2–4–1

_____ 3. 1 Many people think that such issues should be decided by legislation or court decisions.
        2 They need to listen patiently to people who have studied nature's ways.
        3 However, lawyers and judges may not know enough about the realities of nature.
        4 Currently there is much debate in America concerning environmental issues.
          K 2–3–1–4
          L 2–4–1–3
          M 4–1–3–2
          N 4–2–1–3

_____ 4. 1 Tirhakah was king of Ethiopia for a period of 25 years.
        2 For this action Tirhakah earned a place in the Bible.

3 In defense of his ally, Tirhakah led his armies into battle against the Assyrians.

4 When he was sixteen, the Assyrians invaded his friends, the Israelites.

   A 1–2–3–4
   B 1–3–2–4
   C 1–4–3–2
   D 2–1–4–3

_____ 5. 1 Women can and do succeed as business owners.

2 That's the conclusion of a survey by the American Management Association.

3 The second most common reason was a desire for financial independence.

4 The most common reason, the survey showed, for a woman's being in business was having an idea for a product or service to sell.

   F 1–2–4–3
   G 1–4–3–2
   H 4–3–1–2
   J 4–3–2–1

_____ 6. 1 This research is being carried out by government, the military, and universities.

2 Slowly, but steadily, parapsychology is edging toward scientific respectability.

3 However, arguments over the validity of parapsychology are likely to remain unresolved for some time.

4 Carefully controlled research is now being done in ESP, clairvoyance, and telepathy.

   K 2–3–4–1
   L 2–4–1–3
   M 4–1–3–2
   N 4–2–1–3

_____ 7. 1 The starfish moves towards its prey by using its many small appendages.

2 These are called tube feet, or podia, and each of them ends in a small sucker disc.

3 The combined sucker discs on large numbers of podia provide a powerful grip.

4 This grip enables the starfish, not only to cling to rocks, but also to open bivalves.

   A 1–2–3–4
   B 1–2–4–3
   C 3–2–4–1
   D 3–4–1–2

_____ 8. 1 Therefore, he is not a prisoner of war under the rules of the Geneva Convention.

2 A prisoner may be dressed in civilian clothes when captured.

3 The Geneva Convention sets up rules for the treatment of prisoners of war.

4 Sometimes there is room for debate on how or whether these rules apply.

    F 2–1–4–3

    G 3–4–2–1

    H 4–2–1–3

    J 4–3–2–1

_____ 9. 1 Photographers were present at the accident.

2 For this famous picture he was awarded a Pulitzer Prize.

3 One of them, from the National Broadcasting Company, took some film footage with sound.

4 Another one, from the Associated Press, snapped a still picture.

    K 1–3–2–4

    L 1–3–4–2

    M 3–2–4–1

    N 4–2–3–1

_____ 10. 1 After he was severely wounded, he was flown to a hospital in Honolulu.

2 From there he returned to Virginia and opened a small restaurant.

3 Her uncle had been a pilot during the Korean War.

4 His war injuries kept interfering with his business.

    A 3–1–2–4

    B 3–2–4–1

    C 3–4–1–2

    D 4–1–2–3

ILLUSTRATION CREDITS

Page 61: The Bettman Archive. 68: Jack Weaver. 77: Nicole Hollander. 97: Jack Weaver. 107: The National Safety Council. 114, 123: Jack Weaver. 163: Steve Renick. 185: Dudley Witney. 186: James Hinton. 187: Jorge Romero & Associates; Buckminster Fuller. 190: Ron Tunison. 359, 382, 389, 397: Jack Weaver.

ACKNOWLEDGEMENTS

The American Scholar for permission to reprint an excerpt from "Juvenile Delinquents: The Latter-Day Knights" by Joseph Margolis. Reprinted from *The American Scholar,* Volume 29, Number 2, Spring, 1960. Copyright © 1960 by the United Chapters of Phi Beta Kappa. By permission of the publishers.

John Ciardi for permission to reprint an excerpt from *In Fact* by John Ciardi. Copyright © 1962, Rutgers, The State University. Reprinted by permission of the author.

Career Institute for permission to reprint two entries from *Roget's Thesaurus*.

Chicago Tribune—New York News Syndicate, Inc., for permission to reprint a "Dear Abby" letter. Copyright © 1974 by the Chicago Tribune—New York News Syndicate, Inc. All rights reserved.

Curtis Brown, Ltd, for permission to reprint an excerpt from "La Situación" by Edward Rivera which appeared in the August 7, 1972 issue of *New York Magazine*. Reprinted by permission of New York Magazine and Curtis Brown, Ltd. Copyright © 1972, New York Magazine Corporation.

Farrar, Straus and Giroux, Inc., for permission to reprint a selection from *Afrodisia* by Ted Joans. Copyright © 1970 by Ted Joans. Reprinted with the permission of Hill and Wang (now a division of Farrar, Straus and Giroux, Inc.).

Alfred A. Knopf, Inc., for permission to reprint an excerpt from "Half a Grapefruit," from *The Beggar Maid* by Alice Munro. Copyright © 1979 by Alice Munro. Reprinted by permission of the publisher.

McGraw-Hill, Inc., for permission to reprint excerpts from the *Reference Manual for Stenographers and Typists,* Fourth Edition, by Ruth E. Gavin and William A. Sabin; from *Business English Essentials* by Greta La Follete Henderson and Price A. Voiles; and from *Business English and Communication,* Fifth Edition, by Marie M. Stewart.

INDEX

Numerals in italics indicate illustrations. Charts are identified in the Index.

HANDBOOK KEY

WORDS

SENTENCES

COMPOSITION